כל הנשמה

כל הנשמה

Kol Haneshamah

לימות חל

Daily

With readings for use in a house
of mourning and throughout the year

SECOND EDITION

The Reconstuctionist Press
Elkins Park, Pennsylvania
2002

THIRD PRINTING, 2002

Library of Congress Catalog Card Number: 95-78994

International Standard Book Number 0-935457-47-X

Art by Betsy Platkin Teutsch

Book Design by Alvin Schultzberg

Composition by El Ot Printing Enterprises Ltd. (Tel Aviv)

Printed in the United States of America

Lovingly dedicated to the family of
Aaron Ziegelman and the Jews
of his hometown, Luboml (Libivne), Poland
who were murdered by the Germans
during the *Shoah*:

Grandmothers
Chava Eiger
Sime Ziegelman

Aunts & Uncles
Avram & Elke Peltz
Joseph & Sheindel Ziegelman

Cousins
Aaron & Brucha Peltz
Chaya Liba & Tova Ziegelman

108 relatives
and
Over 8,000 Jewish men, women and children

May their memory be for a blessing

Prayerbook Commission

Adina Abramowitz
Rabbi Ronald Aigen
Rabbi Devora Bartnoff
Milton Bienenfeld
Rabbi Daniel Ehrenkrantz
Lillian S. Kaplan
Marlene J. Kunin
Leroy C. Shuster
Rabbi Reena Spicehandler
Rabbi David A. Teutsch, Chairperson

Ex Officio

Rabbi Lee M. Friedlander
Rabbi Mordechai Liebling
Valerie Kaplan

Editorial Committee

Rabbi David A. Teutsch, *Editor-in-Chief*

Joseph Blair, *Editorial Assistant*
Dr. Joel Rosenberg, *Translation*
Rabbi Reena Spicehandler, *Research*

Betsy Platkin Teutsch, *Art*

Rabbi Mordechai Liebling, *Publisher's Representative*

TABLE OF CONTENTS

Commentators viii
Preface ix
Acknowledgments xi
Introduction xv
Notes on Usage xviii
Shaḥarit/Morning Service
- Birḥot Hashaḥar/Morning Blessings 2
- Pesukey Dezimrah/Verses of Praise 32
- Shema and its Blessings 66
- Amidah 98
- Amidah Meditations 128, 132
- Avinu Malkeynu 136
- Taḥanun/Supplication 424
- Netilat Lulav/Waving the Lulav (Sukkot) 358
- Hallel (Rosh Ḥodesh, Ḥol Hamo'ed, Ḥanukah, Yom Ha'atzma'ut) 360
- Torah Service 146
- Hoshanot (Sukkot) 394
- Psalm for the Day 176
- Psalm for the Month of Elul 196
- Psalm for a House of Mourning 200
- Aleynu 168
- Mourners' Kaddish 204

Minḥah/Afternoon Service
- Amidah 218
- Avinu Malkeynu 136
- Taḥanun/Supplication 424
- Aleynu 250
- Mourners' Kaddish 256

Ma'ariv/Evening Service
- Shema and its Blessings 260
- Amidah 294
- Amidah Meditations 292
- Psalm for the Day 176

Ma'ariv/Evening Service (continued)
Psalm for the Month of Elul 196
Psalm for a House of Mourning 200
Counting the Omer 414
Aleynu 326
Mourners' Kaddish 334
Keriat Shema Al Hamitah/The Bedtime Shema 346
Havdalah 350
Netilat Lulav/Waving the Lulav 358
Hallel 360
Hadlakat Nerot Shel Ḥanukah/Ḥanukah Candlelighting 386
Purim 388
Hoshanot 394
Sefirat Ha'omer/Counting the Omer 414
Taḥanun 424
Conclusion of Shivah 428
Readings
Prayer 431
Nature 433
Social Action 435
Torah Study 436
Exodus 438
Elul and Teshuvah 440
Tu Bishevat 448
Yom Hasho'ah 449
Yom Ha'atzma'ut 457
Tisha Be'av 472
New Year's Day 478
Martin Luther King Day 479
Presidents' Day 480
Memorial Day/Veterans' Day 482
Fourth of July 483
Labor Day 485
Thanksgiving 487
Death, Mourning and Memory 490
Loss of a Parent 497
Loss of a Grandparent 508

Readings (continued)
Loss of a Gay or Lesbian Lover 509
Loss of a Loved One 510
Life and Death 512
Sources 533
Index 547

Commentators

At the end of each section in the commentary, the authors' initials appear. Their full names are:

Ronald S. Aigen
Leila Gal Berner
Joseph Blair
Martin Buber
Daniel Ehrenkrantz
Everett Gendler
Arthur Green
Abraham Joshua Heschel
Mordecai M. Kaplan
Levi Weiman-Kelman
Herbert Levine
Mordechai Liebling
Hershel Matt
Eric Mendelsohn
Marcia Prager
Joel Rosenberg
Steven Sager
Sandy Eisenberg Sasso
Mel Scult
Rami M. Shapiro
Reena Spicehandler
William Strongin
David A. Teutsch
Sheila Peltz Weinberg

See also SOURCES, pages 533-546, for citations of previously published materials.

PREFACE

This daily prayerbook resulted from the unique partnership among its editors and the rabbis and laypeople, women and men of the Reconstructionist Prayerbook Commission. It draws upon the Jewish liturgical tradition formed by generations of nameless Jews as well as dozens of contemporary poets and commentators.

Joel Rosenberg has again brought his extraordinary poetic talents to the translation. David Golomb and Uri Melammed have consulted on matters of Hebrew grammar. Joe Blair has worked diligently to assemble the drafts and see the manuscript through the press. Reena Spicehandler, Jeremy Schwartz, and Shoshee Larkey have helped with research. Mel Scult has assembled commentary from the writings of Mordecai M. Kaplan. Proofreaders include Joe Blair, Karen Blair, Judy Gary, Lillian Kaplan, Uri Melammed, Reena Spicehandler, and David Steinberg. Betsy Platkin Teutsch brought her artistic vision to the task of illustration. Ezra Spicehandler has helped with sources for modern Hebrew literature. David Tilman and Elizabeth Bolton have guided on issues of *nusaḥ*. Mordechai Liebling has managed the finances and distribution of the book. Alvin Schultzberg of Townhouse Press guided the book's design, typesetting at El Ot Printing, and production. Larry Pinsker, who has extraordinary liturgy files, suggested many of the readings.

Others who have contributed to this volume include: Dee Einhorn, Ari Elon, Sarah Fenner, Wendie Gabay, Lani Moss, Adina Newberg, Seth Riemer, Diane Schwartz, Elaine Snyder, Muriel Weiss, Elie Wise, and Phyllis Zeeman.

The following congregations provided support for this project: Ramat Shalom, Plantation, FL; Jewish Reconstructionist Congregation, Evanston, IL; Bet Am Shalom, White Plains, NY; Reconstructionist Synagogue of the North Shore, Plandome, NY; Temple Sinai, Amherst, NY; Mishkan Shalom, Havertown, PA; Or Ḥadash, Fort Washington, PA; Darchei Noam, Downsview, ONT, Canada.

Funding was also provided in honor of Rabbi Jacob Neustader by his grandson, Harvey Nixon, and his family.

ACKNOWLEDGMENTS

We wish to express our thanks to authors, translators, adaptors, and other copyright holders for permission to include or quote from works indicated below. Every effort has been made to identify copyright holders and obtain permission from them. Works are listed by title in alphabetical order. For additional information, see Sources, *pages 533-546.*

"About My Father" from *A Few Words in the Mother Tongue – Poems Selected and New*, by Irena Klepfisz. Reprinted with permission of the author. Copyright © 1990. Published by Eighth Mt. Press, Portland, Oregon.

"Above Everything" from *New and Collected Poems, 1970-1985* by David Ignatow. Copyright © 1986 by David Ignatow, Wesleyan University Press. Used with permission of University Press of New England.

"All the Generations Before Me" from *Songs of Jerusalem and Myself* by Yehuda Amichai. Copyright © 1973 by Yehuda Amichai. English translation copyright © 1973 by Harold Schimmel. Reprinted by permission of HarperCollins Publishers Inc.

"Birth is a Beginning" by Alvin I. Fine. From *Gates of Repentance.* Copyright © 1978 by Central Conference of American Rabbis and Union of Liberal and Progressive Synagogues (London) and used by permission.

"Chorus of the Rescued" from *O the Chimneys* by Nelly Sachs, translated by Michael Roloff. Copyright © 1967 by Ferrar, Strauss & Giroux, Inc. Reprinted by permission of Farrar, Straus & Giroux, Inc.

Days of Awe/Yamim Noraim, by S. Y. Agnon. Copyright © 1948, 1965 by Schocken Books Inc. Copyright renewed 1975 by Schocken Books Inc. Reprinted by permission of Schocken Books, published by Pantheon Books, a division of Random House, Inc.

"The Death of a Parent" is reprinted from *A Fraction of Darkness: Poems by Linda Pastan*, by permission of W. W. Norton & Company, Inc. Copyright © 1985 by Linda Pastan.

"Dirge Without Music" by Edna St. Vincent Millay. From *Collected Poems*, Harper & Row. Copyright © 1928, 1955 by Edna St. Vincent Millay and Norma Millay Ellis. Reprinted by permission.

"Do not come when I am dead..." by Juanita de Long from *The World's Greatest Religious Poetry*, ed. Caroline Miles Hill. Published by MacMillan, reprinted by Greenwood Press 1973.

"Fish Crier" from *Chicago Poems* by Carl Sandburg, reprinted by permission of Harcourt Brace & Co.

"The Five Stages of Grief" is reprinted from *The Five Stages of Grief: Poems by Linda Pastan*, by permission of W. W. Norton & Company, Inc. Copyright © 1978 by Linda Pastan.

"Funeral" from *Cemetery Nights* by Stephen Dobyns. Copyright © 1987 by Stephen Dobyns. Used by permission of Viking Penguin, a division of Penguin Books USA Inc.

"God, help me..." from *Forms of Prayer for Jewish Worship* Vol. III, © 1985. Reproduced with the kind permission of the Reform Synagogues of Great Britain.

"Gramma" reprinted from *The Night Train and the Golden Bird* by Peter Meinke, by permission of the University of Pittsburgh Press. Copyright © 1977 by Peter Meinke.

"Gravy" by Raymond Carver from *A New Path to the Waterfall*. Copyright © 1989 by The Estate of Raymond Carver. Used by permission of Grove/Atlantic, Inc.

"Heirloom" from *A. M. Klein Collected Poems*, compiled and edited by Miriam Waddington. Reprinted with permission of University of Toronto Press Incorporated.

"Hold on to What is Good" in *Many Winters* by Nancy Wood. Copyright © 1974 by Nancy Wood, Illustrations © 1974 by Frank Howell. Used by permission of Doubleday, a division of Bantam Doubleday Dell Publishing Group, Inc.

"In Praise of the Living" by Rabbi Harvey J. Fields, Senior Rabbi, Wilshire Boulevard Temple. Used with kind permission of the author.

"The Intention" by Margaret Torrie. Taken from *All in the End is Harvest* edited by Agnes Whitaker, published and copyright© 1986 by Darton, Longman and Todd Ltd./CRUSE and is used by permission of the publisher.

"Kaddish" from *CCAR Journal*, Autumn 1972, by Hannah Kahn. Used with kind permission of the CCAR.

"Kaddish" from *New and Collected Poems, 1970-1985* by David Ignatow. Copyright © 1986 by David Ignatow, Wesleyan University Press. Used with permission of University Press of New England.

"Lament for the European Exile" by A. L. Strauss from *Voices Within the Ark* edited by Howard Schwartz and Anthony Rudolf, 1980. Avon Books.

"Learning from Trees" by Grace Butcher from *Child, House, World* (*Hiram Poetry Review* 1991), originally in *Poetry*, April 1991. Used with the kind permission of the author.

"Legacy" by Dana D. Shuster. Used with kind permission of the author.

"*Leḥol Ish Yesh Shem*/Each of Us Has A Name" by Zelda Mishkowsky. Translation copyright © 1983 by Marcia Lee Falk. Excerpted from Marcia Falk, *The Book of Blessings: A Feminist-Jewish Reconstruction of Prayer* (forthcoming, Harper San Francisco, 1994). Used by permission of the translator. Hebrew original used by permission of Acum.

"Life After Death" by Laura Gilpin in *The Hocus-Pocus of the Universe.* Copyright © 1977 by Doubleday & Company. Used by permission of Doubleday, a division of Bantam, Doubleday, Dell Publishing Group, Inc.

"Living Memory" from *Time's Power: Poems 1985-1988*, by Adrienne Rich. Reprinted with permission of the author and W. W. Norton & Company, Inc. © 1989 by Adrienne Rich.

"Merger" by Judy Chicago from *The Dinner Party.* Copyright © 1979 by Judy Chicago. Reprinted by permission of Doubleday, a division of Bantam, Doubleday, Dell Publishing Group, Inc.

"Metamorphosis" by Louise Gluck from *The Triumph of Achilles.* Copyright © 1985 by Louise Gluck. First published by the Ecco Press in 1985. Reprinted by permission.

"Morning Poem" in *Dream Work* by Mary Oliver. Grove/Atlantic Press, 1986.

"The Operator" by Naftali Gross, translated by Aaron Kramer from *A Century of Yiddish Poetry.* Edited by Aaron Kramer. Reprinted by permission of Associated University Presses.

"Songs of Those Who Died In Vain" by Primo Levi from *Collected Poems*, translated by Ruth Feldman and Brian Swann. Copyright © 1992 by Ruth Feldman. Reprinted by permission of Faber and Faber Publishers, Inc.

"Tattered Kaddish" from *An Atlas of the Difficult World: Poems 1988-1991* by Adrienne Rich. Reprinted by permission of the author and W. W. Norton & Company, Inc. © 1991 by Adrienne Rich.

Ten Rungs: Hasidic Sayings, collected and edited by Martin Buber, translated by Olga Mark, Schocken Books, copyright © 1977.

"Teach me my God..." by Leah Goldberg, translated by Pnina Peli. Reprinted from *Shirey Sof Hadereḥ*. Courtesy of Sifriat Poalim Publishing House of Hakibbutz Ha'Artzi Ltd.

"They" by Mani Leyb. Translated from the Yiddish by David G. Roskies and Hillel Schwartz. Used with permission.

"To open eyes..." by Emmanel Eydoux, translated by Rabbi Jonathan Magonet in *Forms of Prayer for Jewish Worship*, Vol. III, Reform Synagogues of Great Britain. Copyright © 1985. Used with permission of the translator.

"To Touch Hands in Peace" by Nahum Waldman in *Likrat Shabbat*, edited by Sidney Greenberg and Jonathan D. Levine, Augmented Edition, © 1992, The Prayer Book Press of Media Judaica, Inc., Bridgeport, CT.

"We Gather Together" by Pearl Kazin. Reprinted by permission. Copyright © 1955, 1983 The New Yorker Magazine, Inc.

"We Mothers" from *The Seeker* by Nelly Sachs and translated by Ruth and Matthew Mead. Copyright © 1970 by Farrar, Straus & Giroux, Inc. Reprinted by permission of Farrar, Straus & Giroux, Inc.

"*Ye'iruni Se'ipay Laḥazoteḥ*/My Thoughts Awaken Me to See You" translation adapted from *The Gazelle: Medieval Hebrew Poems on God, Israel and the Soul*, The Jewish Publication Society. Copyright © 1991 by Raymond P. Scheindlin.

"*Yerushalayim Shel Zahav*/Jerusalem Jerusalem." Lyrics and music by Naomi Shemer. Copyright © 1967 Chappel & Co., Inc. All rights reserved. Used by permission.

"The Young Dead Soldiers" is reprinted from *Collected Poems 1917-1982* by Archibald MacLeish. Copyright © 1985 by the Estate of Archibald MacLeish. Reprinted by permission of Houghton Mifflin Co. All rights reserved.

Sylvia Heschel gave permission for use of works by Abraham Joshua Heschel.

INTRODUCTION

This daily siddur is intended for several different uses: worship in a weekday minyan in the synagogue, personal prayer and devotion at home, as a tool for study, and at *shivah* and *yahrtzeit minyanim* (with particular support from the readings in the back of the book).

In addition to extensive readings for the shivah house, this siddur provides readings on themes suitable for such secular holidays as Thanksgiving and Memorial Day. It is designed for use on Purim, Ḥanukah, *Tisha Be'Av*, *Yom Hasho'ah*, and *Yom Ha'atzma'ut* as well. This book's use of commentary, transliteration, guided meditation, readings, and song creates a wonderfully flexible approach to Jewish worship adaptable to a wide variety of settings, purposes and skill levels.

It is not an easy task to acquire the liturgical skill, intellectual understanding and spiritual clarity needed to make daily prayer an easy and comfortable part of living. This prayerbook is meant to serve as a bridge into daily worship by providing an easy transition for each of those tasks. Achieving a daily devotional life not only provides perspective on the activities that fill our days; it also provides a moral anchor for making the choices that we face hour by hour. And it provides the source of strength we need during times of adversity. When we have lost loved ones, or when we simply have lost touch with ourselves, we need solace, the support of community, and later on, solitude for sorting things out. This book can help us find them.

It is our hope that, as has occurred with other volumes in the *Kol Haneshamah* series, service leaders will feel free to blend Hebrew and English text, commentary and readings, song and silence as they construct a worship experience that reflects the aspirations and previous experience of the worshippers. That is

as it should be. This prayerbook is designed for maximum flexibility.

It is suggested that beginners at daily worship start with relatively small parts of the liturgy and get to know them slowly rather than feel an obligation to race through an amount of text too large to absorb. It is better to make a modest commitment to pray for ten minutes a day that to attempt a grand plan that might collapse when your schedule becomes more demanding.

Each person will find that a different combination of melody and text, readings, study and meditation will provide the best personal nurturance and growth. Each individual should seek out his or her own way and expect that it will change over time. Growing depth and skill make that inevitable. This siddur allows for many different changes as the worshipper grows. And, of course, it is not always just a question of growth. At different times in our lives, we face different struggles, both internal and external. The resources are here for reflecting and responding to them.

Occasionally people ask how Reconstructionist theology combines with the commitment to a significant spiritual life. The simplest answer is that there does not need to be a conflict. Taking a rational approach to moral, intellectual and personal issues is not in conflict with the recognition that human beings have spiritual needs and aptitudes. We pray in pursuit of different perspectives on our encounter with the world. Prayer can help us to achieve a fresh relationship to the world and find our place in it.

Seeking the unity in nature and the transcendent in the world is an important part of discovering the divine in ourselves. This takes skill, discipline and effort just as intellectual achievement does. Doing this in a Reconstructionist manner, however,

requires that we not abandon what we rationally understand, and that we cling to our moral vision. Parts of this vision, embodied both in the Reconstructionist movement in general and in this book in particular, are a commitment to egalitarian language, a recognition that many peoples in the world seek to make it a better place and seek to encounter the divine, awareness that the Torah was not dictated to Moses at Sinai, and dedication to strengthening community while recognizing the need for individual fulfillment. May you find here a source of sustenance and a challenge to better our world.

DAVID A. TEUTSCH
Chair, Prayerbook Commission

NOTES ON USAGE

Hebrew Pronunciation. The pronunciation in this book follows current Israeli usage. Accordingly, Hebrew words are accented on the final syllable unless otherwise noted. Where the stress is not on the last syllable of a word, the stressed syllable is marked with a caret ($\overset{<}{\times}$). In biblical passages where there are cantillation marks, those marks replace the caret in marking the stressed syllable. *The kamatz katan* (pronounced "o" as in "store") is marked with this sign: $\underset{\top}{\times}$.

Transliteration. Where Hebrew words are not accented on the final syllable, this is indicated by underlining the accented syllable in the transliteration. Use of periods and capital letters roughly follows Hebrew sentence structure. Generally, no other punctuation will occur. Below is a table of Hebrew letters and vowels with their English equivalents.

Consonants

א	(not pronounced)	ל	l
בּ	b	ם מ	m
ב	v	ן נ	n
ג	g (as in "go")	ס	s
ד	d	ע	(not pronounced)
ה	h	פּ	p
ו	v	ף פ	f
ז	z (as in "Zion")	ץ צ	tz (as in "mitzvah")
ח	ḥ (as in "*ḥazan*")	ק	k
ט	t	ר	r
י	y	שׁ	sh
ךּ כּ	k	שׂ	s
ך כ	ḥ (as in "*baruḥ*")	תּ ת	t

Vowels

אֵ / אֶ / אֱ / אְ	e (as in "bed")
אַ / אֲ / אָ	a (as in "are")
אוֹ / אֹ / אָ / אֳ	o (as in "store")
אוּ / אֻ	u (as in "put")
אִי / אִ	i (as in "sit")

Diphthongs and Glides

אֵי / אֵא / אֵה	ey (as in "they")
אַי	ay (as in "bayou")
וּי	uwi (u + i, pronounced rapidly together)
וֹי	oy (as in "toy")

Those transliterations that have become accepted as standard or familiar English have not been changed. Examples: Shabbat, siddur, sukkah, Kiddush. In these cases the doubling of the middle consonant has been kept even though the system of transliteration used here does not require it.

* Indicates where it is traditional for the cantor or service leader to begin chanting in a prayer.

← and ↩ indicate that a prayer continues on the next page.

שחרית

BIRḤOT HASHAḤAR / MORNING BLESSINGS

This translation can be sung to the same melody as the Hebrew.

How lovely are your tents, O Ya'akov,
how fine your encampments, Yisrael!

And as for me, drawn by your love,
I come into your house.

I lay me down in a humble surrender,
before your holy shrine in awe.

GREAT ONE, how I love your house's site,
adore your Glory's dwelling place.

And as for me, I fall in prayer,
my body I bend down,

I greet, I bless, I bend the knee,
before THE ONE who fashions me.

And as for me, my prayer is for you, GENTLE ONE,
may it be for you a time of desire,

O God, in the abundance of your love,
respond to me in truth with your help.

COMMENTARY. *Mah Tovu* begins with a historical progression—the tents of our earliest ancestors, then the sanctuary of the years of wandering in the wilderness, then the Temple in Jerusalem. Each of these is linked to the synagogue, for it too is "your house." And I, the contemporary soul, seeking the right moment to encounter the divine there, am thus not alone. I am a link in the chain of tradition bearing the truth of your salvation. D.A.T.

בִּרְכוֹת הַשַּׁחַר

מַה טֹּבוּ אֹהָלֶיךָ יַעֲקֹב מִשְׁכְּנֹתֶיךָ יִשְׂרָאֵל: וַאֲנִי בְּרֹב חַסְדְּךָ אָבוֹא
בֵיתֶךָ אֶשְׁתַּחֲוֶה אֶל הֵיכַל קָדְשְׁךָ בְּיִרְאָתֶךָ: יהוה אָהַבְתִּי מְעוֹן בֵּיתֶךָ
וּמְקוֹם מִשְׁכַּן כְּבוֹדֶךָ: וַאֲנִי אֶשְׁתַּחֲוֶה וְאֶכְרָעָה אֶבְרְכָה לִפְנֵי יהוה
עֹשִׂי וַאֲנִי תְפִלָּתִי לְךָ יהוה עֵת רָצוֹן אֱלֹהִים בְּרָב חַסְדֶּךָ עֲנֵנִי בֶּאֱמֶת
יִשְׁעֶךָ:

Mah tovu ohaleḥa ya'akov mishkenoteḥa yisra'el. Va'ani berov hasdeḥa avo veyteḥa eshtaḥaveh el heyḥal kodsheḥa beyirateḥa. Adonay ahavti me'on beyteḥa umkom mishkan kevodeḥa. Va'ani eshtaḥaveh ve'eḥra'ah evreḥah lifney adonay osi va'ani tefilati leḥa adonay et ratzon elohim berov ḥasdeḥa aneni be'emet yisheḥa.

ואני תפלתי / as for me, my prayer is for you. The Hebrew text has often been creatively misread to mean "I am my prayer." All I have to offer in prayer is myself. We begin our prayers with a feeling of humility, knowing that the vaunted words we are about to speak are no greater than the person who speaks them. Most of the prayers in our liturgy are phrased in the first person plural, in which *we* as a community stand before the Divine presence. But here they are introduced in the halting and somewhat unsure voice of the individual, expressing some of that inadequacy that each of us feels as we enter the place and hour of prayer. A.G.

NOTE. The *Mah Tovu* prayer is composed entirely of biblical verses: Numbers 24:5; Psalms 5:8, 26:8, 95:6 and 69:14.

ATIFAT TALLIT / DONNING THE TALLIT

It is customary to wrap oneself in the tallit before reciting the blessing that follows. After the blessing is recited, the tallit is placed across the shoulders. In some congregations the blessing is said in unison.

Bless, O my soul, THE ONE!
ABUNDANT ONE, my God, how great you grow!
In majesty and beauty you are dressed,
wrapping yourself in light as in a garment,
stretching out the heavens like a shawl! (Psalm 104:1-2)

Blessed are You, VEILED ONE, our God, the sovereign of all worlds, who has made us holy with your mitzvot, and commanded us to wrap ourselves amid the fringed tallit.

DERASH. The tallit is a very personal ritual object. Usually I wrap it around myself when joining in a prayer community. For the tallit both creates a private space for me and links me with Jewish tradition. It emphasizes my connection to my people while also offering me spiritual privacy. I am alone and in community at the same time. L.B.

COMMENTARY. According to rabbinic tradition, Psalm 104:1-2 describes how God, robed in splendor, wrapped in light, began to create the world. The radiance of God's light-robe (one source says that God donned a white tallit) illumined the world before the creation of sun, moon, and stars. This meditation invites the worshipper to consider the act of donning the tallit to be the first step in the daily renewal of the world. God's wrapping in light becomes Israel's enlightened wrapping at the outset of a new day. It encourages Israel to celebrate world renewing creativity as an unfailing sign of the divine presence within humankind. S.S.

עֲטִיפַת טַלִּית

It is customary to wrap oneself in the tallit before reciting the blessing that follows. After the blessing is recited, the tallit is placed across the shoulders. In some congregations the blessing is said in unison.

בָּרְכִי נַפְשִׁי אֶת יהוה אֱלֹהַי גָּדַלְתָּ מְּאֹד הוֹד וְהָדָר לָבָשְׁתָּ: עֹטֶה אוֹר כַּשַּׂלְמָה נוֹטֶה שָׁמַיִם כַּיְרִיעָה:

בָּרוּךְ אַתָּה יהוה אֱלֹהֵינוּ מֶלֶךְ הָעוֹלָם
אֲשֶׁר קִדְּשָׁנוּ בְּמִצְוֹתָיו
וְצִוָּנוּ לְהִתְעַטֵּף בַּצִּיצִית:

Baruḥ atah adonay eloheynu meleḥ ha'olam
asher kideshanu bemitzvotav
vetzivanu lehit'atef batzitzit.

Many contemporary Jews are reciting *beraḥot*/blessings in ways that reflect their theological outlooks and ethical concerns. At any place where a blessing occurs in the liturgy, the following elements can be combined to create alternative formulas for *beraḥot*. This can be done by selecting one phrase from each group to form the introductory clause.

I	Baruḥ atah adonay	בָּרוּךְ אַתָּה יהוה	Blessed are you Adonay
	Beruḥah at yah	בְּרוּכָה אַתְּ יָהּ	Blessed are you Yah
	Nevareḥ et	נְבָרֵךְ אֶת	Let us bless
II	eloheynu	אֱלֹהֵינוּ	our God
	hasheḥinah	הַשְּׁכִינָה	Sheḥinah
	eyn haḥayim	עֵין הַחַיִּים	Source of Life
III	meleḥ ha'olam	מֶלֶךְ הָעוֹלָם	Sovereign of all worlds
	ḥey ha'olamim	חֵי הָעוֹלָמִים	Life of all the worlds
	ruaḥ ha'olam	רוּחַ הָעוֹלָם	Spirit of the world

How precious is your love, O God,
when earthborn find the shelter of your wing!
They're nourished from the riches of your house.
Give drink to them from your Edenic stream.
For with you is the fountain of all life,
in your Light do we behold all light.
Extend your love to those who know you,
and your justice to those honest in their hearts. (Psalm 36:8-11)

כי עמך מקור חיים / for with you is the fountain of all life, in your light do we behold all light. The flow of light represented by the tallit is joined to the blessing of life itself. God is described here in the psalmist's most delicate and abstract phrasing. We reach forth to the source of life and are bathed in its light as it flows forth to meet us. A.G.

DERASH. The tallit is a "garment of brightness." It links us with the whole universe, with the whole of Nature. The blue thread within it (Numbers 15:37-41) reminds us that heaven and earth can touch, that the elements of our universe are all wondrously connected. L.B.

COMMENTARY. The order of *Birḥot Hashaḥar* varies from prayerbook to prayerbook because this was not a set part of the public service. Individuals originally recited these blessings as they went about rising, washing and dressing in the morning. Later they were recited privately as a prelude to public prayer.

The order of the blessings here begins with the universal act of waking up and becoming aware of the world. It continues with greater wakefulness, addressing sight, clothing, and the act of standing upright. It then shifts to particulars reflecting Jewish uniqueness. Only then does it turn to the full awareness of the mind and spirit expressed in *Elohay Neshamah*.
D.A.T.

מַה יָּקָר חַסְדְּךָ אֱלֹהִים וּבְנֵי אָדָם בְּצֵל כְּנָפֶיךָ יֶחֱסָיוּן׃
יִרְוְיֻן מִדֶּשֶׁן בֵּיתֶךָ וְנַחַל עֲדָנֶיךָ תַשְׁקֵם׃
כִּי עִמְּךָ מְקוֹר חַיִּים בְּאוֹרְךָ נִרְאֶה אוֹר׃
מְשֹׁךְ חַסְדְּךָ לְיֹדְעֶיךָ וְצִדְקָתְךָ לְיִשְׁרֵי לֵב׃

COMMENTARY. The wearing of the tallit has its origins in the biblical commandment (Numbers 15:37-41) that a fringe should be attached to each corner of a garment to remind the Israelites of the mitzvot. This garment, resembling a poncho, was the basic garment worn every day. When clothing without such defined corners came to be customary, the tallit became a special ritual garment. In our time, a large tallit is worn only during the morning prayer, while traditional Jews wear a small tallit, also known as *arba kanfot* / four corners, underneath their outer clothes. In the biblical commandment the fringe was a color called תכלת / *teḥelet*, a particular shade of purple-blue. When this was no longer available, the rabbis ruled that the fringes should be an undyed white. Some contemporary Jews have reinstituted the inclusion of blue in the fringe. Today in Reconstructionist congregations, women are encouraged to wear tallitot as well. D.A.T.

HANAḤAT TEFILLIN: PUTTING ON TEFILLIN

For the union
of the blessed Holy One
with all that is divine within the world,
in awe and reverence for the task
of bringing into harmony and perfect oneness
all the ways that God is manifest
in speech and deed,
and in the name of all the people Israel,
I hereby place upon myself tefillin,
to fulfill the mitzvah of my Creator,
who commanded us to wear tefillin,
as is written in the Torah:
"You shall bind them as a sign upon your hand,
and keep them visible before your eyes."
And God commanded us to wear them on the hand
in remembrance of God's outstretched hand—
placed near the heart in order to direct
our heart's desires and thoughts
to service of the blessed divine name—
and on the head, placed near the brain,
so that the spirit which resides there,
and all my other powers and senses,
shall be harnessed to God's worship.
Blessed be God's name!
And through the flow of divine strength
which I partake of through the mitzvah of tefillin,
may I be granted long life,
and abundant holiness,
and knowledge of the sacred.

KAVANAH: A sign of holiness is placed upon the head, and the arm is bound. This crown of holiness is not accompanied by a scepter that affirms unlimited power but by a binding which restricts the use of it. Jewish empowering implies the responsibility to use power humbly and justly.

E.M.

הַנָּחַת תְּפִלִּין

לְשֵׁם יִחוּד קֻדְשָׁא בְּרִיךְ הוּא וּשְׁכִינְתֵּהּ בִּדְחִילוּ וּרְחִימוּ לְיַחֵד שֵׁם י״ה בְּו״ה (יהוה) בְּיִחוּדָא שְׁלִים בְּשֵׁם כָּל יִשְׂרָאֵל:

הִנְנִי מְכַוֵּן בְּהַנָּחַת תְּפִלִּין לְקַיֵּם מִצְוַת בּוֹרְאִי שֶׁצִּוָּנוּ לְהָנִיחַ תְּפִלִּין כַּכָּתוּב בְּתוֹרָתוֹ: וּקְשַׁרְתָּם לְאוֹת עַל יָדֶךָ וְהָיוּ לְטֹטָפֹת בֵּין עֵינֶיךָ: וְצִוָּנוּ לְהָנִיחַ עַל הַיָּד לְזִכְרוֹן זְרוֹעַ הַנְּטוּיָה וְשֶׁהִיא נֶגֶד הַלֵּב לְשַׁעְבֵּד בָּזֶה מַחְשְׁבוֹת לִבֵּנוּ וְתַאֲווֹתָיו לַעֲבוֹדָתוֹ יִתְבָּרַךְ שְׁמוֹ: וְעַל הָרֹאשׁ נֶגֶד הַמֹּחַ שֶׁהַנְּשָׁמָה שֶׁבְּמוֹחִי עִם שְׁאָר הוּשַׁי וְכֹחוֹתַי כֻּלָּם יִהְיוּ מְשֻׁעְבָּדִים לַעֲבוֹדָתוֹ יִתְבָּרַךְ שְׁמוֹ: וּמִשֶּׁפַע מִצְוַת תְּפִלִּין יִתְמַשֵּׁךְ עָלַי לִהְיוֹת לִי חַיִּים אֲרֻכִּים וְשֶׁפַע קֹדֶשׁ, וּמַחֲשָׁבוֹת קְדוֹשׁוֹת:

COMMENTARY. Men have traditionally worn *tefillin* during worship on weekday mornings. Throughout history women have occasionally worn *tefillin* as well, a trend accelerated by women's increasing equality in the contemporary period.

Tefillin are not worn on Shabbat and holidays, as they are understood to be an אוֹת / *ot* / sign of our relationship to the divine. Since Shabbat and holidays are also "signs," wearing *tefillin* on those days would be redundant. On Tisha Be'Av, *tefillin* are worn for the afternoon service instead of the morning.

Each set of *tefillin* has two parts, one for the head and one for the arm. *Tefillin* straps for both parts are made from the skin of kosher animals and dyed black. The box for the head has four compartments, each containing a scroll with one biblical passage (Ex. 13:1-10, 11-16; Deut. 6:4-9, and 11:13-21). The box worn on the arm contains these same passages on a single parchment. This arrangement suggests freedom of thought and openness of debate while urging unity of action.

Discussion regarding the proper way to wear *tefillin* usually hinges upon *gematriya* (number/word play) and mystical symbolism. There are many minor variations in local customs as a result. The best way to learn how to put on *tefillin* is by imitating a trusted teacher. D.A.T.

When placing the tefillin *on the arm:*

Blessed are you, ALMIGHTY ONE, our God, the sovereign of all worlds, who has made us holy through mitzvot, and has commanded us to wear *tefillin.*

When placing the tefillin *on the forehead:*

Blessed are you, COMPASSIONATE ONE, our God, the sovereign of all worlds, who has made us holy through mitzvot, and has bestowed on us the mitzvah of *tefillin.*

Blessed be the name and glory of God's realm forever!

When winding the retzuah *three times around the middle finger:*

"And I betroth you to me everlastingly,
and I betroth you to me with righteousness and justice,
and I betroth you to me with loving and compassion,
and you shall know THE FOUNT OF LIFE."

NOTE: Right-handed people have traditionally worn the *tefillin* on the left arm; left-handed people wear *tefillin* on the right arm. The rabbis deduced this from *Devarim* / Deuteronomy 6:8-9, which suggests that binding the *tefillin* is done with the same hand with which one writes. It makes sense to put on *tefillin* with one's stronger, defter hand. D.A.T.

When placing the tefillin *on the left arm:*

בָּרוּךְ אַתָּה יהוה אֱלֹהֵינוּ מֶלֶךְ הָעוֹלָם אֲשֶׁר קִדְּשָׁנוּ בְּמִצְוֹתָיו וְצִוָּנוּ לְהָנִיחַ תְּפִלִּין:

When placing the tefillin *on the forehead:*

בָּרוּךְ אַתָּה יהוה אֱלֹהֵינוּ מֶלֶךְ הָעוֹלָם אֲשֶׁר קִדְּשָׁנוּ בְּמִצְוֹתָיו וְצִוָּנוּ עַל מִצְוַת תְּפִלִּין:

בָּרוּךְ שֵׁם כְּבוֹד מַלְכוּתוֹ לְעוֹלָם וָעֶד:

When winding the retzuah *three times round the middle finger:*

וְאֵרַשְׂתִּיךְ לִי לְעוֹלָם וְאֵרַשְׂתִּיךְ לִי בְּצֶדֶק וּבְמִשְׁפָּט וּבְחֶסֶד וּבְרַחֲמִים:
וְאֵרַשְׂתִּיךְ לִי בֶּאֱמוּנָה וְיָדַעַתְּ אֶת יהוה:

COMMENTARY. The *tefillin* straps are arranged to form the "*shaday*" name of God on the hand, arm and head. Thus, seeing or wearing *tefillin* reminds us of God's presence and of our constant duty to serve the divine. Because of their importance as a visible sign, *tefillin* are worn only during daylight hours, when they can be seen.

The rabbis understood the wearing of *tefillin* to be a fulfillment of the commandment from Deuteronomy 6:8 quoted in the *Shema*, וקשרתם לאות על ידך והיו לטטפת בין עיניך / You shall bind them as a sign upon your hand, and keep them visible before your eyes. While the original meaning of the biblical passage has been lost in the mists of time, the custom of putting on *tefillin* has been hallowed by over 2000 years of daily practice.

D.A.T.

וארשתיך...וידעת את יהוה / And I betroth you to me... the FOUNT OF LIFE (Hosea 2:21-22).

For the sake of the union of the blessed Holy One with the Sheḥinah, I stand here, ready in body and mind, to take upon myself the mitzvah, "You shall love your fellow human being as yourself," and by this merit may I open up my mouth.

Some congregations sing Adon Olam (page 343) or Yigdal (page 206) here.

COMMENTARY. This *kavanah* before the morning service was introduced by the kabbalists of Safed. Only by accepting upon ourselves the obligation to love others as ourselves are we allowed to enter the human community of prayer. It is as members of that community, and specifically as Jews, that we come before God in worship. A.G.

לְשֵׁם יִחוּד קֻדְשָׁא בְּרִיךְ הוּא וּשְׁכִינְתֵּהּ
הִנְנִי מוּכָן וּמְזֻמָּן לְקַבֵּל עָלַי
מִצְוַת עֲשֵׂה שֶׁל

וְאָהַבְתָּ לְרֵעֲךָ כָּמוֹךָ

וּבִזְכוּת זֶה אֶפְתַּח פִּי:

Some congregations sing Adon Olam (page 343) or Yigdal (page 206) here.

ואהבת...כמוך / You shall...yourself (Leviticus 19:18).

BIRḤOT HASHAḤAR / MORNING BLESSINGS

Blessed are you, AWAKENER, our God, life of all the worlds, who removes sleep from my eyes, and slumber from my eyelids. ↩

Many contemporary Jews are reciting *beraḥot*/blessings in ways that reflect their theological outlooks and ethical concerns. At any place where a blessing occurs in the liturgy, the following elements can be combined to create alternative formulas for *beraḥot*. This can be done by selecting one phrase from each group to form the introductory clause.

I	Baruḥ atah adonay	בָּרוּךְ אַתָּה יהוה	Blessed are you Adonay
	Beruḥah at yah	בְּרוּכָה אַתְּ יָהּ	Blessed are you Yah
	Nevareḥ et	נְבָרֵךְ אֶת	Let us bless
II	eloheynu	אֱלֹהֵינוּ	our God
	hasheḥinah	הַשְּׁכִינָה	Sheḥinah
	eyn haḥayim	עֵין הַחַיִּים	Source of Life
III	meleḥ ha'olam	מֶלֶךְ הָעוֹלָם	Sovereign of all worlds
	ḥey ha'olamim	חֵי הָעוֹלָמִים	Life of all the worlds
	ruaḥ ha'olam	רוּחַ הָעוֹלָם	Spirit of the world

בִּרְכוֹת הַשַּׁחַר

בָּרוּךְ אַתָּה יהוה אֱלֹהֵינוּ חֵי הָעוֹלָמִים
הַמַּעֲבִיר שֵׁנָה מֵעֵינַי וּתְנוּמָה מֵעַפְעַפָּי: ←

Baruḥ atah adonay elo<u>hey</u>nu ḥey ha'olamim
hama'avir shenah me'eynay utnumah me'afapay

COMMENTARY. The familiar introductory formula for blessings including the phrase *meleḥ ha'olam* / sovereign of the world, was adopted by the rabbis during the talmudic era and universally accepted by later Jews. Substituting another rabbinic phrase, *ḥey ha'olamim* / life of all the worlds, expresses the idea that as Judaism continues to evolve, alternatives to the ancient metaphor of God as divine ruler should emerge. This alternative blessing formulation may be used throughout the siddur by those who prefer it, just as the traditional *meleḥ ha'olam* may be substituted here. A.G.

COMMENTARY. Various editions of the prayerbook offer different orders of the morning blessings. Here the first blessing is that on awakening. Then comes a blessing on the first sounds of dawn, followed by thanksgiving for the return of waking consciousness ("who establishes the dry land upon the waters"), and then the blessing on opening our eyes and seeing our world, freshly created with the dawn, around us. The cycle is completed with the final blessing "who gives strength to the weary" as we prepare to begin our day. A.G.

Blessed are you, THE PROVIDENT, our God, life of all the worlds, who gives the bird of dawn discernment to tell day from night.

Blessed are you, THE FASHIONER, our God, life of all the worlds, who stretches forth the earth upon the waters.

Blessed are you, THE LAMP, our God, life of all the worlds, who makes the blind to see.

Blessed are you, THE COMPASSIONATE, our God, life of all the worlds, who clothes the naked.

Blessed are you, REDEEMING ONE, our God, life of all the worlds, who makes the captive free.

Blessed are you, THE HELPING HAND, our God, life of all the worlds, who raises up the humble. ↩

KAVANAH. We give thanks that we are restored whole and healthy to consciousness and to an orderly universe. That is why, in the second blessing, we give thanks that, when we stepped out of bed our feet encountered not the watery chaos which preceded creation, but the solid earth which God spread over the waters. The daily emergence from unconsciousness reminds us of our fragility as human creatures and our need for support and care. R.A.

KAVANAH. Those of us who live in plenty are grateful for the clothing on our bodies, the warmth of a garment that shields us from the elements. We pray for a time when this blessing may be spoken by *all* people, a time when *all* humans are "clothed" with warmth and safety, enwrapped in God's love. L.B.

בָּרוּךְ אַתָּה יהוה אֱלֹהֵינוּ חֵי הָעוֹלָמִים
הַנּוֹתֵן לַשֶּׂכְוִי בִינָה לְהַבְחִין בֵּין יוֹם וּבֵין לָיְלָה:

בָּרוּךְ אַתָּה יהוה אֱלֹהֵינוּ חֵי הָעוֹלָמִים
רוֹקַע הָאָרֶץ עַל הַמָּיִם:

בָּרוּךְ אַתָּה יהוה אֱלֹהֵינוּ חֵי הָעוֹלָמִים פּוֹקֵחַ עִוְרִים:

בָּרוּךְ אַתָּה יהוה אֱלֹהֵינוּ חֵי הָעוֹלָמִים מַלְבִּישׁ עֲרֻמִּים:

בָּרוּךְ אַתָּה יהוה אֱלֹהֵינוּ חֵי הָעוֹלָמִים מַתִּיר אֲסוּרִים:

בָּרוּךְ אַתָּה יהוה אֱלֹהֵינוּ חֵי הָעוֹלָמִים זוֹקֵף כְּפוּפִים: ←

Baruḥ atah adonay eloheynu ḥey ha'olamim
hanoten laseḥvi vinah lehavḥin beyn yom uveyn laylah.

Baruḥ atah adonay eloheynu ḥey ha'olamim
roka ha'aretz al hamayim.

Baruḥ atah adonay eloheynu ḥey ha'olamim poke'aḥ ivrim.

Baruḥ atah adonay eloheynu ḥey ha'olamim malbish arumim.

Baruḥ atah adonay eloheynu ḥey ha'olamim matir asurim.

Baruḥ atah adonay eloheynu ḥey ha'olamim zokef kefufim.

Blessed are you, THE WAY, our God, life of all the worlds, who makes firm a person's steps.

Blessed are you, THE GENEROUS, our God, life of all the worlds, who acts for all my needs.

Blessed are you, THE MIGHTY ONE, our God, life of all the worlds, who girds Israel with strength.

Blessed are you, THE BEAUTIFUL, our God, life of all the worlds, who crowns Israel with splendor.

Blessed are you, THE IMAGELESS, our God, life of all the worlds, who made me in your image.

Blessed are you, THE FREE, our God, life of all the worlds, who made me free.

Blessed are you, THE ANCIENT ONE, our God, life of all the worlds, who made me of the people Israel.

Blessed are you, RENEWING ONE, our God, life of all the worlds, who gives strength to the weary.

שעשני בצלמו / who made me in your image. When a human being is slain, the very image of God is shattered. We revere human life because it is a spark of the life that animates the universe. Only after we have acquired the principle of reverence for each person is it possible to love each other as we should love, not merely "as thyself" but as a reflection of the divine. "Beloved are human beings," said R. Akiba, "for they were made in the image of God." M.M.K. (Adapted)

שעשני בן/בת חורין / who made me free. Literally, son/daughter of freedom. J.B.

בָּרוּךְ אַתָּה יהוה אֱלֹהֵֽינוּ חֵי הָעוֹלָמִים הַמֵּכִין מִצְעֲדֵי גָֽבֶר׃

בָּרוּךְ אַתָּה יהוה אֱלֹהֵֽינוּ חֵי הָעוֹלָמִים שֶׁעָשָׂה לִי כׇּל צׇרְכִּי׃

בָּרוּךְ אַתָּה יהוה אֱלֹהֵֽינוּ חֵי הָעוֹלָמִים אוֹזֵר יִשְׂרָאֵל בִּגְבוּרָה׃

בָּרוּךְ אַתָּה יהוה אֱלֹהֵֽינוּ חֵי הָעוֹלָמִים עוֹטֵר יִשְׂרָאֵל בְּתִפְאָרָה׃

בָּרוּךְ אַתָּה יהוה אֱלֹהֵֽינוּ חֵי הָעוֹלָמִים שֶׁעָשַֽׂנִי בְּצַלְמוֹ׃

בָּרוּךְ אַתָּה יהוה אֱלֹהֵֽינוּ חֵי הָעוֹלָמִים שֶׁעָשַֽׂנִי בֶּן/בַּת חוֹרִין׃

בָּרוּךְ אַתָּה יהוה אֱלֹהֵֽינוּ חֵי הָעוֹלָמִים שֶׁעָשַֽׂנִי יִשְׂרָאֵל׃

בָּרוּךְ אַתָּה יהוה אֱלֹהֵֽינוּ חֵי הָעוֹלָמִים הַנּוֹתֵן לַיָּעֵף כֹּֽחַ׃ ←

Baruḥ atah adonay eloheynu ḥey ha'olamim
hameḥin mitzadey gaver.

Baruḥ atah adonay eloheynu ḥey ha'olamim
she'asah li kol tzorki.

Baruḥ atah adonay eloheynu ḥey ha'olamim
ozer yisra'el bigvurah.

Baruḥ atah adonay eloheynu ḥey ha'olamim
oter yisra'el betifarah.

Baruḥ atah adonay eloheynu ḥey ha'olamim she'asani
betzalmo.

Baruḥ atah adonay eloheynu ḥey ha'olamim
she'asani ben/bat ḥorin.

Baruḥ atah adonay eloheynu ḥey ha'olamim she'asani yisra'el.

Baruḥ atah adonay eloheynu ḥey ha'olamim
hanoten laya'ef ko'aḥ.

I give thanks before you,
sovereign who lives and who endures,
because you have renewed my breath of life,
with providential kindness.
How abundant is your faithful care!

Blessed are you, THE ARCHITECT, our God, the sovereign of all worlds, who shaped the human being with wisdom, making for us all the openings and vessels of the body. It is revealed and known before your Throne of Glory that if one of these passage-ways be open when it should be closed, or blocked up when it should be free, one could not stay alive or stand before you. Blessed are you, MIRACULOUS, the wondrous healer of all flesh.

COMMENTARY. This blessing expresses wonder at the simple but necessary functioning of the human body. We do not need to stand before any greater wonder of nature than our own bodies in order to appreciate the intricacy and beauty with which our world is endowed. A sense of awe at our own creation is a starting point of prayer. A.G.

KAVANAH: Gratitude, with its overtones of serenity and indebtedness, is the most effective way of experiencing the reality of God. M.M.K. (Adapted)

מוֹדֶה / מוֹדָה אֲנִי

לְפָנֶֽיךָ מֶֽלֶךְ חַי וְקַיָּם שֶׁהֶחֱזַֽרְתָּ בִּי נִשְׁמָתִי בְּחֶמְלָה רַבָּה אֱמוּנָתֶֽךָ׃

Modeh/Modah ani lefaneḥa meleḥ ḥay vekayam sheheḥezarta bi nishmati beḥemlah rabah emunateḥa.

בָּרוּךְ אַתָּה יהוה אֱלֹהֵֽינוּ מֶֽלֶךְ הָעוֹלָם אֲשֶׁר יָצַר אֶת הָאָדָם בְּחָכְמָה
וּבָרָא בוֹ נְקָבִים נְקָבִים חֲלוּלִים חֲלוּלִים׃
גָּלוּי וְיָדֽוּעַ לִפְנֵי כִסֵּא כְבוֹדֶֽךָ שֶׁאִם יִפָּתֵֽחַ אֶחָד מֵהֶם אוֹ יִסָּתֵם אֶחָד
מֵהֶם אִי אֶפְשָׁר לְהִתְקַיֵּם וְלַעֲמֹד לְפָנֶֽיךָ׃
בָּרוּךְ אַתָּה יהוה רוֹפֵא כָל בָּשָׂר וּמַפְלִיא לַעֲשׂוֹת׃

Baruḥ atah adonay eloheynu meleḥ ha'olam asher yatzar et ha'adam beḥoḥmah uvara vo nekavim nekavim ḥalulim ḥalulim. Galuwi veyadu'a lifney ḥisey ḥevodeḥa she'im yipate'aḥ eḥad mehem o yisatem eḥad mehem i efshar lehitkayem vela'amod lefaneḥa. Baruḥ atah adonay rofey ḥol basar umafli la'asot.

COMMENTARY: According to the Talmud's teaching, "sleep is one-sixtieth part of death"—that is, the experience of awakening each day is considered a new creation of life, a miracle to be greeted with wonderment and gratitude. This passage (*Modeh/Modah ani*) also associates the notion of a person's soul or spirit with the physical experience of breathing, an activity one is especially capable of appreciating in those first moments of awakening. J.R.

My God, the soul you gave to me is pure. You have created it, you shaped it, and you breathed it into me, and you preserve it deep inside of me. And someday you will take it from me, restoring it to everlasting life.

As long as spirit breathes in me, I offer thanks before you, BREATH DIVINE, my God, God of my ancestors, the master of all deeds, and source of every life. Blessed are you, THE HOLY SPIRIT, in whose possession is the breath of every living thing, the animation of all flesh.

COMMENTARY. The word *neshamah*, which means both "breath" and "soul," provides a linguistic connection between the blessings for body and soul. The blessing for the soul uses the vocabulary of the Creation story, especially Genesis 2:6, which describes how God created the human form and then animated it with the breath of life. Hence, the language of celebrating each awakening carries an echo of the primal joining of human form to life force. Every awakening is nothing less than a rehearsal of the mystery of creation.

The traditional version of the blessing for the soul acknowledges the daily renewal of life as a recollection of creation and also as a foretaste of resurrection. The current version concludes instead by acknowledging God as the power that renews life each day. S.S.

DERASH. This short and beautiful prayer starts each day and offers comfort in times of stress. Self-esteem is a precious gift. Even though we may lose it in the tragedies of the present, it will be restored to us in our future. God, the healer, returns our souls to us. E.M.

אֱלֹהַי נְשָׁמָה שֶׁנָּתַתָּ בִּי טְהוֹרָה הִיא׃

אַתָּה בְרָאתָהּ אַתָּה יְצַרְתָּהּ אַתָּה נְפַחְתָּהּ בִּי וְאַתָּה מְשַׁמְּרָהּ בְּקִרְבִּי
וְאַתָּה עָתִיד לִטְּלָהּ מִמֶּנִּי לְחַיֵּי עוֹלָם׃ כָּל זְמַן שֶׁהַנְּשָׁמָה בְקִרְבִּי
מוֹדֶה/מוֹדָה אֲנִי לְפָנֶיךָ יהוה אֱלֹהַי וֵאלֹהֵי אֲבוֹתַי וְאִמּוֹתַי רִבּוֹן כָּל
הַמַּעֲשִׂים אֲדוֹן כָּל הַנְּשָׁמוֹת׃ בָּרוּךְ אַתָּה יהוה אֲשֶׁר בְּיָדוֹ נֶפֶשׁ כָּל
חָי וְרוּחַ כָּל בְּשַׂר׃

Elohay neshamah shenatata bi tehorah hi.

לחיי עולם / restoring it [the soul] to everlasting life. The traditional Hebrew text says, "and restore it to me in the future to come." The text in our siddur, rather than stressing the traditional notion of individual afterlife, or of personal resurrection in the messianic End of Days, reverses the emphasis: the soul, having sojourned in the physical life, is restored to the everlasting stream of life—to the continuum of being that is the sum-total of all transitory lives, when viewed from the perspective of eternity. J.R.

אשר בידו נפש כל חי / in whose possession is the breath of every living thing. We gratefully acknowledge God as the source of life itself and of the constant renewal of our spirit. The traditional formula of this blessing, referring to the future resurrection of the dead, has been emended. As Reconstructionists, we accept both the finality of death and the infinite wondrousness of life. Our religion is about the balancing of these two realities, neither of which may be allowed to negate the other. A.G.

BIRKAT LIMUD TORAH / BLESSING PRECEDING TORAH STUDY

The following blessing is said only when it precedes Jewish study. Any Jewish sources may be selected.

Blessed are you, THE ONE OF SINAI, our God, the sovereign of all worlds, who made us holy with your mitzvot, and commanded us to occupy ourselves with words of Torah.

Transmit to us, WISE ONE, our God, your Torah's words, into our mouths, and to the mouths of all the House of Israel, who called you kin. May we, and our children, and all the children of your people, the House of Israel, all of us, be knowers of your Name and learners of your Torah, for its sake alone. Blessed are you, THE SAGE, who teaches Torah to your people Israel.

COMMENTARY. Blessings and texts for Torah study are a traditional part of *Birḥot Hashaḥar.* Like body and soul, Torah study is a daily part of Jewish living. Rabbinic literature records more than a half dozen versions of Torah blessings. The ornate Torah blessing in our text both begins and ends with the formula "*Baruḥ atah.*" In the first instance, the formula of blessing acknowledges that Torah study is essential to Jewish life. The concluding phrase of blessing praises God as the teacher of Torah. From a Reconstructionist perspective, the metaphor of God as teacher is an invitation and challenge to discern the divine presence in learning. A talmudic passage appears between the two blessings. It offers the hope that we, the people Israel, will always see Torah as an intrinsic part of ourselves. S.S.

בְּרָכַּת לִמּוּד תּוֹרָה

The following blessing is said only when it precedes Jewish study. Any Jewish sources may be selected.

בָּרוּךְ אַתָּה יהוה אֱלֹהֵינוּ מֶלֶךְ הָעוֹלָם אֲשֶׁר קִדְּשָׁנוּ בְּמִצְוֹתָיו וְצִוָּנוּ לַעֲסֹק בְּדִבְרֵי תוֹרָה:

Baruḥ atah adonay eloheynu meleḥ ha'olam asher kideshanu bemitzvotav vetzivanu la'asok bedivrey torah.

וְהַעֲרֶב־נָא יהוה אֱלֹהֵינוּ אֶת דִּבְרֵי תוֹרָתְךָ בְּפִינוּ וּבְפִי עַמְּךָ בֵּית יִשְׂרָאֵל וְנִהְיֶה אֲנַחְנוּ וְצֶאֱצָאֵינוּ וְצֶאֱצָאֵי עַמְּךָ בֵּית יִשְׂרָאֵל כֻּלָּנוּ יוֹדְעֵי שְׁמֶךָ וְלוֹמְדֵי תוֹרָתְךָ לִשְׁמָהּ:
בָּרוּךְ אַתָּה יהוה הַמְלַמֵּד תּוֹרָה לְעַמּוֹ יִשְׂרָאֵל:

Veha'arev na adonay eloheynu et divrey torateḥa befinu uvefi ameḥa beyt yisra'el venihyeh anaḥnu vetze'etza'eynu vetze'etza'ey ameḥa beyt yisra'el kulanu yod'ey shemeḥa velomdey torateḥa lishmah. Baruḥ atah adonay hamelamed torah le'amo yisra'el.

NOTE. Traditionally, brief sections of classical texts are studied as part of Birḥot Hashaḥar. Together these comprised the daily minimum of Jewish study. While there has been disagreement within Jewish tradition about which sources must be included, passages of Torah, Mishnah and Talmud have come to dominate. More contemporary sources can be used in our time as well. What matters is making Jewish study a daily activity.

D.A.T.

KADDISH DERABANAN/THE SAGES' KADDISH

This kaddish *is recited after study when a minyan is present.*
The English translation is on page 28.

Yitgadal veyitkadash shemeh raba be'alma di vera ḥirutey veyamliḥ malḥuteh beḥayeyḥon uveyomeyḥon uveḥayey deḥol beyt yisra'el ba'agala uvizman kariv ve'imeru amen.

Yehey shemey raba mevaraḥ le'alam ulalmey almaya.

Yitbaraḥ veyishtabaḥ veyitpa'ar veyitromam veyitnasey veyit-hadar veyitaleh veyit-halal shemey dekudesha beriḥ hu le'e̱la (*Between Rosh Hashanah and Yom Kippur, add:* le'e̱la) min kol birḥata veshirata tushbeḥata veneḥemata da'amiran be'alma ve'imeru amen.

Al yisra'el ve'al rabanan ve'al talmideyhon ve'al kol talmidey talmideyhon ve'al kol man de'askin be'orayta di be'atra hadeyn vedi beḥol atar ve'atar yehey lehon uleḥon shelama rabah ḥina veḥisda veraḥamin veḥayin ariḥin umezoney reviḥey ufurkana min kadam avuhon di vishmaya ve'ara ve'imeru amen.

Yehey shelama rabah min shemaya veḥayim a̱le̱ynu ve'al kol yisra'el ve'imeru amen.

Oseh shalom bimromav hu ya'aseh shalom a̱le̱ynu ve'al kol yisra'el ve'al kol yoshvey tevel ve'imeru amen.

KAVANAH. Adding the rabbinic phrase "*ve'al kol yoshvey tevel*" (and for all who dwell on earth) logically completes the concentric circles of our aspirations—our care starts with our minyan, extends to the entire Jewish people, and radiates outward from there to all who share our planet. D.A.T

קַדִּישׁ דְּרַבָּנָן

This kaddish *is recited after study when a minyan is present.*

יִתְגַּדַּל וְיִתְקַדַּשׁ שְׁמֵהּ רַבָּא בְּעָלְמָא דִּי בְרָא כִרְעוּתֵהּ וְיַמְלִיךְ
מַלְכוּתֵהּ בְּחַיֵּיכוֹן וּבְיוֹמֵיכוֹן וּבְחַיֵּי דְכָל בֵּית יִשְׂרָאֵל בַּעֲגָלָא וּבִזְמַן
קָרִיב וְאִמְרוּ אָמֵן:

יְהֵא שְׁמֵהּ רַבָּא מְבָרַךְ לְעָלַם וּלְעָלְמֵי עָלְמַיָּא:

יִתְבָּרַךְ וְיִשְׁתַּבַּח וְיִתְפָּאַר וְיִתְרוֹמַם וְיִתְנַשֵּׂא וְיִתְהַדַּר וְיִתְעַלֶּה
וְיִתְהַלַּל שְׁמֵהּ דְּקֻדְשָׁא בְּרִיךְ הוּא
לְעֵֽלָּא (*Between Rosh Hashanah and Yom Kippur add:* לְעֵֽלָּא) מִן כָּל בִּרְכָתָא
וְשִׁירָתָא תֻּשְׁבְּחָתָא וְנֶחֱמָתָא דַּאֲמִירָן בְּעָלְמָא וְאִמְרוּ אָמֵן:

עַל יִשְׂרָאֵל וְעַל רַבָּנָן וְעַל תַּלְמִידֵיהוֹן וְעַל כָּל תַּלְמִידֵי תַלְמִידֵיהוֹן
וְעַל כָּל מַאן דְּעָסְקִין בְּאוֹרַיְתָא דִּי בְּאַתְרָא הָדֵין וְדִי בְכָל אֲתַר
וַאֲתַר יְהֵא לְהוֹן וּלְכוֹן שְׁלָמָא רַבָּא חִנָּא וְחִסְדָּא וְרַחֲמִין וְחַיִּין אֲרִיכִין
וּמְזוֹנֵי רְוִיחֵי וּפֻרְקָנָא מִן קֳדָם אֲבוּהוֹן דְּבִשְׁמַיָּא וְאַרְעָא וְאִמְרוּ אָמֵן:

יְהֵא שְׁלָמָא רַבָּא מִן שְׁמַיָּא וְחַיִּים עָלֵֽינוּ וְעַל כָּל יִשְׂרָאֵל וְאִמְרוּ אָמֵן:
עוֹשֶׂה שָׁלוֹם בִּמְרוֹמָיו הוּא יַעֲשֶׂה שָׁלוֹם עָלֵֽינוּ וְעַל כָּל יִשְׂרָאֵל וְעַל
כָּל יוֹשְׁבֵי תֵבֵל וְאִמְרוּ אָמֵן:

NOTE. It is the custom in some communities for remembrances and/or teachings of those who have died to be shared aloud prior to the recitation of the Kaddish Derabanan. Sometimes others share teachings as well.

D.A.T.

COMMENTARY. Most scholars agree that Kaddish Derabanan is the most ancient form of the Kaddish prayer. It was used at the conclusion of study long before the Kaddish became a prayer for mourners. Its prayer is that the efforts of both students and teachers bring holiness and a sense of the divine presence into the world. This in turn should help them formulate a vision of peace that they can spread to all Israel, and ultimately to all the world. Kaddish Derabanan, like all forms of the Kaddish, thus brings us in touch with the central purpose of prayer. D.A.T.

Reader: Let God's name be made great and holy in the world that was created as God willed. May God complete the holy realm in your own lifetime, in your days, and in the days of all the house of Israel, quickly and soon. And say: Amen.

Congregation: May God's great name be blessed, forever and as long as worlds endure.

Reader: May it be blessed, and praised, and glorified, and held in honor, viewed with awe, embellished and revered; and may the blessed name of holiness be hailed, though it be higher (*Between Rosh Hashanah and Yom Kippur, add:* by far) than all the blessings, songs, praises, and consolations that we utter in this world. And say; Amen.

For Israel and her sages, for their pupils and all pupils of their pupils, and for all who occupy themselves with Torah, whether in this place or any other place, may God grant them and you abundant peace, and grace, and love, and mercy, and long life, and ample sustenance, and saving acts, all flowing from divine abundance in the worlds beyond. And say: Amen.

May heaven grant a universal peace and life for us and for all Israel. And say: Amen.

May the one who creates harmony above make peace for us, and for all Israel, and for all who dwell on earth. And say: Amen.

From the cowardice that shrinks from new truth,
From the laziness that is content with half-truths,
From the arrogance that thinks it knows all truth,
O, God of truth, deliver us. M.M.K.

DERASH. When we recite the Kaddish Derabanan, we are thankful for the teachings of Torah (in its widest sense). We have received from those who have come before us—and we accept our own place as links in the chain of tradition. Every student becomes a teacher—what we have learned we will teach. We celebrate our sense of accomplishment, our feeling that we have gained richness from our study. We re-affirm with this Kaddish the honorable endeavor in which we have been engaged. We are a people of study and learning, teaching and receiving—*this* is critical to our collective Jewish life. L.B.

שלום
Shalom
עלינו
for us
ועל כל ישראל
and for all Israel
ועל כל יושבי תבל
and for all who dwell on earth

A psalm. A song for dedication of the house. Of David.

I exalt you, GLORIOUS ONE, because you have delivered me; you gave my enemies no joy on my account.

DEAR ONE, my God, I have cried out to you, and you have made me whole.

REDEEMER, you have raised my spirit from the land of no return, you revived me from among those fallen in a pit.

Sing out to THE ALMIGHTY, fervent souls, be thankful when you call God's holiness to mind.

For God is angry for a moment, but shows favor for a lifetime; though one goes to bed in weeping, one awakes in song.

And I, how I exclaimed in my security: I cannot fail!

PROTECTOR, when you wished, you raised my mountain's strength, and when you hid your face, I was afraid.

To you, THE FOUNT OF LIFE, I used to call, and from my benefactor I sought help unmerited:

"What use in my blood's waste?
What benefit, my going down into the pit?
Can dust acknowledge you? Can it declare your truth?

Hear, O HIDDEN ONE, deal graciously with me,
SUPERNAL ADVOCATE, become a help for me!"

You changed my mourning to an ecstatic dance,
you loosed my sackcloth, and girded me with joy,

that glory might sing out to you, and not be still!
To you, my God, I always shall give thanks.

Psalm 30

מִזְמוֹר שִׁיר־חֲנֻכַּת הַבַּיִת לְדָוִד׃
אֲרוֹמִמְךָ יהוה כִּי דִלִּיתָנִי וְלֹא־שִׂמַּחְתָּ אֹיְבַי לִי׃
יהוה אֱלֹהָי שִׁוַּעְתִּי אֵלֶיךָ וַתִּרְפָּאֵנִי׃
יהוה הֶעֱלִיתָ מִן־שְׁאוֹל נַפְשִׁי חִיִּיתַנִי מִיָּרְדִי־בוֹר׃
זַמְּרוּ לַיהוה חֲסִידָיו וְהוֹדוּ לְזֵכֶר קָדְשׁוֹ׃
כִּי רֶגַע בְּאַפּוֹ חַיִּים בִּרְצוֹנוֹ בָּעֶרֶב יָלִין בֶּכִי וְלַבֹּקֶר רִנָּה׃
וַאֲנִי אָמַרְתִּי בְשַׁלְוִי בַּל־אֶמּוֹט לְעוֹלָם׃
יהוה בִּרְצוֹנְךָ הֶעֱמַדְתָּה לְהַרְרִי עֹז הִסְתַּרְתָּ פָנֶיךָ הָיִיתִי נִבְהָל׃
אֵלֶיךָ יהוה אֶקְרָא וְאֶל־אֲדֹנָי אֶתְחַנָּן׃
מַה־בֶּצַע בְּדָמִי בְּרִדְתִּי אֶל שָׁחַת הֲיוֹדְךָ עָפָר הֲיַגִּיד אֲמִתֶּךָ׃
שְׁמַע־יהוה וְחָנֵּנִי יהוה הֱיֵה־עֹזֵר לִי׃
הָפַכְתָּ מִסְפְּדִי לְמָחוֹל לִי פִּתַּחְתָּ שַׂקִּי וַתְּאַזְּרֵנִי שִׂמְחָה׃
*לְמַעַן יְזַמֶּרְךָ כָבוֹד וְלֹא יִדֹּם יהוה אֱלֹהַי לְעוֹלָם אוֹדֶךָּ׃

Eleḥa adonay ekra ve'el adonay et-ḥanan.
Shema adonay veḥoneni adonay heyey ozer li.

COMMENTARY. According to the Mishnah some Jews regularly meditated for an hour before beginning public prayer. As the public prayer service expanded, this time of personal preparation became filled with a collection of psalms and other biblical selections that became known as *Pesukey Dezimrah*—"Verses of Song." The major theme of *Pesukey Dezimrah* is the praise (*hallel*) of God. Indeed the Talmud sometimes refers to *Pesukey Dezimrah* as the Daily *Hallel*. S.S.

PESUKEY DEZIMRAH / VERSES OF PRAISE

Blessed is the one who spoke and all things came to be!
  Blessed are you!
Blessed, who created all in the beginning!
  Blessed is your name!
Blessed is the one who speaks and acts!
  Blessed are you!
Blessed, who determines and fulfills!
  Blessed is your name!
Blessed, who deals kindly with the world!
  Blessed are you!
Blessed, who acts kindly toward all creatures!
  Blessed is your name!
Blessed, who responds with good to those in awe!
  Blessed are you!
Blessed, who removes the dark and brings the light!
  Blessed is your name!
Blessed is the one who lives eternally and lasts forever!
  Blessed are you!
Blessed, who delivers and redeems!
  Blessed are you and your name!

COMMENTARY. The God affirmed in the words of *Baruḥ She'amar* may be understood in either concrete anthropomorphic terms or in a more abstract manner. It is the latter view with which we Reconstructionists are most comfortable. Our God is not a person who promises and fulfills as a human being would. In speaking of a God who fulfills promises, we express our basic trust in life and our affirmation that goodness and godliness have their own reward. A.G.

COMMENTARY. *Baruḥ She'amar* is the rabbinic composition that introduces *Pesukey Dezimrah*/Verses of Praise, which traditionally is compiled from biblical passages, primarily from Psalms.

The focus of *Birḥot Hashaḥar* is on physical awakening. In *Pesukey Dezimrah* the kaleidoscopic imagery awakens our emotions. Just as we find our own pace walking through art museums, so *Pesukey Dezimrah* invites each of us to wander amidst its visions. On different days, different imagery comes to life. *Pesukey Dezimrah* moves us toward prayerfulness, toward readiness to join in spiritual community. D.A.T.

פְּסוּקֵי דְזִמְרָה

בָּרוּךְ שֶׁאָמַר וְהָיָה הָעוֹלָם	בָּרוּךְ הוּא:
בָּרוּךְ עוֹשֶׂה בְרֵאשִׁית	בָּרוּךְ שְׁמוֹ:
בָּרוּךְ אוֹמֵר וְעוֹשֶׂה	בָּרוּךְ הוּא:
בָּרוּךְ גּוֹזֵר וּמְקַיֵּם	בָּרוּךְ שְׁמוֹ:
בָּרוּךְ מְרַחֵם עַל הָאָֽרֶץ	בָּרוּךְ הוּא:
בָּרוּךְ מְרַחֵם עַל־הַבְּרִיּוֹת	בָּרוּךְ שְׁמוֹ:
בָּרוּךְ מְשַׁלֵּם שָׂכָר טוֹב לִירֵאָיו	בָּרוּךְ הוּא:
בָּרוּךְ מַעֲבִיר אֲפֵלָה וּמֵבִיא אוֹרָה	בָּרוּךְ שְׁמוֹ:
בָּרוּךְ חַי לָעַד וְקַיָּם לָנֶֽצַח	בָּרוּךְ הוּא:
בָּרוּךְ פּוֹדֶה וּמַצִּיל	בָּרוּךְ הוּא וּבָרוּךְ שְׁמוֹ: ←

Baruḥ she'amar vehayah ha'olam.	Baruḥ hu.
Baruḥ oseh vereyshit.	Baruḥ shemo.
Baruḥ omer ve'oseh.	Baruḥ hu.
Baruḥ gozer umkayem.	Baruḥ shemo.
Baruḥ meraḥem al ha'aretz.	Baruḥ hu.
Baruḥ meraḥem al haberiyot.	Baruḥ shemo.
Baruḥ meshalem saḥar tov lire'av.	Baruḥ hu.
Baruḥ ma'avir afelah umevi orah.	Baruḥ shemo.
Baruḥ ḥay la'ad vekayam lanetzaḥ	Baruḥ hu.
Baruḥ podeh umatzil.	Baruḥ hu uvaruḥ shemo. ↩

Blessed are you, THE EVERLASTING ONE, our God, the sovereign of all worlds. Divine one, who gave birth to all, the merciful, subject of praise upon our people's mouths, lauded and glorified upon the tongues of all who love and serve you. And through these, the songs sung by your servant David, may we hail you, SOURCE OF BEING. With praises and with melodies we celebrate your greatness, and we praise you, glorify you, call to mind your Name, and crown you as our sovereign, God of ours, the only one, the living one, throughout all worlds. The one who reigns, lauded and glorified unto the end of time, whose name is ever great. Blessed are you, THE ONE, the sovereign hailed in songs of praise.

COMMENTARY. Although the patchwork of psalms and praises known as *Pesukey Dezimrah* is said to have evolved centuries after the prayer service itself, one can sense in this preface to the service an important echo of worship in biblical times—both the daily service of priests and Levites in the Temple, and the prayers of pilgrims ascending to the Holy City for the seasonal festivals. This bold appropriation of historical memory, undertaken in a period of exile and dispersion, affirms the continuity of biblical Israel with the later people Israel—in effect, inscribing the image of the former upon the latter. All of the themes and moods of the service are present in *Pesukey Dezimraḥ*. J.R.

בָּרוּךְ אַתָּה יהוה אֱלֹהֵינוּ מֶלֶךְ הָעוֹלָם: הָאֵל הָאָב הָרַחֲמָן הַמְהֻלָּל בְּפִי עַמּוֹ: מְשֻׁבָּח וּמְפֹאָר בִּלְשׁוֹן חֲסִידָיו וַעֲבָדָיו: וּבְשִׁירֵי דָוִד עַבְדֶּךָ נְהַלֶּלְךָ יהוה אֱלֹהֵינוּ: בִּשְׁבָחוֹת וּבִזְמִירוֹת נְגַדֶּלְךָ וּנְשַׁבֵּחֲךָ וּנְפָאֶרְךָ וְנַזְכִּיר שִׁמְךָ וְנַמְלִיכְךָ מַלְכֵּנוּ אֱלֹהֵינוּ *יָחִיד חֵי-הָעוֹלָמִים: מֶלֶךְ מְשֻׁבָּח וּמְפֹאָר עֲדֵי-עַד שְׁמוֹ הַגָּדוֹל: בָּרוּךְ אַתָּה יהוה מֶלֶךְ מְהֻלָּל בַּתִּשְׁבָּחוֹת:

Baruḥ atah adonay elo<u>hey</u>nu <u>me</u>leḥ ha'olam. Ha'el ha'av haraḥaman hamhulal befi amo. Meshubaḥ umfo'ar bilshon ḥasidav va'avadav. Uvshirey david av<u>de</u>ḥa nehalelḥa adonay elo<u>hey</u>nu. Bishvaḥot uvizmirot negadelḥa unshabeḥaḥa unfa'ereḥa venazkir shimḥa venamliḥeḥa mal<u>ke</u>nu elo<u>hey</u>nu yaḥid ḥey ha'olamim. <u>Me</u>leḥ meshubaḥ umfo'ar adey ad shemo hagadol. Baruḥ atah adonay <u>me</u>leḥ mehulal batishbaḥot.

DERASH. Rabbi Simlay said: "A person should arrange praise of the Holy One and then pray" (Talmud Beraḥot 32a). *Pesukey Dezimrah* is a preparation. It helps our transition into prayer. L.W.K. (Adapted)

Give thanks to THE MAGNIFICENT, call on the name,
make known among all peoples, God's great deeds.

Sing songs of God, make melody for God,
converse about God's wondrous acts.

Celebrate the holy name,
God will delight the heart of those who seek THE ONE.

Inquire of THE HOLY ONE and gather strength,
search out the divine presence always.

Call to mind the wondrous things God did,
the acts of wonderment, the judgments of God's mouth.

Sing to THE INCOMPARABLE throughout the earth,
bring news, from one day to the next, of divine help.

Tell among the nations of God's glory,
amid all peoples, of God's wondrous acts.

For great is THE ETERNAL, celebrated mightily,
and awesome, above all false gods,

for all the gods of popular imaginings are mere idols,
but THE CREATOR alone made the heavens.

I Chronicles 16:8-12, 23-26

הוֹדוּ· לַיהוה קִרְאוּ בִשְׁמוֹ הוֹדִיעוּ בָעַמִּים עֲלִילוֹתָיו׃
שִׁירוּ לוֹ זַמְּרוּ־לוֹ שִׂיחוּ בְּכָל־נִפְלְאוֹתָיו׃
הִתְהַלְלוּ בְּשֵׁם קָדְשׁוֹ יִשְׂמַח לֵב מְבַקְשֵׁי יהוה׃
דִּרְשׁוּ יהוה וְעֻזּוֹ בַּקְּשׁוּ פָנָיו תָּמִיד׃
זִכְרוּ נִפְלְאֹתָיו אֲשֶׁר עָשָׂה מֹפְתָיו וּמִשְׁפְּטֵי־פִיהוּ׃

שִׁירוּ לַיהוה כָּל־הָאָרֶץ בַּשְּׂרוּ מִיּוֹם־אֶל־יוֹם יְשׁוּעָתוֹ׃
סַפְּרוּ בַגּוֹיִם אֶת־כְּבוֹדוֹ בְּכָל־הָעַמִּים נִפְלְאוֹתָיו׃
כִּי גָדוֹל יהוה וּמְהֻלָּל מְאֹד וְנוֹרָא הוּא עַל־כָּל־אֱלֹהִים׃
* כִּי כָּל־אֱלֹהֵי הָעַמִּים אֱלִילִים וַיהוה שָׁמַיִם עָשָׂה׃

בקשו פניו תמיד / search out the divine presence always. The Hebrew literally reads "Seek His face always." The religious person is one who knows in each situation how to seek "the face of God." Whatever befalls us and wherever life may lead, we find ourselves still seeking. Each unique human situation calls upon us to find God's presence and act upon it in a unique way.
A.G.

DERASH. The service of gratitude is eternal. As the Rabbis put it (Leviticus Rabah 9), though in the time to come all sacrifices will cease, the thank-offering will never cease. It will last on in eternity; thanksgiving will never become obsolete in the realms of spiritual bliss. A world full of praise—how near to heaven it would be! We must bring ourselves into line with such ideals. Our worship must not be impatient supplication, but patient praise. We must think less of what we lack, more of what we have.
M.M.K./M.S.

A psalm of thanksgiving.

Sing out to THE CREATOR, all the earth,
worship THE ALL-SEEING ONE in joy,
approach God's presence with a ringing cry!

Know that THE ABUNDANT ONE is God,
the one who made us, our beginning and our source.
We are God's kin, the flock God feeds.

Enter God's gates with thankful prayers,
God's courtyards with a song of praise.
Give thanks to God, give blessing to the Name,

for the love of THE COMPASSIONATE will last forever,
God's faithful care, throughout all generations.

Psalm 100

KAVANAH. In the biblical consonantal text, the phrase is ולא אנחנו / "and we are not," which is traditionally read ולו אנחנו /and to God we belong." A medieval mystic, however, preferring the original reading, rendered it *ule-Alef-anaḥnu*, "and to Aleph we belong"—that is to the divine source of all things, whose name is Aleph, the silent unpronounceable letter that begins the *Alefbet*, and which is also the initial letter of אנכי, "I am...," the first word of the Ten Commandments. J.R.

KAVANAH: The ultimate joy in life is to be
filled with gratitude
for Creation and to
know my place and purpose in it;
Then I feel secure; bathed in the
endless flow of Grace,
Enduring from generation to generation.

S.P.W.

מִזְמוֹר לְתוֹדָה

הָרִֽיעוּ לַיהוה כׇּל הָאָֽרֶץ׃
עִבְדוּ אֶת יהוה בְּשִׂמְחָה בֹּֽאוּ לְפָנָיו בִּרְנָנָה׃
דְּעוּ כִּי יהוה הוּא אֱלֹהִים הוּא עָשָֽׂנוּ וְלוֹ אֲנַֽחְנוּ
עַמּוֹ וְצֹאן מַרְעִיתוֹ׃
בֹּֽאוּ שְׁעָרָיו בְּתוֹדָה חֲצֵרֹתָיו בִּתְהִלָּה
הֽוֹדוּ לוֹ בָּרְכוּ שְׁמוֹ׃
*כִּי טוֹב יהוה לְעוֹלָם חַסְדּוֹ וְעַד דֹּר וָדֹר אֱמוּנָתוֹ׃

COMMENTARY. What does it mean to work joyfully? Serving higher ends gives meaning to the work, and that is a source of joy. Joyous work brings its own reward, and a sense of thankfulness follows. The prayer of our daily deeds is that they should be in faithful service, linking the generations in joy and thankfulness. D.A.T.

COMMENTARY. The heading of this psalm, *Mizmor letodah*, indicates that it was probably used to accompany the thanksgiving offerings in the ancient Temple. Not only did our ancestors bring sheep for offerings to God; they also compared themselves to sheep. Why does this comparison belong in a song of thanksgiving? Because the psalm wants us to acknowledge that we too are creatures. We were made by God, and we are nurtured by God. At a moment of gratitude for life itself, we surrender our individuality to become members of God's flock. H.L.

Happy are they who dwell within your house,
  may they continue to give praise to you.
Happy is the people for whom life is thus,
  happy is the people with THE EVERLASTING for its God!

A Psalm of David

א All exaltations do I raise to you, my sovereign God,
  and I give blessing to your name, forever and eternally.
ב Blessings do I offer you each day,
  I hail your name, forever and eternally.
ג Great is THE ETERNAL, to be praised emphatically,
  because God's greatness has no measure.
ד Declaring praises for your deeds one era to the next,
  people describe your mighty acts.
ה Heaven's glorious splendor is my song,
  words of your miracles I eagerly pour forth.
ו Wondrous are your powers—people tell of them,
  and your magnificence do I recount.
ז Signs of your abundant goodness they express,
  and in your justice they rejoice.
ח How gracious and how merciful is THE ABUNDANT ONE,
  slow to anger, great in love.
ט To all God's creatures, goodness flows,
  on all creation, divine love.
י Your creatures all give thanks to you,
  your fervent ones bless you emphatically. ↩

אשרי...סלה / Happy...you (Psalm 84:5).
אשרי...אלהיו / Happy...God (Psalm 144:15).

אַשְׁרֵי

אַשְׁרֵי יוֹשְׁבֵי בֵיתֶךָ עוֹד יְהַלְלוּךָ סֶּלָה׃
אַשְׁרֵי הָעָם שֶׁכָּכָה לּוֹ אַשְׁרֵי הָעָם שֶׁיהוה אֱלֹהָיו׃

תְּהִלָּה לְדָוִד

אֲרוֹמִמְךָ אֱלוֹהַי הַמֶּלֶךְ וַאֲבָרְכָה שִׁמְךָ לְעוֹלָם וָעֶד׃
בְּכָל־יוֹם אֲבָרְכֶךָּ וַאֲהַלְלָה שִׁמְךָ לְעוֹלָם וָעֶד׃
גָּדוֹל יהוה וּמְהֻלָּל מְאֹד וְלִגְדֻלָּתוֹ אֵין חֵקֶר׃
דּוֹר לְדוֹר יְשַׁבַּח מַעֲשֶׂיךָ וּגְבוּרֹתֶיךָ יַגִּידוּ׃
הֲדַר כְּבוֹד הוֹדֶךָ וְדִבְרֵי נִפְלְאֹתֶיךָ אָשִׂיחָה׃
וֶעֱזוּז נוֹרְאוֹתֶיךָ יֹאמֵרוּ וּגְדֻלָּתְךָ אֲסַפְּרֶנָּה׃
זֵכֶר רַב־טוּבְךָ יַבִּיעוּ וְצִדְקָתְךָ יְרַנֵּנוּ׃
חַנּוּן וְרַחוּם יהוה אֶרֶךְ אַפַּיִם וּגְדָל־חָסֶד׃
טוֹב־יהוה לַכֹּל וְרַחֲמָיו עַל־כָּל־מַעֲשָׂיו׃
יוֹדוּךָ יהוה כָּל־מַעֲשֶׂיךָ וַחֲסִידֶיךָ יְבָרְכוּכָה׃ ←

Ashrey yoshvey veyteḥa od yehaleluḥa selah.
Ashrey ha'am shekaḥah lo ashrey ha'am she'adonay elohav.
Tehilah ledavid.
Aromimeḥa elohay hameleḥ va'avareḥah shimeḥa le'olam va'ed.
Beḥol yom avareḥeka va'ahalela shimeḥa le'olam va'ed.
Gadol adonay umhulal me'od veligdulato eyn ḥeker.
Dor ledor yeshabaḥ ma'aseḥa ugvuroteḥa yagidu.
Hadar kevod hodeḥa vedivrey nifle'oteḥa asiḥah.
Ve'ezuz noroteḥa yomeru ugdulateḥa asaperenah.
Zeḥer rav tuveḥa yabi'u vetzidkateḥa yeranenu.
Ḥanun veraḥum adonay ereḥ apayim ugdol ḥased.
Tov adonay lakol veraḥamav al kol ma'asav.
Yoduḥa adonay kol ma'aseḥa veḥasideḥa yevareḥuḥah. ↵

COMMENTARY. Psalm 145 is an alphabetical acrostic. The translation roughly preserves the sound of the Hebrew initials of each line. The line for the letter *nun* is missing from this psalm, for unknown reasons. J.R.

כ Calling out the glory of your sovereignty,
of your magnificence they speak,
ל Letting all people know your mighty acts,
and of your sovereignty's glory and splendor.
מ May your sovereignty last all eternities,
your dominion for era after era.
ס Strong support to all who fall,
GOD raises up the humble and the lame.
ע All hopeful gazes turn toward you,
as you give sustenance in its appointed time.
פ Providing with your open hand,
you satisfy desire in all life.
צ So just is God in every way,
so loving amid all the divine deeds.
ק Close by is God to all who call,
to all who call to God in truth.
ר Responding to the yearning of all those who fear,
God hears their cry and comes to rescue them.
ש Showing care to all who love God, THE ETERNAL
brings destruction to all evildoers.
ת The praise of THE ALL-KNOWING does my mouth declare,
and all flesh give blessing to God's holy name, unto eternity.

Psalm 145

And as for us, we bless the name of Yah,
from now until the end of time. Halleluyah!

ואנחנו...הללויה / And...Halleluyah! (Psalm 115:18).

כְּבוֹד מַלְכוּתְךָ יֹאמֵרוּ   וּגְבוּרָתְךָ יְדַבֵּרוּ:
לְהוֹדִיעַ לִבְנֵי הָאָדָם גְּבוּרֹתָיו   וּכְבוֹד הֲדַר מַלְכוּתוֹ:
מַלְכוּתְךָ מַלְכוּת כָּל־עֹלָמִים   וּמֶמְשַׁלְתְּךָ בְּכָל־דּוֹר וָדוֹר:
סוֹמֵךְ יהוה לְכָל־הַנֹּפְלִים   וְזוֹקֵף לְכָל־הַכְּפוּפִים:
עֵינֵי כֹל אֵלֶיךָ יְשַׂבֵּרוּ   וְאַתָּה נוֹתֵן־לָהֶם אֶת־אָכְלָם בְּעִתּוֹ:
פּוֹתֵחַ אֶת־יָדֶךָ   וּמַשְׂבִּיעַ לְכָל־חַי רָצוֹן:
צַדִּיק יהוה בְּכָל־דְּרָכָיו   וְחָסִיד בְּכָל־מַעֲשָׂיו:
קָרוֹב יהוה לְכָל־קֹרְאָיו   לְכֹל אֲשֶׁר יִקְרָאֻהוּ בֶאֱמֶת:
רְצוֹן יְרֵאָיו יַעֲשֶׂה   וְאֶת־שַׁוְעָתָם יִשְׁמַע וְיוֹשִׁיעֵם:
שׁוֹמֵר יהוה אֶת־כָּל־אֹהֲבָיו   וְאֵת כָּל־הָרְשָׁעִים יַשְׁמִיד:
*תְּהִלַּת יהוה יְדַבֶּר פִּי   וִיבָרֵךְ כָּל־בָּשָׂר שֵׁם קָדְשׁוֹ
לְעוֹלָם וָעֶד:
וַאֲנַחְנוּ נְבָרֵךְ יָהּ   מֵעַתָּה וְעַד־עוֹלָם   הַלְלוּיָהּ

Kevod malḥuteḥa yomeru ugvurateḥa yedaberu.
Lehodi'a livney ha'adam gevurotav uḥvod hadar malḥuto.
Malḥuteḥa malḥut kol olamim umemshalteḥa beḥol dor vador.
Someḥ adonay leḥol hanofelim vezokef leḥol hakefufim.
Eyney ḥol eleḥa yesaberu
ve'atah noten lahem et oḥlam be'ito.
Pote'aḥ et yadeḥa umasbi'a leḥol ḥay ratzon.
Tzadik adonay beḥol deraḥav veḥasid beḥol ma'asav.
Karov adonay leḥol korav leḥol asher yikra'uhu ve'emet.
Retzon yere'av ya'aseh ve'et shavatam yishma veyoshi'em.
Shomer adonay et kol ohavav ve'et kol harsha'im yashmid.
Tehilat adonay yedaber pi
vivareḥ kol basar shem kodsho le'olam va'ed.
Va'anaḥnu nevareḥ yah me'atah ve'ad olam halleluyah.

A Song for the Ascents.

I lift my eyes up to the hills.
From where does my help come?

My help is from THE UNSEEN ONE,
the maker of the heavens and the earth,

who will not cause your foot to fail.
Your protector never slumbers.

Behold the one who slumbers not, who never sleeps,
the guardian of Israel.

THE ABUNDANT ONE preserves you,
THE WATCHFUL ONE, your shelter, at your right hand a support.

By day, the sun will not afflict you,
nor the moonlight by the night.

THE VIGILANT shall guard you from all evil,
and will keep your lifebreath safe.

THE SHEPHERD guard your going out and coming in,
from now unto eternity.

Psalm 121

NOTE. Several psalms and anthologies of psalms that are often found in *Pesukey Dezimrah* have been omitted from *Kol Haneshamah* in favor of Psalms 121, 128 and 130, which are more commonly found in the Sephardic liturgy.
D.A.T.

שִׁיר לַמַּעֲלוֹת אֶשָּׂא עֵינַי אֶל־הֶהָרִים מֵאַיִן יָבֹא עֶזְרִי׃
עֶזְרִי מֵעִם יהוה עֹשֵׂה שָׁמַיִם וָאָרֶץ׃
אַל־יִתֵּן לַמּוֹט רַגְלֶךָ אַל־יָנוּם שֹׁמְרֶךָ׃
הִנֵּה לֹא־יָנוּם וְלֹא יִישָׁן שׁוֹמֵר יִשְׂרָאֵל׃
יהוה שֹׁמְרֶךָ יהוה צִלְּךָ עַל־יַד יְמִינֶךָ׃
יוֹמָם הַשֶּׁמֶשׁ לֹא־יַכֶּכָּה וְיָרֵחַ בַּלָּיְלָה׃
יהוה יִשְׁמָרְךָ מִכָּל־רָע יִשְׁמֹר אֶת־נַפְשֶׁךָ׃
יהוה יִשְׁמָר־צֵאתְךָ וּבוֹאֶךָ מֵעַתָּה וְעַד־עוֹלָם הַלְלוּיָהּ׃

Esa eynay el heharim me'ayin yavo ezri.
Ezri me'im adonay oseh shamayim va'aretz.

COMMENTARY. The psalm's image of help coming from the mountains, from the maker of heaven and earth, anchors us in the natural world, in the majesty and orderliness of creation. But the psalm also has a jarring image: "the Guardian of Israel neither slumbers nor sleeps." It is hard to hear this phrase without thinking of all the times that while God seemed to slumber, the Jewish people were slaughtered on account of their religious beliefs. We constantly need to translate such ancient images of God through the lens of our contemporary theology. The Guardian of Israel can then be understood as the eternal source of unity in the world or the vision of goodness that cannot be snuffed out even by unspeakable evil and suffering. H.L.

A song of the Ascents.

Happy are all those in awe of THE ALMIGHTY ONE,
who walk in paths that God established.

When you enjoy the fruits of your own labors,
happy are you, how good it is for you!

When from within your household grows a fruiting vine,
when children of your household grow like sprouting olive
branches,
filling seats around your table,

this is a way those in awe of God are blessed.
May THE ABUNDANT ONE bless you from Zion,

and may you, in turn, behold Jerusalem's prosperity
throughout your life,

and may you live to see your children's children,
and well-being over Israel.

Psalm 128

COMMENTARY. Blessings flow to us as creatures on a planet sustained by love. Respecting the power of that love, we pray for the grace to channel that flow of blessing back to our partners, our families, and our people's eternal home, Zion. In this psalm, we celebrate those who revere God, and thereby provide for the continuity of the Jewish people. H.L.

שִׁיר הַמַּעֲלוֹת

אַשְׁרֵי כָּל־יְרֵא יהוה הַהֹלֵךְ בִּדְרָכָיו׃
יְגִיעַ כַּפֶּיךָ כִּי תֹאכֵל אַשְׁרֶיךָ וְטוֹב לָךְ׃
אֶשְׁתְּךָ כְּגֶפֶן פֹּרִיָּה בְּיַרְכְּתֵי בֵיתֶךָ
בָּנֶיךָ כִּשְׁתִלֵי זֵיתִים סָבִיב לְשֻׁלְחָנֶךָ׃
הִנֵּה כִּי־כֵן יְבֹרַךְ גָּבֶר יְרֵא יהוה׃
יְבָרֶכְךָ יהוה מִצִּיּוֹן
וּרְאֵה בְּטוּב יְרוּשָׁלָםִ כֹּל יְמֵי חַיֶּיךָ׃
וּרְאֵה־בָנִים לְבָנֶיךָ שָׁלוֹם עַל־יִשְׂרָאֵל הַלְלוּיָהּ׃

Yevareheha adonay mitziyon urey betuv yerushalayim kol yemey hayeha. Urey vanim levaneha shalom al yisra'el.

COMMENTARY. Psalms beginning with the words "שיר המעלות / A Song of Ascents" were sung as Jews ascended toward the Temple mount, primarily on the pilgrimage festivals. The Temple mount is one of the highest points in Jerusalem, which itself is nestled high in the hills. When many Jews came to offer sacrifices, a long line of pilgrims must have moved slowly upward as they awaited a turn at the altar. These psalms might well have been sung by the people in the slowly ascending line. D.A.T.

A song of the Ascents.

From the depths I have called out to you, REDEEMING ONE,
please listen, my provider, to my voice!
May you harken to my voice of supplication.
Were you to pay careful attention to a person's sins,
who could endure, almighty one?
With you alone originates all power to forgive;
for this you are revered.
So I have hoped, MERCIFUL ONE! My soul has hoped,
and for your word I have looked forward in my yearning.
My spirit yearns for my protector more than people watch for daybreak,
truly, more than watching for the dawn.
So does Israel eagerly anticipate THE MERCIFUL,
for from THE MERCIFUL all kindness comes,
from God alone comes all deliverance,
yes, God alone delivers Israel from its wrongful acts.

Psalm 130

שִׁיר הַמַּעֲלוֹת

מִמַּעֲמַקִּים קְרָאתִיךָ יהוה: אֲדֹנָי שִׁמְעָה בְקוֹלִי
תִּהְיֶינָה אָזְנֶיךָ קַשֻּׁבוֹת לְקוֹל תַּחֲנוּנָי:
אִם־עֲוֹנוֹת תִּשְׁמָר־יָהּ אֲדֹנָי מִי יַעֲמֹד:
כִּי־עִמְּךָ הַסְּלִיחָה לְמַעַן תִּוָּרֵא:
קִוִּיתִי יהוה קִוְּתָה נַפְשִׁי וְלִדְבָרוֹ הוֹחָלְתִּי:
נַפְשִׁי לַאדֹנָי מִשֹּׁמְרִים לַבֹּקֶר שֹׁמְרִים לַבֹּקֶר:
יַחֵל יִשְׂרָאֵל אֶל־יהוה
כִּי־עִם־יהוה הַחֶסֶד וְהַרְבֵּה עִמּוֹ פְדוּת:
וְהוּא יִפְדֶּה אֶת־יִשְׂרָאֵל מִכֹּל עֲוֹנוֹתָיו **הַלְלוּיָהּ**

COMMENTARY. ממעמקים / "From the depths." The phrase calls us back to the inner sources of our personal and collective pain. Through psalms like this one, we express our yearning for a place beyond pain. We have not been the best we could have been. We long for forgiveness. We know ourselves forgiven, however, only when we have turned our lives back toward the holy. Our word for this process is atonement, or at-one-ment, a movement toward reconciliation with the holiness we know as God. H.L.

Halleluyah!
Hail, my soul, THE OMNIPRESENT!

I hail THE INNERMOST my whole life through,
I sing out to my God as long as I endure.

Trust not in human benefactors,
in mortal beings, who have no power to help.

Their spirit leaves, they go back to the ground,
on that day, all their thoughts are lost.

Happy is the one who has the God of Jacob for a help,
whose hopeful thought is for THE LIVING ONE, our God,

the maker of the heavens and the earth,
the seas and all that they contain,

the world's true guardian,

who musters justice on behalf of the oppressed,
who gives bread to the hungry,

ADVOCATE, who sets the captive free,

THE UNSEEN ONE, who makes the blind to see,
SUPPORTING ONE, who helps the lame to stand,

THE WATCHFUL ONE, who loves the just,

THE BOUNTIFUL, protector of the stranger,
and in whom the orphan and the widow find their strength,

By whom the evildoers' route is set awry.

The ALL-EMBRACING reigns eternally,
your God, O Zion, from one generation to the next.
Halleluyah!

Psalm 146

הַלְלוּיָהּ

הַלְלִי נַפְשִׁי אֶת־יְהוָה׃

אֲהַלְלָה יְהוָה בְּחַיָּי אֲזַמְּרָה לֵאלֹהַי בְּעוֹדִי׃

אַל־תִּבְטְחוּ בִנְדִיבִים בְּבֶן־אָדָם שֶׁאֵין לוֹ תְשׁוּעָה׃

תֵּצֵא רוּחוֹ יָשֻׁב לְאַדְמָתוֹ בַּיּוֹם הַהוּא אָבְדוּ עֶשְׁתֹּנֹתָיו׃

אַשְׁרֵי שֶׁאֵל יַעֲקֹב בְּעֶזְרוֹ שִׂבְרוֹ עַל־יהוה אֱלֹהָיו׃

עֹשֶׂה שָׁמַיִם וָאָרֶץ אֶת־הַיָּם וְאֶת־כָּל־אֲשֶׁר־בָּם

הַשֹּׁמֵר אֱמֶת לְעוֹלָם׃

עֹשֶׂה מִשְׁפָּט לָעֲשׁוּקִים נֹתֵן לֶחֶם לָרְעֵבִים

יהוה מַתִּיר אֲסוּרִים׃

יהוה פֹּקֵחַ עִוְרִים יהוה זֹקֵף כְּפוּפִים

יהוה אֹהֵב צַדִּיקִים׃

יהוה שֹׁמֵר אֶת־גֵּרִים יָתוֹם וְאַלְמָנָה יְעוֹדֵד

וְדֶרֶךְ רְשָׁעִים יְעַוֵּת׃

*יִמְלֹךְ יהוה לְעוֹלָם אֱלֹהַיִךְ צִיּוֹן לְדֹר וָדֹר **הַלְלוּיָהּ׃**

COMMENTARY. The latter part of this psalm lists divine actions worthy of human emulation. The approach of predicate theology treats divine attributes as models for human conduct. In praising God this way we are not attempting to make factual statements about God's conduct. We are stating values that we hope to make manifest through the way we lead our lives. D.A.T.

DERASH. אל תבטחו בנדיבים / Trust not in human benefactors. At first the message catches us off guard. Do not put your trust in other people. Even leaders—born or chosen. Then we recall that ours is a program of sacred principles, not sacred personalities. We should not rely on the good will of even the noblest and most generous. (The root נ ד ב is the same for noble and generous.) The principle of protecting the weak and defenseless is far too important to entrust to any regime, ruler or promising politician. It is a principle encoded in the very structure of the universe. It demands our individual obedience. S.P.W.

Halleluyah! How good it is to sing out to our God!
How much a pleasure and how fitting is our praise!

The builder of Jerusalem is ZION'S GOD,
may those of Israel gone astray be gathered there.

The healer of the broken-hearted,
the one who bandages their bones,

who alone reckons the number of the stars,
while giving names to every one of them—

how great is our protector, and how powerful,
whose understanding has no limit!

THE COMPASSIONATE encourages the humble,
and brings down the wicked to the earth,

sing choruses of thanks to THE MAGNIFICENT,
sing out to our God with instrument of strings,

the one who covers up the sky with clouds,
who prepares the rainfall for the earth,

who causes grass to sprout upon the mountains,

who gives the beast its sustenance,
young ravens, what they clamor for,

who is indifferent to the horse's power,
who takes no pleasure in the muscle's might, ↩

הַלְלוּיָהּ

כִּי־טוֹב זַמְּרָה אֱלֹהֵינוּ כִּי־נָעִים נָאוָה תְהִלָּה׃
בֹּנֵה יְרוּשָׁלַםִ יהוה נִדְחֵי יִשְׂרָאֵל יְכַנֵּס׃
הָרוֹפֵא לִשְׁבוּרֵי לֵב וּמְחַבֵּשׁ לְעַצְּבוֹתָם׃
מוֹנֶה מִסְפָּר לַכּוֹכָבִים לְכֻלָּם שֵׁמוֹת יִקְרָא׃
גָּדוֹל אֲדוֹנֵינוּ וְרַב־כֹּחַ לִתְבוּנָתוֹ אֵין מִסְפָּר׃
מְעוֹדֵד עֲנָוִים יְהוָה מַשְׁפִּיל רְשָׁעִים עֲדֵי־אָרֶץ׃
עֱנוּ לַיהוה בְּתוֹדָה זַמְּרוּ לֵאלֹהֵינוּ בְכִנּוֹר׃
הַמְכַסֶּה שָׁמַיִם בְּעָבִים הַמֵּכִין לָאָרֶץ מָטָר
הַמַּצְמִיחַ הָרִים חָצִיר׃
נוֹתֵן לִבְהֵמָה לַחְמָהּ לִבְנֵי עֹרֵב אֲשֶׁר יִקְרָאוּ׃
לֹא בִגְבוּרַת הַסּוּס יֶחְפָּץ לֹא־בְשׁוֹקֵי הָאִישׁ יִרְצֶה׃ ←

COMMENTARY. Psalm 147 has three majestic interlacing themes. The divine is present in the ordered universe of galaxies and creatures. The divine is present, too, in the broken human heart, in those humbled by loss and disappointment. Finally, the divine is present in the capacity of our senses and in our ability to appreciate the world around us. S.P.W.

The Just One values only those in awe of God,
only the ones who yearn for God's kind love.

Give praise, Jerusalem, to The Eternal,
hail your God, O Zion,

for God has fortified the bars upon your gates,
has blessed your brood amid your breast,

and sets your borderlands at peace,
and satisfies you with the choicest wheat,

the one who sends an utterance to earth,
whose word runs swiftest in the world,

the giver of a snow like fleece,
who strews a frost like frigid ash,

who casts down hail like crumbs of bread
—before such chill, who can endure?—

but who, with but a word, can melt them all,
and by whose breath the waters flow.

God tells the words of tale to Jacob,
laws and judgments to the people Israel.

Has God not done so for all nations?
Are there any who do not know such laws?

Halleluyah!

Psalm 147

רוֹצֶה יהוה אֶת־יְרֵאָיו אֶת־הַמְיַחֲלִים לְחַסְדּוֹ׃
שַׁבְּחִי יְרוּשָׁלַ͏ִם אֶת־יְהוָה הַלְלִי אֱלֹהַיִךְ צִיּוֹן׃
כִּי־חִזַּק בְּרִיחֵי שְׁעָרָיִךְ בֵּרַךְ בָּנַיִךְ בְּקִרְבֵּךְ׃
הַשָּׂם־גְּבוּלֵךְ שָׁלוֹם חֵלֶב חִטִּים יַשְׂבִּיעֵךְ׃
הַשֹּׁלֵחַ אִמְרָתוֹ אָרֶץ עַד־מְהֵרָה יָרוּץ דְּבָרוֹ׃
הַנֹּתֵן שֶׁלֶג כַּצָּמֶר כְּפוֹר כָּאֵפֶר יְפַזֵּר׃
מַשְׁלִיךְ קַרְחוֹ כְפִתִּים לִפְנֵי קָרָתוֹ מִי יַעֲמֹד׃
יִשְׁלַח דְּבָרוֹ וְיַמְסֵם יַשֵּׁב רוּחוֹ יִזְּלוּ־מָיִם׃
*מַגִּיד דְּבָרָיו לְיַעֲקֹב חֻקָּיו וּמִשְׁפָּטָיו לְיִשְׂרָאֵל׃
לֹא עָשָׂה כֵן לְכָל־גּוֹי וּמִשְׁפָּטִים בַּל־יְדָעוּם

הַלְלוּיָהּ

Halleluyah!

Hail! THE OMNIPRESENT from the heavens,
praise God in the heights,

sing out your praises, all you angels,
praise God, all you multitudes,

give praise to God, you sun and moon,
praise God, all you stars of light,

praise God, heavens upon heavens,
and you, the waters up above the heavens!

Let all praise the name of THE ETERNAL,
who commanded, and all things became,

who raised them up forever and an aeon,
who affixed a limit none could pass. ←

COMMENTARY. The stanzas in this psalm outline its organization. First, a group of lines directed to heavenly beings; second, a group of lines directed to terrestrial beings; and finally, a shorter group of concluding lines that build up to a climactic focus on Israel, God's faithful people who are enjoined to praise God. The liturgy's poetic structure provides a map of religious experience. Psalms like this one reveal that Israel's religious experience derives from seeing itself as the center and apogee of God's world. This psalm poses a challenge to contemporary Jewish spirituality: to reconcile the special heritage of Judaism with our awareness of living in a nonhierarchical world of many centers. H.L.

הַלְלוּיָהּ

הַלְלוּ אֶת־יהוה מִן־הַשָּׁמַיִם הַלְלוּהוּ בַּמְּרוֹמִים׃
הַלְלוּהוּ כָל־מַלְאָכָיו הַלְלוּהוּ כָּל־צְבָאָיו׃
הַלְלוּהוּ שֶׁמֶשׁ וְיָרֵחַ הַלְלוּהוּ כָּל־כּוֹכְבֵי אוֹר׃
הַלְלוּהוּ שְׁמֵי הַשָּׁמָיִם וְהַמַּיִם אֲשֶׁר מֵעַל הַשָּׁמָיִם׃
יְהַלְלוּ אֶת־שֵׁם יהוה כִּי הוּא צִוָּה וְנִבְרָאוּ׃
וַיַּעֲמִידֵם לָעַד לְעוֹלָם חָק־נָתַן וְלֹא יַעֲבוֹר׃ ←

COMMENTARY. This psalm and the tradition it represents stand as an important counterweight to the first chapter in Genesis. That chapter gives us the impression that humans are separate from the world around us, we alone having been created in God's image as "the crown of creation." Here we see a different vision. The human community is an integral part of the natural realm. "You young men, and you maidens, elders sitting with the young," sing and dance before the Lord as do mountains and hills, fruit trees and cedars. A.G.

Give praise to THE ALL-POWERFUL throughout the earth,
you dragons and torrential depths,

you fire and hail and snow, and smoke,
you raging wind, all acting by God's word,

you mountains, all you hills,
you fruit trees, bearing every seed,

you wild animals, and every beast,
you creeping thing, and bird of wing,

you rulers of the earth, and all the nations,
nobles, and you judges of the land,

you young men, and you maidens,
elders sitting with the young!

Let all bless the name of THE ETERNAL
for God's name alone is to be exalted.

God's majesty is in the earth and heavens,

God has raised the fortunes of our people,
praises for the fervent ones,

for Israel's children, people near to God,
Halleluyah!

Psalm 148

הַלְלוּ אֶת־יהוה מִן־הָאָרֶץ   תַּנִּינִים וְכָל־תְּהֹמוֹת:
אֵשׁ וּבָרָד שֶׁלֶג וְקִיטוֹר   רוּחַ סְעָרָה עֹשָׂה דְבָרוֹ:
הֶהָרִים וְכָל־גְּבָעוֹת   עֵץ פְּרִי וְכָל־אֲרָזִים:
הַחַיָּה וְכָל־בְּהֵמָה   רֶמֶשׂ וְצִפּוֹר כָּנָף:
מַלְכֵי־אֶרֶץ וְכָל־לְאֻמִּים   שָׂרִים וְכָל־שֹׁפְטֵי אָרֶץ:
בַּחוּרִים וְגַם־בְּתוּלוֹת   זְקֵנִים עִם־נְעָרִים:
יְהַלְלוּ אֶת־שֵׁם יהוה   כִּי־נִשְׂגָּב שְׁמוֹ לְבַדּוֹ
הוֹדוֹ עַל־אֶרֶץ וְשָׁמָיִם:
*וַיָּרֶם קֶרֶן לְעַמּוֹ   תְּהִלָּה לְכָל־חֲסִידָיו
לִבְנֵי יִשְׂרָאֵל עַם קְרֹבוֹ

הַלְלוּיָהּ

Hallelu/Yah!
Call out to Yah in Heaven's holy place!
Boom out to Yah across the firmament!
Shout out for Yah, for all God's mighty deeds!
Cry out for Yah, as loud as God is great!
Blast out for Yah with piercing shofar note!
Pluck out for Yah with lute and violin!
Throb out for Yah with drum and writhing dance!
Sing out for Yah with strings and husky flute!
Ring out for Yah with cymbals that resound!
Clang out for Yah with cymbals that rebound!
Let every living thing Yah's praises sing, Hallelu/Yah!
Let every living thing Yah's praises sing, Hallelu/Yah!

Psalm 150

Blessed is THE ONE eternally.
Amen! Amen!
Blessed is THE OMNIPRESENT,
dwelling in Jerusalem, Halleluyah!
Blessed is THE MIGHTY ONE divine,
The God of Israel who alone works wonders,
and blessed is the glorious name forever,
and may God's glory fill the earth.
Amen! Amen!

COMMENTARY. Psalm 150 as it appears in the biblical text does not repeat its concluding line as it does in the liturgy. The repetition here makes this concluding verse parallel to all the preceding ones, allowing it to fit a variety of musical settings. The repetition also emphasizes the psalm's essential message. D.A.T.

הַלְלוּיָהּ הַלְלוּ אֵל בְּקָדְשׁוֹ הַלְלֽוּהוּ בִּרְקִֽיעַ עֻזּוֹ׃
הַלְלֽוּהוּ בִגְבוּרֹתָיו הַלְלֽוּהוּ כְּרֹב גֻּדְלוֹ׃
הַלְלֽוּהוּ בְּתֵֽקַע שׁוֹפָר הַלְלֽוּהוּ בְּנֵֽבֶל וְכִנּוֹר׃
הַלְלֽוּהוּ בְתֹף וּמָחוֹל הַלְלֽוּהוּ בְּמִנִּים וְעֻגָב׃
הַלְלֽוּהוּ בְצִלְצְלֵי שָֽׁמַע הַלְלֽוּהוּ בְּצִלְצְלֵי תְרוּעָה׃
*כֹּל הַנְּשָׁמָה תְּהַלֵּל יָהּ הַלְלוּיָהּ׃
כֹּל הַנְּשָׁמָה תְּהַלֵּל יָהּ הַלְלוּיָהּ

Halleluyah halelu el bekodsho. Haleluhu birki'a uzo.
Haleluhu bigvurotav. Haleluhu kerov gudlo.
Haleluhu beteka shofar.
Haleluhu benevel veḥinor.
Haleluhu betof umaḥol.
Haleluhu beminim ve'ugav.
Haleluhu betziltzeley shama.
Haleluhu betziltzeley teru'ah.
Kol haneshamah tehalel yah. Halleluyah.

בָּרוּךְ יהוה לְעוֹלָם אָמֵן וְאָמֵן׃ בָּרוּךְ יהוה מִצִּיּוֹן שֹׁכֵן יְרוּשָׁלָֽיִם
הַלְלוּיָהּ׃ בָּרוּךְ יהוה אֱלֹהִים אֱלֹהֵי יִשְׂרָאֵל עֹשֵׂה נִפְלָאוֹת לְבַדּוֹ׃
*וּבָרוּךְ שֵׁם כְּבוֹדוֹ לְעוֹלָם וְיִמָּלֵא כְבוֹדוֹ אֶת־כָּל־הָאָֽרֶץ אָמֵן וְאָמֵן׃

וימלא כבודו את כל הארץ / and may God's glory fill all the earth. The meaning of the Hebrew phrase is rich in ambiguity. All earth is filled with divine glory, but divine glory itself is filled up with earthliness. It is the reality of this world that fills God's presence, as it is the presence that gives the world its glory. A.G.

ברוך...ואמן / Blessed...Amen! (Psalms 89:53, 135:21, 72:18-19).

Your name be praised eternally, our sovereign, you who are divine, and powerful, and great, and holy, throughout all the heavens and the earth. For unto you, RESPLENDENT ONE, our God, our ancients' God, it is appropriate to offer song, and to ascribe all greatness, might, and praise, all splendor, holiness, and royalty, all blessings and all thanks, from now unto eternity. Blessed are you, ETERNAL ONE, the sovereign divine, so great in praises, God of all thanksgiving, source of wondrous deeds, who takes pleasure in our song and melody. Blessed is the one who lives eternally!

Every morning
the world
is created.
Under the orange

sticks of the sun
the heaped
ashes of the night
turn into leaves again

and fasten themselves to the high branches—
and the ponds appear
like black cloth
on which are painted islands

of summer lilies.
If it is your nature
to be happy
you will swim away along the soft trails

for hours, your imagination
alighting everywhere.
And if your spirit
carries with it

the thorn
that is heavier than lead—
if it's all you can do
to keep on trudging—

(continued on page 63)

*יִשְׁתַּבַּח שִׁמְךָ לָעַד מַלְכֵּנוּ הָאֵל הַמֶּלֶךְ הַגָּדוֹל וְהַקָּדוֹשׁ בַּשָּׁמַיִם וּבָאָרֶץ כִּי לְךָ נָאֶה יהוה אֱלֹהֵינוּ וֵאלֹהֵי אֲבוֹתֵינוּ וְאִמּוֹתֵינוּ שִׁיר וּשְׁבָחָה הַלֵּל וְזִמְרָה עֹז וּמֶמְשָׁלָה נֶצַח גְּדֻלָּה וּגְבוּרָה תְּהִלָּה וְתִפְאֶרֶת קְדֻשָּׁה וּמַלְכוּת *בְּרָכוֹת וְהוֹדָאוֹת מֵעַתָּה וְעַד עוֹלָם: בָּרוּךְ אַתָּה יהוה אֵל מֶלֶךְ גָּדוֹל בַּתִּשְׁבָּחוֹת אֵל הַהוֹדָאוֹת אֲדוֹן הַנִּפְלָאוֹת הַבּוֹחֵר בְּשִׁירֵי זִמְרָה מֶלֶךְ אֵל חֵי הָעוֹלָמִים:

(continued from page 62)

there is still
somewhere deep within you
a beast shouting that the earth
is exactly what it wanted—

each pond with its blazing lilies
is a prayer heard and answered
lavishly,
every morning,

whether or not
you have ever dared to be happy,
whether or not
you have ever dared to pray.

Mary Oliver

COMMENTARY. This rabbinic composition, which serves as the conclusion of the daily *Pesukey Dezimrah*, The Verses of Praise, reminds us that all blessing is elusive. By its very nature, it is a time-bound marker pointing to the dimension in life which is *beyond* time—to Ḥey Ha'olamim—the one that lives eternally. D.A.T.

חי העולמים / who lives eternally. This Hebrew phrase literally means life of the worlds. This prayerbook also uses this phrase for the morning blessings. The word *olam* can refer either to space or to time. A God who is "the life of the *olamim*" can be one who lives eternally, one who inhabits all of many worlds, or one who joins space and time together. Space and time are the two essential categories that are sanctified by religion. Our understanding of God as *ḥey ha'olamim* cuts through the distinction between space and time and binds them together in cosmic oneness. A.G.

ḤATZI KADDISH / SHORT KADDISH

Reader: Let God's name be made great and holy in the world that was created as God willed. May God complete the holy realm in your own lifetime, in your days, and in the days of all the house of Israel, quickly and soon. And say: Amen.

Congregation: May God's great name be blessed, forever and as long as worlds endure.

Reader: May it be blessed, and praised, and glorified and held in honor, viewed with awe, embellished and revered; and may the blessed name of holiness be hailed, though it be higher (*Between Rosh Hashanah and Yom Kippur add:* by far) than all the blessings, songs, praises, and consolations that we utter in this world, and say: Amen.

COMMENTARY. Holiness is the quality or value that things or persons have when they help people to become fully human. M.M.K. (Adapted)

חֲצִי קַדִּישׁ

יִתְגַּדַּל וְיִתְקַדַּשׁ שְׁמֵהּ רַבָּא בְּעָלְמָא דִּי בְרָא כִרְעוּתֵהּ וְיַמְלִיךְ מַלְכוּתֵהּ בְּחַיֵּיכוֹן וּבְיוֹמֵיכוֹן וּבְחַיֵּי דְכָל בֵּית יִשְׂרָאֵל בַּעֲגָלָא וּבִזְמַן קָרִיב וְאִמְרוּ: אָמֵן:

יְהֵא שְׁמֵהּ רַבָּא מְבָרַךְ לְעָלַם וּלְעָלְמֵי עָלְמַיָּא:

יִתְבָּרַךְ וְיִשְׁתַּבַּח וְיִתְפָּאַר וְיִתְרוֹמַם וְיִתְנַשֵּׂא וְיִתְהַדַּר וְיִתְעַלֶּה וְיִתְהַלָּל שְׁמֵהּ דְּקֻדְשָׁא בְּרִיךְ הוּא

לְעֵֽלָּא (*Between Rosh Hashanah and Yom Kippur, add:* לְעֵֽלָּא) מִן כָּל בִּרְכָתָא וְשִׁירָתָא תֻּשְׁבְּחָתָא וְנֶחֱמָתָא דַּאֲמִירָן בְּעָלְמָא וְאִמְרוּ: אָמֵן:

Reader: Yitgadal veyitkadash shemey raba be'alma di vera ḥirutey veyamliḥ malḥutey beḥayeyḥon uvyomeyḥon uvḥayey deḥol beyt yisra'el ba'agala uvizman kariv ve'imru amen.

Congregation: Yehey shemey raba mevaraḥ le'alam ulalmey almaya.

Reader: Yitbaraḥ veyishtabaḥ veyitpa'ar veyitromam veyitnasey veyit-hadar veyitaleh veyit-halal shemey dekudsha beriḥ hu le'e̱la (*Between Rosh Hashanah and Yom Kippur add:* le'e̱la) min kol birḥata veshirata tushbeḥata veneḥemata da'amiran be'alma ve'imru amen.

THE SHEMA AND ITS BLESSINGS

When a minyan is present, the Bareḥu *is said. The congregation rises and faces the ark. It is customary to bow. The reader chants the first line, and the congregation responds with the second, which the reader then repeats.*

Bless THE INFINITE, the blessed One!
Blessed is THE INFINITE, the blessed One, now and forever!

YOTZER / GOD IN NATURE

Blessed are you, ETERNAL ONE, our God, the sovereign of all worlds, who fashions light and creates darkness, maker of peace and creator of all. ↩

KAVANNAH. As we bless the Source of Life, so we are blessed. And the blessing gives us strength and makes our visions clear. And the blessing gives us peace, and the courage to dare. FAITH ROGOW

COMMENTARY. *Bareḥu* calls the congregation together for formal worship. The sections that precede it in the morning service, *Birḥot Hashaḥar* and *Pesukey Dezimrah*, have brought individuals gradually closer together until they could reach the mutual connection needed for joining together in prayer. The emotional stirring and heightened awareness brought by these earlier sections now become focused in the tighter intellectual structure of the Shema and its blessings and the *Amidah*. D.A.T.

COMMENTARY. The first major theme following *Bareḥu* is that of Creation. We wonder at the order, the complexity, the vastness of our world. Struck by our own smallness, we are nonetheless also caught up in the grace of having a home amidst the splendor that is nature. Our wonder and our sense of smallness give way to thankfulness for the gift of life in this world. D.A.T.

קְרִיאַת שְׁמַע וּבִרְכוֹתֶיהָ

When a minyan is present, the Bareḥu *is said. The congregation rises and faces the ark. It is customary to bow. The reader chants the first line, and the congregation responds with the second, which the reader then repeats.*

בָּרְכוּ אֶת יהוה הַמְבֹרָךְ׃

בָּרוּךְ יהוה הַמְבֹרָךְ לְעוֹלָם וָעֶד׃

Bareḥu et adonay hamvoraḥ.
Baruḥ adonay hamvoraḥ le'olam va'ed.

יוֹצֵר

בָּרוּךְ אַתָּה יהוה אֱלֹהֵינוּ מֶלֶךְ הָעוֹלָם יוֹצֵר אוֹר וּבוֹרֵא חֹשֶׁךְ עֹשֶׂה שָׁלוֹם וּבוֹרֵא אֶת־הַכֹּל׃ ←

Baruḥ atah adonay eloheynu meleḥ ha'olam yotzer or uvorey ḥosheḥ oseh shalom uvorey et hakol.

Many contemporary Jews are reciting *beraḥot*/blessings in ways that reflect their theological outlooks and ethical concerns. At any place where a blessing occurs in the liturgy, the following elements can be combined to create alternative formulas for *beraḥot*. This can be done by selecting one phrase from each group to form the introductory clause.

I	Baruḥ atah adonay	בָּרוּךְ אַתָּה יהוה	Blessed are you Adonay
	Beruḥah at yah	בְּרוּכָה אַתְּ יָהּ	Blessed are you Yah
	Nevareḥ et	נְבָרֵךְ אֶת	Let us bless
II	eloheynu	אֱלֹהֵינוּ	our God
	hasheḥinah	הַשְּׁכִינָה	Sheḥinah
	eyn haḥayim	עֵין הַחַיִּים	Source of Life
III	meleḥ ha'olam	מֶלֶךְ הָעוֹלָם	Sovereign of all worlds
	ḥey ha'olamim	חֵי הָעוֹלָמִים	Life of all the worlds
	ruaḥ ha'olam	רוּחַ הָעוֹלָם	Spirit of the world

For additional readings, see pages 433-434.

You who in your mercy give light to the earth and its inhabitants, and in your goodness do perpetually renew each day Creation's wondrous work, how great your deeds, ETERNAL ONE! In wisdom you have made them all. The earth is filled with your accomplishments. You are the world's sole sovereign, dwelling in the highest heights before the dawn of time, praised and magnified and held in awe from days of old. God of the world, in your abundant mercy, care for us. Source of our strength, our stronghold rock, our shield of help, the fortress over us! **A**ll-powerful and **b**lessed, **g**reat in **d**iscernment, you **h**ave prepared and **w**rought the **s**unlight's **h**ealing rays; **t**rue good **y**ou have **c**reated; **l**uminaries you have **m**ade, in honor of your **n**ame, **s**urrounding for divine **o**mnipotence; your **p**rincipal **c**elestial ones, **q**uaking in holiness, **r**evere the **s**haper of the heavens, **t**o eternity. They tell of divine glory and the holiness of God. Be blessed, redeeming power, in celebration of your handiwork, and for the luminaries that you made. Let all declare your greatness! ↩

הַמֵּאִיר לָאָֽרֶץ וְלַדָּרִים עָלֶֽיהָ בְּרַחֲמִים וּבְטוּבוֹ מְחַדֵּשׁ בְּכָל־יוֹם תָּמִיד מַעֲשֵׂה־בְרֵאשִׁית: מָה־רַבּוּ מַעֲשֶֽׂיךָ יהוה כֻּלָּם בְּחָכְמָה עָשִֽׂיתָ מָלְאָה הָאָֽרֶץ קִנְיָנֶֽךָ: הַמֶּֽלֶךְ הַמְרוֹמָם לְבַדּוֹ מֵאָז הַמְשֻׁבָּח וְהַמְפֹאָר וְהַמִּתְנַשֵּׂא מִימוֹת עוֹלָם אֱלֹהֵי עוֹלָם בְּרַחֲמֶֽיךָ הָרַבִּים רַחֵם עָלֵֽינוּ אֲדוֹן עֻזֵּֽנוּ צוּר מִשְׂגַּבֵּֽנוּ מָגֵן יִשְׁעֵֽנוּ מִשְׂגָּב בַּעֲדֵֽנוּ: **אֵל** **בָּרוּךְ** **גְּדוֹל** **דֵּעָה** **הֵכִין** **וּפָעַל** **זָהֳרֵי** **חַמָּה** **טוֹב** **יָצַר** **כָּבוֹד** **לִשְׁמוֹ** **מְאוֹרוֹת** **נָתַן** **סְבִיבוֹת** **עֻזּוֹ** **פִּנּוֹת** **צְבָאָיו** **קְדוֹשִׁים** **רוֹמְמֵי** **שַׁדַּי** **תָּמִיד** מְסַפְּרִים כְּבוֹד־אֵל וּקְדֻשָּׁתוֹ: *תִּתְבָּרַךְ יהוה אֱלֹהֵֽינוּ עַל־שֶֽׁבַח מַעֲשֵׂה יָדֶֽיךָ וְעַל־מְאוֹרֵי אוֹר שֶׁעָשִֽׂיתָ יְפָאֲרֽוּךָ סֶּֽלָה: ←

NOTE. An early acrostic version of the *Yotzer* became a part of this expanded rabbinic text. In both Hebrew and English, bold letters here indicate the location of the acrostic.
D.A.T

May you be blessed, our rock, our sovereign, our champion, creator of the holy beings, and let your name be praised eternally, majestic one, the fashioner of ministering angels. All of them are standing in the heavens' highest realms, and giving voice, in awestruck unison, to words of the living God, the sovereign of all worlds. All of them adored, all brilliant in light, all great and mighty—all of them perform, in awe and dread, the will of their creator. And all open their mouths in holiness and purity. With song and melody, they bless, they praise, they magnify, they raise aloft, and sanctify, and proclaim sovereign: ↩

COMMENTARY. This passage pictures an angelic chorus singing God's praises. In Jewish tradition, angels have had a long and varied history—messengers warning Abraham of Sodom's destruction, the heavenly choir of Isaiah, the Talmud's host of heavenly functionaries, the impersonal forces of medieval philosophy, the presences of the Kabbalists. The tradition leaves ample room for each generation to understand angels as it will, whether as natural forces or revealing moments in our lives, the divine in the people we meet, or manifestations of the goodness in our world or in the inner workings of the human heart. D.A.T.

תִּתְבָּרַךְ צוּרֵנוּ מַלְכֵּנוּ וְגוֹאֲלֵנוּ בּוֹרֵא קְדוֹשִׁים יִשְׁתַּבַּח שִׁמְךָ לָעַד מַלְכֵּנוּ יוֹצֵר מְשָׁרְתִים וַאֲשֶׁר מְשָׁרְתָיו כֻּלָּם עוֹמְדִים בְּרוּם עוֹלָם וּמַשְׁמִיעִים בְּיִרְאָה יַחַד בְּקוֹל דִּבְרֵי אֱלֹהִים חַיִּים וּמֶלֶךְ עוֹלָם *כֻּלָּם אֲהוּבִים כֻּלָּם בְּרוּרִים כֻּלָּם גִּבּוֹרִים וְכֻלָּם עֹשִׂים בְּאֵימָה וּבְיִרְאָה רְצוֹן קוֹנָם וְכֻלָּם פּוֹתְחִים אֶת־פִּיהֶם בִּקְדֻשָּׁה וּבְטָהֳרָה בְּשִׁירָה וּבְזִמְרָה וּמְבָרְכִים וּמְשַׁבְּחִים וּמְפָאֲרִים וּמַעֲרִיצִים וּמַקְדִּישִׁים וּמַמְלִיכִים←

Who are holy beings?
They are beloved, clear of mind and courageous.
Their will and God's are one.
Raising their voices in constant gratitude
they marvel at every detail of life,
Granting each other loving permission to be exactly who they are.
When we listen for their sweet voices, we can hear the echo within our own souls.

S.P.W.

The name of God, the regal, grand, and awesome one! Holy is God!
And all of them receive upon themselves, from each to each, the yoke of heaven's rule, and lovingly they give to one another the permission to declare their maker holy. In an ecstasy of spirit, with pure speech and holy melody, all of them respond in awe as one, and cry: "Holy, holy, holy is THE RULER of the multitudes of heaven. The whole world overflows with divine glory!"

The angels of the chariot and holy creatures of the heavens, in great quaking, rise to face the seraphim. And, facing them, they sing in praise, and cry: "Blessed be the glory of THE ONE, wherever God may dwell!" ↩

NOTE. Several forms of *kedushah* exist in our liturgy. Here we have the *Kedushah Diyeshivah*, which we recite without standing. We remember that, according to the Bible, the angels proclaim God's holiness, but we do not yet rise to do so ourselves. Proclaiming the holiness of the divine unity takes more preparation and concentration. We strive to be ready to move from remembering to proclaiming when we recite the *Kedushah* of the *Amidah*. D.A.T.

מלא כל הארץ כבודו Literally, the fullness of the earth is God's glory. In this we recognize that there are barren places and empty lives. When we turn despair to hope, cry out for justice, pursue peace, we fill the earth with what is holy, and then the fullness of the earth is God's glory.

S.E.S.

אֶת שֵׁם הָאֵל הַמֶּלֶךְ הַגָּדוֹל הַגִּבּוֹר וְהַנּוֹרָא קָדוֹשׁ הוּא *וְכֻלָּם מְקַבְּלִים עֲלֵיהֶם עֹל מַלְכוּת שָׁמַיִם זֶה מִזֶּה וְנוֹתְנִים בְּאַהֲבָה רְשׁוּת זֶה לָזֶה לְהַקְדִּישׁ לְיוֹצְרָם בְּנַחַת רוּחַ בְּשָׂפָה בְרוּרָה וּבִנְעִימָה קְדֻשָּׁה כֻּלָּם כְּאֶחָד עוֹנִים וְאוֹמְרִים בְּיִרְאָה:

קָדוֹשׁ קָדוֹשׁ קָדוֹשׁ

יהוה צְבָאוֹת מְלֹא כָל הָאָרֶץ כְּבוֹדוֹ:

*וְהָאוֹפַנִּים וְחַיּוֹת הַקֹּדֶשׁ בְּרַעַשׁ גָּדוֹל מִתְנַשְּׂאִים לְעֻמַּת שְׂרָפִים לְעֻמָּתָם מְשַׁבְּחִים וְאוֹמְרִים:

בָּרוּךְ כְּבוֹד יהוה מִמְּקוֹמוֹ: ←

Kadosh kadosh kadosh adonay tzeva'ot melo ḥol ha'a̲retz kevodo.

Baruḥ kevod adonay mimekomo. ↵

ונותנים באהבה / and lovingly they give to one another the permission. Here our text follows the Sephardic version by adding the word *be'ahavah* (in love). It is only in our love for one another that we are truly capable of granting to each other "permission" to pray. A community of Jews who stand together in real prayer must be one where each individual is known and cared for as a person. Only when such love exists among us are we a community whose members can truly "grant permission" to one another to seek or to sanctify God. A.G.

To blessed God they offer melodies. To the sovereign and enduring God they utter songs, and make their praises heard, for God alone is holy and revered, enactor of all mighty deeds, the fashioner of all new things, the seeder of all righteousness, the grower of all saving acts, creator of all healing, awesome in praises, source of every wonder, who renews each day, with constant good, Creation's work—as it is said: "The maker of the skies' great lights, whose love is everlasting!"

Let a new light shine forever upon Zion. Soon, may everyone of us be worthy of its light. Blessed are you, ETERNAL ONE, the shaper of the heavens' lights.

Every day, Creation is renewed.
Wake up and see unfolding
In the spreading light of dawn,
The world and all it contains
Coming into being, new, fresh,
Filled with divine goodness
And love.
Every day, Creation is renewed.
Reflected in the great lights
We see a new day,
One precious day,
Eternity.

S.P.W.

לָאֵל בָּרוּךְ נְעִימוֹת יִתֵּנוּ לַמֶּלֶךְ אֵל חַי וְקַיָּם זְמִירוֹת יֹאמֵרוּ וְתִשְׁבָּחוֹת יַשְׁמִיעוּ כִּי הוּא לְבַדּוֹ מָרוֹם וְקָדוֹשׁ פּוֹעֵל גְּבוּרוֹת עוֹשֶׂה חֲדָשׁוֹת זוֹרֵעַ צְדָקוֹת מַצְמִיחַ יְשׁוּעוֹת בּוֹרֵא רְפוּאוֹת נוֹרָא תְהִלּוֹת אֲדוֹן הַנִּפְלָאוֹת הַמְחַדֵּשׁ בְּטוּבוֹ בְּכָל יוֹם תָּמִיד מַעֲשֵׂה בְרֵאשִׁית כָּאָמוּר: לְעֹשֵׂה אוֹרִים גְּדֹלִים כִּי לְעוֹלָם חַסְדּוֹ:

*אוֹר חָדָשׁ עַל צִיּוֹן תָּאִיר וְנִזְכֶּה כֻלָּנוּ בִמְהֵרָה לְאוֹרוֹ: בָּרוּךְ אַתָּה יהוה יוֹצֵר הַמְּאוֹרוֹת:

Or ḥadash al tziyon ta'ir venizkeh ḥulanu bimherah le'oro. Baruḥ atah adonay yotzer hame'orot.

לעשה...חסדו / The...everlasting (Psalm 136:7).

INTERPRETIVE VERSION: YOTZER

Blessed is our God, sovereign of the universe, who in love illuminates the earth and those who dwell on it. With the dawn, nature's familiar shapes and colors emerge from the darkness to delight us afresh with their variety and beauty. And with our awakening from slumber, our senses and our spirits respond anew to the splendor of the world. Reborn with the day, we hail our God, who renews continually the work of creation. Blessed is our God, for the light of day.

And blessed is our God, for the light of understanding with which we read the meaning of nature and discover the laws by which we can live. The more we delve into the mysteries of creation, the more we marvel at the order, the power, the wonder and the beauty of the universe. The heavens declare the glory of God, and the earth proclaims God's handiwork.

Our God, you have created us in your image and have made us to share in your work of creation. You have given to each generation the task of shaping the future of humanity. May our gratitude for all the beauty, order and power that reveal you in nature impel us to serve you. May nothing that we do mar the holiness of life by causing any other creature to lose the joy of living. May all our acts conform with your law and bring blessing to us and to all whose lives touch ours. Give us of your light that we may walk in your way. Blessed are you, our God, creator of luminaries.

1945 Reconstructionist Prayer Book (Adapted)

INTERPRETIVE VERSION: AHAVAH RABAH

Abounding is the love that God has shown the house of Israel in giving us the Torah. Through Torah we have come to know the power of righteousness. Truly your word has been our life and the length of our days, enabling us to outlive powerful nations that have sought to enslave or destroy us. For it has taught us to put our trust not in force and violence, in aggression and domination, but in justice and truth, in kindness and compassion. Torah has helped curb in us the lust and greed, vindictiveness and cruelty that mar human life. It has filled us with a yearning for a world permeated with love, in which people live in peace and security, in mutual loyalty and friendship. It has inspired us with the faith that the ultimate destiny of humanity is to achieve the triumph of righteousness.

Therefore we will not despair even in life's darkest moments, for we possess in Torah the token of God's love. May our hearts be ever open to love! With grateful awareness of all the kindness and good will in the world, let us reach out to others. Then, whatever befalls us in life, we shall not feel forlorn or forsaken. May you never withdraw your love from us! Blessed are you, our God, who has shown eternal love to the people of Israel.

1945 Reconstructionist Prayer Book (Adapted)

AHAVAH RABAH / LOVE AND TORAH

For additional readings, see pages 436-437.

With an abounding love, you love us, NURTURER, our God; with great compassion do you care for us. Our source, our sovereign, just as our ancestors placed their trust in you, and you imparted to them laws of life, so be gracious to us, too, and teach us. Our fount, our loving parent, caring one, be merciful with us, and place into our hearts ability to understand, to see, to hear, to learn, to teach, to keep, to do, and to uphold with love all that we study of your Torah. ↩

אהבה רבה / With an abounding love, you love us. *Ahavah Rabah* may be called the quintessentially Jewish prayer. In boundless love for Israel, God gives the greatest gift imaginable: teachings that will help us to live. What more could we want from the loving parent, combining attributes of both father and mother, who here becomes the compassionate teacher, sharing the gift of true knowledge with children who have become disciples? We pray that we may have the open and understanding heart to receive these teachings, to make them real by our deeds, and to pass them on to others. This is our response to God's love: a commitment to study, to live the life of Torah, and to carry it forward to future generations. A.G.

ותלמדם חקי חיים / you imparted to them laws of life. This second *beraḥah* prior to the Shema moves us from the cosmic realm of God as experienced in nature to the particular Jewish experience of God, as transmitted through our culture. Our Torah records those laws of life that reflect our people's collective experience of God. R.S.A.

אַהֲבָה רַבָּה

אַהֲבָה רַבָּה אֲהַבְתָּנוּ יהוה אֱלֹהֵינוּ חֶמְלָה גְדוֹלָה וִיתֵרָה חָמַלְתָּ
עָלֵינוּ: אָבִינוּ מַלְכֵּנוּ בַּעֲבוּר אֲבוֹתֵינוּ וְאִמּוֹתֵינוּ שֶׁבָּטְחוּ בְךָ וַתְּלַמְּדֵם
חֻקֵּי חַיִּים כֵּן תְּחָנֵּנוּ וּתְלַמְּדֵנוּ: אָבִינוּ הָאָב הָרַחֲמָן הַמְרַחֵם רַחֵם
עָלֵינוּ וְתֵן בְּלִבֵּנוּ לְהָבִין וּלְהַשְׂכִּיל לִשְׁמֹעַ לִלְמֹד וּלְלַמֵּד לִשְׁמֹר
וְלַעֲשׂוֹת וּלְקַיֵּם אֶת כָּל דִּבְרֵי תַלְמוּד תּוֹרָתֶךָ בְּאַהֲבָה: ←

Ahavah rabah ahavtanu adonay eloheynu ḥemlah gedolah viterah ḥamalta aleynu. Avinu malkenu ba'avur avoteynu ve'imoteynu shebateḥu veḥa vatelamdem ḥukey ḥayim ken teḥonenu utlamdenu. Avinu ha'av haraḥaman hamraḥem raḥem aleynu veten belibenu lehavin ulhaskil lishmo'a lilmod ulelamed lishmor vela'asot ulkayem et kol divrey talmud torateḥa be'ahavah.

Commentary. In the preceding pages (66-75) we offered an extended blessing for Creation. We accepted our creatureliness, our place in nature. Now we shift to concern with what gives our creaturely lives transcendent meaning.

We learn of our own significance through the love that is freely offered to us first by parents and later by others as well. We learn our ultimate worth in this love, which is rooted in the divine love. This is truly essential teaching! This love teaches us what to do with our lives, how to serve others, how to do the divine bidding. Thus loving and learning are inseparable parts of our tie to the divine. D.A.T.

הרחמן המרחם רחם / loving...caring...be merciful. These three consecutive words are based on the same root רחם, which is related to the Hebrew word *reḥem*/womb. J.R.

Enlighten us with your Torah, cause our hearts to cling to your mitzvot. Make our hearts one, to love your name and be in awe of it. Keep us from shame, and from humiliation, and from stumbling, today and always. For we have trusted in your holy, great, and awesome name. May we be glad, rejoicing in your saving power, and may you reunite our people from all corners of the earth, leading us proudly independent to our land. For you are the redeeming God and have brought us near to your great name, to offer thanks to you, and lovingly declare your unity. Blessed are you, ABUNDANT ONE, who lovingly cares for your people Israel.

KAVANAH. In gathering together the four corners of the tallit, we gather our scattered thoughts and focus on unity—uniting our people, uniting the disparate elements of our lives, uniting with the oneness that links all that is. This inner unity is the place out of which our hearts speak the Shema. D.A.T.

NOTE. Jews traditionally have gathered in the four *tzitziyot* at the corners of their tallitot when they reach *vahavi'enu* / reunite. The *tzitziyot* are then held throughout the Shema. D.A.T.

וְהָאֵר עֵינֵינוּ בְּתוֹרָתֶךָ וְדַבֵּק לִבֵּנוּ בְּמִצְוֹתֶיךָ וְיַחֵד לְבָבֵנוּ לְאַהֲבָה
וּלְיִרְאָה אֶת שְׁמֶךָ וְלֹא נֵבוֹשׁ וְלֹא נִכָּלֵם וְלֹא נִכָּשֵׁל לְעוֹלָם וָעֶד:
כִּי בְשֵׁם קָדְשְׁךָ הַגָּדוֹל וְהַנּוֹרָא בָּטָחְנוּ: נָגִילָה וְנִשְׂמְחָה בִּישׁוּעָתֶךָ:

*וַהֲבִיאֵנוּ לְשָׁלוֹם מֵאַרְבַּע כַּנְפוֹת הָאָרֶץ וְתוֹלִיכֵנוּ קוֹמְמִיּוּת לְאַרְצֵנוּ:
כִּי אֵל פּוֹעֵל יְשׁוּעוֹת אָתָּה: וְקֵרַבְתָּנוּ לְשִׁמְךָ הַגָּדוֹל סֶלָה בֶּאֱמֶת:
לְהוֹדוֹת לְךָ וּלְיַחֶדְךָ בְּאַהֲבָה: בָּרוּךְ אַתָּה יהוה אוֹהֵב עַמּוֹ יִשְׂרָאֵל:

Veha'er eyneynu betorateḥa vedabek libenu bemitzvoteḥa veyaḥed levavenu le'ahavah ulyirah et shemeḥa. Velo nevosh velo nikalem velo nikashel le'olam va'ed. Ki veshem kodsheḥa hagadol vehanora bataḥnu. Nagilah venismeḥah bishu'ateḥa.

Vahavi'enu leshalom me'arba kanfot ha'aretz vetoliḥeynu komemiyut le'artzeynu. Ki el po'el yeshu'ot atah vekeravtanu le'shimeḥa hagadol selah be'emet. Lehodot leḥa ulyaḥedeḥa be'ahavah.
Baruḥ atah adonay ohev amo yisra'el.

שמע ישראל יהוה אלהינו יהוה אחד

Listen, Israel: THE ETERNAL is our God, THE ETERNAL ONE alone!
Blessed be the name and glory of God's realm forever!

And you must love THE ONE, your God, with your whole heart, with every breath, with all you have. Take these words that I command you now to heart. Teach them intently to your children. Speak them when you sit inside your house or walk upon the road, when you lie down and when you rise. And bind them as a sign upon your hand, and keep them visible before your eyes. Inscribe them on the doorposts of your house and on your gates. ↩

שמע ישראל / Listen, Israel. The core of our worship is not a prayer at all, but a cry to our fellow-Jews and fellow-humans. In it we declare that God is one—which is also to say that humanity is one, that life is one, that joys and sufferings are all one—for God is the force that binds them all together. There is nothing obvious about this truth, for life as we experience it seems infinitely fragmented. Human beings seem isolated from one another, divided by all the fears and hatreds that make up human history. Even within a single life, one moment feels cut off from the next, memories of joy and fullness offering us little consolation when we are depressed or lonely. To assert that all is one in God is our supreme act of faith. No wonder that the Shema, the first "prayer" we learn in childhood, is also the last thing we are to say before we die. The memory of these words on the lips of martyrs deepens our faith as we call them out each day. A.G.

COMMENTARY. From recognition of our place in nature in the first blessing of this part of the service, we shifted to concern with our moral place in the second blessing. As creatures made conscious of our ultimate worth by love, we recite the Shema. We thereby enter into a partnership aimed at transforming the world and ourselves in the light of that vision of ultimate worth. D.A.T.

שְׁמַע יִשְׂרָאֵל יהוה אֱלֹהֵינוּ יהוה אֶחָד׃

בָּרוּךְ שֵׁם כְּבוֹד מַלְכוּתוֹ לְעוֹלָם וָעֶד׃

וְאָהַבְתָּ֗ אֵ֚ת יְהוָ֣ה אֱלֹהֶ֑יךָ בְּכָל־לְבָבְךָ֥ וּבְכָל־נַפְשְׁךָ֖ וּבְכָל־מְאֹדֶֽךָ׃
וְהָי֞וּ הַדְּבָרִ֣ים הָאֵ֗לֶּה אֲשֶׁ֨ר אָנֹכִ֧י מְצַוְּךָ֛ הַיּ֖וֹם עַל־לְבָבֶֽךָ׃
וְשִׁנַּנְתָּ֣ם לְבָנֶ֔יךָ וְדִבַּרְתָּ֖ בָּ֑ם בְּשִׁבְתְּךָ֤ בְּבֵיתֶ֙ךָ֙ וּבְלֶכְתְּךָ֣ בַדֶּ֔רֶךְ
וּֽבְשָׁכְבְּךָ֖ וּבְקוּמֶֽךָ׃ וּקְשַׁרְתָּ֥ם לְא֖וֹת עַל־יָדֶ֑ךָ וְהָי֥וּ לְטֹטָפֹ֖ת בֵּ֥ין
עֵינֶֽיךָ׃ וּכְתַבְתָּ֛ם עַל־מְזֻז֥וֹת בֵּיתֶ֖ךָ וּבִשְׁעָרֶֽיךָ׃

Shema yisra'el adonay eloheynu adonay eḥad.
Baruḥ shem kevod malḥuto le'olam va'ed.

Ve'ahavta et adonay eloheḥa
beḥol levaveḥa uvḥol nafsheḥa uvḥol me'odeḥa.
Vehayu hadevarim ha'eleh asher anoḥi metzaveḥa hayom al levaveḥa,
Veshinantam levaneḥa vedibarta bam
beshivteḥa beveyteḥa uvleḥteḥa vadereḥ uvshoḥbeḥa uvkumeḥa.
Ukshartam le'ot al yadeḥa vehayu letotafot beyn eyneḥa.
Uḥtavtam al mezuzot beyteḥa uvishareḥa.

ואהבת / And you must love. You shall love your God intellectually, emotionally and with all your deeds. Whatever you love most in these ways is your god. For the Jewish people, the deepest love should be for freedom, justice and peace. M.M.K./M.S.

For the second paragraph of the Shema, read either the version below or the alternative biblical selection beginning on page 88, then continue with the third paragraph, page 90.

BIBLICAL SELECTION I

It came to pass, and will again,
that if you truly listen
to the voice of THE ETERNAL ONE, your God,
being sure to do whatever has been asked of you today,
THE ONE, your God, will make of you a model
for all nations of the earth,
and there will come upon you all these blessings,
as you listen to the call of THE ABUNDANT ONE, your God:
Blessed be you in the city,
blessed be you upon the field.
Blessed be the fruit of your womb,
the fruit of your land, the fruit of your cattle,
the calving of your oxen, and the lambing of your sheep.
Blessed be your basket and your kneading-trough.
Blessed be you when you come home,
and blessed be you when you go forth.

See, I have placed in front of you today
both life and good, both death and ill,
commanding you today to love THE BOUNDLESS ONE, your God,
to walk in ways I have ordained,
keeping the commandments, laws, and judgments,
so that you survive and multiply.
THE BOUNTIFUL, your God, will bless you
on the land you are about to enter and inherit. ↩

For the second paragraph of the Shema, read either the version below or the biblical selection beginning on page 89, then continue with the third paragraph, page 91.

BIBLICAL SELECTION I

וְהָיָה אִם־שָׁמוֹעַ תִּשְׁמַע בְּקוֹל יהוה אֱלֹהֶיךָ לִשְׁמֹר לַעֲשׂוֹת אֶת־
כָּל־מִצְוֹתָיו אֲשֶׁר אָנֹכִי מְצַוְּךָ הַיּוֹם וּנְתָנְךָ יהוה אֱלֹהֶיךָ עֶלְיוֹן
עַל כָּל־גּוֹיֵי הָאָרֶץ: וּבָאוּ עָלֶיךָ כָּל־הַבְּרָכוֹת הָאֵלֶּה וְהִשִּׂיגֻךָ
כִּי תִשְׁמַע בְּקוֹל יהוה אֱלֹהֶיךָ: בָּרוּךְ אַתָּה בָּעִיר וּבָרוּךְ אַתָּה
בַּשָּׂדֶה: בָּרוּךְ פְּרִי־בִטְנְךָ וּפְרִי אַדְמָתְךָ וּפְרִי בְהֶמְתֶּךָ שְׁגַר
אֲלָפֶיךָ וְעַשְׁתְּרוֹת צֹאנֶךָ: בָּרוּךְ טַנְאֲךָ וּמִשְׁאַרְתֶּךָ: בָּרוּךְ אַתָּה
בְּבֹאֶךָ וּבָרוּךְ אַתָּה בְּצֵאתֶךָ:

רְאֵה נָתַתִּי לְפָנֶיךָ הַיּוֹם אֶת־הַחַיִּים וְאֶת־הַטּוֹב וְאֶת־הַמָּוֶת וְאֶת־
הָרָע: אֲשֶׁר אָנֹכִי מְצַוְּךָ הַיּוֹם לְאַהֲבָה אֶת־יהוה אֱלֹהֶיךָ לָלֶכֶת
בִּדְרָכָיו וְלִשְׁמֹר מִצְוֹתָיו וְחֻקֹּתָיו וּמִשְׁפָּטָיו וְחָיִיתָ וְרָבִיתָ וּבֵרַכְךָ
יהוה אֱלֹהֶיךָ בָּאָרֶץ אֲשֶׁר־אַתָּה בָא־שָׁמָּה לְרִשְׁתָּהּ: ←

COMMENTARY. The traditional wording of Biblical Selection II presents detailed bountiful or devastating consequences of Israel's collective relationship to the mitzvot. That biblical section (Deuteronomy 11:13-21) offers a supernatural theology that many contemporary Jews find difficult. The first part of this biblical selection (Deuteronomy 28:1-6, 30:15-19) was included in the 1945 Reconstructionist siddur. It begins by encouraging observance in the same language, but concentrates on the positive ways in which observance of mitzvot focuses our attention on God's presence as perceived through productivity and the pursuit of abundant life. The second part was first used in the Israeli Progressive siddur, *Ha-avodah Shebalev.* S.S.

DERASH. A person must acquire a religious faith, not by being reasoned to about God, but by experiencing God's power in making life worthwhile.
M.M.K./M.S. (Adapted)

But if your heart should turn away,
and you not heed, and go astray,
and you submit to other gods and serve them,
I declare to you today that you shall be
destroyed completely; you shall not live out
a great expanse of days upon the land
that you now cross the Jordan to possess.
I call as witnesses concerning you
both heaven and earth, both life and death,
that I have placed in front of you
a blessing and a curse.
Choose life, that you may live,
you and your seed!

Continue on page 90.

וְאִם־יִפְנֶה לְבָבְךָ וְלֹא תִשְׁמָע וְנִדַּחְתָּ וְהִשְׁתַּחֲוִיתָ לֵאלֹהִים אֲחֵרִים
וַעֲבַדְתָּם: הִגַּדְתִּי לָכֶם הַיּוֹם כִּי אָבֹד תֹּאבֵדוּן לֹא־תַאֲרִיכֻן יָמִים
עַל־הָאֲדָמָה אֲשֶׁר אַתָּה עֹבֵר אֶת־הַיַּרְדֵּן לָבוֹא שָׁמָּה לְרִשְׁתָּהּ:
הַעִדֹתִי בָכֶם הַיּוֹם אֶת־הַשָּׁמַיִם וְאֶת־הָאָרֶץ הַחַיִּים וְהַמָּוֶת נָתַתִּי
לְפָנֶיךָ הַבְּרָכָה וְהַקְּלָלָה וּבָחַרְתָּ בַּחַיִּים לְמַעַן תִּחְיֶה אַתָּה וְזַרְעֶךָ:

Continue with ויאמר, *page 91.*

BIBLICAL SELECTION II

And if you truly listen to my bidding, as I bid you now—loving THE FOUNT OF LIFE, your God, and serving God with all your heart, with every breath—then I will give you rain upon your land in its appointed time, the early rain and later rain, so you may gather in your corn, your wine and oil. And I will give you grass upon your field to feed your animals, and you will eat and be content. Beware, then, lest your heart be led astray, and you go off and worship other gods, and you submit to them, so that the anger of THE MIGHTY ONE should burn against you, and seal up the heavens so no rain would fall, so that the ground would not give forth her produce, and you be forced to leave the good land I am giving you.

So place these words upon your heart, into your lifebreath. Bind them as a sign upon your hand, and let them rest before your eyes. Teach them to your children, speaking of them when you sit at home, and when you walk upon the road, when you lie down, and when you rise, inscribing them on the doorposts of your house and on your gates—so that your days and your children's days be many on the land THE FAITHFUL ONE promised to give your ancestors, as long as heaven rests above the earth.

DERASH. The traditional second paragraph of the Shema (Deuteronomy 11:13-21) offers an account of the natural process by which the blessings of God themselves lead to pride, self-satisfaction, and ingratitude on the part of those who receive them. Ironically, the more we are blessed, so it seems, the less grateful and aware of blessing we become. It is when we are most sated, Scripture warns us, that we should be most careful. Fullness can lead to ingratitude, and ingratitude to idolatry—primarily in the form of worship of our own accomplishments. Then, indeed, "the heavens might close up and no rain fall." For, once we begin to worship our achievements, we will never find satisfaction. A.G.

BIBLICAL SELECTION II

וְהָיָה אִם־שָׁמֹעַ תִּשְׁמְעוּ אֶל־מִצְוֹתַי אֲשֶׁר אָנֹכִי מְצַוֶּה
אֶתְכֶם הַיּוֹם לְאַהֲבָה אֶת־יהוה אֱלֹהֵיכֶם וּלְעָבְדוֹ בְּכָל־לְבַבְכֶם
וּבְכָל־נַפְשְׁכֶם׃ וְנָתַתִּי מְטַר־אַרְצְכֶם בְּעִתּוֹ יוֹרֶה וּמַלְקוֹשׁ
וְאָסַפְתָּ דְגָנֶךָ וְתִירֹשְׁךָ וְיִצְהָרֶךָ׃ וְנָתַתִּי עֵשֶׂב בְּשָׂדְךָ לִבְהֶמְתֶּךָ
וְאָכַלְתָּ וְשָׂבָעְתָּ׃ הִשָּׁמְרוּ לָכֶם פֶּן־יִפְתֶּה לְבַבְכֶם וְסַרְתֶּם
וַעֲבַדְתֶּם אֱלֹהִים אֲחֵרִים וְהִשְׁתַּחֲוִיתֶם לָהֶם׃ וְחָרָה אַף־יהוה
בָּכֶם וְעָצַר אֶת־הַשָּׁמַיִם וְלֹא־יִהְיֶה מָטָר וְהָאֲדָמָה לֹא תִתֵּן אֶת־
יְבוּלָהּ וַאֲבַדְתֶּם מְהֵרָה מֵעַל הָאָרֶץ הַטֹּבָה אֲשֶׁר יהוה נֹתֵן לָכֶם׃

וְשַׂמְתֶּם אֶת־דְּבָרַי אֵלֶּה עַל־לְבַבְכֶם וְעַל־נַפְשְׁכֶם וּקְשַׁרְתֶּם אֹתָם
לְאוֹת עַל־יֶדְכֶם וְהָיוּ לְטוֹטָפֹת בֵּין עֵינֵיכֶם׃ וְלִמַּדְתֶּם אֹתָם אֶת־
בְּנֵיכֶם לְדַבֵּר בָּם בְּשִׁבְתְּךָ בְּבֵיתֶךָ וּבְלֶכְתְּךָ בַדֶּרֶךְ וּבְשָׁכְבְּךָ
וּבְקוּמֶךָ׃ וּכְתַבְתָּם עַל־מְזוּזוֹת בֵּיתֶךָ וּבִשְׁעָרֶיךָ׃ לְמַעַן יִרְבּוּ
יְמֵיכֶם וִימֵי בְנֵיכֶם עַל הָאֲדָמָה אֲשֶׁר נִשְׁבַּע יהוה לַאֲבֹתֵיכֶם
לָתֵת לָהֶם כִּימֵי הַשָּׁמַיִם עַל־הָאָרֶץ׃

COMMENTARY. What human action could result in the destruction of the rains, the onset of crop failure and famine? Abuse of the eco-system upon which our very lives depend. And how could such an event occur? When we lose sight of our place in the world and the wondrous gift in all that is. The traditional second paragraph of the Shema was replaced by another biblical selection in earlier Reconstructionist liturgy because the traditional paragraph was understood as literal reward and punishment. However, today in the light of our awareness of the human abuse of the environment, we recognize that often this reward and punishment rest in our own hands. This ancient and yet vital message of the Torah urges us to choose life.

D.A.T.

THE BOUNDLESS ONE told Moses: Speak to the Israelites—tell them to make themselves *tzitzit* upon the corners of their clothes, throughout their generations. Have them place upon the corner *tzitzit* a twine of royal blue. This is your *tzitzit*. Look at it and remember all the mitzvot of the ETERNAL ONE. And do them, so you won't go off after the lusts of your heart or after what catches your eye, so that you remember to do all my mitzvot and be holy for your God. I am THE FAITHFUL ONE, your God, who brought you from Mitzrayim to be for you a God. I am THE INFINITE, your God.

למען תזכרו / so that you remember. The *tzitzit*, like all the forms of religion, are there as reminders for us as we go about our daily lives. All of us have had moments when we most became ourselves, liberated from the bonds holding us back, or when we discovered those great inner truths that lend meaning to our lives. But such moments are forgotten, covered over by the petty angers and frustrations of daily living, by the hard shell we think we need about us to protect our most precious feelings.

Our tradition calls upon us to bring such moments back to mind and make them part of our worship. Our own innermost liberation is our "coming out of Egypt"; our own moment of deepest truth is our "standing before Sinai". Let us remember these as we look at our *tzitzit*, and join them to the ancient memories of our people. A.G.

DERASH. The four *tzitziyot* represent the four corners of the world. The divine presence spans the entire area from one corner of the world to the other. So too do the inescapable moral obligations extend throughout our lives no matter where we are. D.A.T.

וַיֹּאמֶר יְהוָה אֶל־מֹשֶׁה לֵּאמֹר׃ דַּבֵּר אֶל־בְּנֵי יִשְׂרָאֵל וְאָמַרְתָּ
אֲלֵהֶם וְעָשׂוּ לָהֶם צִיצִת עַל־כַּנְפֵי בִגְדֵיהֶם לְדֹרֹתָם וְנָתְנוּ עַל־
צִיצִת הַכָּנָף פְּתִיל תְּכֵלֶת׃ וְהָיָה לָכֶם לְצִיצִת וּרְאִיתֶם אֹתוֹ
וּזְכַרְתֶּם אֶת־כָּל־מִצְוֹת יְהוָה וַעֲשִׂיתֶם אֹתָם וְלֹא תָתוּרוּ אַחֲרֵי
לְבַבְכֶם וְאַחֲרֵי עֵינֵיכֶם אֲשֶׁר־אַתֶּם זֹנִים אַחֲרֵיהֶם׃ לְמַעַן תִּזְכְּרוּ
וַעֲשִׂיתֶם אֶת־כָּל־מִצְוֹתָי וִהְיִיתֶם קְדֹשִׁים לֵאלֹהֵיכֶם׃ אֲנִי יְהוָה
אֱלֹהֵיכֶם אֲשֶׁר הוֹצֵאתִי אֶתְכֶם מֵאֶרֶץ מִצְרַיִם לִהְיוֹת לָכֶם
לֵאלֹהִים אֲנִי יְהוָה אֱלֹהֵיכֶם׃ יהוה אֱלֹהֵיכֶם **אמת**

Vayomer adonay el moshe leymor. Daber el beney yisra'el ve'amarta aleyhem ve'asu lahem tzitzit al kanfey vigdeyhem ledorotam venatenu al tzitzit hakanaf petil tehelet. Vehayah laḥem letzitzit uritem oto uzḥartem et kol mitzvot adonay va'asitem otam velo taturu aḥarey levaveḥem ve'aḥarey eyneyḥem asher atem zonim aḥareyhem. Lema'an tizkeru va'asitem et kol mitzvotay vihe-yitem kedoshim leyloheyḥem. Ani adonay eloheyḥem asher hotzeyti etḥem me'eretz mitzrayim lihyot laḥem leylohim ani adonay eloheyḥem. Adonay eloheyḥem emet.

ויאמר...אמת / The Boundless One...God (Numbers 15:37-41).

EMET VEYATZIV / TRUE AND ESTABLISHED

For additional readings, see pages 435, 438-439.

True, and established, and correct,
enduring and straightforward,
steadfast, good, and beautiful
one fundamental principle shall be—
as for our ancestors, for us,
and for the generations after us,
and for all the generations that the seed of Israel,
your servants, shall exist—
the truth for early eras and for later ones,
a thing most excellent and real,
forever and as long as time endures,
a true and faithful law that cannot pass away.
The truth that you are THE ETERNAL ONE,
our God, our ancients' God,
our sovereign one, our ancients' sovereign one,
our champion, our ancients' champion,
our rock, the rock of our salvation,
our redeemer and our rescuer,
your name has always been,
there is no God but you.
Help of our ancestors you have always been,
shield and savior to their children after them,
in each and every generation.
In heaven's heights your dwelling sits,
but your judgments and your justice
fill the farthest reaches of the earth.
Happy is the one who pays heed to your mitzvot,
who takes your Torah and your word to heart!
True it is that you are sovereign to your people,
and a mighty ruler who is quick to plead their cause. ↩

אֱמֶת וְיַצִּיב

אֱמֶת: וְיַצִּיב וְנָכוֹן וְקַיָּם וְיָשָׁר וְנֶאֱמָן וְטוֹב וְיָפֶה הַדָּבָר הַזֶּה: *עַל אֲבוֹתֵינוּ וְעַל אִמּוֹתֵינוּ וְעָלֵינוּ וְעַל בָּנֵינוּ וְעַל דּוֹרוֹתֵינוּ וְעַל כָּל־דּוֹרוֹת זֶרַע יִשְׂרָאֵל עֲבָדֶיךָ:

עַל הָרִאשׁוֹנִים וְעַל הָאַחֲרוֹנִים דָּבָר טוֹב וְקַיָּם לְעוֹלָם וָעֶד אֱמֶת וֶאֱמוּנָה חֹק וְלֹא יַעֲבוֹר: *אֱמֶת שָׁאַתָּה הוּא יהוה אֱלֹהֵינוּ וֵאלֹהֵי אֲבוֹתֵינוּ וְאִמּוֹתֵינוּ מַלְכֵּנוּ מֶלֶךְ אֲבוֹתֵינוּ גּוֹאֲלֵנוּ גּוֹאֵל אִמּוֹתֵינוּ צוּרֵנוּ צוּר יְשׁוּעָתֵנוּ פּוֹדֵנוּ וּמַצִּילֵנוּ מֵעוֹלָם הוּא שְׁמֶךָ: אֵין אֱלֹהִים זוּלָתֶךָ:

עֶזְרַת אֲבוֹתֵינוּ וְאִמּוֹתֵינוּ אַתָּה הוּא מֵעוֹלָם מָגֵן וּמוֹשִׁיעַ לִבְנֵיהֶם אַחֲרֵיהֶם בְּכָל דּוֹר וָדוֹר: בְּרוּם עוֹלָם מוֹשָׁבֶךָ וּמִשְׁפָּטֶיךָ וְצִדְקָתְךָ עַד אַפְסֵי־אָרֶץ: אַשְׁרֵי אִישׁ שֶׁיִּשְׁמַע לְמִצְוֹתֶיךָ וְתוֹרָתְךָ וּדְבָרְךָ יָשִׂים עַל לִבּוֹ: אֱמֶת אַתָּה הוּא אָדוֹן לְעַמֶּךָ וּמֶלֶךְ גִּבּוֹר לָרִיב רִיבָם: ←

DERASH. *Emet Veyatziv* is an affirmation of the Shema. We join the last words of the Shema to אמת as a statement of our ongoing commitment to their truth. Both אמת / truth and אמן / Amen are derived from a root meaning "strong" or "firm". It has also been noted that the three letters of אמת span the Hebrew alphabet; they are its beginning, middle, and end. In contrast, the letters of שקר / lie are all huddled together in a single corner of the alphabet. Truth is broad and all-encompassing; we have to expand our minds in order to embrace it. Lies, like gossip and malicious talk, bring out the narrowness within us. Let us commit ourselves, in affirming the Shema, to breadth of vision and the ongoing search for truth.

L.W.K./A.G.

True it is that you are first and last,
and without you, we have no ruler, champion, or savior.
From servitude and bondage you redeemed us, BOUNDLESS ONE, our God,
and from a house of slavery you set us free.
For this your loved ones celebrated you,
and held divinity in reverence,
and your beloved ones gave forth their melodies,
their songs and exaltations, blessings and thanks,
to the sovereign, living, and enduring God,
the lofty, the exalted, and the awesome one,
who casts the prideful down, and lifts the lowly,
who sets the captive free, and saves the humble,
and who helps the poor, responding to our people
when they cry aloud to God.
Give praises to the highest God!
Blessed is God, the one to bless!
So Moses, Miriam and the Israelites came forth with song to you,
in boundless happiness, and they all cried: ↩

אֱמֶת אַתָּה הוּא רִאשׁוֹן וְאַתָּה הוּא אַחֲרוֹן וּמִבַּלְעָדֶֽיךָ אֵין לָֽנוּ מֶֽלֶךְ
גּוֹאֵל וּמוֹשִֽׁיעַ׃ מִמִּצְרַֽיִם גְּאַלְתָּֽנוּ יהוה אֱלֹהֵֽינוּ וּמִבֵּית עֲבָדִים
פְּדִיתָֽנוּ׃

עַל־זֹאת שִׁבְּחוּ אֲהוּבִים וְרוֹמְמוּ אֵל׃ וְנָתְנוּ יְדִידִים זְמִירוֹת שִׁירוֹת
וְתִשְׁבָּחוֹת בְּרָכוֹת וְהוֹדָאוֹת לְמֶֽלֶךְ אֵל חַי וְקַיָּם׃ רָם וְנִשָּׂא גָּדוֹל
וְנוֹרָא מַשְׁפִּיל גֵּאִים וּמַגְבִּֽיהַּ שְׁפָלִים מוֹצִיא אֲסִירִים וּפוֹדֶה עֲנָוִים
וְעוֹזֵר דַּלִּים וְעוֹנֶה לְעַמּוֹ בְּעֵת שַׁוְּעָם אֵלָיו׃
*תְּהִלּוֹת לְאֵל עֶלְיוֹן בָּרוּךְ הוּא וּמְבוֹרָךְ׃ מֹשֶׁה וּמִרְיָם וּבְנֵי יִשְׂרָאֵל
לְךָ עָנוּ שִׁירָה בְּשִׂמְחָה רַבָּה וְאָמְרוּ כֻלָּם׃ ←

Mosheh umiryam uvney yisra'el leḥa anu shirah besimḥah rabah ve'ameru ḥulam.

Commentary. The sequence of this part of the service moves from Creation (*Yotzer*) to love and revelation (*Ahavah Rabah*), to affirmation of our commitment (Shema) and now to redemption. In this way the idea is expressed that redemption becomes possible only if we participate in making it happen.

The symbol of redemption in the mythic life of the Jewish people is the crossing of the Sea. In the rabbinic imagination, the ancient Israelites slog through mud up to their knees, their waists, even their chests. It falls to us to continue the task of redemption—to face the contemporary morass and find the resolve to wade through it with waves threatening to submerge us on either hand. We wade toward a future that at our darkest moments seems but a dim hope. The hint of the Promised Land is in our loving moments.

We join in singing what the Israelites proclaimed after they had successfully crossed the Sea and find in their redemption the strength to seek our own. This struggle carries us into the *Amidah*, a prayer of becoming, of transformation, of divine-human partnership that brings grace into our lives and into our world.

D.A.T.

"Who among the mighty can compare
  to you, ETERNAL ONE?
    Who can compare to you,
      adorned in holiness,
        awesome in praises,
          acting wondrously!"

A new song did the redeemed ones sing out to your name,
  beside the Sea.
Together, all of them gave thanks, declared your sovereignty.
  and said:
"THE HOLY ONE will reign forever!"

Rock of Israel, rise up to the help of Israel,
redeem, according to your word, Judah and Israel.
Blessed are you, ETERNAL ONE, the champion of Israel.

DERASH. Rabbi Judah said: [At the sea] each tribe said to the other, "You go into the sea first!" As they stood there bickering, Naḥshon ben Aminadav jumped into the water. God said to Moses, who had been praying, "My friend is drowning—and you pray!" "What can I do?" Moses asked. God responded, "Speak to the people of Israel and tell them to go! Raise your staff..." TALMUD SOTAH 37a

מִי־כָמֹכָה בָּאֵלִם יהוה מִי כָּמֹכָה נֶאְדָּר בַּקֹּדֶשׁ נוֹרָא תְהִלֹּת
עֹשֵׂה־פֶלֶא:

*שִׁירָה חֲדָשָׁה שִׁבְּחוּ גְאוּלִים לְשִׁמְךָ עַל־שְׂפַת הַיָּם:

יַחַד כֻּלָּם הוֹדוּ וְהִמְלִיכוּ וְאָמְרוּ:

יהוה יִמְלֹךְ לְעֹלָם וָעֶד:

*צוּר יִשְׂרָאֵל קוּמָה בְּעֶזְרַת יִשְׂרָאֵל: וּפְדֵה כִנְאֻמֶךָ יְהוּדָה וְיִשְׂרָאֵל:

גֹּאֲלֵנוּ יהוה צְבָאוֹת שְׁמוֹ קְדוֹשׁ יִשְׂרָאֵל:

בָּרוּךְ אַתָּה יהוה גָּאַל יִשְׂרָאֵל:

Mi ḥamoḥah ba'elim adonay. Mi kamoḥah nedar bakodesh nora tehilot osey feleh.
Shirah ḥadashah shibeḥu ge'ulim leshimeḥa al sefat hayam.
Yaḥad kulam hodu vehimliḥu ve'ameru.
Adonay yimloḥ le'olam va'ed.
Tzur yisra'el kumah be'ezrat yisra'el. Ufdey ḥinumeḥa yehudah veyisrael. Go'aleynu adonay tzeva'ot shemo kedosh yisra'el.
Baruḥ atah adonay ga'al yisra'el.

DERASH. Most congregations stand at *tzur yisra'el* rather than wait for the blessing. Thus we are already on our feet when we request that God קומה / arise. We cannot ask God to rise up to help Israel unless we have done so ourselves.

E.M.

AMIDAH

The traditional Amidah *follows here. The* Shiviti *meditation begins on page 132. A guided meditation begins on page 128. The* Amidah *is traditionally recited while standing, beginning with three short steps forward and bowing left and right, a reminder of our entry into the divine presence.*

Open my lips, BELOVED ONE,
and let my mouth declare your praise.

1. AVOT VE'IMOT / ANCESTORS

Blessed are you, ANCIENT ONE, our God, God of our ancestors,

God of Abraham	God of Sarah
God of Isaac	God of Rebekah
God of Jacob	God of Rachel
	and God of Leah; ↵

DERASH. Acknowledging our ancestors reminds us that what we are is shaped by who they were. Just as an acorn is shaped by the oak that preceded it and yet gives birth to a tree uniquely its own, so we are shaped by our ancestors yet give rise to a Judaism all our own. R.M.S.

KAVANAH. The opening of the *Amidah* calls to mind previous generations, near as well as distant. Take a few moments to think about your parents, your grandparents, other relatives about whom you may have heard stories. What is your connection with them? L.B.

COMMENTARY. The *Amidah* or "standing prayer" is also called "*Hatefilah* / The Prayer," because of its centrality in every one of the daily services. The *Amidah* in its weekday form is also known as the "*Shemoneh Esrey* / The Eighteen (benedictions)." This name dates from a very early period; nineteen blessings have been included for the last 2000 years. Most liturgy scholars agree that the weekday *Amidah* is structured as a prayer for the arrival of messianic times. The thirteen middle blessings of the weekday *Amidah* are petitions for success and wellbeing that reflect the concerns that occupy our daily circumstances. The *Amidah* always concludes with a prayer for completeness and peace, uniting workday concerns with messianic hope. D.A.T. / R.S.

אדוני...תהלתך / Open...praise (Psalm 51:17).

עֲמִידָה

The traditional Amidah *follows here. The* Shiviti *meditation begins on page 132. A guided meditation begins on page 128. The* Amidah *is traditionally recited while standing, beginning with three short steps forward and bowing left and right, a reminder of our entry into the divine presence.*

אֲדֹנָי שְׂפָתַי תִּפְתָּח וּפִי יַגִּיד תְּהִלָּתֶךָ׃

Adonay sefatay tiftaḥ ufi yagid tehilateḥa.

א 1 אָבוֹת וְאִמּוֹת

בָּרוּךְ אַתָּה יהוה אֱלֹהֵינוּ וֵאלֹהֵי אֲבוֹתֵינוּ וְאִמּוֹתֵינוּ

אֱלֹהֵי אַבְרָהָם	אֱלֹהֵי שָׂרָה
אֱלֹהֵי יִצְחָק	אֱלֹהֵי רִבְקָה
אֱלֹהֵי יַעֲקֹב	אֱלֹהֵי רָחֵל
	וֵאלֹהֵי לֵאָה׃ ←

Baruḥ atah adonay eloheynu veylohey avoteynu ve'imoteynu

elohey avraham	elohey sarah
elohey yitzḥak	elohey rivkah
elohey ya'akov	elohey raḥel
	veylohey le'ah ↵

COMMENTARY. Throughout the centuries the pursuit of meaningful communal prayer has led to variations in the *Amidah*. These variations reflect the attitudes and beliefs of different prayer communities. In the ongoing pursuit of meaningful prayer for a Reconstructionist prayer community, changes have been introduced into this *Amidah*, most notably in the first two of the nineteen *beraḥot* which comprise the weekday *Amidah*. The first *beraḥah* has been expanded to include the matriarchs along with the patriarchs as exemplars of God's presence in human lives. By concentrating on examples of healing forces and life-sustaining rains, the second *beraḥah* acknowledges God as the power that sustains life. The traditional emphasis on God's ability to resurrect the dead has been replaced here by a celebration of God as the power that sustains all life. S.S.

great, heroic, awesome God, supreme divinity,
imparting deeds of kindness, begetter of all;
mindful of the loyalty of Israel's ancestors,
bringing, with love, redemption to their children's children
for the sake of the divine name.

Between Rosh Hashanah and Yom Kippur, add:

(Remember us for life,
our sovereign, who wishes us to live,
and write us in the Book of Life,
for your sake, ever-living God.)

Regal One, our help, salvation, and protector:
Blessed are you, KIND ONE,
the shield of Abraham and help of Sarah. ↩

NOTE. The *Amidah* is made up of three sections. The first and last remain the same for all services, but the central portion differs, containing thirteen blessings on weekdays, and only one on Shabbat and Festivals. The central section on weekdays contains petitions or requests. These workday concerns are set aside on Shabbat and Festivals, when the focus shifts to the joy and holiness of the day. J.B.

וזוכר חסדי אבות ואמות / mindful of the loyalty of Israel's ancestors. The Hebrew phrase can also be translated, "who remembers the love of parents." The legacy each generation gives to its children inevitably contains within it pain and hurt, a sense of inadequacy and of task unfulfilled. Some children are hurt when parents are taken from them too early, others by parents who did not know how to show their love. We say that God "remembers the love of parents;" God is the one who sees to it that the love as well is remembered, even when parents are unable to transmit it.
DANIEL KAMESAR

כל חי / every living thing, gives and renews life. The traditional siddur affirms מחיה המתים / revival of the dead. We substitute כל חי, demonstrating an understanding that all of life is rooted in the world's divine order and avoiding affirmation of life after death. We cannot know what happens to us after we die, but we can, by our thought and action, affirm the possibility of this-worldly salvation. (See pages 103-106). D.A.T.

הָאֵל הַגָּדוֹל הַגִּבּוֹר וְהַנּוֹרָא אֵל עֶלְיוֹן גּוֹמֵל חֲסָדִים טוֹבִים וְקוֹנֵה הַכֹּל וְזוֹכֵר חַסְדֵי אָבוֹת וְאִמּוֹת וּמֵבִיא גְאֻלָּה לִבְנֵי בְנֵיהֶם לְמַעַן שְׁמוֹ בְּאַהֲבָה:

Between Rosh Hashanah and Yom Kippur, add:

(זָכְרֵנוּ לְחַיִּים מֶלֶךְ חָפֵץ בַּחַיִּים וְכָתְבֵנוּ בְּסֵפֶר הַחַיִּים לְמַעַנְךָ אֱלֹהִים חַיִּים:)

מֶלֶךְ עוֹזֵר וּמוֹשִׁיעַ וּמָגֵן: בָּרוּךְ אַתָּה יהוה מָגֵן אַבְרָהָם וְעֶזְרַת שָׂרָה: ←

Ha'el hagadol hagibor vehanora el elyon gomel ḥasadim tovim vekoney hakol vezoḥer ḥasdey avot ve'imot umevi ge'ulah livney veneyhem lema'an shemo be'ahavah.

(Zoḥrenu leḥayim meleḥ ḥafetz baḥayim veḥotvenu besefer haḥayim lema'aneḥa elohim ḥayim.)

Meleḥ ozer umoshi'a umagen. Baruḥ atah adonay magen avraham ve'ezrat sarah. ↵

COMMENTARY. This version of the first *beraḥah* in the *Amidah* includes the matriarchs as well as the patriarchs. The phrase "help of Sarah," *ezrat sarah*, comes from a Hebrew root (עזר) which can mean either "save" or "be strong." This parallels the meaning of *magen* / shield. The biblical text says that Abraham experienced God as a shield and that Sarah experienced God as a helper. Their experience and the example of their lives can enrich our own. Just as Abraham and Sarah found the strength to face the unknown physical and spiritual dangers of their journey, so we seek to find the courage and inspiration to meet the challenges of our time. R.S.

2. GEVUROT / DIVINE POWER

You are forever powerful, ALMIGHTY ONE,
abundant in your saving acts.
In summer: You send down the dew.
In winter: You cause the wind to blow and rain to fall.

In loyalty you sustain the living,
nurturing the life of every living thing,
upholding those who fall,
healing the sick, freeing the captive,
and remaining faithful to all life
held dormant in the earth.
Who can compare to you, almighty God,
who can resemble you, the source of life and death,
who makes salvation grow?

Between Rosh Hashanah and Yom Kippur, add:
(Who can compare to you, source of all mercy,
remembering all creatures mercifully, decreeing life!)

Faithful are you in giving life to every living thing.
Blessed are you, THE FOUNT OF LIFE,
who gives and renews life.
When chanting aloud in a minyan, continue with the Kedushah, page 104.
When praying silently, continue here.

3. KEDUSHAT HASHEM / HALLOWING GOD'S NAME

Recited when praying silently:
Holy are you. Your name is holy.
And all holy beings hail you each day.
Blessed are you, THE AWESOME ONE, the holy God.

(*Between Rosh Hashanah and Yom Kippur, conclude:* the holy sovereign.)

For a shortened form of the Amidah turn to the Abbreviated Amidah, page 106. For the full Amidah, continue on page 108.

2 גְּבוּרוֹת

אַתָּה גִּבּוֹר לְעוֹלָם אֲדֹנָי רַב לְהוֹשִׁיעַ:

In summer: מוֹרִיד הַטָּל:

In winter: מַשִּׁיב הָרוּחַ וּמוֹרִיד הַגָּשֶׁם:

מְכַלְכֵּל חַיִּים בְּחֶסֶד מְחַיֵּה כָּל חַי בְּרַחֲמִים רַבִּים סוֹמֵךְ נוֹפְלִים וְרוֹפֵא חוֹלִים וּמַתִּיר אֲסוּרִים וּמְקַיֵּם אֱמוּנָתוֹ לִישֵׁנֵי עָפָר: מִי כָמוֹךָ בַּעַל גְּבוּרוֹת וּמִי דּוֹמֶה לָּךְ מֶלֶךְ מֵמִית וּמְחַיֶּה וּמַצְמִיחַ יְשׁוּעָה:

Atah gibor le'olam adonay rav lehoshi'a.

In summer: Morid hatal.

In winter: Mashiv haru'aḥ umorid hagashem.

Meḥalkel ḥayim beḥesed meḥayey kol ḥay beraḥamim rabim someḥ noflim verofey ḥolim umatir asurim umkayem emunato lisheney afar. Mi ḥamoḥa ba'al gevurot umi domeh laḥ meleḥ memit umḥayeh umatzmi'aḥ yeshu'ah.

Between Rosh Hashanah and Yom Kippur, add:

(מִי כָמוֹךָ אַב הָרַחֲמִים זוֹכֵר יְצוּרָיו לְחַיִּים בְּרַחֲמִים:)

וְנֶאֱמָן אַתָּה לְהַחֲיוֹת כָּל חָי: בָּרוּךְ אַתָּה יהוה מְחַיֵּה כָּל חָי:

(Mi ḥamoḥa av haraḥamim zoḥer yetzurav leḥayim beraḥamim.)

Vene'eman atah lehaḥayot kol ḥay. Baruḥ atah adonay meḥayey kol ḥay.

When chanting aloud in a minyan, continue with the Kedushah, page 105. When praying silently, continue here.

3 קְדֻשַּׁת הַשֵּׁם

Recited when praying silently:

אַתָּה קָדוֹשׁ וְשִׁמְךָ קָדוֹשׁ וּקְדוֹשִׁים בְּכָל יוֹם יְהַלְלוּךָ סֶּלָה: בָּרוּךְ אַתָּה יהוה הָאֵל הַקָּדוֹשׁ:

(*Between Rosh Hashanah and Yom Kippur, conclude:* הַמֶּלֶךְ הַקָּדוֹשׁ)

For a shortened form of the Amidah turn to the Abbreviated Amidah, page 107. For the full Amidah, continue on page 109.

3. KEDUSHAH / SANCTIFICATION

The Kedushah *is chanted aloud in a minyan.*

We sanctify your name throughout this world,
as it is sanctified in the heavens above,
as it is written by your prophet:
"And each celestial being calls to another, and exclaims
Holy, holy, holy is THE RULER of the Multitudes of Heaven!
All the world is filled with divine glory!"
And they are answered with a blessing:
"Blessed is the glory of THE HOLY ONE,
wherever God may dwell!"
And as is written in your sacred words of psalm:
"May THE ETERNAL reign forever,
your God, O Zion, from one generation to the next.
Halleluyah!"
From one generation to the next may we declare your greatness,
and for all eternities may we affirm your holiness,
And may your praise, our God, never be absent from our
mouths, now and forever.
For you are a great and holy God.
Blessed are you, THE AWESOME ONE, the holy God.
(*Between Rosh Hashanah and Yom Kippur, conclude:* the holy sovereign.)

The traditional Amidah *continues on page 108. For the abbreviated* Amidah *continue on page 106.*

וקרא...כבודו / And...glory! (Isaiah 6:3).
ברוך...ממקומו / Blessed...dwell! (Ezekiel 3:12).
ימלך...הללויה / May...Halleluyah! (Psalm 146:10).

DERASH. Holiness is the manner in which we react to persons, objects, places and events which we regard as indispensable to human welfare and self-realization. M.M.K.

KAVANAH. To be holy means for power and goodness to exist in perfect harmony. M.M.K. (Adapted)

קְדֻשָּׁה

The Kedushah *is chanted aloud in a minyan.*

*נְקַדֵּשׁ אֶת־שִׁמְךָ בָּעוֹלָם כְּשֵׁם שֶׁמַּקְדִּישִׁים אוֹתוֹ בִּשְׁמֵי מָרוֹם: כַּכָּתוּב
עַל־יַד נְבִיאֶךָ וְקָרָא זֶה אֶל־זֶה וְאָמַר:

קָדוֹשׁ קָדוֹשׁ קָדוֹשׁ

יהוה צְבָאוֹת מְלֹא כָל־הָאָרֶץ כְּבוֹדוֹ:

*לְעֻמָּתָם בָּרוּךְ יֹאמֵרוּ:

בָּרוּךְ כְּבוֹד־יהוה מִמְּקוֹמוֹ:

*וּבְדִבְרֵי קָדְשְׁךָ כָּתוּב לֵאמֹר:

יִמְלֹךְ יהוה לְעוֹלָם אֱלֹהַיִךְ צִיּוֹן לְדֹר וָדֹר הַלְלוּיָהּ:

*לְדוֹר וָדוֹר נַגִּיד גָּדְלֶךָ וּלְנֵצַח נְצָחִים קְדֻשָּׁתְךָ נַקְדִּישׁ וְשִׁבְחֲךָ
אֱלֹהֵינוּ מִפִּינוּ לֹא יָמוּשׁ לְעוֹלָם וָעֶד כִּי אֵל מֶלֶךְ גָּדוֹל וְקָדוֹשׁ אָתָּה:
בָּרוּךְ אַתָּה יהוה הָאֵל הַקָּדוֹשׁ:

Between Rosh Hashanah and Yom Kippur, conclude:

(בָּרוּךְ אַתָּה יהוה הַמֶּלֶךְ הַקָּדוֹשׁ:)

Nekadesh et shimeḥa ba'olam keshem shemakdishim oto bishmey marom kakatuv al yad nevi'eḥa vekara zeh el zeh ve'amar:

Kadosh kadosh kadosh adonay tzeva'ot melo ḥol ha'aretz kevodo. le'umatam baruḥ yomeru:

Baruḥ kevod adonay mimekomo. Uvedivrey kodsheḥa katuv lemor: Yimloḥ adonay le'olam elohayiḥ tziyon ledor vador halleluyah.

Ledor vador nagid godleḥa ulnetzaḥ netzaḥim Kedushateḥa nakdish veshivḥaḥa eloheynu mipinu lo yamush le'olam va'ed ki el meleḥ gadol vekadosh atah. Baruḥ atah adonay ha'el hakadosh.

(Baruḥ atah adonay hameleḥ hakadosh.)

The traditional Amidah *continues on page 109. For the abbreviated* Amidah *continue on page 107.*

AMIDAH KETZURAH / ABBREVIATED AMIDAH

This shortened form of the Amidah was originally intended for those on a journey or unable to allot the amount of time to say the traditional Amidah. It is suitable for those less adept at the liturgy as well. It replaces the middle thirteen blessings of the weekday Amidah. It is preceded by the first three blessings of the full Amidah.

Open my eye, that it may look upon the goodness of your plan,
and turn my knowledge into knowledge of your ways,
my will into your will.
May all that I do be like an offering received into your presence,
and may you forgive me all I have done wrong.
Enable me to see your light in all whom I encounter,
and please heal the pain within my heart.
For you are one who listens to the prayer of all who speak.
Blessed are you, ETERNAL ONE,
who hears all prayer.

Continue with the seventeenth blessing (Shaḥarit page 118, Minḥah page 236, or Ma'ariv page 312).

NOTE. The abridging of the weekday Amidah by summarizing its middle thirteen blessings in a single paragraph is described in the Mishnah (*Beraḥot* 4:3-6). The version presented here was composed by Rabbi Edward Feld. It is followed by the last three blessings of the full Amidah.

J.B.

KAVANAH. You are eternal, the life of all that lives, the love in all that loves. You animate lifeless matter. You are the courage of those who conquer adversity. You are in the health of those who overcome sickness. You are the hope of those who now sleep in the dust. Yet you are more than all these, O master of life and death and salvation. You are holy and those who strive after holiness worship you. M.M.K./M.S. (Adapted)

עֲמִידָה קְצָרָה

This shortened form of the Amidah was originally intended for those on a journey or unable to allot the amount of time to say the traditional Amidah. It is suitable for those less adept at the liturgy as well. It replaces the middle thirteen blessings of the weekday Amidah. It is preceded by the first three blessings of the full Amidah.

פְּקַח עֵינַי לִרְאוֹת בְּטוּב יִצְרֶךָ
וַהֲפֹךְ דַּעְתִּי לְדַעְתְּךָ וּרְצוֹנִי לִרְצוֹנֶךָ.
יִהְיוּ כָּל מַעֲשַׂי כְּקָרְבָּן רָצוּי לְפָנֶיךָ
וְתִסְלַח לְכָל פְּשָׁעַי.
תֵּן לִי לִרְאוֹת אוֹרְךָ בְּכָל פְּגִישׁוֹתַי
וּרְפָא נָא מַכְאוֹבוֹת לִבִּי.
כִּי אַתָּה שׁוֹמֵעַ תְּפִלַּת כָּל פֶּה.
בָּרוּךְ אַתָּה יהוה שׁוֹמֵעַ תְּפִלָּה.

Continue with the seventeenth blessing (Shaḥarit page 119, Minḥah page 237, or Ma'ariv page 313).

4. BINAH / UNDERSTANDING

You graciously endow the human being
with the power to know;
you teach a person understanding.
So may you provide us now
with knowledge, understanding, and intelligence.
Blessed are you, THE FOUNT OF WISDOM
who graciously bestows all knowledge.

5. TESHUVAH / REPENTANCE

Return us, divine source, to your Torah,
bring us nearer, our sovereign, to your service.
And restore us, in complete return, into your presence.
Blessed are you, RECEPTIVE ONE,
who takes joy in our return.

6. SELIḤAH / FORGIVENESS

Forgive us, our Creator, for we have done wrong.
Deal mercifully with us, our protector, though we have rebelled.
For you are truly kind and merciful.
Blessed are you, ALL-MERCIFUL,
who graciously abounds in power to forgive.

7. GE'ULAH / REDEMPTION

Behold our need, and plead our cause,
and speedily redeem us, as your name demands,
for you are called a powerful redeemer.
Blessed are you, ALMIGHTY ONE,
redeemer of the people Israel. ↩

ד 4 בִּינָה

אַתָּה חוֹנֵן לְאָדָם דַּעַת וּמְלַמֵּד לֶאֱנוֹשׁ בִּינָה:
חָנֵּנוּ מֵאִתְּךָ דֵּעָה בִּינָה וְהַשְׂכֵּל: בָּרוּךְ אַתָּה יהוה חוֹנֵן הַדָּעַת:

ה 5 תְּשׁוּבָה

הֲשִׁיבֵנוּ מְקוֹרֵנוּ לְתוֹרָתֶךָ: וְקָרְבֵנוּ עֲטַרְתֵּנוּ לַעֲבוֹדָתֶךָ: וְהַחֲזִירֵנוּ
בִּתְשׁוּבָה שְׁלֵמָה לְפָנֶיךָ: בָּרוּךְ אַתָּה יהוה הָרוֹצֶה בִּתְשׁוּבָה:

ו 6 סְלִיחָה

סְלַח־לָנוּ אָבִינוּ כִּי חָטָאנוּ: מְחַל־לָנוּ מַלְכֵּנוּ כִּי פָשָׁעְנוּ: כִּי מוֹחֵל
וְסוֹלֵחַ אָתָּה: בָּרוּךְ אַתָּה יהוה חַנּוּן הַמַּרְבֶּה לִסְלוֹחַ:

ז 7 גְּאֻלָּה

רְאֵה בְעָנְיֵנוּ וְרִיבָה רִיבֵנוּ וּגְאָלֵנוּ מְהֵרָה לְמַעַן שְׁמֶךָ: כִּי גוֹאֵל חָזָק
אָתָּה: בָּרוּךְ אַתָּה יהוה גּוֹאֵל יִשְׂרָאֵל: ←

NOTE. The fifth blessing of the weekday *Amidah* focuses on the call to *teshuvah* – return to the path of Torah and the divine presence. Like the High Holy Day liturgy, this blessing invokes the imagery of kingship. This imagery is male and hierarchical, which is problematical for many contemporary Jews. Even more difficult for some is the image of an external God pronouncing individual judgments. This contradicts our sense of the divinity within ourselves that we strive to keep in our awareness and to bring into harmony with our lives. These difficulties have led to emendation of the traditional wording. אָבִינוּ / Our Father has been replaced by מְקוֹרֵנוּ / Divine Source, and מַלְכֵּנוּ / Our King has been replaced by עֲטַרְתֵּנוּ / literally, Our Crown, but here translated figuratively as "our sovereign." Compare the alternative and interpretive versions of *Avinu Malkenu*, pages 136-143. D.A.T./J.B.

The truth is that our belief in God is not based upon God's self-revelation but on our discovery of God. According to the modern way of thinking and speaking, it is more correct to say that we discover God than to say that God reveals the divine self to us. M.M.K. (Adapted)

8. REFU'AH / HEALING

Heal us, NURTURING ONE, so that we may be healed,
help us to restore ourselves to a state of health,
and bring upon us complete cure of all our ailments.

Optional prayer for one who is ill:

(May it be your will, COMPASSIONATE ONE, my God,
God of my ancestors,
that you quickly send forth thorough healing,
a healing of the body and a healing of the spirit,
to the one who ails,

for a female:

to __________ daughter of __________

for a male:

to __________ son of __________
among all others of the people Israel who are ailing.)
And remove from us all suffering and grief,
for you are a sovereign divine power
and a faithful and compassionate healer.
Blessed are you, RESTORER OF ALL LIFE,
who heals the sick among the people Israel.

9. BIRKAT HASHANIM / BLESSING FOR ABUNDANCE

Grant blessing over us, ABUNDANT ONE,
upon this year, and all its forms of produce;
let it be a year of good.

From December 4 till Pesaḥ say:
And grant us dew and rain,
for blessing

From Pesaḥ till December 4 say:
And give blessing

on the earth, and satisfy us with your goodness,
and give blessing to this year
as in the good years of the past.
Blessed are you, ALL BOUNTIFUL,
who gives blessing to the years. ↩

8 רְפוּאָה

רְפָאֵנוּ יהוה וְנֵרָפֵא הוֹשִׁיעֵנוּ וְנִוָּשֵׁעָה: וְהַעֲלֵה רְפוּאָה שְׁלֵמָה לְכָל מַכּוֹתֵינוּ

Optional prayer for one who is ill:

(יְהִי רָצוֹן מִלְּפָנֶיךָ יהוה אֱלֹהַי וֵאלֹהֵי אֲבוֹתַי וְאִמּוֹתַי שֶׁתִּשְׁלַח מְהֵרָה רְפוּאָה שְׁלֵמָה מִן הַשָּׁמַיִם רְפוּאַת הַנֶּפֶשׁ וּרְפוּאַת הַגּוּף

for a female – לַחוֹלָה *(patient's name)* בַּת *(parents' names)* בְּתוֹךְ שְׁאָר חוֹלֵי יִשְׂרָאֵל.

for a male – לַחוֹלֶה *(patient's name)* בֶּן *(parents' names)* בְּתוֹךְ שְׁאָר חוֹלֵי יִשְׂרָאֵל.)

וְהָסֵר מִמֶּנּוּ יָגוֹן וַאֲנָחָה כִּי אֵל מֶלֶךְ רוֹפֵא נֶאֱמָן וְרַחֲמָן אָתָּה: בָּרוּךְ אַתָּה יהוה רוֹפֵא חוֹלֵי עַמּוֹ יִשְׂרָאֵל:

9 בִּרְכַּת הַשָּׁנִים

בָּרֵךְ עָלֵינוּ יהוה אֱלֹהֵינוּ אֶת הַשָּׁנָה הַזֹּאת וְאֶת כָּל מִינֵי תְבוּאָתָהּ לְטוֹבָה

From Pesaḥ till December 4 say:

וְתֵן בְּרָכָה

From December 4 till Pesaḥ say:

וְתֵן טַל וּמָטָר לִבְרָכָה

עַל פְּנֵי הָאֲדָמָה וְשַׂבְּעֵנוּ מִטּוּבֶךָ וּבָרֵךְ שְׁנָתֵנוּ כַּשָּׁנִים הַטּוֹבוֹת: בָּרוּךְ אַתָּה יהוה מְבָרֵךְ הַשָּׁנִים: ←

COMMENTARY. As a God of lovingkindness, God not only teaches us how to conduct ourselves so as to elicit the best in each other, but also calls upon the transgressor to repent. When human beings repent, God forgives, and by forgiveness enables individuals to use their own powers as God would have them do. M.M.K. (Adapted)

NOTE. Our hope for rain in its season, which sustains crops throughout the year, is expressed in a subtle change of words. "Provide blessing," which is used most of the year, becomes "provide dew and rain for a blessing." Pesaḥ marks the beginning of the spring grain-planting season in Israel. The rabbis used the sun calendar date of December 4 for this prayer for rain to adjust to agricultural conditions in Babylonia. In following their lead, we recognize the need to adjust Jewish practice in response to local climactic, cultural, and political conditions. D.A.T.

10. KIBUTZ GALUYOT / INGATHERING OF THE JEWISH PEOPLE

Sound the great shofar for our freedom,
raise up the banner for the gathering-in of those in exile,
and gather us together from the earth's four corners.
Blessed are you, REDEEMING ONE,
who gathers Israel's dispossessed.

11. DIN / RESTORING JUSTICE

Restore our judges, as of old,
our counselors, as in the beginning,
and remove from us all suffering and grief.
Rule over us, OUR SOVEREIGN, you alone,
with love and with compassion.
Help us achieve justice through the rule of law.

Blessed are you, WISE ONE,
the sovereign who loves righteousness and justice.

Between Rosh Hashanah and Yom Kippur, conclude:

(Blessed are you, ENTHRONED IN MAJESTY,
the sovereign, the source of all just law.)

12. BIRKAT HAMINIM / OVERCOMING DIVISIONS

Let all who speak and act unjustly
find no hope for ill intentions.
Let all wickedness be lost.
Blessed are you, JUST ONE,
who subdues the evildoers. ↩

10 קִבּוּץ גָּלֻיּוֹת

תְּקַע בְּשׁוֹפָר גָּדוֹל לְחֵרוּתֵֽנוּ וְשָׂא נֵס לְקַבֵּץ גָּלֻיּוֹתֵֽינוּ וְקַבְּצֵֽנוּ יַֽחַד
מֵאַרְבַּע כַּנְפוֹת הָאָֽרֶץ: בָּרוּךְ אַתָּה יהוה מְקַבֵּץ נִדְחֵי עַמּוֹ יִשְׂרָאֵל:

11 דִּין

הָשִֽׁיבָה שׁוֹפְטֵֽינוּ כְּבָרִאשׁוֹנָה וְיוֹעֲצֵֽינוּ כְּבַתְּחִלָּה וְהָסֵר מִמֶּֽנּוּ יָגוֹן
וַאֲנָחָה וּמְלוֹךְ עָלֵֽינוּ אַתָּה יהוה לְבַדְּךָ בְּחֶֽסֶד וּבְרַחֲמִים וְצַדְּקֵֽנוּ
בַּמִּשְׁפָּט: בָּרוּךְ אַתָּה יהוה מֶֽלֶךְ אוֹהֵב צְדָקָה וּמִשְׁפָּט:

Between Rosh Hashanah and Yom Kippur, conclude:

(בָּרוּךְ אַתָּה יהוה הַמֶּֽלֶךְ הַמִּשְׁפָּט:)

12 בִּרְכַּת הַמִּינִים

וְלַמַּלְשִׁינִים אַל תְּהִי תִקְוָה וְכָל הָרִשְׁעָה כְּרֶֽגַע תֹּאבֵד: בָּרוּךְ אַתָּה
יהוה מַכְנִֽיעַ זֵדִים: ←

13. TZADIKIM / COMPASSION FOR THE RIGHTEOUS

For the righteous, and for the pious,
and for the elders of your people, the house of Israel,
and for the remnant of their scholars,
and for the righteous who have chosen to be Jews,
let your compassion be aroused, DEAR ONE, our God,
and give proper recompense to all
who truly have found shelter in your name,
and give us a portion in their midst,
that we may never be ashamed,
for in you we place our trust.
Blessed are you, THE SOURCE OF TRUST,
support and stronghold for the righteous.

14. BINYAN YERUSHALAYIM / REBUILDING JERUSALEM

And to Jerusalem, your city,
may you turn with mercy,
and come home to dwell there,
as you have promised.
And rebuild the city, soon and in our days,
with everlasting peace.
Blessed are you, THE GOD OF ZION,
builder of Jerusalem. ↩

יג 13 צַדִּיקִים

עַל הַצַּדִּיקִים וְעַל הַחֲסִידִים וְעַל זִקְנֵי עַמְּךָ בֵּית יִשְׂרָאֵל וְעַל פְּלֵיטַת סוֹפְרֵיהֶם וְעַל גֵּרֵי הַצֶּדֶק וְעָלֵינוּ יֶהֱמוּ נָא רַחֲמֶיךָ יהוה אֱלֹהֵינוּ וְתֵן שָׂכָר טוֹב לְכָל הַבּוֹטְחִים בְּשִׁמְךָ בֶּאֱמֶת וְשִׂים חֶלְקֵנוּ עִמָּהֶם וּלְעוֹלָם לֹא נֵבוֹשׁ כִּי בְךָ בָּטָחְנוּ: בָּרוּךְ אַתָּה יהוה מִשְׁעָן וּמִבְטָח לַצַּדִּיקִים:

יד 14 בִּנְיַן יְרוּשָׁלַיִם

וְלִירוּשָׁלַיִם עִירְךָ בְּרַחֲמִים תָּשׁוּב וְתִשְׁכּוֹן בְּתוֹכָהּ כַּאֲשֶׁר דִּבַּרְתָּ וּבְנֵה אוֹתָהּ בְּקָרוֹב בְּיָמֵינוּ בִּנְיַן שָׁלוֹם: בָּרוּךְ אַתָּה יהוה בּוֹנֵה יְרוּשָׁלָיִם:←

NOTE. The fourteenth blessing of the *Amidah* focuses on the rebuilding of Jerusalem. For centuries the rebuilding of Jerusalem has stood for an end to Jewish suffering and a return to Jewish sovereignty, as well as for the mythic end of days in which Jerusalem would become all that generations of longing Jews could imagine. For us, the rebuilding of Jerusalem signifies a world at peace and in which all human need is fulfilled.

D.A.T.

15. YESHU'AH / SALVATION

May you speedily redeem your people Israel,
and raise their stronghold with your help,
for we await with hope throughout our days
the coming of your help.
Blessed are you, THE GOD OF ISRAEL,
who plants the stronghold of your help.

16. KABBALAT TEFILAH / ACCEPTING PRAYER

Hear our voice, ATTENTIVE ONE, our God,
have mercy and compassion for us,
and accept our prayer
with kindness and with favor,
for you are the God who harkens
to the words of prayer and supplication.
Do not turn us from your presence empty-handed.
For you are one who listens
to the prayer of your people Israel
with compassion.

Blessed are you, COMPASSIONATE ONE,
who listens to the words of prayer. ↵

At this point in the Amidah it is customary to add personal petitions for healing or safety, for successfully earning a living, and for other hopes and needs. For Tefilat Hadereḥ */ The Travelers' Prayer, see page 174. For* Parnasah */ Sustenance and well-being, see page 234.*

COMMENTARY. We plead that our prayer be accepted. That plea can only have meaning if we listen to it ourselves. If we are to find grace in *teshuvah*, then it is we who must turn our hearts. If we are to be forgiven, we must forgive ourselves. If our families or our communities need changing, then it is we who must change them. Thus we cry out to the divine within. We call upon the strength, the insight, the spiritual vision hidden in our hearts: hear our voice that we may give meaning to our words.

D.A.T.

15 יְשׁוּעָה

אֶת עַמְּךָ יִשְׂרָאֵל מְהֵרָה תִגְאַל וְקַרְנוֹ תָּרוּם בִּישׁוּעָתֶךָ כִּי לִישׁוּעָתְךָ
קִוִּינוּ כָּל הַיּוֹם: בָּרוּךְ אַתָּה יהוה מַצְמִיחַ קֶרֶן יְשׁוּעָה:

16 קַבָּלַת תְּפִלָּה

שְׁמַע קוֹלֵנוּ יהוה אֱלֹהֵינוּ חוּס וְרַחֵם עָלֵינוּ וְקַבֵּל בְּרַחֲמִים וּבְרָצוֹן
אֶת תְּפִלָּתֵנוּ כִּי אֵל שׁוֹמֵעַ תְּפִלּוֹת וְתַחֲנוּנִים אָתָּה: וּמִלְּפָנֶיךָ מַלְכֵּנוּ
רֵיקָם אַל תְּשִׁיבֵנוּ כִּי אַתָּה שׁוֹמֵעַ תְּפִלַּת עַמְּךָ יִשְׂרָאֵל בְּרַחֲמִים:
בָּרוּךְ אַתָּה יהוה שׁוֹמֵעַ תְּפִלָּה: ←

At this point in the Amidah it is customary to add personal petitions for healing or safety, for successfully earning a living and for other hopes and needs. For Tefilat Hadereḥ */ The Travelers' Prayer, see page 175. For* Parnasah */ Sustenance and well-being, see page 235. For other optional prayers, see pages 154-157, the* Mi Sheberaḥ, *for an explanation of how to incorporate other events and occasions.*

שמע קולנו / Hear our voice. After all these specific requests and petitions why do we still ask God to hear our prayers? Don't we assume God has been listening to our voice all along? All prayer is about opening. The Shema Kolenu / Hear our voice indicates how wide and expansive we have become. No longer is content expressed. It is pure compassion—pure opening alone that we seek—our innermost hopes have been expressed through the specific litany of needs—now our voice rises from the tender core of our beings. We are one with all Israel whose cries have been heard in love. We cannot return empty. The opening itself is the filling. S.P.W.

Both the full Amidah *and the abbreviated* Amidah *continue here.*

17. AVODAH / WORSHIP

Take pleasure, GRACIOUS ONE, our God,
in Israel your people;
lovingly accept their fervent prayer.
May Israel's worship always be acceptable to you.

(*On a Rosh Ḥodesh or Festival add:*
Our God, our ancients' God,
may our prayer arise and come to you,
and be beheld, and be acceptable.
Let it be heard, acted upon, remembered
—the memory of us and all our needs,
the memory of our ancestors,
the memory of messianic hopes,
the memory of Jerusalem your holy city,
and the memory of all your kin, the house of Israel,
all surviving in your presence.
Act for goodness and grace, for love and care,
for life, well-being, and peace, on this day of
On Rosh Ḥodesh: the new moon.
On Pesaḥ: the festival of matzot.
On Sukkot: the festival of sukkot.
Remember us this day,
ALL-KNOWING ONE, our God, for goodness.
Favor us this day with blessing.
Preserve us this day for life.
With your redeeming, nurturing word,
be kind and generous. Act tenderly on our behalf,
and grant us victory over all our trials.
Truly, our eyes are turned toward you,
for you are a providing God,
gracious and merciful are you.)

And may our eyes behold your homecoming,
with merciful intent, to Zion.
Blessed are you, THE FAITHFUL ONE,
who brings your presence home to Zion. ↩

Both the full Amidah *and the abbreviated* Amidah *continue here.*

דו עֲבוֹדָה

רְצֵה יהוה אֱלֹהֵינוּ בְּעַמְּךָ יִשְׂרָאֵל וְלַהַב תְּפִלָּתָם בְּאַהֲבָה תְקַבֵּל בְּרָצוֹן וּתְהִי לְרָצוֹן תָּמִיד עֲבוֹדַת יִשְׂרָאֵל עַמֶּךָ׃

On a Rosh Ḥodesh or Festival, add:

(אֱלֹהֵינוּ וֵאלֹהֵי אֲבוֹתֵינוּ וְאִמּוֹתֵינוּ יַעֲלֶה וְיָבוֹא וְיַגִּיעַ וְיֵרָאֶה וְיֵרָצֶה וְיִשָּׁמַע וְיִפָּקֵד וְיִזָּכֵר זִכְרוֹנֵנוּ וּפִקְדוֹנֵנוּ וְזִכְרוֹן אֲבוֹתֵינוּ וְאִמּוֹתֵינוּ וְזִכְרוֹן יְמוֹת הַמָּשִׁיחַ וְזִכְרוֹן יְרוּשָׁלַיִם עִיר קָדְשֶׁךָ וְזִכְרוֹן כָּל עַמְּךָ בֵּית יִשְׂרָאֵל לְפָנֶיךָ לִפְלֵיטָה וּלְטוֹבָה לְחֵן וּלְחֶסֶד וּלְרַחֲמִים לְחַיִּים וּלְשָׁלוֹם בְּיוֹם

רֹאשׁ הַחֹדֶשׁ הַזֶּה	*On Rosh Ḥodesh:*
חַג הַמַּצּוֹת הַזֶּה	*On Pesaḥ*
חַג הַסֻּכּוֹת הַזֶּה	*On Sukkot:*

זָכְרֵנוּ יהוה אֱלֹהֵינוּ בּוֹ לְטוֹבָה׃ וּפָקְדֵנוּ לִבְרָכָה וְהוֹשִׁיעֵנוּ בוֹ לְחַיִּים׃ וּבִדְבַר יְשׁוּעָה וְרַחֲמִים חוּס וְחָנֵּנוּ וְרַחֵם עָלֵינוּ וְהוֹשִׁיעֵנוּ כִּי אֵלֶיךָ עֵינֵינוּ כִּי אֵל מֶלֶךְ חַנּוּן וְרַחוּם אָתָּה׃)

וְתֶחֱזֶינָה עֵינֵינוּ בְּשׁוּבְךָ לְצִיּוֹן בְּרַחֲמִים׃ בָּרוּךְ אַתָּה יהוה הַמַּחֲזִיר שְׁכִינָתוֹ לְצִיּוֹן׃ ←

18. HODA'AH / THANKS

We give thanks to you that you are THE ALL-MERCIFUL, our God, God of our ancestors, today and always. A firm, enduring source of life, a shield to us in time of trial, you are ever there, from age to age. We acknowledge you, declare your praise, and thank you for our lives entrusted to your hand, our souls placed in your care, for your miracles that greet us every day, and for your wonders and the good things that are with us every hour, morning, noon, and night. Good One, whose kindness never stops, Kind One, whose loving acts have never failed—always have we placed our hope in you.

(*On Ḥanukah add:* For the miracles, for the redemption, for heroic acts, for saving deeds, for consolations, all of which you have enacted for our ancestors at this time of year in days gone by —as in the days of Matthew, son of Yoḥanan, Hasmonean High Priest, and Matthew's sons: a wicked Hellenistic government arose against your people Israel, forcing them to shun your Torah and to leave off from the laws your will ordained. And you, in your abundant mercy, stood up for Israel in their hour of distress. You pressed their claim, exacted justice for them. You delivered armed might to the weak, the many to the power of the few, the wicked to the power of the just, the vicious to the power of those occupied with Torah. You made known your name that day, and made it holy in your world. And for your people Israel you enacted great deliverance, as in our own time. Afterward, your children came into your Temple's inner room. They cleared your sanctuary, purified your holy place, kindled lights inside your holy courtyards, and established these eight days of Ḥanukah, for giving thanks and praise to your great name.) ↩

18 הוֹדָאָה

מוֹדִים אֲנַחְנוּ לָךְ שָׁאַתָּה הוּא יהוה אֱלֹהֵינוּ וֵאלֹהֵי אֲבוֹתֵינוּ
וְאִמּוֹתֵינוּ לְעוֹלָם וָעֶד צוּר חַיֵּינוּ מָגֵן יִשְׁעֵנוּ אַתָּה הוּא לְדוֹר וָדוֹר:
נוֹדֶה לְּךָ וּנְסַפֵּר תְּהִלָּתֶךָ עַל חַיֵּינוּ הַמְּסוּרִים בְּיָדֶךָ וְעַל נִשְׁמוֹתֵינוּ
הַפְּקוּדוֹת לָךְ וְעַל נִסֶּיךָ שֶׁבְּכָל יוֹם עִמָּנוּ וְעַל נִפְלְאוֹתֶיךָ וְטוֹבוֹתֶיךָ
שֶׁבְּכָל־עֵת עֶרֶב וָבֹקֶר וְצָהֳרָיִם: הַטּוֹב כִּי לֹא כָלוּ רַחֲמֶיךָ וְהַמְרַחֵם
כִּי לֹא תַמּוּ חֲסָדֶיךָ מֵעוֹלָם קִוִּינוּ לָךְ:

On Ḥanukah add:

(עַל הַנִּסִּים וְעַל הַפֻּרְקָן וְעַל הַגְּבוּרוֹת וְעַל הַתְּשׁוּעוֹת וְעַל הַנֶּחָמוֹת
שֶׁעָשִׂיתָ לַאֲבוֹתֵינוּ וְאִמּוֹתֵינוּ בַּיָּמִים הָהֵם בַּזְּמַן הַזֶּה: בִּימֵי מַתִּתְיָהוּ
בֶּן יוֹחָנָן כֹּהֵן גָּדוֹל חַשְׁמוֹנַאי וּבָנָיו כְּשֶׁעָמְדָה מַלְכוּת יָוָן הָרְשָׁעָה
עַל עַמְּךָ יִשְׂרָאֵל לְהַשְׁכִּיחָם תּוֹרָתֶךָ וּלְהַעֲבִירָם מֵחֻקֵּי רְצוֹנֶךָ וְאַתָּה
בְּרַחֲמֶיךָ הָרַבִּים עָמַדְתָּ לָהֶם בְּעֵת צָרָתָם רַבְתָּ אֶת רִיבָם דַּנְתָּ אֶת
דִּינָם מָסַרְתָּ גִּבּוֹרִים בְּיַד חַלָּשִׁים וְרַבִּים בְּיַד מְעַטִּים וּרְשָׁעִים בְּיַד
צַדִּיקִים וְזֵדִים בְּיַד עוֹסְקֵי תוֹרָתֶךָ: וּלְךָ עָשִׂיתָ שֵׁם גָּדוֹל וְקָדוֹשׁ
בְּעוֹלָמֶךָ וּלְעַמְּךָ יִשְׂרָאֵל עָשִׂיתָ תְּשׁוּעָה גְדוֹלָה וּפֻרְקָן כְּהַיּוֹם הַזֶּה:
וְאַחַר כֵּן בָּאוּ בָנֶיךָ לִדְבִיר בֵּיתֶךָ וּפִנּוּ אֶת הֵיכָלֶךָ וְטִהֲרוּ אֶת מִקְדָּשֶׁךָ
וְהִדְלִיקוּ נֵרוֹת בְּחַצְרוֹת קָדְשֶׁךָ וְקָבְעוּ שְׁמוֹנַת יְמֵי חֲנֻכָּה אֵלּוּ
לְהוֹדוֹת וּלְהַלֵּל לְשִׁמְךָ הַגָּדוֹל:) ←

KAVANAH. This prayer helps us to get in touch with our gratitude for the extraordinary yet often overlooked daily workings of the world, and through them to recognize the insignificance of our own roles, to feel humble. In becoming aware of our smallness, we become able to grasp our relatedness to the All. This in turn makes it possible to overcome the loneliness of claiming we have all the answers and the anxiety of always needing to be in control. At these moments the pain of our unfulfilled needs is swept away in the wondrous goodness we feel in the world about us. We give thanks.

S.P.W.

(*On Purim, add:* For the miracles, and for deliverance,
and for the mighty deeds, and for the saving acts,
and for the consolations
you enacted for our ancestors
in ancient times, and in our own time.

In the days of Mordechai and Esther
in Shushan, the mighty capital [of Persia],
when the wicked Haman rose against them,
seeking to destroy, to kill, and to eradicate
all Jews, the young and old alike,
in a single day,
the thirteenth of the twelfth month,
that is, the month of Adar,
and take as plunder all they owned.

But you, in your abundant mercies,
thwarted his conspiracy, destroyed his plan.
And to the Jews came light and happiness,
and joy and glory.)

For all these things, let your name be blessed and raised in honor always, sovereign of ours, forever.

(*Between Rosh Hashanah and Yom Kippur, add:* And write down for a good life all the people of your covenant.)

Let all of life acknowledge you! May all beings praise your name in truth, O God, our rescue and our aid. Blessed are you THE GRACIOUS ONE, whose name is good, to whom all thanks are due. ↩

On Purim add:

(עַל הַנִּסִּים וְעַל הַפֻּרְקָן וְעַל הַגְּבוּרוֹת וְעַל הַתְּשׁוּעוֹת וְעַל הַנֶּחָמוֹת שֶׁעָשִׂיתָ לַאֲבוֹתֵינוּ וְאִמּוֹתֵינוּ בַּיָּמִים הָהֵם בַּזְּמַן הַזֶּה:

בִּימֵי מָרְדְּכַי וְאֶסְתֵּר בְּשׁוּשַׁן הַבִּירָה כְּשֶׁעָמַד עֲלֵיהֶם הָמָן הָרָשָׁע: בִּקֵּשׁ לְהַשְׁמִיד לַהֲרוֹג וּלְאַבֵּד אֶת כָּל הַיְּהוּדִים מִנַּעַר וְעַד זָקֵן בְּיוֹם אֶחָד בִּשְׁלוֹשָׁה עָשָׂר לְחֹדֶשׁ שְׁנֵים עָשָׂר הוּא חֹדֶשׁ אֲדָר וּשְׁלָלָם לָבוֹז: וְאַתָּה בְּרַחֲמֶיךָ הָרַבִּים הֵפַרְתָּ אֶת עֲצָתוֹ וְקִלְקַלְתָּ אֶת מַחֲשַׁבְתּוֹ וְלַיְּהוּדִים הָיְתָה אוֹרָה וְשִׂמְחָה וְשָׂשׂוֹן וִיקָר)

וְעַל כֻּלָּם יִתְבָּרַךְ וְיִתְרוֹמַם שִׁמְךָ מַלְכֵּנוּ תָּמִיד לְעוֹלָם וָעֶד:

Between Rosh Hashanah and Yom Kippur, add:

(וּכְתֹב לְחַיִּים טוֹבִים כָּל־בְּנֵי בְרִיתֶךָ:)

וְכֹל הַחַיִּים יוֹדוּךָ סֶּלָה וִיהַלְלוּ אֶת שִׁמְךָ בֶּאֱמֶת הָאֵל יְשׁוּעָתֵנוּ וְעֶזְרָתֵנוּ סֶלָה: בָּרוּךְ אַתָּה יהוה הַטּוֹב שִׁמְךָ וּלְךָ נָאֶה לְהוֹדוֹת: ←

19. BIRKAT HASHALOM / BLESSING FOR PEACE

When praying silently, continue on page 126.
The following paragraph is said only when the congregation recites aloud together.

Our God, our ancients' God,
bless us with the threefold blessing
spoken from the mouth of Aaron and his sons, as is said:

Reader:	*Congregation:*
May THE ETERNAL bless you and protect you.	Let it be God's will!
May THE ETERNAL'S face give light to you, and show you favor.	Let it be God's will!
May THE ETERNAL'S face be lifted toward you, and bestow upon you peace.	Let it be God's will!

COMMENTARY. Traditionally the Priestly Blessing was done by the male descendants of the *kohanim*. In some congregations the *sheliaḥ tzibur* (service leader) recites the blessing, and the congregation responds with "*Ken yehi ratzon.*" In other communities all the members of the congregation wrap arms and tallitot around each other and recite the blessing together. Another way to enact the Priestly Blessing is for each congregant to turn to a neighbor and recite the first half of each blessing, while the neighbor responds with the second half of the blessing. MICHAEL M. COHEN

COMMENTARY. Rabbi Lavy Becker of Montreal noticed that when this blessing was pronounced in the synagogue of Pisa, all the children gathered under the sheltering wings of their fathers' tallitot to receive it. He recognized this "as a reconstruction of the ancient priestly ceremony." He modified that custom so that those wearing a tallit share it with their neighbors and all are under the sheltering wings of the Sheḥinah as we bless each other. It is now an established part of Canadian Reconstructionist practice. E.M.

בִּרְכַּת הַשָּׁלוֹם

When praying silently, continue on page 127.
The following paragraph is said only when the congregation recites aloud together.

אֱלֹהֵינוּ וֵאלֹהֵי אֲבוֹתֵינוּ וְאִמּוֹתֵינוּ בָּרְכֵנוּ בַּבְּרָכָה הַמְשֻׁלֶּשֶׁת הָאֲמוּרָה מִפִּי אַהֲרֹן וּבָנָיו כָּאָמוּר:

יְבָרֶכְךָ יְיָ וְיִשְׁמְרֶךָ׃

כֵּן יְהִי רָצוֹן׃

יָאֵר יְיָ פָּנָיו אֵלֶיךָ וִיחֻנֶּךָּ׃

כֵּן יְהִי רָצוֹן׃

יִשָּׂא יְיָ פָּנָיו אֵלֶיךָ וְיָשֵׂם לְךָ שָׁלוֹם׃

כֵּן יְהִי רָצוֹן׃ ←

Eloheynu veylohey avoteynu ve'imoteynu
bareḥenu baberaḥah hamshuleshet
ha'amurah mipi aharon uvanav ka'amur:
Yevareḥeḥa adonay veyishmereḥa. Ken yehi ratzon.
Ya'er adonay panav eleḥa viḥuneka. Ken yehi ratzon.
Yisa adonay panav eleḥa veyasem leḥa shalom. Ken yehi ratzon. ↵

יברכך...שלום / May...peace. (Numbers 6:24-26).

Grant peace, goodness and blessing in the world,
grace, love, and mercy
over us and over all your people Israel.
Bless us, source of being, all of us, as one
amid your light,
for by your light,
WISE ONE, our God, you give to us
Torah of life, and love of kindness,
justice, blessing, mercy, life, and peace.
So may it be a good thing in your eyes,
to bless your people Israel, and all peoples,
with abundant strength and peace.

(*Between Rosh Hashanah and Yom Kippur, add:*
In the book of life, blessing, and peace, and proper sustenance,
may we be remembered and inscribed,
we and all your people, the house of Israel,
for a good life and for peace.)

Blessed are you, COMPASSIONATE ONE, maker of peace.

The Amidah *traditionally concludes with bowing and taking three steps back.*

Continue on page 134.

KAVANAH. Try to imagine a time of true peace and tranquility, and think about your part in helping this time to come about. What can you do? What can you commit to? How will *you* be a peacemaker? L.B.

שִׂים שָׁלוֹם טוֹבָה וּבְרָכָה בָּעוֹלָם חֵן וָחֶסֶד וְרַחֲמִים עָלֵינוּ וְעַל
כָּל־יִשְׂרָאֵל עַמֶּךָ: בָּרְכֵנוּ אָבִינוּ כֻּלָּנוּ כְּאֶחָד בְּאוֹר פָּנֶיךָ: כִּי בְאוֹר
פָּנֶיךָ נָתַתָּ לָּנוּ יהוה אֱלֹהֵינוּ תּוֹרַת חַיִּים וְאַהֲבַת חֶסֶד וּצְדָקָה וּבְרָכָה
וְרַחֲמִים וְחַיִּים וְשָׁלוֹם: וְטוֹב בְּעֵינֶיךָ לְבָרֵךְ אֶת עַמְּךָ יִשְׂרָאֵל וְאֶת
כָּל הָעַמִּים בְּרֹב עֹז וְשָׁלוֹם.

Between Rosh Hashanah and Yom Kippur, add:

(בְּסֵפֶר חַיִּים בְּרָכָה וְשָׁלוֹם וּפַרְנָסָה טוֹבָה נִזָּכֵר וְנִכָּתֵב לְפָנֶיךָ אֲנַחְנוּ
וְכָל־עַמְּךָ בֵּית יִשְׂרָאֵל לְחַיִּים טוֹבִים וּלְשָׁלוֹם:)
בָּרוּךְ אַתָּה יהוה עוֹשֵׂה הַשָּׁלוֹם:

Sim shalom tovah uvraḥah ba'olam ḥen vaḥesed veraḥamim aleynu ve'al kol yisrael ameḥa. Bareḥenu avinu kulanu ke'eḥad be'or paneḥa. Ki ve'or paneḥa natata lanu adonay eloheynu torat ḥayim ve'ahavat ḥesed utzedakah uvraḥah veraḥamim veḥayim veshalom. Vetov be'eyneḥa levareḥ et ameḥa yisra'el ve'et kol ha'amim berov oz veshalom.

Between Rosh Hashanah and Yom Kippur, add:

(Besefer ḥayim beraḥah veshalom ufarnasah tovah nizaḥer venikatev lefaneḥa anaḥnu veḥol ameḥa beyt yisra'el leḥayim tovim ulshalom.)
Baruḥ atah adonay osey hashalom.

The Amidah *traditionally concludes with bowing and taking three steps back.*

Continue on page 135.

A GUIDED MEDITATION FOR THE WEEKDAY AMIDAH

(*Slowly*) Close your eyes and breathe deeply. As you breathe in, be aware of the solidity of your body. Then breathe out, letting the breath lead the way for tension to leave the center of your body...Breathe in again, and as you breathe out, feel the tension leaving your limbs, all the way from your fingertips and from the tips of your toes...As you breathe out again, feel yourself getting lighter and lighter and more and more relaxed...

Become aware of your legs...your hips...your torso...your arms...shoulders...neck...and head...Feel the length of you...Be aware of the busy-ness of the many complex systems inside your body. Be aware of your body's outside edges, of where it ends, of your skin and anything touching your skin—the floor, the arms of your chair, the air...

Imagine within you a point of light, a point of holiness and peacefulness...This point of light becomes brighter as you focus on it, and it begins to fill you...It glows outward from you and begins to surround you in a cocoon of light...Savor that light, cradle it within you and let it cradle you.

From inside your cradle of light, feel yourself supported by many gentle hands...Imagine all of the people—these are people from generations past—who are keeping you aloft. They, too, have light emanating from within them, and they join together to support and cradle you, gently but securely...They, too, are being supported by generations who came before them, who, in turn, are being supported by generations who came before them... ↩

You become aware of your head—the thickness of your skull, armored plating for the most complex device we know of. Notice your mind. Notice the thoughts going through it. Allow your thoughts to come and go without following them. For every thought you think, a million microscopic explosions occur, making connections between seemingly unrelated things...But your brain does not function on its own; at its best, it operates in conjunction with the heart. Take note of what you are feeling. Let your feelings float by...Focus on the connection between your mind and your heart. Watch the pulses of light, of thoughts and emotion, travel in both directions along the telegraph wire of your soul.

Be aware that the two ends of that line of communication are connected not only to each other but to a third entity, outside or inside of you, which represents the sum total of your ideals, your hopes, your dreams...Feel the connectedness along all three sides of this triangle, the yearning toward that third point.

Feel the boundaries around you. Feel the boundaries between you and what is outside of you melt away, recede into the distance...You begin to feel a sense of boundlessness...Within you, the point of light, of holiness and peace, still glows, but that light is now a glow of strength, and it pulses with energy. The light streams off into that boundlessness, filling it and pulsing further outward. Feel your body fill with strength and light and energy.

The energy begins to ebb away into the distance around you, and very slowly, your whole being becomes still...You can rest in this place of stillness, feeling it encompass you...Deep within you, you begin to feel the stirrings of new energy...Around you, a light rain begins to fall, warm and pattering. It brings you back a sense of gentle vigor, reviving the very essence of your soul. ↩

And you feel grateful. Grateful for the light and strength and holiness in you. Grateful for your life. Little green shoots of gratitude sprout, and tendrils of gratefulness creep and grow and wind their ways out from your heart...Your gratitude is boundless, overflowing, and it makes your heart want to dance, makes your toes want to go frolicking, makes your head want to soar, makes you want to fling out your arms to embrace the giver of this wonderful gift of being filled with life.

And slowly, this feeling of gratitude is not flung outward any more but begins to turn inward, to point to your very center, to transform itself into a quiet bubbling calm which possesses within it the memory of the light you felt glowing within you and around you, and the weightlessness, the feeling of being supported, the pulses of light in your mind and your soul, the boundless energy and the stillness, and the revivifying rain, and the unbounded gratitude for being alive. You will carry the awareness of all of these with you as you open your eyes to go on with your day.

Judith Kummer

Continue on page 134.

I will be ever aware of the SOURCE OF LIFE's presence.
יהוה
שויתי יהוה לנגדי תמיד
In loyalty you sustain the living, nurturing the life of each living thing, upholding those who fall, healing the sick.
May my words of prayer and my heart's meditation be seen favorably, God, my rock and my redeemer.
יהיו לרצון אמרי פי והגיון לבי לפניך יהוה צורי וגואלי
How precious is your love, O God, when earthborn find the shelter of your wing.
Guard our going forth each day for life and peace.
Spread over us your shelter of peace.
ברוך
אתה
יהוה
מחיה
כל חי
Blessed are you,
THE FOUNT OF LIFE,
who gives
and renews life.
כי עמך
מקור חיים
באורך
נראה
אור
For with you is
the Fountain of all life;
in your Light
do we behold all light.
השכיבנו
יהוה
אלהינו
לשלום
והעמידנו
מלכנו
לחיים
על מי מנוחות ינהלני נפשי ישובב
You are with me, God. Your power and support are there to comfort me.
כי אתה עמדי שבטך ומשענתך
המה ינחמוני
ברוך
אתה
בצאתך
ברוך
אתה
בבאך
For it is a tree of life- עץ חיים היא למחזיקים בה
©Betsy Platkin Teutsch

SHIVITI MEDITATION

The *Shiviti* is a spiritual tool. It provides a visual focus for efforts to sense the divine presence. Facing that presence through the *Shiviti* design, feeling surrounded by the divine, embracing the divine within ourselves leads to awareness of the fullness of God—and to the godliness which fills us. The *Shiviti* meditation can yield new insight—a sense of harmony and balance. It can give us a sense of our place in the order of things. It can provide fresh perspective, clarity, and energy. The *Shiviti* design is on page 131. The first-time user can begin by exploring the *Shiviti*—responding to its overall shape, reading its words, contemplating their meanings. More focused meditations on the *Shiviti* appear below.

(a) Let the fullness of this *Shiviti* flow over you...Slowly begin to focus on one of the psalm verses on the *Shiviti* page. Breathe in and out slowly and steadily...Now close your eyes. Visualize the *yud hey vav hey*...Slowly chant to yourself the words of your verse. Let all extraneous thoughts flow away from you. Allow yourself to feel the presence of God.

(b) Let the fullness of this *Shiviti* flow over you. Breathe steadily. Begin to focus on the *yud hey vav hey.* Close your eyes. Visualize the יהוה...See it vertically with the *yud* on top. Reach for the holiness it embodies...Now begin to focus on the *yud.* Visualize your head as a *yud*...Focus on the *hey.* Visualize your shoulders as a *hey*...Focus on the *vav.* Visualize your trunk as a *vav*...Focus on the final *hey.* Now visualize your legs as a *hey*...Breathe slowly. Feel the godliness rise and fall within you, with each breath. Focus on your sense of oneness, of unity, with the divine.

(c) Let the fullness of this *Shiviti* flow over you. Breathe steadily. Begin to focus on the יהוה...Close your eyes. As you focus on the *yud*, empty your breath slowly, for a count of four...As you focus on the *hey*, breathe in slowly for a count of four, softly making the sound of *hey*...As you focus on the *vav*, hold your breath for a count of four...As you focus on the final *hey*, begin to breathe out for a count of four, softly making the sound of *hey*...Repeat this breathing exercise several times, holding each point for a count of four. Feel godliness flowing in and out of you, and flowing all around you. Feel the links to all other breathing vessels of God...Now feel the godliness in all the other vessels of the divine, the divine bridges through all creation, the bridges that make us one. Devora Bartnoff

ELOHAY NETZOR / A CONCLUDING MEDITATION

Dear God, protect my tongue from evil,
and my lips from telling lies.
May I turn away from evil
and do what is good in your sight.
Let me be counted among those who seek peace.
May my words of prayer
and my heart's meditation be seen favorably,
BELOVED ONE, my rock and my redeemer.
May the one who creates harmony above
make peace
for us and for all Israel,
and for all who dwell on earth.
And say: Amen.

On Sukkot continue with Netilat Lulav, *page 358.*
On Rosh Ḥodesh, Ḥanukah, Yom Ha'atzma'ut, and Ḥol Hamo'ed *continue with Hallel, page 360.*
On fast days and during the days between Rosh Hashanah and Yom Kippur, continue with Avinu Malkenu *or alternatives, pages 136-143.*
On other days, some congregations continue with Taḥanun, *page 424.*
Otherwise, continue with Kaddish Titkabal, *page 144.*

COMMENTARY. The Talmud lists twelve examples of personal meditations that could follow the *Amidah*. If this one does not speak to you, compose your own, or stand or sit in silent meditation. L.W.K.

NOTE. Like the opening verse of the *Amidah*, this prayer employs the singular and deals with the power of words. But here the concern is for words between people, not for those directed to God. Some people find it easier to talk to God than to talk to others. L.W.K.

KAVANAH. Sin is the failure to live up to the best that is in us. It means that our souls are not attuned to the divine—that we have betrayed God. M.M.K. (Adapted)

יהיו...וגואלי / May...redeemer (Psalm 19:15).

אֱלֹהַי נְצוֹר

אֱלֹהַי נְצוֹר לְשׁוֹנִי מֵרָע
וּשְׂפָתַי מִדַּבֵּר מִרְמָה:

יְהִי רָצוֹן שֶׁאָסוּר מֵרָע
וְהַטּוֹב בְּעֵינֶֽיךָ אֶעֱשֶׂה
יְהִי חֶלְקִי עִם מְבַקְשֵׁי שָׁלוֹם וְרוֹדְפָיו:

יִהְיוּ לְרָצוֹן אִמְרֵי פִי
וְהֶגְיוֹן לִבִּי לְפָנֶֽיךָ
יהוה צוּרִי וְגוֹאֲלִי:

עוֹשֶׂה שָׁלוֹם בִּמְרוֹמָיו
הוּא יַעֲשֶׂה שָׁלוֹם
עָלֵֽינוּ וְעַל כָּל יִשְׂרָאֵל
וְעַל כָּל יוֹשְׁבֵי תֵבֵל
וְאִמְרוּ אָמֵן:

Yihyu leratzon imrey fi
vehegyon libi lefaneḥa
adonay tzuri vego'ali.
Oseh shalom bimromav
hu ya'aseh shalom
aleynu ve'al kol yisra'el
ve'al kol yoshvey tevel
ve'imru amen.

On Sukkot continue with Netilat Lulav, *page 359.*
On Rosh Ḥodesh, Ḥanukah, Yom Ha'atzma'ut, and Ḥol Hamo'ed *continue with Hallel, page 361.*
On fast days and during the days between Rosh Hashanah and Yom Kippur, continue with Avinu Malkenu *or alternatives, pages 136-143.*
On other days, some congregations continue with Taḥanun, *page 425.*
Otherwise continue with Kaddish Titkabal, *page 145.*

AVINU MALKENU / OUR CREATOR, OUR SOVEREIGN

Avinu Malkenu is traditionally recited between Rosh Hashanah and Yom Kippur, and on fast days. On fast days, substitute "bless" for "renew" and "remember" for "inscribe." For an alternative version see pages 140-143.

Our creator, our sovereign, we have done wrong in your presence.
Our creator, our sovereign, we have no one to rule over us but you.
Our creator, our sovereign, help us for the honor of your name.
Our creator, our sovereign, renew for us a good year.
Our creator, our sovereign, nullify the plans of any who may seek to do us harm.
Our creator, our sovereign, grant forgiveness and atonement for all of our transgressions.
Our creator, our sovereign, help us to return wholeheartedly into your presence.
Our creator, our sovereign, send thorough healing to all those who ail.
Our creator, our sovereign, inscribe us for good fortune in the Book of Life.
Our creator, our sovereign, inscribe us in the Book of Redemption and Salvation.
Our creator, our sovereign, inscribe us in the Book of Sustenance and Livelihood.
Our creator, our sovereign, inscribe us in the Book of Merit.
Our creator, our sovereign, inscribe us in the Book of Forgiveness and Atonement.
Our creator, our sovereign, let grow for us the tree of imminent redemption. ↩

אָבִינוּ מַלְכֵּנוּ

Avinu Malkenu is traditionally recited between Rosh Hashanah and Yom Kippur, and on fast days. On fast days, substitute "בָּרֵךְ" for "חַדֵּשׁ" and "זָכְרֵנוּ" for "כָּתְבֵנוּ." For an alternative version see pages 141-143.

אָבִינוּ מַלְכֵּנוּ חָטָאנוּ לְפָנֶיךָ:
אָבִינוּ מַלְכֵּנוּ אֵין לָנוּ מֶלֶךְ אֶלָּא אָתָּה:
אָבִינוּ מַלְכֵּנוּ עֲשֵׂה עִמָּנוּ לְמַעַן שְׁמֶךָ:
אָבִינוּ מַלְכֵּנוּ חַדֵּשׁ עָלֵינוּ שָׁנָה טוֹבָה:
אָבִינוּ מַלְכֵּנוּ הָפֵר עֲצַת אוֹיְבֵינוּ:
אָבִינוּ מַלְכֵּנוּ סְלַח וּמְחַל לְכָל־עֲוֹנוֹתֵינוּ:
אָבִינוּ מַלְכֵּנוּ הַחֲזִירֵנוּ בִּתְשׁוּבָה שְׁלֵמָה לְפָנֶיךָ:
אָבִינוּ מַלְכֵּנוּ שְׁלַח רְפוּאָה שְׁלֵמָה לַחוֹלִים:
אָבִינוּ מַלְכֵּנוּ כָּתְבֵנוּ בְּסֵפֶר חַיִּים טוֹבִים:
אָבִינוּ מַלְכֵּנוּ כָּתְבֵנוּ בְּסֵפֶר גְּאֻלָּה וִישׁוּעָה:
אָבִינוּ מַלְכֵּנוּ כָּתְבֵנוּ בְּסֵפֶר פַּרְנָסָה וְכַלְכָּלָה:
אָבִינוּ מַלְכֵּנוּ כָּתְבֵנוּ בְּסֵפֶר זְכֻיּוֹת:
אָבִינוּ מַלְכֵּנוּ כָּתְבֵנוּ בְּסֵפֶר סְלִיחָה וּמְחִילָה:
אָבִינוּ מַלְכֵּנוּ הַצְמַח לָנוּ יְשׁוּעָה בְּקָרוֹב: ←

Our creator, our sovereign, remember us, though we are made of dust.

Our creator, our sovereign, be merciful to us and to all our offspring.

Our creator, our sovereign, act in memory of all those who have been killed while honoring your name.

Our creator, our sovereign, act in honor of your great and mighty, awe-inspiring name, which has been called out over us for our protection.

Our creator, our sovereign, be gracious with us and respond to us, for we have no deeds to justify us; deal with us in righteousness and love, and save us now.

Continue on page 144.

COMMENTARY. Perhaps more than any other prayer, *Avinu Malkenu* invokes the image of a long-bearded king sitting in judgment upon his throne. How many are the ways that this image can trouble us! Some Jews are struggling to recover from the harsh judgments of parents or peers, or from harsh self-judgments. Some are struggling to escape the transcendent imagery of God and replace it with the divine within. Some have trouble with the maleness of the image.

Despite these very real difficulties, there is a powerful core of truth in the *Avinu Malkenu* that transcends the trouble many of us have with its imagery: we must grapple with standards of justice that are external to us. Social responsibility is not merely a matter of personal conscience. Chanting the *Avinu Malkenu* reminds us of standards by which we ought to judge ourselves.

Furthermore, it reminds us of forces infinitely greater than ourselves upon which our very lives depend. While our lives depend upon our inner resources, we cannot exist without the aid of natural and social forces. Knowing who we are means accepting the limits of our power and knowledge and the inevitability of our dependency. D.A.T.

אָבִֽינוּ מַלְכֵּֽנוּ זְכוֹר כִּי עָפָר אֲנָֽחְנוּ׃
אָבִֽינוּ מַלְכֵּֽנוּ חֲמוֹל עָלֵֽינוּ וְעַל־עוֹלָלֵֽינוּ וְטַפֵּֽינוּ׃
אָבִֽינוּ מַלְכֵּֽנוּ עֲשֵׂה לְמַֽעַן הֲרוּגִים עַל־שֵׁם קָדְשֶֽׁךָ׃
אָבִֽינוּ מַלְכֵּֽנוּ עֲשֵׂה לְמַֽעַן שִׁמְךָ הַגָּדוֹל הַגִּבּוֹר וְהַנּוֹרָא שֶׁנִּקְרָא עָלֵֽינוּ׃
אָבִֽינוּ מַלְכֵּֽנוּ חָנֵּֽנוּ וַעֲנֵֽנוּ כִּי אֵין בָּֽנוּ מַעֲשִׂים עֲשֵׂה עִמָּֽנוּ צְדָקָה וָחֶֽסֶד וְהוֹשִׁיעֵֽנוּ׃

Avinu malkenu ḥonenu va'anenu ki eyn banu ma'asim, aseh imanu tzedakah vaḥesed vehoshi'enu.

Continue on page 145.

In *Avinu Malkenu* we seek the strength to do justice, the inner harmony needed to find forgiveness, and the acceptance of the small place we have amidst the tumult of the world. It is in that context that we express the hopes embodied in this prayer. Whether or not the worshipper chooses to change the words of *Avinu Malkenu*, the fervently expressed pleas it contains transcend the constraints of time and place. D.A.T.

AVINU MALKENU / OUR CREATOR, OUR SOVEREIGN

Our source, our God, we have done wrong in your presence.
Our source, our God, we have no one to rule over us but you.
Our source, our God, help us for the honor of your name.
Our source, our God, renew for us a good year.
Our source, our God, nullify the plans of any who may seek to do us harm.
Our source, our God, grant forgiveness and atonement for all of our transgressions.
Our source, our God, help us to return wholeheartedly into your presence.
Our source, our God, send thorough healing to all those who ail.
Our source, our God, inscribe us for good fortune in the Book of Life.
Our source, our God, inscribe us in the Book of Redemption and Salvation.
Our source, our God, inscribe us in the Book of Sustenance and Livelihood.
Our source, our God, inscribe us in the Book of Merit.
Our source, our God, inscribe us in the Book of Forgiveness and Atonement.
Our source, our God, let grow for us the tree of imminent redemption. ↩

אָבִֽינוּ מַלְכֵּֽנוּ

מְקוֹרֵֽנוּ אֱלֹהֵֽינוּ חָטָֽאנוּ לְפָנֶֽיךָ׃

מְקוֹרֵֽנוּ אֱלֹהֵֽינוּ אֵין לָֽנוּ מֶֽלֶךְ אֶלָּא אָֽתָּה׃

מְקוֹרֵֽנוּ אֱלֹהֵֽינוּ עֲשֵׂה עִמָּֽנוּ לְמַֽעַן שְׁמֶֽךָ׃

מְקוֹרֵֽנוּ אֱלֹהֵֽינוּ חַדֵּשׁ עָלֵֽינוּ שָׁנָה טוֹבָה׃

מְקוֹרֵֽנוּ אֱלֹהֵֽינוּ הָפֵר עֲצַת אוֹיְבֵֽינוּ׃

מְקוֹרֵֽנוּ אֱלֹהֵֽינוּ סְלַח וּמְחַל לְכָל־עֲוֹנוֹתֵֽינוּ׃

מְקוֹרֵֽנוּ אֱלֹהֵֽינוּ הַחֲזִירֵֽנוּ בִּתְשׁוּבָה שְׁלֵמָה לְפָנֶֽיךָ׃

מְקוֹרֵֽנוּ אֱלֹהֵֽינוּ שְׁלַח רְפוּאָה שְׁלֵמָה לַחוֹלִים׃

מְקוֹרֵֽנוּ אֱלֹהֵֽינוּ כָּתְבֵֽנוּ בְּסֵֽפֶר חַיִּים טוֹבִים׃

מְקוֹרֵֽנוּ אֱלֹהֵֽינוּ כָּתְבֵֽנוּ בְּסֵֽפֶר גְּאֻלָּה וִישׁוּעָה׃

מְקוֹרֵֽנוּ אֱלֹהֵֽינוּ כָּתְבֵֽנוּ בְּסֵֽפֶר פַּרְנָסָה וְכַלְכָּלָה׃

מְקוֹרֵֽנוּ אֱלֹהֵֽינוּ כָּתְבֵֽנוּ בְּסֵֽפֶר זְכוּת׃

מְקוֹרֵֽנוּ אֱלֹהֵֽינוּ כָּתְבֵֽנוּ בְּסֵֽפֶר סְלִיחָה וּמְחִילָה׃

מְקוֹרֵֽנוּ אֱלֹהֵֽינוּ הַצְמַח לָֽנוּ יְשׁוּעָה בְּקָרוֹב׃ ←

NOTE. מקורנו אלהינו / *Mekorenu Eloheynu* / Our source, our God. This alternative version changes the first two words of each line from "Our creator, our sovereign" to "Our source, our God." Many other versions can be constructed to reflect different theological outlooks and ethical concerns. This can be done by selecting one word from each group to form the introductory phrase.

I	Imeynu	אִמֵּֽינוּ	Our mother
	Eloheynu	אֱלֹהֵֽינוּ	Our God
	Mekorenu	מְקוֹרֵֽנוּ	Our source
	Avinu	אָבִֽינוּ	Our creator (literally, father)
	Sheḥinatenu	שְׁכִינָתֵֽנוּ	Our presence
II	Malkatenu	מַלְכָּתֵֽנוּ	Our queen
	Shebashamayim	שֶׁבַּשָּׁמַֽיִם	In heaven
	Atartenu	עֲטַרְתֵּֽנוּ	Our crown
	Sheḥinatenu	שְׁכִינָתֵֽנוּ	Our presence
	Malkenu	מַלְכֵּֽנוּ	Our sovereign

Our source, our God, remember us, though we are made of dust.
Our source, our God, be merciful to us and to all our offspring.
Our source, our God, act in memory of all those who have been killed while honoring your name.
Our source, our God, act in honor of your great and mighty, awe-inspiring name, which has been called out over us for our protection.
Our creator, our sovereign, be gracious with us and respond to us, for we have no deeds to justify us; deal with us in righteousness and love, and save us now.

מְקוֹרֵנוּ אֱלֹהֵינוּ זְכוֹר כִּי עָפָר אֲנָחְנוּ׃
מְקוֹרֵנוּ אֱלֹהֵינוּ חֲמוֹל עָלֵינוּ וְעַל־עוֹלָלֵינוּ וְטַפֵּינוּ׃
מְקוֹרֵנוּ אֱלֹהֵינוּ עֲשֵׂה לְמַעַן הֲרוּגִים עַל־שֵׁם קָדְשֶׁךָ׃
מְקוֹרֵנוּ אֱלֹהֵינוּ עֲשֵׂה לְמַעַן שִׁמְךָ הַגָּדוֹל הַגִּבּוֹר וְהַנּוֹרָא שֶׁנִּקְרָא עָלֵינוּ׃
אָבִינוּ מַלְכֵּנוּ חָנֵּנוּ וַעֲנֵנוּ כִּי אֵין בָּנוּ מַעֲשִׂים עֲשֵׂה עִמָּנוּ צְדָקָה וָחֶסֶד וְהוֹשִׁיעֵנוּ׃

Avinu malkenu ḥonenu va'anenu ki eyn banu ma'asim aseh imanu tzedakah vaḥesed vehoshi'enu.

KADDISH TITKABAL / KADDISH FOR THE COMPLETION OF PRAYER

Reader: Let God's name be made great and holy in the world that was created as God willed. May God complete the holy realm in your own lifetime, in your days, and in the days of all the house of Israel, quickly and soon. And say: Amen.

Congregation: May God's great name be blessed forever and as long as worlds endure.

Reader: May it be blessed, and praised, and glorified, and held in honor, viewed with awe, embellished, and revered; and may the blessed name of holiness be hailed, though it be higher (*Between Rosh Hashanah and Yom Kippur, add:* by far) than all the blessings, songs, praises, and consolations that we utter in this world. And say: Amen.

And may the prayer and supplication of the whole house of Israel be acceptable to their creator in the heavens. And say: Amen.

May Heaven grant a universal peace, and life for us, and for all Israel. And say: Amen.

May the one who creates harmony above make peace for us and for all Israel, and for all who dwell on earth. And say: Amen.

On Monday, Thursday, holidays and Rosh Ḥodesh, continue with the Torah Service, page 146. On other days, continue with Aleynu, page 168.

NOTE. Kaddish Titkabal concludes the section of the service containing an *Amidah* / silent prayer. It therefore contains a request for the acceptance of prayer, which is omitted in the Mourner's Kaddish that follows *Aleynu*. D.A.T.

קַדִּישׁ תִּתְקַבַּל

יִתְגַּדַּל וְיִתְקַדַּשׁ שְׁמֵהּ רַבָּא בְּעָלְמָא דִּי בְרָא כִרְעוּתֵהּ וְיַמְלִיךְ
מַלְכוּתֵהּ בְּחַיֵּיכוֹן וּבְיוֹמֵיכוֹן וּבְחַיֵּי דְכָל בֵּית יִשְׂרָאֵל בַּעֲגָלָא וּבִזְמַן
קָרִיב וְאִמְרוּ אָמֵן:
יְהֵא שְׁמֵהּ רַבָּא מְבָרַךְ לְעָלַם וּלְעָלְמֵי עָלְמַיָּא:
יִתְבָּרַךְ וְיִשְׁתַּבַּח וְיִתְפָּאַר וְיִתְרוֹמַם וְיִתְנַשֵּׂא וְיִתְהַדָּר וְיִתְעַלֶּה
וְיִתְהַלַּל שְׁמֵהּ דְּקֻדְשָׁא בְּרִיךְ הוּא
לְעֵֽלָּא (*Between Rosh Hashanah and Yom Kippur, add:* לְעֵֽלָּא) מִן כָּל בִּרְכָתָא
וְשִׁירָתָא תֻּשְׁבְּחָתָא וְנֶחֱמָתָא דַּאֲמִירָן בְּעָלְמָא וְאִמְרוּ אָמֵן:

תִּתְקַבַּל צְלוֹתְהוֹן וּבָעוּתְהוֹן דְּכָל בֵּית יִשְׂרָאֵל קֳדָם אֲבוּהוֹן דִּי
בִשְׁמַיָּא וְאִמְרוּ אָמֵן:
יְהֵא שְׁלָמָא רַבָּא מִן שְׁמַיָּא וְחַיִּים עָלֵֽינוּ וְעַל כָּל יִשְׂרָאֵל וְאִמְרוּ אָמֵן:
עוֹשֶׂה שָׁלוֹם בִּמְרוֹמָיו הוּא יַעֲשֶׂה שָׁלוֹם עָלֵינוּ וְעַל כָּל יִשְׂרָאֵל וְעַל
כָּל יוֹשְׁבֵי תֵבֵל וְאִמְרוּ אָמֵן:

Yehey shemey raba mevaraḥ le'alam ulalmey almaya.
Oseh shalom bimromav hu ya'aseh shalom aleynu ve'al kol
yisra'el ve'al kol yoshvey tevel ve'imru amen.

On Monday, Thursday, holidays and Rosh Ḥodesh, continue with the Torah service, page 147. On other days continue with Aleynu, page 169.

HOTZA'AT SEFER TORAH / THE TORAH SERVICE

The ark is opened.

And it happened, when the Ark began its journey,
that Moses said: Arise, ASCENDANT ONE,
and may your enemies be scattered,
May the ones who oppose you
Be afraid of your might!
Behold, out of Zion emerges our Torah,
and the word of THE WISE ONE from Jerusalem's heights.
Blessed is God who has given us Torah,
to Israel, our people, with holy intent.

The leader faces the ark, bows and says:

Declare with me the greatness of THE INFINITE,
together let us raise God's name.

The leader carries the Torah around the room as the leader and congregation sing:

To you, ETERNAL ONE, is all majesty,
and might and splendor, and eternity, and power!
For everything that is, in the heavens and the earth,
is yours, ALMIGHTY ONE, as is all sovereignty,
and highest eminence above all beings.

ויהי...מפניך / And...might! (Numbers 10:35).
כי...ירושלים / Behold...Jerusalem's heights (Isaiah 2:3).

הוֹצָאַת סֵפֶר תּוֹרָה

The ark is opened.

וַיְהִי בִּנְסֹעַ הָאָרֹן וַיֹּאמֶר מֹשֶׁה קוּמָה יהוה וְיָפֻצוּ אֹיְבֶיךָ וְיָנֻסוּ מְשַׂנְאֶיךָ מִפָּנֶיךָ׃

כִּי מִצִּיּוֹן תֵּצֵא תוֹרָה וּדְבַר יהוה מִירוּשָׁלָיִם׃

בָּרוּךְ שֶׁנָּתַן תּוֹרָה לְעַמּוֹ יִשְׂרָאֵל בִּקְדֻשָּׁתוֹ׃

Vayehi binso'a ha'aron vayomer mosheh kumah adonay veyafutzu oyveḥa veyanusu mesaneḥa mipaneḥa.
Ki mitziyon tetzey torah udvar adonay mirushalayim.
Baruḥ shenatan torah le'amo yisra'el bikdushato.

The leader faces the ark, bows and says:

גַּדְּלוּ לַיהוה אִתִּי וּנְרוֹמְמָה שְׁמוֹ יַחְדָּו׃

Gadelu ladonay iti unromemah shemo yaḥdav.

The leader carries the Torah around the room as the leader and congregation sing:

לְךָ יהוה הַגְּדֻלָּה וְהַגְּבוּרָה וְהַתִּפְאֶרֶת וְהַנֵּצַח וְהַהוֹד כִּי כֹל בַּשָּׁמַיִם וּבָאָרֶץ לְךָ יהוה הַמַּמְלָכָה וְהַמִּתְנַשֵּׂא לְכֹל לְרֹאשׁ׃

רוֹמְמוּ יהוה אֱלֹהֵינוּ וְהִשְׁתַּחֲווּ לַהֲדֹם רַגְלָיו קָדוֹשׁ הוּא׃

רוֹמְמוּ יהוה אֱלֹהֵינוּ וְהִשְׁתַּחֲווּ לְהַר קָדְשׁוֹ כִּי קָדוֹשׁ יהוה אֱלֹהֵינוּ׃

Leḥa adonay hagedulah vehagevurah vehatiferet vehanetzaḥ vehahod ki ḥol bashamayim uva'aretz leḥa adonay hamamlaḥah vehamitnasey leḥol lerosh.
Romemu adonay eloheynu vehishtaḥavu lahadom raglav kadosh hu.
Romemu adonay eloheynu vehishtaḥavu lehar kodsho ki kadosh adonay eloheynu.

The Torah is placed on the reading table and opened. The gabay *says:*

May God help, protect, and save
all who seek refuge in God's shelter,
and let us say: Amen.
Let everyone declare the greatness of our God,
let all give honor to the Torah.
May ________________ arise,
as first (second, third, fourth) one called up to the Torah.
Blessed is the one who has given Torah to the people Israel!

COMMENTARY. The public reading of the Torah is a form of ritualized study designed to actively engage the participants. During the Torah reading, one person reads from the scroll. There are also two *gabayim*. One *gabay* assigns the Torah honors, calls people up to the Torah, and recites additional prayers, including the *mi sheberaḥ* prayers. The second *gabay* follows the Torah reading closely and corrects errors.

Traditionally, seven adult Jews were called on Shabbat morning, six on Yom Kippur, five on Pilgrimage Festivals and Rosh Hashanah, four on Rosh Ḥodesh and three on Monday and Thursday, *Ḥol Hamo'ed*, Purim, Ḥanukah and Shabbat afternoon. On days when the *Haftarah* is chanted, an additional *aliyah*, known as the *maftir*, is given to the person who reads the *Haftarah*. In many contemporary synagogues, there are fewer *aliyot* on Shabbat and holidays.

D.A.T.

The Torah is placed on the reading table and opened. The gabay *says:*

וְיַעֲזוֹר וְיָגֵן וְיוֹשִׁיעַ לְכֹל הַחוֹסִים בּוֹ וְנֹאמַר אָמֵן:
הַכֹּל הָבוּ גֹדֶל לֵאלֹהֵינוּ וּתְנוּ כָבוֹד לַתּוֹרָה:
יַעֲמוֹד/תַּעֲמוֹד/יַעַמְדוּ ______ בֶּן/בַּת ______ לָעֲלִיָּה/לַמַּפְטִיר
[הָרִאשׁוֹנָה, הַשֵּׁנִית, הַשְּׁלִישִׁית, הָרְבִיעִית, הַחֲמִישִׁית, הַשִּׁשִּׁית, הַשְּׁבִיעִית, הוֹסָפָה]
בָּרוּךְ שֶׁנָּתַן תּוֹרָה לְעַמּוֹ יִשְׂרָאֵל בִּקְדֻשָּׁתוֹ:

Congregation and gabay *continue:*

And you who cling to THE ETERNAL ONE your God,
are all alive today!

COMMENTARY. The *aliyah* is the public enactment of an individual's commitment to Judaism, reiterated in the words of the hallowed formula. It is an enactment of belonging and an enactment of belief.

The *aliyah* is always a numinous moment when the experience of divinity is strong. Even though this numinous quality often is dimmed by repetition or by our increased informality, we still experience the power of standing on the *bimah* before the Torah ark, *ner tamid* (eternal light), Jewish officiants, and fellow Jews. The act links us in the living moment to the mythic event of God's calling the Jewish people at Sinai, as well as to all other moments of calling in Jewish and human experience. When we chant new words, rather than the words of the tradition, we are doing more than merely changing a formula of words; we are enacting our own calling to a new and no longer traditional way of being Jewish. Whereas saying *asher baḥar banu* links us to the biblical drama at Sinai, chanting *asher kervanu* links us both to that drama and to the Reconstructionist movement's root metaphor of Judaism as an evolving religious civilization.

ROBIN GOLDBERG

ואתם הדבקים...היום / And you who cling...today. The people to whom this verse was originally spoken (Deuteronomy 4:4) live on through their place in the chain of tradition. We touch the past by bringing the ancient words to life. And when future generations recite this verse, we, who have kept the chain alive, will be present. You who cleave to Adonay your God, you are *all* alive today.

D.E.

Congregation and gabay *continue:*

וְאַתֶּם הַדְּבֵקִים בַּיהוה אֱלֹהֵיכֶם חַיִּים כֻּלְּכֶם הַיּוֹם׃

Ve'atem hadevekim badonay eloheyḥem ḥayim kuleḥem hayom.

The last part of the blessing preceding the Torah reading has been the subject of considerable discussion. Below are several current variants. You can use these by selecting one from section I, one from II, and then III:

I. בָּרוּךְ אַתָּה יהוה אֱלֹהֵינוּ מֶלֶךְ הָעוֹלָם

Baruḥ atah adonay eloheynu meleḥ ha'olam

Blessed are you, ETERNAL ONE, our God, sovereign of all worlds

בָּרוּךְ אַתָּה יהוה אֱלֹהֵינוּ חֵי הָעוֹלָמִים

Baruḥ atah adonay eloheynu ḥey ha'olamim

Blessed are you, ETERNAL ONE, our God, life of all the worlds

נְבָרֵךְ אֶת עֵין הַחַיִּים

Nevareḥ et eyn haḥayim

Let us bless the source of life

II. אֲשֶׁר קֵרְבָנוּ לַעֲבוֹדָתוֹ וְנָתַן־לָנוּ אֶת־תּוֹרָתוֹ.

asher kervanu la'avodato venatan lanu et torato.

who has drawn us to your service, and given us your Torah.

אֲשֶׁר בָּחַר בָּנוּ מִכָּל הָעַמִּים וְנָתַן לָנוּ אֶת תּוֹרָתוֹ

asher baḥar banu mikol ha'amim venatan lanu et torato.

who has singled us out from all the peoples and given us your Torah.

III. בָּרוּךְ אַתָּה יהוה נוֹתֵן הַתּוֹרָה

Baruḥ atah adonay noten hatorah

Blessed are you, ETERNAL ONE, giver of the Torah.

BIRḤOT HATORAH / TORAH BLESSINGS

Those who receive an aliyah *to the Torah say the following blessing:*

Bless THE INFINITE, the blessed One!

Congregation:

Blessed is THE INFINITE, the blessed One, now and forever!

The response of the congregation is repeated, and the blessing continues as follows:

Blessed are you, ETERNAL ONE, our God, the sovereign of all worlds, who has drawn us to your service, and has given us your Torah. Blessed are you, ETERNAL ONE, who gives the Torah.

After the section of the Torah is read, the following blessing is recited:

Blessed are you, ETERNAL ONE, our God, the sovereign of all worlds, who has given us a Torah of truth, and planted in our midst eternal life. Blessed are you, ETERNAL ONE, who gives the Torah.

DERASH. *Aliyah* is ascent. We ascend to the Torah to acknowledge that we choose to live under its laws and principles. We ascend to the Torah to affirm that we are part of a people and a story that is much greater than ourselves. We ascend to the Torah to represent those who remain below. We ascend to the Torah to risk receiving an honor, to risk being known and seen, to risk being at Sinai again. We ascend to the Torah with slow steps, or in haste, with enthusiasm or reluctance, in awe or in fear, in hope and in love. S.P.W.

COMMENTARY. The blessing over the Torah recalls the *Bareḥu*, the call to worship, the beginning of the morning service recited only in the presence of the minyan, ten adult Jews. The blessing encircles the Torah reading in a familiar liturgical pattern of blessing and study. Through blessing, study, and community we manifest God, Torah and Israel. S.P.W.

בִּרְכוֹת הַתּוֹרָה

Those who receive an aliyah *to the Torah say the following blessing:*

בָּרְכוּ אֶת יהוה הַמְבֹרָךְ:

Bareḥu et adonay hamvoraḥ.

Congregation:

בָּרוּךְ יהוה הַמְבֹרָךְ לְעוֹלָם וָעֶד:

Baruḥ adonay hamvoraḥ le'olam va'ed.

The response of the congregation is repeated, and the blessing continues as follows:

בָּרוּךְ אַתָּה יהוה אֱלֹהֵינוּ מֶלֶךְ הָעוֹלָם אֲשֶׁר קֵרְבָנוּ לַעֲבוֹדָתוֹ וְנָתַן־לָנוּ אֶת־תּוֹרָתוֹ: בָּרוּךְ אַתָּה יהוה נוֹתֵן הַתּוֹרָה:

Baruḥ atah adonay eloheynu meleḥ ha'olam asher kervanu la'avodato venatan lanu et torato. Baruḥ atah adonay noten hatorah.

After the section of the Torah is read, the following blessing is recited:

בָּרוּךְ אַתָּה יהוה אֱלֹהֵינוּ מֶלֶךְ הָעוֹלָם אֲשֶׁר נָתַן־לָנוּ תּוֹרַת אֱמֶת וְחַיֵּי עוֹלָם נָטַע בְּתוֹכֵנוּ: בָּרוּךְ אַתָּה יהוה נוֹתֵן הַתּוֹרָה:

Baruḥ atah adonay eloheynu meleḥ ha'olam asher natan lanu torat emet veḥayey olam nata betoḥenu. Baruḥ atah adonay noten hatorah.

BIRKAT HAGOMEL / BLESSING FOR DELIVERANCE AND GOOD FORTUNE

If the person called up to the Torah has recently escaped danger or returned safely from a journey, he or she recites as follows:

Blessed are you, ABUNDANT ONE, our God, the sovereign of all worlds, who bestows good things on one in debt to you, and who has granted me all good.

Congregational response to one who offers this blessing:

Amen. And may the one who has bestowed upon you good, continue to bestow upon you good.

Individual mi sheberaḥ *prayers for anyone called to the Torah can be inserted here. They may be recited for those who are ill, a newborn child, a birthday, a trip to Israel, or for aliyah to Israel. Other* mi sheberaḥ *prayers can be created by adapting the individual* mi sheberaḥ *form. For additional* mi sheberaḥ *prayers, see the Shabbat and Festivals volume of* Kol Haneshamah.

COMMENTARY. *Mi sheberaḥ* prayers announce to the whole community individual times of joy and need. When *birkat hagomel* or a *mi sheberaḥ* is recited, it is customary to contribute to *tzedakah*. Often this offering is directed to the synagogue. On happy occasions this serves as an offering of thanksgiving. A *mi sheberaḥ* in the form of petition, such as a prayer for healing, was traditionally offered in the hope that a good deed would encourage divine intervention. More recently the act of *tzedakah* has been understood as a tangible way of expressing gratitude for the support and good wishes of the community. Just as the community supports the individual in times of need, so does the community depend upon the support of each individual. D.A.T.

בִּרְכַּת הַגּוֹמֵל

If the person called up to the Torah has recently escaped danger or returned safely from a journey, he or she recites as follows:

בָּרוּךְ אַתָּה יהוה אֱלֹהֵינוּ מֶלֶךְ הָעוֹלָם הַגּוֹמֵל לְחַיָּבִים טוֹבוֹת שֶׁגְּמָלַנִי כָּל טוֹב׃

Baruḥ atah adonay eloheynu meleḥ ha'olam hagomel leḥayavim tovot shegemalani kol tov.

Congregational response to a man who offers this blessing:

אָמֵן. מִי שֶׁגְּמָלְךָ טוֹב הוּא יִגְמָלְךָ כָּל טוֹב סֶלָה׃

Amen. Mi shegemaleḥa tov hu yigmoleḥa kol tov selah.

Congregational response to a woman who offers this blessing:

אָמֵן. מִי שֶׁגְּמָלֵךְ טוֹב הוּא יִגְמְלֵךְ כָּל טוֹב סֶלָה׃

Amen. Mi shegemaleḥ tov hu yigmeleḥ kol tov selah.

Individual mi sheberaḥ *prayers for anyone called to the Torah can be inserted here. They may be recited for those who are ill, a newborn child, a birthday, a trip to Israel, or for aliyah to Israel. Other* mi sheberaḥ *prayers can be created by adapting the individual* mi sheberaḥ *form. For additional* mi sheberaḥ *prayers, see the Shabbat and Festivals volume of* Kol Haneshamah.

COMMENTARY. At the mysterious edges of life we seek the embrace of our community past and present. Hence individuals marking recovery from illness or the birth of a child are blessed before the open Torah. This process can build community as news is communicated and support mobilized. Most significantly it counteracts the devastating possibility of isolation in times of vulnerability. The practice gives voice to gratitude and anxiety in a forum where it can be shared and transformed into connectedness and faith.

S.P.W.

COLLECTIVE BLESSING FOR THOSE WHO HAVE RECEIVED *ALIYOT*

May the one who blessed our ancestors, Abraham, Isaac, and Jacob, Sarah, Rebekah, Rachel, and Leah, bless all those here who have risen today to honor the Omnipresent, and to honor the Torah, (*on a festival:* and to honor the Festival). And by this merit, may they be granted life and kept from all trouble and affliction, and from every harm or sickness, and may they find blessing and success in all their labors (*on a festival:* and may they be worthy to ascend as pilgrims on this day), along with all of Israel, all their brothers and their sisters, and let us say: Amen.

מִי שֶׁבֵּרַךְ

מִי שֶׁבֵּרַךְ אֲבוֹתֵינוּ אַבְרָהָם יִצְחָק וְיַעֲקֹב וְאִמּוֹתֵינוּ שָׂרָה רִבְקָה רָחֵל
וְלֵאָה הוּא יְבָרֵךְ אֶת כָּל אֵלֶּה שֶׁעָלוּ הַיּוֹם לִכְבוֹד הַמָּקוֹם וְלִכְבוֹד
הַתּוֹרָה (*on a festival:* וְלִכְבוֹד הָרֶגֶל) בִּשְׂכַר זֶה הַקָּדוֹשׁ בָּרוּךְ הוּא יְחַיֵּים
וְיִשְׁמְרֵם מִכָּל צָרָה וְצוּקָה וּמִכָּל נֶגַע וּמַחֲלָה וְיִשְׁלַח בְּרָכָה וְהַצְלָחָה
בְּכָל מַעֲשֵׂה יְדֵיהֶם וִיבָרְכֵם (*on a festival:* וִיזַכֵּם לַעֲלוֹת לָרֶגֶל) עִם כָּל
יִשְׂרָאֵל אֲחֵיהֶם וְאַחְיוֹתֵיהֶם וְנֹאמַר אָמֵן:

ḤATZI KADDISH / SHORT KADDISH

In some congregations, Ḥatzi Kaddish *is recited at the conclusion of the Torah reading. On days when portions from two Torah scrolls are read, both scrolls are placed on the reading table after the reading from the first scroll.* Ḥatzi Kaddish *is then recited.*

Transliteration is on page 217.

Reader: Let God's name be made great and holy in the world that was created as God willed. May God complete the holy realm in your own lifetime, in your days, and in the days of all the house of Israel, quickly and soon. And say: Amen.

Congregation: May God's great name be blessed, forever and as long as worlds endure.

Reader: May it be blessed, and praised, and glorified, and held in honor, viewed with awe, embellished, and revered; and may the blessed name of holiness be hailed, though it be higher (*On Shabbat Shuvah add:* by far) than all the blessings, songs, praises, and consolations that we utter in this world. And say: Amen.

חֲצִי קַדִּישׁ

In some congregations, Ḥatzi Kaddish *is recited at the conclusion of the Torah reading. On days when portions from two Torah scrolls are read, both scrolls are placed on the reading table after the reading from the first scroll.* Ḥatzi Kaddish *is then recited.*

Transliteration is on page 217.

יִתְגַּדַּל וְיִתְקַדַּשׁ שְׁמֵהּ רַבָּא בְּעָלְמָא דִּי בְרָא כִרְעוּתֵהּ וְיַמְלִיךְ
מַלְכוּתֵהּ בְּחַיֵּיכוֹן וּבְיוֹמֵיכוֹן וּבְחַיֵּי דְכָל בֵּית יִשְׂרָאֵל בַּעֲגָלָא וּבִזְמַן
קָרִיב וְאִמְרוּ אָמֵן׃

יְהֵא שְׁמֵהּ רַבָּא מְבָרַךְ לְעָלַם וּלְעָלְמֵי עָלְמַיָּא׃

יִתְבָּרַךְ וְיִשְׁתַּבַּח וְיִתְפָּאַר וְיִתְרוֹמַם וְיִתְנַשֵּׂא וְיִתְהַדַּר וְיִתְעַלֶּה וְיִתְהַלַּל
שְׁמֵהּ דְּקֻדְשָׁא בְּרִיךְ הוּא לְעֵֽלָּא (לְעֵֽלָּא) מִן כָּל בִּרְכָתָא וְשִׁירָתָא
תֻּשְׁבְּחָתָא וְנֶחֱמָתָא דַּאֲמִירָן בְּעָלְמָא וְאִמְרוּ אָמֵן׃

The Torah is lifted, and one of the following is recited:

This is the Torah.
It is a Tree of Life to those who hold fast to it.
Those who uphold it may be counted fortunate!

This is the Torah which Moses placed before the children of Israel,
by the word of THE ALMIGHTY ONE, and by the hand of Moses.

On days when portions from two Torah scrolls are read, the second reading takes place here. After that, the second scroll is lifted as above.

COMMENTARY. The 1945 Reconstructionist Prayerbook puts *Etz ḥayim hi* / It is a tree of life in place of *asher sam moshe lifney beney yisra'el* / which Moses placed before the children of Israel. Earlier Reconstructionists were concerned that it be made clear that while affirming the holiness of Torah, they did not believe that it was given to Moses at Mount Sinai. Many current Reconstructionists believe the evolutionary nature of the Torah to be self-evident and have returned to the traditional line for the sake of its rich mythic imagery. Both options are included here. D.A.T.

עץ חיים היא / It is a Tree of Life. The book of Genesis tells us that the tree of life is in the garden of Eden. The Torah is our tree of life; it is our way back to the garden. D.E.

The Torah is lifted, and one of the following is recited:

וְזֹאת הַתּוֹרָה עֵץ חַיִּים הִיא לַמַּחֲזִיקִים בָּהּ וְתֹמְכֶיהָ מְאֻשָּׁר:

Vezot hatorah etz ḥayim hi lamaḥazikim bah vetomẖeha me'ushar.

וְזֹאת הַתּוֹרָה אֲשֶׁר שָׂם מֹשֶׁה לִפְנֵי בְּנֵי יִשְׂרָאֵל עַל פִּי יהוה בְּיַד מֹשֶׁה:

Vezot hatorah asher sam mosheh lifney beney yisra'el al pi adonay beyad mosheh.

On days when portions from two Torah scrolls are read, the second reading takes place here. After that, the second scroll is lifted as above.

עץ...מאשר / It...fortunate! (Proverbs 3:18).
וזאת...ישראל / This...Israel (Deuteronomy 4:44).
על...משה / by...Moses (Numbers 9:23).

A PRAYER FOR PEACE

May it be your will, ETERNAL ONE, our God, God of our ancestors, that wars and bloodshed be abolished from the world, and bring into the world a great and wonderful and lasting peace. And let no nation lift a sword against a nation—let them learn no more the ways of war!

Let all who dwell on earth simply acknowledge the truth of truths: that we have not come into this world for the sake of quarreling and war, nor for the sake of hatred, jealousy, anger, or bloodshed; rather, we have come into this world only to know you—may you be blessed eternally!

Therefore, have mercy on us, and fulfill among us what is written in your Scripture: "I shall give peace upon the earth, and you shall lie down with none to make you afraid. I shall abolish from the earth the predatory beast. The sword shall never come upon your land. Justice shall roll down like the waters, and righteousness like a mighty stream. For the earth shall be filled with knowledge of THE OMNIPRESENT, as the waters fill the seas."

On Sukkot continue with Hoshanot, *page 394.*

תְּפִלָּה לְשָׁלוֹם

יְהִי רָצוֹן מִלְּפָנֶיךָ יהוה אֱלֹהֵינוּ וֵאלֹהֵי אֲבוֹתֵינוּ וְאִמּוֹתֵינוּ שֶׁתְּבַטֵּל מִלְחָמוֹת וּשְׁפִיכוּת דָּמִים מִן הָעוֹלָם וְתַמְשִׁיךְ שָׁלוֹם גָּדוֹל וְנִפְלָא בָּעוֹלָם וְלֹא יִשָּׂא גוֹי אֶל גּוֹי חֶרֶב וְלֹא יִלְמְדוּ עוֹד מִלְחָמָה׃

רַק יַכִּירוּ וְיֵדְעוּ כָּל־יוֹשְׁבֵי תֵבֵל הָאֱמֶת לַאֲמִתּוֹ אֲשֶׁר לֹא בָּאנוּ לָזֶה הָעוֹלָם בִּשְׁבִיל רִיב וּמַחֲלֹקֶת וְלֹא בִּשְׁבִיל שִׂנְאָה וְקִנְאָה וְקִנְתּוּר וּשְׁפִיכוּת דָּמִים׃ רַק בָּאנוּ לָעוֹלָם כְּדֵי לְהַכִּיר אוֹתְךָ תִּתְבָּרַךְ לָנֶצַח׃

וּבְכֵן תְּרַחֵם עָלֵינוּ וִיקֻיַּם בָּנוּ מִקְרָא שֶׁכָּתוּב וְנָתַתִּי שָׁלוֹם בָּאָרֶץ וּשְׁכַבְתֶּם וְאֵין מַחֲרִיד וְהִשְׁבַּתִּי חַיָּה רָעָה מִן הָאָרֶץ וְחֶרֶב לֹא תַעֲבֹר בְּאַרְצְכֶם׃ וְיִגַּל כַּמַּיִם מִשְׁפָּט וּצְדָקָה כְּנַחַל אֵיתָן כִּי מָלְאָה הָאָרֶץ דֵּעָה אֶת־יהוה כַּמַּיִם לַיָּם מְכַסִּים׃

Rabbi Nathan Sternhartz of Nemirov

On Sukkot continue with Hoshanot, *page 395.*

ולא ישא...מלחמה / And let no...war (Micah 4:3, Isaiah 2:4).

ונתתי...בארצכם / I shall give you...upon your land (Leviticus 26:6).

ויגל...איתן / Justice...stream (Amos 5:24).

כי...מכסים / For the earth...seas (Isaiah 11:9).

HAḤNASAT SEFER TORAH / RETURNING THE TORAH TO THE ARK

Let all bless the name of THE ETERNAL,
for it alone is to be exalted.

Congregation:
God's splendor dwells on earth and in the heavens,
God has lifted up our people's strength.
Praise to all God's fervent ones,
to the children of Israel, people near to God.
Halleluyah! ↩

The Torah is traditionally carried around the room, although some congregations immediately place it in the ark and continue with Etz Ḥayim Hi.

הַכְנָסַת סֵפֶר תּוֹרָה

יְהַלְלוּ אֶת־שֵׁם יהוה כִּי־נִשְׂגָּב שְׁמוֹ לְבַדּוֹ:

Congregation:

הוֹדוֹ עַל־אֶרֶץ וְשָׁמָיִם וַיָּרֶם קֶרֶן לְעַמּוֹ תְּהִלָּה לְכָל־חֲסִידָיו לִבְנֵי יִשְׂרָאֵל עַם קְרוֹבוֹ הַלְלוּיָהּ: ←

Yehalelu et shem adonay ki nisgav shemo levado.
Hodo al eretz veshamayim vayarem keren le'amo tehilah leḥol ḥasidav livney yisra'el am kerovo halleluyah.

יהללו...הללויה / Let...Halleluyah! (Psalm 148:13-14).

The ark is opened and the Torah placed inside.

And when the Ark was set at rest, they would proclaim:
Restore, ETERNAL ONE, the many thousand troops of Israel!

For it is a precious teaching I have given you,
my Torah: Don't abandon it!

It is a Tree of Life to those that hold fast to it,
all who uphold it may be counted fortunate.

Its ways are ways of pleasantness,
and all its paths are peace.

Return us, PRECIOUS ONE, let us return!
Renew our days, as you have done of old!

The ark is closed.

COMMENTARY. Renew our days as you have done of old.
We may read:
Renew our days as when we were young.
Revive us with the wonder of your world,
  with the enthusiasm of our youth.
Help us to recover something of the child within
  that knew you in the desert
  and trembled at the foot of the mountain.
Grant us, once again, the sacred vision
  and the courage of new beginnings.
Do not return us to days past:
Renew our days as when we were young. S.E.S.

The Torah is traditionally carried around the room, although some congregations immediately place it in the ark and continue with Etz Ḥayim Hi.

The ark is opened and the Torah placed inside.

וּבְנֻחֹה יֹאמַר: שׁוּבָה יהוה רִבְבוֹת אַלְפֵי יִשְׂרָאֵל:
כִּי לֶקַח טוֹב נָתַתִּי לָכֶם תּוֹרָתִי אַל־תַּעֲזֹבוּ:
עֵץ־חַיִּים הִיא לַמַּחֲזִיקִים בָּהּ וְתֹמְכֶיהָ מְאֻשָּׁר:
דְּרָכֶיהָ דַרְכֵי־נֹעַם וְכָל־נְתִיבוֹתֶיהָ שָׁלוֹם:
הֲשִׁיבֵנוּ יהוה אֵלֶיךָ וְנָשׁוּבָה חַדֵּשׁ יָמֵינוּ כְּקֶדֶם:

Etz ḥayim hi lamaḥazikim bah vetomḥeha me'ushar.
Deraḥeha darḥey no'am veḥol netivoteha shalom.
Hashivenu adonay eleyḥa venashuva ḥadesh yameynu kekedem.

The ark is closed.

ובנחה...ישראל / And...Israel (Numbers 10:36).
כי...תעזבו / For...it (Proverbs 4:2).
עץ...מאשר / It...fortunate (Proverbs 3:18).
דרכיה...שלום / Its...peace (Proverbs 3:17).
השיבנו...כקדם / Return...old (Lamentations 5:21).
עץ חיים היא / It is a Tree of Life. At the end of the Garden story, Adam and Eve are forbidden access to the mysterious Tree of Life, whose fruit confers immortality. Yet over the generations to follow, humankind itself *becomes* a Tree of Life. The Torah is handed on from one generation to another, binding the generations in a commonwealth of time and conferring the norms on which the survival of civilization depends. Thus the Torah is compared to the Tree of Life. J.R.

ALEYNU

We rise for Aleynu. *It is customary to bow at "bend the knee." For an alternative version see page 332. Choose one of the following:*

It is up to us to offer praises to the Source of all,
to declare the greatness of the author of Creation,
who gave us teachings of truth
and planted eternal life within us.

It is up to us to offer praises to the Source of all,
to declare the greatness of the author of Creation,
who created heaven's heights and spread out its expanse,
who laid the earth's foundation and brought forth its offspring,
giving life to all its peoples,
the breath of life to all who walk about.

COMMENTARY. This siddur offers several versions of the *Aleynu*. The first, which appeared in the 1945 Reconstructionist siddur, emphasizes that the gift of God's Torah or teaching demands our committed response. The second version, based on Isaiah 42:5 and fit into the *Aleynu* by Rabbi Max D. Klein, emphasizes that our obligation to God flows from our role as part of Creation. The traditional *Aleynu* that appears below the line has troubled Reconstructionist Jews because it implies the inferiority of other faiths and peoples. D.A.T.

עָלֵינוּ

We rise for Aleynu. *It is customary to bow at* korim. *Choose one of the following.*

עָלֵינוּ לְשַׁבֵּחַ לַאֲדוֹן הַכֹּל
לָתֵת גְּדֻלָּה לְיוֹצֵר בְּרֵאשִׁית
שֶׁנָּתַן לָנוּ תּוֹרַת אֱמֶת
וְחַיֵּי עוֹלָם נָטַע בְּתוֹכֵנוּ:

Aleynu leshabe'aḥ la'adon hakol
latet gedulah leyotzer bereyshit
shenatan lanu torat emet
veḥayey olam nata betoḥenu.

Continue on page 171.

עָלֵינוּ לְשַׁבֵּחַ לַאֲדוֹן הַכֹּל
לָתֵת גְּדֻלָּה לְיוֹצֵר בְּרֵאשִׁית
בּוֹרֵא הַשָּׁמַיִם וְנוֹטֵיהֶם
רֹקַע הָאָרֶץ וְצֶאֱצָאֶיהָ
נֹתֵן נְשָׁמָה לָעָם עָלֶיהָ
וְרוּחַ לַהֹלְכִים בָּהּ:

Aleynu leshabe'aḥ la'adon hakol
latet gedulah leyotzer bereyshit.
bore hashamayim venoteyhem
roka ha'aretz vetze'etza'eha
noten neshamah la'am aleha
veru'aḥ laholeḥim ba.

Continue on page 171.

עָלֵינוּ לְשַׁבֵּחַ לַאֲדוֹן הַכֹּל לָתֵת גְּדֻלָּה לְיוֹצֵר בְּרֵאשִׁית שֶׁלֹּא עָשָׂנוּ כְּגוֹיֵי הָאֲרָצוֹת וְלֹא שָׂמָנוּ כְּמִשְׁפְּחוֹת הָאֲדָמָה שֶׁלֹּא שָׂם חֶלְקֵנוּ כָּהֶם וְגוֹרָלֵנוּ כְּכָל הֲמוֹנָם:

It is up to us to offer praises to the Source of all, to declare the greatness of the author of Creation, who has made us different from the other nations of the earth, and situated us in quite a different spot, and made our daily lot another kind from theirs, and given us a destiny uncommon in this world.

And so, we bend the knee and bow,
acknowledging the sovereign who rules
above all those who rule, the blessed Holy One,
who stretched out the heavens and founded the earth,
whose realm embraces heaven's heights,
whose mighty presence stalks celestial ramparts.
This is our God; there is none else besides,
as it is written in the Torah:
"You shall know this day, and bring it home
inside your heart, that THE SUPREME ONE is God
in the heavens above and on the earth below.
There is no other God." ↩

DERASH. Every person and people that feel they have something to live for, and that are bent on living that life in righteousness, are true witnesses of God. M.M.K.

KAVANAH. As the hand held before the eye hides the tallest mountain, so this small earthly life hides from our gaze the vast radiance and secrets of which the world is full, and if we can take life from before our eyes, as one takes away one's hand, we will see the great radiance within the world. M.B. (Adapted)

וידעת...עוד / You...other God (Deuteronomy 4:39).

וַאֲנַחְנוּ כּוֹרְעִים וּמִשְׁתַּחֲוִים וּמוֹדִים לִפְנֵי מֶלֶךְ מַלְכֵי הַמְּלָכִים
הַקָּדוֹשׁ בָּרוּךְ הוּא:
שֶׁהוּא נוֹטֶה שָׁמַיִם וְיוֹסֵד אָרֶץ וּמוֹשַׁב יְקָרוֹ בַּשָּׁמַיִם מִמַּעַל וּשְׁכִינַת
עֻזּוֹ בְּגָבְהֵי מְרוֹמִים: הוּא אֱלֹהֵינוּ אֵין עוֹד: אֱמֶת מַלְכֵּנוּ אֶפֶס זוּלָתוֹ
כַּכָּתוּב בְּתוֹרָתוֹ: וְיָדַעְתָּ הַיּוֹם וַהֲשֵׁבֹתָ אֶל לְבָבֶךָ כִּי יהוה הוּא
הָאֱלֹהִים בַּשָּׁמַיִם מִמַּעַל וְעַל הָאָרֶץ מִתָּחַת אֵין עוֹד:←

Va'anaḥnu korim umishtaḥavim umodim
lifney meleḥ malḥey hamelaḥim hakadosh baruḥ hu.
Shehu noteh shamayim veyosed aretz umoshav yekaro
bashamayim mima'al
ush-ḥinat uzo begovhey meromim.
Hu eloheynu eyn od.
Emet malkenu efes zulato kakatuv betorato.
Veyadata hayom vahashevota el levaveḥa
ki adonay hu ha'elohim bashamayim mima'al ve'al ha'aretz
mitaḥat eyn od.

And so, we put our hope in you,
The Eminence, our God,
that soon we may behold
the full splendor of your might,
and see idolatry vanish from the earth,
and all material gods be swept away,
and the power of your rule repair the world,
and all creatures of flesh call on your name,
and all the wicked of the earth turn back to you.
Let all who dwell upon the globe perceive and know
that to you each knee must bend, each tongue swear oath,
and let them give the glory of your name its precious due.
Let all of them take upon themselves your rule.
Reign over them, soon and for always.
For this is all your realm, throughout all worlds, across all time—
as it is written in your Torah:
"The Eternal One will reign now and forever."

And it is written:
"The Everlasting One will reign
as sovereign over all the earth.
On that day shall The Many-Named be one,
God's name be one!"

Kavanah. A world of God callers is a world of truth and peace, a world where lust for power, greed, and envy—the idols of pride—is uprooted from the individual and group psyche. S.P.W.

עַל כֵּן נְקַוֶּה לְּךָ יהוה אֱלֹהֵינוּ לִרְאוֹת מְהֵרָה בְּתִפְאֶרֶת עֻזֶּךָ לְהַעֲבִיר
גִּלּוּלִים מִן הָאָרֶץ וְהָאֱלִילִים כָּרוֹת יִכָּרֵתוּן לְתַקֵּן עוֹלָם בְּמַלְכוּת
שַׁדַּי: וְכָל בְּנֵי בָשָׂר יִקְרְאוּ בִשְׁמֶךָ: לְהַפְנוֹת אֵלֶיךָ כָּל רִשְׁעֵי אָרֶץ:
יַכִּירוּ וְיֵדְעוּ כָּל יוֹשְׁבֵי תֵבֵל כִּי לְךָ תִּכְרַע כָּל בֶּרֶךְ תִּשָּׁבַע כָּל־לָשׁוֹן:
לְפָנֶיךָ יהוה אֱלֹהֵינוּ יִכְרְעוּ וְיִפֹּלוּ וְלִכְבוֹד שִׁמְךָ יְקָר יִתֵּנוּ וִיקַבְּלוּ
כֻלָּם אֶת עֹל מַלְכוּתֶךָ וְתִמְלֹךְ עֲלֵיהֶם מְהֵרָה לְעוֹלָם וָעֶד: כִּי
הַמַּלְכוּת שֶׁלְּךָ הִיא וּלְעוֹלְמֵי עַד תִּמְלֹךְ בְּכָבוֹד כַּכָּתוּב בְּתוֹרָתֶךָ:
יהוה יִמְלֹךְ לְעֹלָם וָעֶד: וְנֶאֱמַר: וְהָיָה יהוה לְמֶלֶךְ עַל כָּל הָאָרֶץ
בַּיּוֹם הַהוּא יִהְיֶה יהוה אֶחָד וּשְׁמוֹ אֶחָד:

Kakatuv betorateḥa: Adonay yimloḥ le'olam va'ed.
Vene'emar: Vehayah adonay lemeleḥ al kol ha'aretz.
Bayom hahu yihyeh adonay eḥad ushmo eḥad.

DERASH. When senseless hatred reigns on earth and people hide their faces from one another, then heaven is forced to hide its face. But when love comes to rule the earth and people reveal their faces to one another, then the splendor of God will be revealed. M.B. (Adapted)

DERASH. It is not the seeking after God that divides but the claim to have found God and to have discovered the only proper way of obeying God and communing with God. M.M.K. (Adapted)

יהוה...ועד / THE ETERNAL ONE...forever (Exodus 15:18).

והיה...אחד / THE EVERLASTING ONE...one (Zechariah 14:9).

TEFILAT HADEREḤ / TRAVELER'S PRAYER

May it be your will, SHELTERING ONE, our God, God of our ancestors,
that you lead us on the road in peace,
and protect our footsteps,
and enable us to reach our destination,
alive and well, happy and safe.
Protect us from all harm and mishap on the road,
and grant us favor, kindness, and compassion,
in your own eyes and the eyes of all who may behold us.
May you hear our voice of prayer.

When Tefilat Hadereḥ *is inserted in the* Amidah, *continue* Shaḥarit *on page 118,* Minḥah *on page 234, and* Ma'ariv *on page 312.*

A prayer for the journey
We could say it every day
When we first leave the soft warmth of our beds
And don't know for sure if we'll return at night
When we get in the trains, planes & automobiles
And put our lives in the hands of many strangers.
Or when we leave our homes for a day, a week, a month or more—
Will we return to a peaceful home? Untouched by fire, flood or crime?
How will our travels change us?
What gives us the courage to go through that door?

A prayer for the journey.
For the journey we take in this fragile vessel of flesh.
A finite number of years and we will reach
The unknown, where it all began.
Every life, every day, every hour is a journey.
In the travel is the discovery,
the wisdom, the joy.
Every life, every day, every hour is a journey.
In the travel is the reward,
the peace, the blessing.

S.P.W.

תְּפִלַּת הַדֶּרֶךְ

יְהִי רָצוֹן מִלְּפָנֶיךָ יהוה אֱלֹהֵינוּ וֵאלֹהֵי אֲבוֹתֵינוּ וְאִמּוֹתֵינוּ שֶׁתּוֹלִיכֵנוּ
לְשָׁלוֹם וְתַצְעִידֵנוּ לְשָׁלוֹם וְתַגִּיעֵנוּ אֶל מְחוֹז חֶפְצֵנוּ לְחַיִּים וּלְשִׂמְחָה
וּלְשָׁלוֹם: וְתַצִּילֵנוּ מִכַּף כָּל אוֹיֵב וְאוֹרֵב וְאָסוֹן בַּדֶּרֶךְ וְתִתְּנֵנוּ לְחֵן
וּלְחֶסֶד וּלְרַחֲמִים בְּעֵינֶיךָ וּבְעֵינֵי כָל רוֹאֵינוּ: וְתִשְׁמַע קוֹל תַּחֲנוּנֵינוּ:

When Tefilat Hadereḥ *is inserted in the* Amidah, *continue* Shaḥarit *on page 119,* Minḥah *on page 235, and* Ma'ariv *on page 313.*

NOTE. *Tefilat Hadereḥ* is a prayer for a safe journey. It is similar in form and intent to a *mi sheberaḥ* prayer, which can be adapted to recognize and honor many different times and events in life. See pages 156-157 and the note on page 154 regarding how to modify the text given, or see *Kol Haneshamah: Shabbat and Festivals* for additional *mi sheberaḥ* prayers. J.B.

COMMENTARY. Why do we still pray in Hebrew, when we so often do not understand the language of our prayer? Because Hebrew shapes spiritual communication in a way not paralleled by our various modern languages. A case in point: our prayer begins יהי רצון מלפניך, which is translated above as May it be your will. If translated very literally, the words mean "May it be a want from-to your face." This is a very peculiar expression. "Face" in Hebrew often refers to presence, but it does so by way of direct encounter. מלפני / From-to is a preposition often used to mean "before", but it connotes the back-and-forth motion of dialogue. Thus we are speaking of a powerful exchange between two presences, and a flow of mutuality. What appears idiomatically to be a plea turns out to be, in living Hebrew, a relationship. W.S.

SHIR SHEL YOM / THE DAILY PSALM

On Sunday the following psalm is traditionally recited.

Today is the first day of the week, on which the Temple Levites used to sing the following psalm:

A psalm of David.

The world belongs to GOD in all its fullness,
the earth, and all who dwell on it.

For God has founded it upon the waters,
upon the torrents, God established it.

Who can ascend onto the mount of THE ETERNAL?
who can rise up to the holy place of God?

The one whose hands are clean, whose heart is pure,
the one who has not lifted up his soul in vanity,
the one who never swore deceitfully.

That person reaps a blessing from the OMNIPRESENT,
justice from the God of help.

For many generations now,
the family of Jacob have sought out your presence. It is so!

You city gates, raise up your bolts,
you gates to the eternal, open up,
and let the sovereign of glory come! ↩

שִׁיר שֶׁל יוֹם

On Sunday the following Psalm is traditionally recited.

הַיּוֹם יוֹם רִאשׁוֹן בְּשַׁבָּת שֶׁבּוֹ הָיוּ הַלְוִיִּם אוֹמְרִים בְּבֵית הַמִּקְדָּשׁ:

לְדָוִד מִזְמוֹר

לַיהוה הָאָֽרֶץ וּמְלוֹאָהּ תֵּבֵל וְיֹֽשְׁבֵי בָהּ:

כִּי הוּא עַל יַמִּים יְסָדָהּ וְעַל נְהָרוֹת יְכוֹנְנֶֽהָ:

מִי יַעֲלֶה בְהַר יהוה וּמִי יָקוּם בִּמְקוֹם קָדְשׁוֹ:

נְקִי כַפַּֽיִם וּבַר לֵבָב אֲשֶׁר לֹא נָשָׂא לַשָּׁוְא נַפְשִׁי

וְלֹא נִשְׁבַּע לְמִרְמָה:

יִשָּׂא בְרָכָה מֵאֵת יהוה וּצְדָקָה מֵאֱלֹהֵי יִשְׁעוֹ:

זֶה דּוֹר דֹּרְשָׁיו מְבַקְשֵׁי פָנֶיךָ יַעֲקֹב, סֶֽלָה:

שְׂאוּ שְׁעָרִים רָאשֵׁיכֶם וְהִנָּשְׂאוּ פִּתְחֵי עוֹלָם

וְיָבוֹא מֶֽלֶךְ הַכָּבוֹד: ←

COMMENTARY. The seven psalms designated as daily psalms culminate in the psalm for the Sabbath day. The week begins and ends in harmony, but in the middle we are exposed to a world of terrible suffering. How are we to deal with it? On Sunday harmony is created through a partnership between us and God. God established creation as a perfect unity; our part is to live a pure life and thereby earn the right to enter into God's holy Temple. On Monday the holiness of Jerusalem is attacked, and disaster is only narrowly averted. On Tuesday, not only Jerusalem is threatened; the whole of the earth has been given over to pagan gods who govern with no concern for justice. On Wednesday we reach the nadir of injustice; the Jewish people are oppressed by their enemies. On Thursday Israel's woes are laid on its backsliding. On Friday, waters seem to threaten the stability of the earth, God's voice and plan are mightier still. On Shabbat, the ultimate defeat of the wicked is envisioned. The righteous, who meditate on God's works, know that their faith will be rewarded. Shabbat is the day of true vision, on which all the contradictions of everyday existence are resolved. In this respect, it is a harbinger of the messianic era, a foretaste, as the tradition teaches, of a time that is to be all Shabbat. H.L.

Who is the sovereign of glory?
The MAGNIFICENT, so powerful and mighty!
THE ETERNAL ONE, a champion in battle!

You city gates, raise up your bolts,
you gates to the eternal, open up,
and let the sovereign of glory come!

Who is this one, the sovereign of glory?
THE CREATOR of the Throngs of Heaven is this one,
the sovereign of glory. It is so!

Psalm 24

Continue on page 196 (Psalm 27), 200 (Psalm 49) or 204 (Mourners' Kaddish).

KAVANAH. The Levites' Temple ritual for each day of the week marks the change from an agricultural/herding-centered society to a town/craft-centered society. Farmers' units of time are the moon and seasons. For the craftsperson the regular weekly market days measure and order tasks. The potter must work clay on Sunday, throw it on Monday and fire it on Tuesday in order to sell the pot on Thursday. The daily psalms similarly progress through the week. We can use this point in the service to plan how we will bring Jewish values into today's tasks. E.M.

מִי זֶה מֶ֫לֶךְ הַכָּבוֹד
יהוה עִזּוּז וְגִבּוֹר יהוה גִּבּוֹר מִלְחָמָה:
* שְׂאוּ שְׁעָרִים רָאשֵׁיכֶם וּשְׂאוּ פִּתְחֵי עוֹלָם
וְיָבֹא מֶ֫לֶךְ הַכָּבוֹד:
מִי הוּא זֶה מֶ֫לֶךְ הַכָּבוֹד
יהוה צְבָאוֹת הוּא מֶ֫לֶךְ הַכָּבוֹד סֶ֫לָה:

Continue on page 197 (Psalm 27), 201 (Psalm 49) or 205 (Mourners' Kaddish).

COMMENTARY. This psalm is known by scholars as an Entrance Liturgy, a song used to accompany a procession of worshippers into the Temple. After invoking the earth founded on the waters, the psalm focuses on the Temple, the mountain of Yah, as the goal of each individual's religious aspirations. The psalm asks a basic question of each aspiring worshipper: are you worthy to enter here? As you come in to pray, will you be bringing the best of yourself? If so, your reward will be blessing and righteousness. The psalm upholds an ideal of purity in deeds and thought, leaving to each individual the personal work of self-purification. The conclusion of the psalm offers the excitement of the entrance itself: walking through the massive gates, through which Yah, the Glorious Ruler, is about to enter.

H.L.

On Monday the following psalm is traditionally recited.

Today is the second day of the week, on which the Temple Levites used to sing the following psalm:

A song, a psalm belonging to the clan of Koraḥ.

Great is THE CREATOR, powerful should be our praise,
within God's city, and upon God's mount.

Its view is beautiful, a joy to all the earth,
from Zion's mount to furthest north,
the city of a mighty sovereign.

Within its palaces is God made manifest,
our source of strength.

For, yes, the rulers of the nations met,
united in a league against us.

But they beheld and were amazed;
thrown into fright, they tried to run.

A trembling assailed them;
there they suffered turmoil like one giving birth.

With the east wind you would smash the ships of Tarshish.
As we have heard, so did we see,

within the citadel of THE CREATOR of the Throngs of Heaven,
within the city of our God, may God establish it forever!

We have depicted for ourselves, O God, your steadfast love,
amid your palace. ↩

On Monday the following psalm is traditionally recited.

הַיּוֹם יוֹם שֵׁנִי בְּשַׁבָּת שֶׁבּוֹ הָיוּ הַלְוִיִּם אוֹמְרִים בְּבֵית הַמִּקְדָּשׁ:

שִׁיר מִזְמוֹר לִבְנֵי קֹֽרַח:

גָּדוֹל יהוה וּמְהֻלָּל מְאֹד בְּעִיר אֱלֹהֵינוּ הַר קָדְשׁוֹ:

יְפֵה נוֹף מְשׂוֹשׂ כָּל הָאָֽרֶץ הַר צִיּוֹן יַרְכְּתֵי צָפוֹן

קִרְיַת מֶֽלֶךְ רָב:

אֱלֹהִים בְּאַרְמְנוֹתֶֽיהָ נוֹדַע לְמִשְׂגָּב:

כִּי הִנֵּה הַמְּלָכִים נוֹעֲדוּ עָבְרוּ יַחְדָּו:

הֵמָּה רָאוּ כֵּן תָּמָֽהוּ נִבְהֲלוּ נֶחְפָּֽזוּ:

רְעָדָה אֲחָזָֽתַם שָׁם חִיל כַּיּוֹלֵדָה:

בְּרֽוּחַ קָדִים תְּשַׁבֵּר אֳנִיּוֹת תַּרְשִׁישׁ:

כַּאֲשֶׁר שָׁמַֽעְנוּ כֵּן רָאִינוּ בְּעִיר יהוה צְבָאוֹת

בְּעִיר אֱלֹהֵֽינוּ אֱלֹהִים יְכוֹנְנֶֽהָ עַד עוֹלָם סֶֽלָה:

דִּמִּֽינוּ אֱלֹהִים חַסְדֶּֽךָ בְּקֶֽרֶב הֵיכָלֶֽךָ: ←

COMMENTARY. This psalm, centering on Zion, contrasts the beauty and majesty of the holy city with a great disaster that was narrowly averted: the attempt by distant foreign kings to overthrow Jerusalem. We hear two stories of how they were turned back: miraculously, by the mere sight of God's city, and by an east wind, which broke up their ships in the Mediterranean. Had they made it to land, their siege would have encircled the city. Instead, the psalm invites the pilgrim worshippers to circle it, count its towers, note its ramparts, and take home stories of the city of God to hand down through the ages, as this psalm itself has been handed down to us. H.L.

As is your name, O God, so is your praise,
extending to the furthest reaches of the earth;
filled with justice is your right hand.

Let Zion's mount rejoice! Let Judah's women dance with joy,
in celebration of your justice.

Circle Zion, and surround it,
count its towers,

pay attention to its ramparts,
pass between its palaces,
that you might tell it many generations hence:

that this is God, our God for all eternity,
who guides us for as long as we may live.

Psalm 48

Continue on page 196 (Psalm 27), 200 (Psalm 49) or 204 (Mourners' Kaddish).

כְּשִׁמְךָ אֱלֹהִים כֵּן תְּהִלָּתְךָ

עַל קַצְוֵי אֶרֶץ צֶדֶק מָלְאָה יְמִינֶךָ׃

יִשְׂמַח הַר צִיּוֹן תָּגֵלְנָה בְּנוֹת יְהוּדָה לְמַעַן מִשְׁפָּטֶיךָ׃

סֹבּוּ צִיּוֹן וְהַקִּיפוּהָ סִפְרוּ מִגְדָּלֶיהָ׃

* שִׁיתוּ לִבְּכֶם לְחֵילָה פַּסְּגוּ אַרְמְנוֹתֶיהָ

לְמַעַן תְּסַפְּרוּ לְדוֹר אַחֲרוֹן׃

כִּי זֶה אֱלֹהִים אֱלֹהֵינוּ עוֹלָם וָעֶד הוּא יְנַהֲגֵנוּ עַל מוּת׃

Continue on page 197 (Psalm 27), 201 (Psalm 49), or 205 (Mourners' Kaddish).

Note. Koraḥ is famed for leading a rebellion against the authority of Moses during the forty years of wandering in the wilderness. According to the account in Numbers 16, at the end of the rebellion the earth opened up and swallowed Koraḥ and all of his supporters. How then can it be that some of the psalms are attributed to Koraḥ's descendants? Clearly, they remained welcome among the Israelites! We are judged not by who our ancestors were but for ourselves. D.A.T.

On Tuesday the following psalm is traditionally recited.

Today is the third day of the week, on which the Temple Levites used to sing the following psalm:

A psalm of Asaph.

God takes a stand amid the councils of the mighty;
among the judges, God will render judgment:

"How long will you continue to judge wrongly,
favoring the wicked? Yes, it's so!

Defend the lowly and the orphaned;
for the poor and the impoverished, establish justice.

Rescue the downtrodden,
save them from the clutches of the wicked.

For they know not what to do, they do not understand;
they walk about in darkness.
Let the pillars of the earth be moved!

I say that you have godlike powers,
all of you are children of the highest realm.

And yet, as earthborn, you shall die.
As one, you rulers of the earth shall fall!"

Arise, God, judge the earth,
for all the nations of the world belong to you!

Psalm 82

Continue on page 196 (Psalm 27), 200 (Psalm 49) or 204 (Mourners' Kaddish).

On Tuesday the following psalm is traditionally recited.

הַיּוֹם יוֹם שְׁלִישִׁי בְּשַׁבָּת שֶׁבּוֹ הָיוּ הַלְוִיִּם אוֹמְרִים בְּבֵית הַמִּקְדָּשׁ:

מִזְמוֹר לְאָסָף אֱלֹהִים נִצָּב בַּעֲדַת אֵל בְּקֶרֶב אֱלֹהִים יִשְׁפֹּט:
עַד מָתַי תִּשְׁפְּטוּ עָוֶל וּפְנֵי רְשָׁעִים תִּשְׂאוּ סֶלָה:
שִׁפְטוּ דָל וְיָתוֹם עָנִי וָרָשׁ הַצְדִּיקוּ:
פַּלְּטוּ דַל וְאֶבְיוֹן מִיַּד רְשָׁעִים הַצִּילוּ:
לֹא יָדְעוּ וְלֹא יָבִינוּ בַּחֲשֵׁכָה יִתְהַלָּכוּ יִמּוֹטוּ כָּל מוֹסְדֵי אָרֶץ:
אֲנִי אָמַרְתִּי אֱלֹהִים אַתֶּם וּבְנֵי עֶלְיוֹן כֻּלְּכֶם:
אָכֵן כְּאָדָם תְּמוּתוּן וּכְאַחַד הַשָּׂרִים תִּפֹּלוּ:
*קוּמָה אֱלֹהִים שָׁפְטָה הָאָרֶץ כִּי אַתָּה תִנְחַל בְּכָל־הַגּוֹיִם:

Continue on page 197 (Psalm 27), 201 (Psalm 49) or 205 (Mourners' Kaddish).

COMMENTARY. This psalm describes an imaginary scenario set in heaven. The Supreme God, *Elohim*, has put on trial the whole pantheon of *El*, the gods of the surrounding pagan nations. God challenges these supposed deities to do justice, in exactly the same way that the prophets challenged the Jewish people: Care for the poor, the widow, and the orphan; overturn the sway of the wicked. In an aside, God reveals that these gods are really not gods at all, but simply mighty beings abusing their power, who will lose it when they die. The multiple ironies of the psalm converge in the last line, where the psalmist turns back to *Elohim*, urging God to practice the justice that God has preached. Like Abraham, this psalmist in effect asks: "Shall not the Judge of all the earth deal justly?" (Gen. 18:25) H.L.

NOTE. Asaph, a Levite, had descendants who formed the choir in the Temple (*see* Ezra 2:41, Nehemiah 7:44). The ascription here suggests that this clan had psalms of its own. Whether written by Asaph or his descendants, they have become part of our common heritage. D.A.T.

On Wednesday the following psalm is traditionally recited.

Today is the fourth day of the week, on which the Temple Levites used to sing this psalm:

ETERNAL ONE, God who exacts strict justice,
God exacting justice, show yourself!

Raise yourself, judge of the earth,
render retribution to the proud!

How long, ALMIGHTY ONE, shall evildoers,
yes, how long shall evildoers triumph?

Hear them rant; they speak in arrogance,
all workers of injustice boast aloud.

Your people, HIDDEN ONE, are beaten down,
your heritage is being oppressed.

They kill the widow and the stranger,
they murder orphans.

They say: "Yah doesn't see,
the God of Jacob doesn't care."

You'd better care, you who consume the people!
You fools, when will you understand?

Shall one who plants the ear in us not hear?
Shall the creator of our eye not watch?

Shall the one who has taught nations not give argument,
the one who has taught human beings their knowledge?

THE ALL-SEEING ONE can know a person's thoughts,
and truly those are nothing!

Happy is the person you will chasten, Yah,
the person you will teach from your Torah,

providing rest from days of evil,
while for evildoers shall the grave be dug. ↩

On Wednesday the following psalm is traditionally recited.

הַיּוֹם יוֹם רְבִיעִי בְּשַׁבָּת שֶׁבּוֹ הָיוּ הַלְוִיִּם אוֹמְרִים בְּבֵית הַמִּקְדָּשׁ:

אֵל נְקָמוֹת יהוה אֵל נְקָמוֹת הוֹפִֽיעַ׃
הִנָּשֵׂא שֹׁפֵט הָאָֽרֶץ הָשֵׁב גְּמוּל עַל גֵּאִים׃
עַד מָתַי רְשָׁעִים יהוה עַד מָתַי רְשָׁעִים יַעֲלֹֽזוּ׃
יַבִּֽיעוּ יְדַבְּרוּ עָתָק יִתְאַמְּרוּ כָּל פּוֹעֲלֵי אָֽוֶן׃
עַמְּךָ יהוה יְדַכְּאוּ וְנַחֲלָתְךָ יְעַנּוּ׃
אַלְמָנָה וְגֵר יַהֲרֹֽגוּ וִיתוֹמִים יְרַצֵּֽחוּ׃
וַיֹּאמְרוּ לֹא יִרְאֶה יָּהּ וְלֹא יָבִין אֱלֹהֵי יַעֲקֹב׃
בִּֽינוּ בֹּעֲרִים בָּעָם וּכְסִילִים מָתַי תַּשְׂכִּילוּ׃
הֲנֹטַע אֹֽזֶן הֲלֹא יִשְׁמָע אִם יֹצֵר עַֽיִן הֲלֹא יַבִּיט׃
הֲיֹסֵֽר גּוֹיִם הֲלֹא יוֹכִֽיחַ הַמְלַמֵּד אָדָם דָּֽעַת׃
יהוה יֹדֵֽעַ מַחְשְׁבוֹת אָדָם כִּי הֵֽמָּה הָֽבֶל׃
אַשְׁרֵי הַגֶּֽבֶר אֲשֶׁר תְּיַסְּרֶֽנּוּ יָּהּ וּמִתּוֹרָתְךָ תְלַמְּדֶֽנּוּ׃
לְהַשְׁקִיט לוֹ מִֽימֵי רָע עַד יִכָּרֶה לָרָשָׁע שָֽׁחַת׃ ←

Commentary. The first line of this psalm can easily stop us in our tracks. We may not want to believe in a God of retribution, let alone pray to one. But, there is more at stake in this psalm than the all-too-human desire for vengeance. The paramount issue in the psalm is the nature of justice in the world, and God's relationship to that justice. The psalmist is living in a time of great misfortune for the Jewish people, who are being afflicted and crushed by their enemies. How long can this go on without a response from God? The psalmist needs God to protect against evildoers, to once again bring together *tzedek* and *mishpat*, justice and judgment. Together with its questions and challenges, this psalm retains an abiding faith that God will not forsake the Jewish people. One can easily imagine this psalm being prayed amidst utter destruction. Its combination of stubborn faithfulness and powerful challenge to faith can help our generation of worshippers continue to bring our questions and our yearning to prayer. H.L.

For God shall never spurn this people,
the inheritance of God shall never be forsaken.

For law shall once again serve righteousness,
and all honest of heart shall follow it.

Who can stand against me among evildoers?
Who of all the workers of injustice can prevail against me?

Were THE JUST ONE not a help to me,
my soul by now would be inhabiting the grave.

And when I've said, "My foot has slipped,"
your love, DEAR ONE, has helped sustain me.

With a multitude of anguished thoughts within me,
your consoling has brought pleasure to my soul.

Can the throne of wicked rulers be allied to you?
Can one who wreaks injustice by decree?

Let them try to come in league against the righteous soul!
Let them try to work their bloodshed on the innocent!

THE REDEEMING ONE remains my stronghold,
God is for me a fortress rock,

who pays them back for all their unjust ways,
and for their evil, THE ETERNAL ONE, our God
destroys them, yes, destroys them thoroughly!

Psalm 94

Come, sing in ecstasy to THE ETERNAL ONE,
ring out a fanfare to our rock of rescue!

Hurry forth in thanks before the Presence,
shouting in song to God.

For THE REDEEMER is a generous divinity,
a sovereign greater than all image-gods.

Psalm 95:1-3

Continue on page 196 (Psalm 27), 200 (Psalm 49) or 204 (Mourners' Kaddish).

כִּי לֹא יִטֹּשׁ יהוה עַמּוֹ וְנַחֲלָתוֹ לֹא יַעֲזֹב׃
כִּי עַד צֶדֶק יָשׁוּב מִשְׁפָּט וְאַחֲרָיו כָּל יִשְׁרֵי לֵב׃
מִי יָקוּם לִי עִם מְרֵעִים מִי יִתְיַצֵּב לִי עִם פֹּעֲלֵי אָוֶן׃
לוּלֵי יהוה עֶזְרָתָה לִּי כִּמְעַט שָׁכְנָה דוּמָה נַפְשִׁי׃
אִם אָמַרְתִּי מָטָה רַגְלִי חַסְדְּךָ יהוה יִסְעָדֵנִי׃
בְּרֹב שַׂרְעַפַּי בְּקִרְבִּי תַּנְחוּמֶיךָ יְשַׁעַשְׁעוּ נַפְשִׁי׃
הַיְחָבְרְךָ כִּסֵּא הַוּוֹת יֹצֵר עָמָל עֲלֵי חֹק׃
יָגוֹדּוּ עַל נֶפֶשׁ צַדִּיק וְדָם נָקִי יַרְשִׁיעוּ׃
וַיְהִי יהוה לִי לְמִשְׂגָּב, וֵאלֹהַי לְצוּר מַחְסִי׃
וַיָּשֶׁב עֲלֵיהֶם אֶת אוֹנָם וּבְרָעָתָם יַצְמִיתֵם יַצְמִיתֵם יהוה אֱלֹהֵינוּ׃
*לְכוּ נְרַנְּנָה לַיהוה נָרִיעָה לְצוּר יִשְׁעֵנוּ׃
נְקַדְּמָה פָנָיו בְּתוֹדָה בִּזְמִרוֹת נָרִיעַ לוֹ׃
כִּי אֵל גָּדוֹל יהוה וּמֶלֶךְ גָּדוֹל עַל כָּל־אֱלֹהִים׃

Continue on page 197 (Psalm 27), 201 (Psalm 49), or 205 (Mourners' Kaddish).

COMMENTARY. The rabbis who arranged the text of the siddur added the first verses of Psalm 95 to Psalm 94. Thus, worshippers do not leave God's presence with a prayer for the annihilation of their enemies, but rather with the praise of God on their lips. H.L.

On Thursday the following psalm is traditionally recited.

Today is the fifth day of the week, on which the Temple Levities used to sing the following psalm:

For the chief musician, to a Gathite melody; by Asaph.

Sing joyful song to God, our strength,
make joyous sounds for Jacob's God!

Raise up a song, and strike the tambourine,
pluck sweetly on the strings, accompanied by harp.

Blast piercing notes upon the shofar for the New Moon,
for the full moon, for our festive holiday.

For it is Israel's law,
a statute of the God of Jacob.

God established it in Joseph's clans,
when going forth against the land of Egypt;
I heard a language that I didn't know.

"I have relieved their shoulders from their burdens,
their hands are freed from carrying the basket.

In sorrow you called out, and I released you,
I answered from my hidden place where thunder rolls,
I tried you at Meribah's waters. So it was!

Listen, my people, I admonish you!
Israel, if you only would pay heed to me!

Let you not have among you alien gods,
let you not bow down to exotic gods.

I am THE REDEEMING ONE, your God,
who brings you up out of the land of Egypt,
open up your mouth, and I shall fill it!

But my people did not listen to my voice,
no, Israel did not care for me. ↩

On Thursday the following psalm is traditionally recited.

הַיּוֹם יוֹם חֲמִישִׁי בַּשַּׁבָּת שֶׁבּוֹ הָיוּ הַלְוִיִּם אוֹמְרִים בְּבֵית הַמִּקְדָּשׁ׃

לַמְנַצֵּחַ עַל הַגִּתִּית לְאָסָף׃

הַרְנִינוּ לֵאלֹהִים עוּזֵּנוּ הָרִיעוּ לֵאלֹהֵי יַעֲקֹב׃
שְׂאוּ זִמְרָה וּתְנוּ תֹף כִּנּוֹר נָעִים עִם נָבֶל׃
תִּקְעוּ בַחֹדֶשׁ שׁוֹפָר בַּכֶּסֶה לְיוֹם חַגֵּנוּ׃
כִּי חֹק לְיִשְׂרָאֵל הוּא מִשְׁפָּט לֵאלֹהֵי יַעֲקֹב׃
עֵדוּת בִּיהוֹסֵף שָׂמוֹ בְּצֵאתוֹ עַל אֶרֶץ מִצְרָיִם שְׂפַת לֹא יָדַעְתִּי אֶשְׁמָע׃
הֲסִירוֹתִי מִסֵּבֶל שִׁכְמוֹ כַּפָּיו מִדּוּד תַּעֲבֹרְנָה׃
בַּצָּרָה קָרָאתָ וָאֲחַלְּצֶךָּ אֶעֶנְךָ בְּסֵתֶר רַעַם אֶבְחָנְךָ עַל מֵי מְרִיבָה סֶלָה׃
שְׁמַע עַמִּי וְאָעִידָה בָּךְ יִשְׂרָאֵל אִם תִּשְׁמַע לִי׃
לֹא יִהְיֶה בְךָ אֵל זָר וְלֹא תִשְׁתַּחֲוֶה לְאֵל נֵכָר׃
אָנֹכִי יהוה אֱלֹהֶיךָ הַמַּעַלְךָ מֵאֶרֶץ מִצְרָיִם הַרְחֶב פִּיךָ וַאֲמַלְאֵהוּ׃
וְלֹא שָׁמַע עַמִּי לְקוֹלִי וְיִשְׂרָאֵל לֹא אָבָה לִי׃ ←

COMMENTARY. Much of this psalm is structured around the importance of listening. God heard Israel's strange language in Egypt. Then, at Sinai, "the secret place of thunder," Israel heard and accepted the commandments. Finally, at Meribah, which stands for the entire forty years in the wilderness, Israel rebelled by attacking God for bringing them to die in the wilderness. The psalmist implores the people with the voice of God, "Israel, if you would but listen to me!" This focus on listening suggests Israel's responsibility for its own destiny. Israel's redemption depends on hearing the revelatory command, "You shall have no other god." H.L.

So I sent away the people in their stubbornness of heart,
I let them go according to their own devices.

Would that my people might listen to me,
yes, would that Israel walked according to my ways!

How quickly would I crush their enemies,
on their oppressors would I cast my hand.

Those who hate GOD would cringe before my people;
I would stand beside them always.

God would feed them from the choicest wheat.
Yes, from the rock I'd feed you honey in abundance.

Psalm 81

Continue on page 196 (Psalm 27), 200 (Psalm 49) or 204 (Mourners' Kaddish).

וָאֲשַׁלְּחֵהוּ בִּשְׁרִירוּת לִבָּם יֵלְכוּ בְּמוֹעֲצוֹתֵיהֶם׃
לוּ עַמִּי שֹׁמֵעַ לִי יִשְׂרָאֵל בִּדְרָכַי יְהַלֵּכוּ׃
כִּמְעַט אוֹיְבֵיהֶם אַכְנִיעַ וְעַל צָרֵיהֶם אָשִׁיב יָדִי׃
מְשַׂנְאֵי יהוה יְכַחֲשׁוּ לוֹ וִיהִי עִתָּם לְעוֹלָם׃
*וַיַּאֲכִילֵהוּ מֵחֵלֶב חִטָּה וּמִצּוּר דְּבַשׁ אַשְׂבִּיעֶךָ׃

Continue on page 197 (Psalm 27), 201 (Psalm 49) or 205 (Mourners' Kaddish).

NOTE. The appellation, "For the chief musician, to a Gathite melody," occurs dozens of times at the beginning of psalms, as at the end of the book of Habakuk. Often it occurs alongside references to Asaph, the clan of Levite singers. This suggests that the choir leader either composed or directed the performance of these compositions. D.A.T.

On Friday the following psalm is traditionally recited.

Today is the sixth day of the week, on which the Temple Levites used to sing this psalm:

THE ETERNAL reigns, is clothed in majesty,
THE INVISIBLE is clothed, is girded up with might.

The world is now established,
it cannot give way.

Your Throne was long ago secured,
beyond eternity are You.

The rivers raise, ALMIGHTY ONE,
the rivers raise a roaring sound,
the floods raise up torrential waves,

but louder than the sound of mighty waters,
more exalted than the breakers of the sea,
raised up on high are you, THE INEXPRESSIBLE.

Your precepts have retained their truth,
and holiness befits your house,
ETERNAL ONE, forever and a day.

Psalm 93

Continue on page 196 (Psalm 27), 200 (Psalm 49) or 204 (Mourners' Kaddish).

COMMENTARY. This psalm shows us the universe, not from our perspective, but from God's. It is essentially a glimpse from here to eternity. Waters, earth, heavens; primordial time, present time, future time—all are included in the divine cosmic view. What holds our universe together, in the final image of the psalm, is the divine presence that brings harmony to the world's multiplicity. It is that harmony which the psalm encourages us to seek. H.L.

On Friday the following psalm is traditionally recited.

הַיּוֹם יוֹם שִׁשִּׁי בְּשַׁבָּת שֶׁבּוֹ הָיוּ הַלְוִיִּם אוֹמְרִים בְּבֵית הַמִּקְדָּשׁ:

יְהוָה מָלָךְ גֵּאוּת לָבֵשׁ   לָבֵשׁ יהוה עֹז הִתְאַזָּר
אַף תִּכּוֹן תֵּבֵל בַּל תִּמּוֹט:
נָכוֹן כִּסְאֲךָ מֵאָז   מֵעוֹלָם אָתָּה:
נָשְׂאוּ נְהָרוֹת יהוה   נָשְׂאוּ נְהָרוֹת קוֹלָם
יִשְׂאוּ נְהָרוֹת דָּכְיָם:
מִקֹּלוֹת מַיִם רַבִּים   אַדִּירִים מִשְׁבְּרֵי־יָם
אַדִּיר בַּמָּרוֹם יהוה:
עֵדֹתֶיךָ נֶאֶמְנוּ מְאֹד   לְבֵיתְךָ נַאֲוָה־קֹּדֶשׁ
יהוה לְאֹרֶךְ יָמִים:

Continue on page 197 (Psalm 27), 201 (Psalm 49) or 205 (Mourners' Kaddish).

The following psalm is traditionally recited each morning and evening from Rosh Ḥodesh Elul through Hoshanah Rabah.

[A psalm] of David

THE ETERNAL is my light and my salvation; whom, then, should I fear?
THE ALMIGHTY is my living source of strength; before whom should I tremble?

When evildoers approach to eat my flesh, when tormenters and enemies come after me,
see how they stumble; see how they tumble down!

Should a force encamp against me, my heart shall have no fear;
should a war arise against me, in one thing I shall trust,

one thing have I asked of GOD, one goal do I pursue: to dwell in THE ETERNAL's house throughout my days,
to know the bliss of THE SUBLIME, to visit in God's temple.

Truly, in a day of trouble, I am nestled in God's shelter, hidden in the recess of God's tent.
God sets me high upon a rock. ↩

KAVANAH. Throughout history it has been true that sometimes good people suffer through no fault of their own. The psalmist is not so naive as to be unaware of this reality. How can there be shelter in the midst of swarming enemies? With physical protection unlikely, the shelter invoked here provides not physical but spiritual succor. The psalmist seeks the calm and bliss that come from an awareness of the divine made manifest in the workings of the human heart. With this sense of a greatness that transcends physical peril, enemies' violence causes no fear, and slanderers can do little damage. Living directed to the divine gives us the power not to avoid mortal danger, but to transcend our fear of it. D.A.T.

The following psalm is traditionally recited each morning and evening from Rosh Ḥodesh Elul through Hoshanah Rabah.

לְדָוִד

יהוה אוֹרִי וְיִשְׁעִי מִמִּי אִירָא:
יהוה מָעוֹז חַיַּי מִמִּי אֶפְחָד:
בִּקְרֹב עָלַי מְרֵעִים לֶאֱכֹל אֶת בְּשָׂרִי
צָרַי וְאֹיְבַי לִי הֵמָּה כָשְׁלוּ וְנָפָלוּ:
אִם תַּחֲנֶה עָלַי מַחֲנֶה לֹא יִירָא לִבִּי
אִם תָּקוּם עָלַי מִלְחָמָה בְּזֹאת אֲנִי בוֹטֵחַ:
אַחַת שָׁאַלְתִּי מֵאֵת יהוה אוֹתָהּ אֲבַקֵּשׁ
שִׁבְתִּי בְּבֵית יהוה כָּל יְמֵי חַיַּי לַחֲזוֹת בְּנֹעַם יהוה וּלְבַקֵּר בְּהֵיכָלוֹ:
כִּי יִצְפְּנֵנִי בְּסֻכֹּו בְּיוֹם רָעָה יַסְתִּרֵנִי בְּסֵתֶר אָהֳלוֹ בְּצוּר יְרוֹמְמֵנִי: ←

Aḥat sha'alti me'et adonay otah avakesh, shivti beveyt adonay kol yemey ḥayay laḥazot beno'am adonay ulevaker beheyḥalo.

COMMENTARY. We say this psalm every day from the first of Elul through Hoshanah Rabah. The rabbis doubtless chose it to accompany us through every phase of the fall holiday season because it encompasses such a range of powerful emotions. Identifying with the experience of the speaker can help us to be in touch with our fears of abandonment, our need for security, our yearning for joyful religious experience, our need for guidance from God, or our steadying commitment to never lose hope. Above all, we experience the psalmist's vulnerability. Feeling that it is possible to be hidden and secure within God's presence, the speaker also knows, by contrast, the terrible fear that God can hide the divine countenance and seem utterly unavailable. The psalm delicately balances these two kinds of hiddenness, as it tries to find a metaphoric "level path," the right way of walking in a difficult, dangerous world. The psalm ends by urging that we seek out God, clinging to hope in the return of God's presence. H.L.

And now, my head is raised in triumph on my foes around me,
and I offer sacrifice in celebration in God's tent.
I offer song and melody to MY REDEEMER.

Hear me, PRECIOUS ONE, I call aloud;
be gracious to me, answer me!

To you my heart cries out, to you my face is turned,
your presence, GRACIOUS ONE, I seek.

Hide not your face from me; do not, in anger, turn away your servant.
You have been my help, don't shun me now; do not abandon me, my God who saves!

For my father and my mother have abandoned me,
but THE LIVING ONE shall take me in.

Teach me your way, WISE ONE, and guide me in a just path as I meet my foes.
Don't place me at the mercy of my enemies, for slanderers arise against me, and they fume in violence.

Were it not for my belief that I'll behold GOD's goodness in the Land of Life...
Hope, then, for THE ETERNAL ONE; strengthen your heart with courage, and have hope in THE ETERNAL.

Psalm 27

Continue on page 204.

וְעַתָּה יָרוּם רֹאשִׁי עַל אֹיְבַי סְבִיבוֹתַי וְאֶזְבְּחָה בְאָהֳלוֹ זִבְחֵי תְרוּעָה
אָשִׁירָה וַאֲזַמְּרָה לַיהוה:
שְׁמַע יהוה קוֹלִי אֶקְרָא וְחָנֵּנִי וַעֲנֵנִי:
לְךָ אָמַר לִבִּי בַּקְּשׁוּ פָנָי אֶת פָּנֶיךָ יהוה אֲבַקֵּשׁ:
אַל תַּסְתֵּר פָּנֶיךָ מִמֶּנִּי אַל תַּט בְּאַף עַבְדֶּךָ עֶזְרָתִי הָיִיתָ אַל תִּטְּשֵׁנִי
וְאַל תַּעַזְבֵנִי אֱלֹהֵי יִשְׁעִי:
כִּי אָבִי וְאִמִּי עֲזָבוּנִי וַיהוה יַאַסְפֵנִי:
הוֹרֵנִי יהוה דַּרְכֶּךָ וּנְחֵנִי בְּאֹרַח מִישׁוֹר לְמַעַן שׁוֹרְרָי:
אַל תִּתְּנֵנִי בְּנֶפֶשׁ צָרָי כִּי קָמוּ בִי עֵדֵי שֶׁקֶר וִיפֵחַ חָמָס:
*לוּלֵא הֶאֱמַנְתִּי לִרְאוֹת בְּטוּב יהוה בְּאֶרֶץ חַיִּים:
קַוֵּה אֶל יהוה חֲזַק וְיַאֲמֵץ לִבֶּךָ וְקַוֵּה אֶל יהוה:

Continue on page 205.

KAVANAH. This psalm speaks of evildoers, but also refers to our illness, pain, the trials and tribulations we all suffer, and our concerns and worries with living. The plane on which we focus our everyday consciousness keeps us in touch with all the things that go wrong in our lives—both small and large. This psalm urges an awareness of a different plane, one where we focus on the eternal instead of the everyday. Here we are nurtured by spiritual connection. Here we gain perspective on the whirl of activity that dominates our everyday lives. Here we find the strength and goodness that can sustain us in our daily tasks. D.A.T.

The following psalm is traditionally recited in a mourner's house.

For the chief musician; a psalm of the clan of Koraḥ.

Hear this, all you nations!
Hearken, all you dwellers of the earth,

you human beings of every sort,
the rich and poor alike!

My mouth shall utter words of wisdom,
words of understanding shall my heart conceive.

I'll turn my mind to parable,
my riddle I'll unfold upon the harp.

Why should I fear in times of trouble,
when the treachery of challengers surrounds me,

they who trust in force, who boast of their great wealth?
No, never can such things redeem a person;
that's not the way to clear accounts with God!

Their life cannot be saved so cheaply;
but forever they shall cease, and pass away.

For could one live forever?
Shall one never see the grave?

As one can see, even the wise shall die,
together shall the foolish and the ignorant be lost;
to others shall they leave their wealth.

Their grave is their eternal home,
their dwelling-place throughout all generations,
they whose names were famous in all lands. ←

The following psalm is traditionally recited in a mourner's house.

לַמְנַצֵּחַ לִבְנֵי־קֹרַח מִזְמוֹר׃

שִׁמְעוּ זֹאת כָּל הָעַמִּים הַאֲזִינוּ כָּל יֹשְׁבֵי חָלֶד׃
גַּם בְּנֵי אָדָם גַּם בְּנֵי אִישׁ יַחַד עָשִׁיר וְאֶבְיוֹן׃
פִּי יְדַבֵּר חָכְמוֹת וְהָגוּת לִבִּי תְבוּנוֹת׃
אַטֶּה לְמָשָׁל אָזְנִי אֶפְתַּח בְּכִנּוֹר חִידָתִי׃
לָמָּה אִירָא בִּימֵי רָע עֲוֺן עֲקֵבַי יְסֻבֵּנִי׃
הַבֹּטְחִים עַל חֵילָם וּבְרֹב עָשְׁרָם יִתְהַלָּלוּ׃
אָח לֹא פָדֹה יִפְדֶּה אִישׁ לֹא יִתֵּן לֵאלֹהִים כָּפְרוֹ׃
וְיֵקַר פִּדְיוֹן נַפְשָׁם וְחָדַל לְעוֹלָם׃
וִיחִי עוֹד לָנֶצַח לֹא יִרְאֶה הַשָּׁחַת׃
כִּי יִרְאֶה חֲכָמִים יָמוּתוּ יַחַד כְּסִיל וָבַעַר יֹאבֵדוּ וְעָזְבוּ לַאֲחֵרִים חֵילָם׃
קִרְבָּם בָּתֵּימוֹ לְעוֹלָם מִשְׁכְּנֹתָם לְדוֹר וָדוֹר קָרְאוּ בִשְׁמוֹתָם עֲלֵי אֲדָמוֹת׃ ←

COMMENTARY. In reflecting on the death that awaits everyone, this psalm, like Ecclesiastes, recognizes the transience of earthly existence. The psalmist seems to exclude himself, however, from this inevitable fate, by saying God will "take" him, rather than let him descend to the grave. Does he imagine that he is exempt from the laws of mortality? Ibn Ezra says, obviously not; the poet is aware of an eternal soul that outlasts our physical bodies. Rashi, however, claims that God "takes" him to walk in God's ways during his lifetime. From this perspective, the psalmist's main thrust is not on life after death, but on life itself. Do not focus on material wealth, he urges, because, as popular wisdom has always taught, you can't take it with you. Focus instead on what will truly bring lasting honor. H.L.

No person dwells in honor long;
one perishes the same way as the beasts.

Such is the fate of fools,
the latter end of those who revel in their talk—it shall be so!

Like sheep, they are appointed for the great unknown.
Death is their shepherd; straight to the grave they descend;
it is their fate to waste away; and in Sheol is their abode.

But God redeems my soul from Sheol's power;
it is God who takes me—this, too, shall be so!

Don't be afraid of this: that though a person may grow rich,
and though the glory of one's house grow great,

one doesn't keep a bit of it at death;
one's worldly glory doesn't follow to the grave.

However blessed you may be in life,
however much people might say, "You have done well,"

you'll come to take your place beside your ancestors,
with those who never more behold the light of day.

A person may know honor, yet not understand,
we perish in the same way as the beasts.

Psalm 49

וְאָדָם בִּיקָר בַּל יָלִין נִמְשַׁל כַּבְּהֵמוֹת נִדְמוּ׃
זֶה דַרְכָּם כֵּסֶל לָמוֹ וְאַחֲרֵיהֶם בְּפִיהֶם יִרְצוּ סֶלָה׃
כַּצֹּאן לִשְׁאוֹל שַׁתּוּ מָוֶת יִרְעֵם וַיִּרְדּוּ בָם יְשָׁרִים לַבֹּקֶר וְצוּרָם לְבַלּוֹת
שְׁאוֹל מִזְּבֻל לוֹ׃
אַךְ אֱלֹהִים יִפְדֶּה נַפְשִׁי מִיַּד שְׁאוֹל כִּי יִקָּחֵנִי סֶלָה׃
אַל תִּירָא כִּי יַעֲשִׁר אִישׁ כִּי יִרְבֶּה כְּבוֹד בֵּיתוֹ׃
כִּי לֹא בְמוֹתוֹ יִקַּח הַכֹּל לֹא יֵרֵד אַחֲרָיו כְּבוֹדוֹ׃
כִּי נַפְשׁוֹ בְּחַיָּיו יְבָרֵךְ וְיוֹדֻךָ כִּי תֵיטִיב לָךְ׃
תָּבוֹא עַד־דּוֹר אֲבוֹתָיו עַד נֵצַח לֹא יִרְאוּ אוֹר׃
אָדָם בִּיקָר וְלֹא יָבִין נִמְשַׁל כַּבְּהֵמוֹת נִדְמוּ׃

לשאול / the great unknown—The Biblical word for the place of the dead is *she'ol*, literally "questioning, inquiry." The name arose from the practice, described in 1 Sam. 28, of consulting the spirits of the dead for knowledge about the future. But the name in effect became synonymous with the mystery of the afterlife itself. J.R.

אך אלהים יפדה...סלה / But God redeems...be so! These are the psalm's only words of affirmation of some reality beyond physical death, but no details are given. However vague this affirmation, it forms the premise for the psalmist's contention, in the next verse, that death of the body is not to be feared, but rather accepted as a fact of life. J.R.

Readings suitable for a house of mourning may be added here. *See pages 490-532.*

INTRODUCTION TO THE MOURNERS' KADDISH

In reciting the Kaddish we affirm our awareness of holiness in our world. Much of our experience of divine goodness, grace and love has come to us through those whose lives have touched our own. (Today we remember....) We invoke the transcendent power of love and caring as we sanctify God's name.

KADDISH YATOM /THE MOURNERS' KADDISH

It is customary for mourners, and those observing Yahrzeit, *to stand for Kaddish. In some congregations everyone rises.*

Reader: Let God's name be made great and holy in the world that was created as God willed. May God complete the holy realm in your own lifetime, in your days, and in the days of all the house of Israel, quickly and soon. And say: Amen.

Congregation: May God's great name be blessed, forever and as long as worlds endure.

Reader: May it be blessed, and praised, and glorified, and held in honor, viewed with awe, embellished, and revered; and may the blessed name of holiness be hailed, though it be higher (*Between Rosh Hashanah and Yom Kippur, add:* by far) than all the blessings, songs, praises, and consolations that we utter in this world. And say: Amen.

May Heaven grant a universal peace, and life for us, and for all Israel. And say: Amen.

May the one who creates harmony above, make peace for us and for all Israel, and for all who dwell on earth. And say: Amen.

NOTE. Congregations usually mention the names of congregants and their relatives who have died in the previous week before reciting the Mourners' Kaddish. In many congregations a *Yahrzeit* list is read as well. In more informal settings the leader sometimes invites those present to speak the names of those they wish to be remembered. D.A.T.

Readings suitable for a house of mourning may be added here. *See pages 490-532.*

קַדִּישׁ יָתוֹם

It is customary for mourners, and those observing Yahrzeit, *to stand for Kaddish. In some congregations everyone rises.*

יִתְגַּדַּל וְיִתְקַדַּשׁ שְׁמֵהּ רַבָּא בְּעָלְמָא דִּי בְרָא כִרְעוּתֵהּ וְיַמְלִיךְ
מַלְכוּתֵהּ בְּחַיֵּיכוֹן וּבְיוֹמֵיכוֹן וּבְחַיֵּי דְכָל בֵּית יִשְׂרָאֵל בַּעֲגָלָא וּבִזְמַן
קָרִיב וְאִמְרוּ אָמֵן:

יְהֵא שְׁמֵהּ רַבָּא מְבָרַךְ לְעָלַם וּלְעָלְמֵי עָלְמַיָּא:

יִתְבָּרַךְ וְיִשְׁתַּבַּח וְיִתְפָּאַר וְיִתְרוֹמַם וְיִתְנַשֵּׂא וְיִתְהַדַּר וְיִתְעַלֶּה
וְיִתְהַלַּל שְׁמֵהּ דְּקֻדְשָׁא בְּרִיךְ הוּא
לְעֵֽלָּא (*Between Rosh Hashanah and Yom Kippur, add:* לְעֵֽלָּא) מִן כָּל בִּרְכָתָא
וְשִׁירָתָא תֻּשְׁבְּחָתָא וְנֶחֱמָתָא דַּאֲמִירָן בְּעָלְמָא וְאִמְרוּ אָמֵן:

יְהֵא שְׁלָמָא רַבָּא מִן שְׁמַיָּא וְחַיִּים עָלֵֽינוּ וְעַל כָּל יִשְׂרָאֵל וְאִמְרוּ אָמֵן:

עוֹשֶׂה שָׁלוֹם בִּמְרוֹמָיו הוּא יַעֲשֶׂה שָׁלוֹם עָלֵֽינוּ וְעַל כָּל יִשְׂרָאֵל וְעַל
כָּל יוֹשְׁבֵי תֵבֵל וְאִמְרוּ אָמֵן:

Reader: Yitgadal veyitkadash shemey raba
be'alma di vera ḥirutey veyamliḥ malḥutey
beḥayeyḥon uvyomeyḥon uvḥayey deḥol beyt yisra'el
ba'agala uvizman kariv ve'imru amen.

Congregation: Yehey shemey raba mevaraḥ le'alam ulalmey almaya.

Reader: Yitbaraḥ veyishtabaḥ veyitpa'ar veyitromam veyitnasey veyit-hadar veyitaleh veyit-halal shemey dekudsha beriḥ hu le'e̲la (*Between Rosh Hashanah and Yom Kippur, add:* le'e̲la) min kol birḥata veshirata tushbeḥata veneḥemata da'amiran be'alma ve'imru amen.

Yehey shelama raba min shemaya veḥayim aleynu ve'al kol yisra'el ve'imru amen.

Oseh shalom bimromav hu ya'aseh shalom aleynu ve'al kol yisra'el ve'al kol yoshvey tevel ve'imru amen.

ADON OLAM / Crown of All Time is found on page 342.

YIGDAL / GREAT IS...

This translation can be sung to the same melody as the Hebrew.

Great is the living God,
  to whom we give our praise,
who is, and whose great being
  is timeless, without days,
The One, to whom in oneness
  no one can compare,
invisible, in unity
  unbounded, everywhere,

Who has no body's form,
  has no material dress,
nor can we find the likeness
  of God's awesome holiness,
more ancient than all things
  brought forth in creation,
the first of everything that is,
  Beginning unbegun!

Behold the supreme being,
  whose universal power,
whose greatness and whose rule
  all creatures shall declare,
whose flow of prophecy
  was granted to a few,
the treasured ones who stood amid
  God's splendor ever new. ↩

ADON OLAM / Crown of All Time is found on page 343.

יִגְדַּל

יִגְדַּל אֱלֹהִים חַי וְיִשְׁתַּבַּח נִמְצָא וְאֵין עֵת אֶל מְצִיאוּתוֹ:
אֶחָד וְאֵין יָחִיד כְּיִחוּדוֹ נֶעְלָם וְגַם אֵין סוֹף לְאַחְדוּתוֹ:

אֵין לוֹ דְּמוּת הַגּוּף וְאֵינוֹ גוּף לֹא נַעֲרוֹךְ אֵלָיו קְדֻשָּׁתוֹ:
קַדְמוֹן לְכָל דָּבָר אֲשֶׁר נִבְרָא רִאשׁוֹן וְאֵין רֵאשִׁית לְרֵאשִׁיתוֹ:

הִנּוֹ אֲדוֹן עוֹלָם וְכָל נוֹצָר יוֹרֶה גְדֻלָּתוֹ וּמַלְכוּתוֹ:
שֶׁפַע נְבוּאָתוֹ נְתָנוֹ אֶל אַנְשֵׁי סְגֻלָּתוֹ וְתִפְאַרְתּוֹ: ←

Yigdal elohim ḥay veyishtabaḥ, nimtza ve'eyn et el metzi'uto.
Eḥad ve'eyn yaḥid keyiḥudo, nelam vegam eyn sof le'aḥduto.
Eyn lo demut haguf ve'eyno guf, lo na'aroḥ elav kedushato.
Kadmon leḥol davar asher nivra, rishon ve'eyn reyshit lereyshito.
Hino adon olam veḥol notzar, yoreh gedulato umalḥuto.
Shefa nevu'ato netano el, anshey segulato vetifar-to. ←

NOTE. *Yigdal* was written by Daniel ben Judah, a fourteenth-century poet. He based it upon Maimonides' Thirteen Articles of Faith. We have attempted to make the closing line more acceptable to the contemporary worshipper by referring to the sustenance of life (חיים מכלכל), rather than resurrection of the dead (מתים יחיה), as the true testimony of God's blessing.

A.G.

In Israel none arose
  as prophet like Moshe,
a prophet who would come to see
  the "image" in the *sneh*.
Torah of truth God gave
  the people Isra'el,
by truest prophet's hand
  that in God's house would dwell.

And God will never let
  the Torah pass away,
its doctrine will not change,
  but through all change will stay.
God sees and knows all things,
  and even what we hide,
can look upon how things begin
  the end of things to find,

Rewarding acts of love,
  when love for love we'll find,
and paying to all wickedness
  a recompense in kind,
God shall deliver all,
  upon the end of time,
redeeming all who wait for God,
  who for salvation pine.

God wakes all beings to life,
  abundant love shall reign,
blessed evermore,
  the glory of God's Name!

חיים מכלכל אל / God wakes all beings to life. The original version of this line was מתים יחיה אל / God revives the dead. It was changed to the version above in the 1945 Reconstructionist Prayer Book, which, like this one, avoids references to revival of the dead for ideological reasons. This change parallels those in the second blessing of the Amidah. D.A.T.

לֹא קָם בְּיִשְׂרָאֵל כְּמֹשֶׁה עוֹד נָבִיא וּמַבִּיט אֶת תְּמוּנָתוֹ:
תּוֹרַת אֱמֶת נָתַן לְעַמּוֹ אֵל עַל יַד נְבִיאוֹ נֶאֱמַן בֵּיתוֹ:

לֹא יַחֲלִיף הָאֵל וְלֹא יָמִיר דָּתוֹ לְעוֹלָמִים לְזוּלָתוֹ:
צוֹפֶה וְיוֹדֵעַ סְתָרֵינוּ מַבִּיט לְסוֹף דָּבָר בְּקַדְמָתוֹ:

גּוֹמֵל לְאִישׁ חֶסֶד כְּמִפְעָלוֹ יִתֵּן לְרָשָׁע רָע כְּרִשְׁעָתוֹ:
יִשְׁלַח לְקֵץ יָמִין גְּאֻלָּתוֹ לִפְדּוֹת מְחַכֵּי קֵץ יְשׁוּעָתוֹ:

חַיִּים מְכַלְכֵּל אֵל בְּרֹב חַסְדּוֹ בָּרוּךְ עֲדֵי עַד שֵׁם תְּהִלָּתוֹ:

Lo kam beyisra'el kemosheh od, navi umabit et temunato.
Torat emet natan le'amo el, al yad nevi'o ne'eman beyto.
Lo yaḥalif ha'el velo yamir, dato le'olamim lezulato.
Tzofeh veyode'a setareynu, mabit lesof davar bekadmato.
Gomel le'ish ḥesed kemifalo, yiten lerasha ra kerishato.
Yishlaḥ leketz yamin ge'ulato, lifdot meḥakey ketz yeshu'ato.
Ḥayim meḥalkel el berov ḥasdo, baruḥ adey ad shem tehilato.

מִנְחָה

MINḤAH/ AFTERNOON SERVICE

Happy are they who dwell within your house,
  may they continue to give praise to you.
Happy is the people for whom life is thus,
  happy is the people with THE EVERLASTING for its God!

A Psalm of David
א All exaltations do I raise to you, my sovereign God,
  and I give blessing to your name, forever and eternally.
ב Blessings do I offer you each day,
  I hail your name, forever and eternally.
ג Great is THE ETERNAL, to be praised emphatically,
  because God's greatness has no measure.
ד Declaring praises for your deeds one era to the next,
  people describe your mighty acts.
ה Heaven's glorious splendor is my song,
  words of your miracles I eagerly pour forth.
ו Wondrous are your powers—people tell of them,
  and your magnificence do I recount.
ז Signs of your abundant goodness they express,
  and in your justice they rejoice.
ח How gracious and how merciful is THE ABUNDANT ONE,
  slow to anger, great in love.
ט To all God's creatures, goodness flows,
  on all creation, divine love.
י Your creatures all give thanks to you,
  your fervent ones bless you emphatically. ↩

אשרי...סלה / Happy...you (Psalm 84:5).
אשרי...אלהיו / Happy...God (Psalm 144:15).

מִנְחָה

אַשְׁרֵי יוֹשְׁבֵי בֵיתֶ֫ךָ עוֹד יְהַלְלֽוּךָ סֶּ֫לָה׃
אַשְׁרֵי הָעָם שֶׁכָּ֫כָה לּוֹ אַשְׁרֵי הָעָם שֶׁיהוה אֱלֹהָיו׃
תְּהִלָּה לְדָוִד
אֲרוֹמִמְךָ אֱלוֹהַי הַמֶּ֫לֶךְ וַאֲבָרְכָה שִׁמְךָ לְעוֹלָם וָעֶד׃
בְּכָל־יוֹם אֲבָרְכֶ֫ךָּ וַאֲהַלְלָה שִׁמְךָ לְעוֹלָם וָעֶד׃
גָּדוֹל יהוה וּמְהֻלָּל מְאֹד וְלִגְדֻלָּתוֹ אֵין חֵֽקֶר׃
דּוֹר לְדוֹר יְשַׁבַּח מַעֲשֶׂ֫יךָ וּגְבוּרֹתֶ֫יךָ יַגִּֽידוּ׃
הֲדַר כְּבוֹד הוֹדֶ֫ךָ וְדִבְרֵי נִפְלְאֹתֶ֫יךָ אָשִֽׂיחָה׃
וֶעֱזוּז נוֹרְאוֹתֶ֫יךָ יֹאמֵ֫רוּ וּגְדֻלָּתְךָ אֲסַפְּרֶֽנָּה׃
זֵ֫כֶר רַב־טוּבְךָ יַבִּ֫יעוּ וְצִדְקָתְךָ יְרַנֵּֽנוּ׃
חַנּוּן וְרַחוּם יהוה אֶ֫רֶךְ אַפַּ֫יִם וּגְדָל־חָֽסֶד׃
טוֹב־יהוה לַכֹּל וְרַחֲמָיו עַל־כָּל־מַעֲשָׂיו׃
יוֹדֽוּךָ יהוה כָּל־מַעֲשֶׂ֫יךָ וַחֲסִידֶ֫יךָ יְבָרְכֽוּכָה׃ ←

Ashrey yoshvey veyteḥa od yehaleluḥa selah.
Ashrey ha'am shekaḥah lo ashrey ha'am she'adonay elohav.
Tehilah ledavid.
Aromimeḥa elohay hameleḥ va'avareḥah shimeḥa le'olam va'ed.
Beḥol yom avareḥeka va'ahalela shimeḥa le'olam va'ed.
Gadol adonay umhulal me'od veligdulato eyn ḥeker.
Dor ledor yeshabaḥ ma'aseḥa ugvuroteḥa yagidu.
Hadar kevod hodeḥa vedivrey nifle'oteḥa asiḥah.
Ve'ezuz noroteḥa yomeru ugdulateḥa asaperenah.
Zeḥer rav tuveḥa yabi'u vetzidkateḥa yeranenu.
Ḥanun veraḥum adonay ereḥ apayim ugdol ḥased.
Tov adonay lakol veraḥamav al kol ma'asav.
Yoduḥa adonay kol ma'aseḥa veḥasideḥa yevareḥuḥah. ↩

COMMENTARY. Psalm 145 is an alphabetical acrostic. The translation roughly preserves the sound of the Hebrew initials of each line. The line for the letter *nun* is missing from this psalm, for unknown reasons. J.R.

כ Calling out the glory of your sovereignty,
of your magnificence they speak,
ל Letting all people know your mighty acts,
and of your sovereignty's glory and splendor.
מ May your sovereignty last all eternities,
your dominion for era after era.
ס Strong support to all who fall,
GOD raises up the humble and the lame.
ע All hopeful gazes turn toward you,
as you give sustenance in its appointed time.
פ Providing with your open hand,
you satisfy desire in all life.
צ So just is God in every way,
so loving amid all the divine deeds.
ק Close by is God to all who call,
to all who call to God in truth.
ר Responding to the yearning of all those who fear,
God hears their cry and comes to rescue them.
ש Showing care to all who love God, THE ETERNAL
brings destruction to all evildoers.
ת The praise of THE ALL-KNOWING does my mouth declare,
and all flesh give blessing to God's holy name,
unto eternity.

Psalm 145

And as for us, we bless the name of Yah,
from now until the end of time. Halleluyah!

ואנחנו...הללויה / And...Halleluyah (Psalm 115:18).

כְּבוֹד מַלְכוּתְךָ יֹאמֵרוּ וּגְבוּרָתְךָ יְדַבֵּרוּ׃

לְהוֹדִיעַ לִבְנֵי הָאָדָם גְּבוּרֹתָיו וּכְבוֹד הֲדַר מַלְכוּתוֹ׃

מַלְכוּתְךָ מַלְכוּת כָּל־עֹלָמִים וּמֶמְשַׁלְתְּךָ בְּכָל־דּוֹר וָדוֹר׃

סוֹמֵךְ יהוה לְכָל־הַנֹּפְלִים וְזוֹקֵף לְכָל־הַכְּפוּפִים׃

עֵינֵי כֹל אֵלֶיךָ יְשַׂבֵּרוּ וְאַתָּה נוֹתֵן־לָהֶם אֶת־אָכְלָם בְּעִתּוֹ׃

פּוֹתֵחַ אֶת־יָדֶךָ וּמַשְׂבִּיעַ לְכָל־חַי רָצוֹן׃

צַדִּיק יהוה בְּכָל־דְּרָכָיו וְחָסִיד בְּכָל־מַעֲשָׂיו׃

קָרוֹב יהוה לְכָל־קֹרְאָיו לְכֹל אֲשֶׁר יִקְרָאֻהוּ בֶאֱמֶת׃

רְצוֹן יְרֵאָיו יַעֲשֶׂה וְאֶת־שַׁוְעָתָם יִשְׁמַע וְיוֹשִׁיעֵם׃

שׁוֹמֵר יהוה אֶת־כָּל־אֹהֲבָיו וְאֵת כָּל־הָרְשָׁעִים יַשְׁמִיד׃

* תְּהִלַּת יהוה יְדַבֶּר פִּי וִיבָרֵךְ כָּל־בָּשָׂר שֵׁם קָדְשׁוֹ לְעוֹלָם וָעֶד׃

וַאֲנַחְנוּ נְבָרֵךְ יָהּ מֵעַתָּה וְעַד־עוֹלָם הַלְלוּיָהּ׃

Kevod malḥuteḥa yomeru ugvuroteḥa yedaberu.
Lehodi'a livney ha'adam gevurotav uḥvod hadar malḥuto.
Malḥuteḥa malḥut kol olamim umemshalteḥa beḥol dor vador.
Someḥ adonay leḥol hanofelim vezokef leḥol hakefufim.
Eyney ḥol eleḥa yesaberu
 ve'atah noten lahem et oḥlam be'ito.
Pote'aḥ et yadeḥa umasbi'a leḥol ḥay ratzon.
Tzadik adonay beḥol deraḥav veḥasid beḥol ma'asav.
Karov adonay leḥol korav leḥol asher yikra'uhu ve'emet.
Retzon yere'av ya'aseh ve'et shavatam yishma veyoshi'em.
Shomer adonay et kol ohavav ve'et kol harsha'im yashmid.
Tehilat adonay yedaber pi
 vivareḥ kol basar shem kodsho le'olam va'ed.
Va'anaḥnu nevareḥ yah me'atah ve'ad olam halleluyah.

ḤATZI KADDISH / SHORT KADDISH

Reader: Let God's name be made great and holy in the world that was created as God willed. May God complete the holy realm in your own lifetime, in your days, and in the days of all the house of Israel, quickly and soon. And say: Amen.

Congregation: May God's great name be blessed, forever and as long as worlds endure.

Reader: May it be blessed, and praised, and glorified, and held in honor, viewed with awe, embellished, and revered; and may the blessed name of holiness be hailed, though it be higher (*Between Rosh Hashanah and Yom Kippur add:* by far) than all the blessings, songs, praises, and consolations that we utter in this world. And say: Amen.

חֲצִי קַדִּישׁ

יִתְגַּדַּל וְיִתְקַדַּשׁ שְׁמֵהּ רַבָּא בְּעָלְמָא דִּי בְרָא כִרְעוּתֵהּ וְיַמְלִיךְ מַלְכוּתֵהּ בְּחַיֵּיכוֹן וּבְיוֹמֵיכוֹן וּבְחַיֵּי דְכָל בֵּית יִשְׂרָאֵל בַּעֲגָלָא וּבִזְמַן קָרִיב וְאִמְרוּ אָמֵן:

יְהֵא שְׁמֵהּ רַבָּא מְבָרַךְ לְעָלַם וּלְעָלְמֵי עָלְמַיָּא:

יִתְבָּרַךְ וְיִשְׁתַּבַּח וְיִתְפָּאַר וְיִתְרוֹמַם וְיִתְנַשֵּׂא וְיִתְהַדַּר וְיִתְעַלֶּה וְיִתְהַלַּל שְׁמֵהּ דְּקֻדְשָׁא בְּרִיךְ הוּא

לְעֵֽלָּא (*Between Rosh Hashanah and Yom Kippur add:* לְעֵֽלָּא) מִן כָּל בִּרְכָתָא וְשִׁירָתָא תֻּשְׁבְּחָתָא וְנֶחֱמָתָא דַּאֲמִירָן בְּעָלְמָא וְאִמְרוּ אָמֵן:

Reader: Yitgadal veyitkadash shemey raba
be'alma di vera ḥirutey veyamliḥ malḥutey
beḥayeyḥon uvyomeyḥon uvḥayey deḥol beyt yisra'el
ba'agala uvizman kariv ve'imru amen.

Congregation: Yehey shemey raba mevaraḥ le'alam ulalmey almaya.

Reader: Yitbaraḥ veyishtabaḥ veyitpa'ar veyitromam
veyitnasey veyit-hadar veyitaleh veyit-halal
shemey dekudsha beriḥ hu
le'e̲la (*Between Rosh Hashanah and Yom Kippur add:* le'e̲la) min kol birḥata
veshirata tushbeḥata veneḥemata da'amiran be'alma
ve'imru amen.

AMIDAH

The traditional Amidah *follows here. The* Shiviti *meditation begins on page 132. A guided meditation begins on page 128.*
The Amidah *is traditionally recited while standing, beginning with three short steps forward and bowing left and right, a reminder of our entry into the divine presence.*

Open my lips, BELOVED ONE,
and let my mouth declare your praise.

1. AVOT VE'IMOT / ANCESTORS

Blessed are you, ANCIENT ONE, our God, God of our ancestors,

God of Abraham	God of Sarah
God of Isaac	God of Rebekah
God of Jacob	God of Rachel
	and God of Leah;

DERASH. Acknowledging our ancestors reminds us that what we are is shaped by who they were. Just as an acorn is shaped by the oak that preceded it and yet gives birth to a tree uniquely its own, so we are shaped by our ancestors yet give rise to a Judaism all our own. R.M.S.

COMMENTARY. The *Amidah* or "standing prayer" is also called "*Hatefilah* / The Prayer," because of its centrality in every one of the daily services. The *Amidah* in its weekday form is also known as the "*Shemoneh Esrey* / The Eighteen (benedictions)." This name dates from a very early period; nineteen blessings have been included for the last 2000 years. Most liturgy scholars agree that the weekday *Amidah* is structured as a prayer for the arrival of messianic times. The thirteen middle blessings of the weekday *Amidah* are petitions for success and wellbeing that reflect the concerns that occupy our daily circumstances. The *Amidah* always concludes with a prayer for completeness and peace, uniting workday concerns with messianic hope. D.A.T./R.S.

אדני...תהלתך / Open...praise (Psalm 51:17).

The traditional Amidah *follows here. The* Shiviti *meditation begins on page 131. A guided meditation begins on page 128.*
The Amidah *is traditionally recited while standing, beginning with three short steps forward and bowing left and right, a reminder of our entry into the divine presence.*

אֲדֹנָי שְׂפָתַי תִּפְתָּח וּפִי יַגִּיד תְּהִלָּתֶךָ׃

א 1 אָבוֹת וְאִמּוֹת

בָּרוּךְ אַתָּה יהוה אֱלֹהֵינוּ וֵאלֹהֵי אֲבוֹתֵינוּ וְאִמּוֹתֵינוּ
אֱלֹהֵי אַבְרָהָם אֱלֹהֵי שָׂרָה
אֱלֹהֵי יִצְחָק אֱלֹהֵי רִבְקָה
אֱלֹהֵי יַעֲקֹב אֱלֹהֵי רָחֵל
וֵאלֹהֵי לֵאָה׃ ←

Adonay sefatay tiftaḥ ufi yagid tehilateḥa.
Baruḥ atah adonay eloheynu veylohey
avoteynu ve'imoteynu
elohey avraham elohey sarah
elohey yitzḥak elohey rivkah
elohey ya'akov elohey raḥel
veylohey le'ah. ↵

COMMENTARY. Throughout the centuries the pursuit of meaningful communal prayer has led to variations in the Amidah. These variations reflect the attitudes and beliefs of different prayer communities. In the ongoing pursuit of meaningful prayer for a Reconstructionist prayer community, changes have been introduced into this *Amidah*, most notably in the first two *beraḥot*. The first *beraḥah* acknowledges God as the power that sustains life. The traditional emphasis on God's ability to resurrect the dead has been replaced here by a celebration of God as the power that sustains all life.

S.S.

great, heroic, awesome God, supreme divinity,
imparting deeds of kindness, begetter of all;
mindful of the loyalty of Israel's ancestors,
bringing, with love, redemption to their children's children
for the sake of the divine name.

Between Rosh Hashanah and Yom Kippur, add:
(Remember us for life,
our sovereign, who wishes us to live,
and write us in the Book of Life,
for your sake, ever-living God.)

Regal One, our help, salvation, and protector:
Blessed are you, KIND ONE,
the shield of Abraham and the help of Sarah. ↵

עזרת שרה / *ezrat sarah*. The biblical term *ezer* has two meanings, "rescue" and "be strong." It is commonly translated as "aid" or "help." It also has the sense of power and strength. In Deuteronomy 33:29, *ezer* is parallel to גאוה, majesty. Eve is described as Adam's *ezer kenegdo*, a power equal to him, a strength and majesty to match his. Thus *magen avraham* (shield of Abraham) and *ezrat sarah* (help of Sarah) are parallel images of power and protection. R.S.A.

KAVANAH. God is experienced as עוזר / helper, every time our thought of God furnishes us an escape from the sense of frustration and supplies us with a feeling of permanence in the midst of universal flux.
M.M.K./M.S.

COMMENTARY. This version of the first *beraḥah* in the Amidah includes the matriarchs as well as the patriarchs. The phrase *ezrat Sarah* comes from a Hebrew root (עזר) which can mean either "help," "save" or "be strong." This parallels the meaning of *magen* / shield. The biblical text says that Abraham experienced God as a shield and that Sarah experienced God as a helper. Their experience and the example of their lives can enrich our own. Just as Abraham and Sarah found the strength to face the unknown physical and spiritual dangers of their journey, so we seek to find the courage and inspiration to meet the challenges of our own time. R.S.

הָאֵל הַגָּדוֹל הַגִּבּוֹר וְהַנּוֹרָא אֵל עֶלְיוֹן גּוֹמֵל חֲסָדִים טוֹבִים וְקוֹנֵה הַכֹּל וְזוֹכֵר חַסְדֵי אָבוֹת וְאִמּוֹת וּמֵבִיא גְּאֻלָּה לִבְנֵי בְנֵיהֶם לְמַעַן שְׁמוֹ בְּאַהֲבָה:

Between Rosh Hashanah and Yom Kippur, add:

(זָכְרֵנוּ לְחַיִּים מֶלֶךְ חָפֵץ בַּחַיִּים וְכָתְבֵנוּ בְּסֵפֶר הַחַיִּים לְמַעַנְךָ אֱלֹהִים חַיִּים:)

מֶלֶךְ עוֹזֵר וּמוֹשִׁיעַ וּמָגֵן: בָּרוּךְ אַתָּה יהוה מָגֵן אַבְרָהָם וְעֶזְרַת שָׂרָה: ←

Ha'el hagadol hagibor vehanora el elyon gomel ḥasadim tovim vekoney hakol vezoḥer ḥasdey avot ve'imot umevi ge'ulah livney veneyhem lema'an shemo be'ahavah.

Between Rosh Hashanah and Yom Kippur add:

(Zoḥrenu leḥayim meleḥ ḥafetz baḥayim veḥotvenu besefer haḥayim lema'aneḥa elohim ḥayim.)
Meleḥ ozer umoshi'a umagen. Baruḥ atah adonay magen avraham ve'ezrat sarah. ↩

Many contemporary Jews are reciting *beraḥot* / blessings in ways that reflect their theological outlooks and ethical concerns. At any place where a blessing occurs in the liturgy, the following elements can be combined to create alternative formulas for *beraḥot.* This can be done by selecting one phrase from each group to form the introductory clause.

I	Baruḥ atah adonay	בָּרוּךְ אַתָּה יהוה	Blessed are you Adonay
	Beruḥah at yah	בְּרוּכָה אַתְּ יָהּ	Blessed are you Yah
	Nevareḥ et	נְבָרֵךְ אֶת	Let us bless
II	eloheynu	אֱלֹהֵינוּ	our God
	hasheḥinah	הַשְּׁכִינָה	Sheḥinah
	eyn haḥayim	עֵין הַחַיִּים	Source of Life
III	meleḥ ha'olam	מֶלֶךְ הָעוֹלָם	Sovereign of all worlds
	ḥey ha'olamim	חֵי הָעוֹלָמִים	Life of all the worlds
	ru'aḥ ha'olam	רוּחַ הָעוֹלָם	Spirit of the world

2. GEVUROT / DIVINE POWER

You are forever powerful, ALMIGHTY ONE,
abundant in your saving acts.
In summer: You send down the dew.
In winter: You cause the wind to blow and rain to fall.

In loyalty you sustain the living,
nurturing the life of every living thing,
upholding those who fall,
healing the sick, freeing the captive,
and remaining faithful to all life
held dormant in the earth.
Who can compare to you, almighty God,
who can resemble you, the source of life and death,
who makes salvation grow?

(*Between Rosh Hashanah and Yom Kippur, add:*
Who can compare to you, source of all mercy,
remembering all creatures mercifully, decreeing life!)

Faithful are you in giving life to every living thing.
Blessed are you, THE FOUNT OF LIFE,
who gives and renews life.

When chanting aloud in a minyan, continue with the Kedushah, *page 224.*
When praying silently, continue here.

3. KEDUSHAT HASHEM / HALLOWING GOD'S NAME

Holy are you. Your name is holy.
And all holy beings hail you each day.
Blessed are you, THE AWESOME ONE, the holy God.

(*Between Rosh Hashanah and Yom Kippur, conclude:* the holy sovereign.)

For the abbreviated Amidah, *continue on page 106.*
For the full Amidah, *continue on page 226.*

גְּבוּרוֹת

אַתָּה גִּבּוֹר לְעוֹלָם אֲדֹנָי רַב לְהוֹשִֽׁיעַ:

מוֹרִיד הַטָּל: *In summer*

מַשִּׁיב הָרֽוּחַ וּמוֹרִיד הַגָּֽשֶׁם: *In winter*

מְכַלְכֵּל חַיִּים בְּחֶֽסֶד מְחַיֵּה כָּל חַי בְּרַחֲמִים רַבִּים סוֹמֵךְ נוֹפְלִים וְרוֹפֵא חוֹלִים וּמַתִּיר אֲסוּרִים וּמְקַיֵּם אֱמוּנָתוֹ לִישֵׁנֵי עָפָר:
מִי כָמֽוֹךְ בַּֽעַל גְּבוּרוֹת וּמִי דֽוֹמֶה לָּךְ מֶֽלֶךְ מֵמִית וּמְחַיֶּה וּמַצְמִֽיחַ יְשׁוּעָה:

Atah gibor le'olam adonay rav lehoshi'a.
In summer: Morid hatal.
In winter: Mashiv haru'aḥ umorid hagashem.

Meḥalkel ḥayim beḥesed meḥayey kol ḥay beraḥamim rabim someḥ noflim verofey ḥolim umatir asurim umkayem emunato lisheney afar. Mi ḥamoḥa ba'al gevurot umi domeh laḥ meleḥ memit umḥayeh umatzmi'aḥ yeshu'ah.

Between Rosh Hashanah and Yom Kippur, add:

(מִי כָמֽוֹךְ אַב הָרַחֲמִים זוֹכֵר יְצוּרָיו לְחַיִּים בְּרַחֲמִים:)

(Mi ḥamoḥa av haraḥamim zoḥer yetzurav leḥayim beraḥamim.)

וְנֶאֱמָן אַתָּה לְהַחֲיוֹת כָּל חָי: בָּרוּךְ אַתָּה יהוה מְחַיֵּה כָּל חָי:

Vene'eman atah lehaḥayot kol ḥay. Baruḥ atah adonay meḥayey kol ḥay.

When chanting aloud in a minyan, continue with the Kedushah, *page 225.*
When praying silently, continue here.

קְדֻשַּׁת הַשֵּׁם

אַתָּה קָדוֹשׁ וְשִׁמְךָ קָדוֹשׁ וּקְדוֹשִׁים בְּכָל יוֹם יְהַלְלֽוּךָ סֶּֽלָה:
בָּרוּךְ אַתָּה יהוה הָאֵל הַקָּדוֹשׁ:

(*Between Rosh Hashanah and Yom Kippur, conclude:* הַמֶּֽלֶךְ הַקָּדוֹשׁ)

For the abbreviated Amidah, *continue on page 107.*
For the full Amidah, *continue on page 227.*

3. KEDUSHAH / SANCTIFICATION

The kedushah *is chanted aloud in a minyan.*

We sanctify your name throughout this world,
as it is sanctified in the heavens above,
as it is written by your prophet:
"And each celestial being calls to another, and declares:
Holy, holy, holy is THE RULER of the Multitudes of Heaven!
All the world is filled with divine glory!"
And they are answered with a blessing:
"Blessed is the glory of THE HOLY ONE,
wherever God may dwell!"
And as is written in your sacred words of psalm:
"May THE ETERNAL reign forever,
your God, O Zion, from one generation to the next. Hallelulyah!"
From one generation to the next may we declare your greatness,
and for all eternities may we affirm your holiness,
and may your praise, our God, never be absent from our mouths,
now and forever.
For you are a great and holy God.
Blessed are you, THE AWESOME ONE, the holy God.
(*Between Rosh Hashanah and Yom Kippur, conclude:* the holy sovereign.)

The traditional Amidah *continues on page 226. For the abbreviated* Amidah *continue on page 106.*

וקרא...כבודו / And...glory (Isaiah: 6:3).
ברוך...ממקומו / Blessed...dwell (Ezekiel 3:12).
ימלך...הללויה / May...Halleluyah (Psalm 146:10).

כל חי / every living thing, gives and renews life. The traditional siddur affirms מחיה המתים / revival of the dead. We substitute כל חי, demonstrating an understanding that all of life is rooted in the world's divine order and avoiding affirmation of life after death. We cannot know what happens to us after we die, but we can, by our thought and action, affirm the possibility of this-worldly salvation. D.A.T.

קְדֻשָּׁה

The kedushah *is chanted aloud in a minyan.*

* נְקַדֵּשׁ אֶת שִׁמְךָ בָּעוֹלָם כְּשֵׁם שֶׁמַּקְדִּישִׁים אוֹתוֹ בִּשְׁמֵי מָרוֹם כַּכָּתוּב
עַל יַד נְבִיאֶךָ: וְקָרָא זֶה אֶל זֶה וְאָמַר:
קָדוֹשׁ קָדוֹשׁ קָדוֹשׁ יהוה צְבָאוֹת מְלֹא כָל הָאָרֶץ כְּבוֹדוֹ:
* לְעֻמָּתָם בָּרוּךְ יֹאמֵרוּ: בָּרוּךְ כְּבוֹד יהוה מִמְּקוֹמוֹ:
* וּבְדִבְרֵי קָדְשְׁךָ כָּתוּב לֵאמֹר:
יִמְלֹךְ יהוה לְעוֹלָם אֱלֹהַיִךְ צִיּוֹן לְדֹר וָדֹר הַלְלוּיָהּ:
לְדוֹר וָדוֹר נַגִּיד גָּדְלֶךָ וּלְנֵצַח נְצָחִים קְדֻשָּׁתְךָ נַקְדִּישׁ וְשִׁבְחֲךָ
אֱלֹהֵינוּ מִפִּינוּ לֹא יָמוּשׁ לְעוֹלָם וָעֶד כִּי אֵל מֶלֶךְ גָּדוֹל וְקָדוֹשׁ אָתָּה:
בָּרוּךְ אַתָּה יהוה הָאֵל הַקָּדוֹשׁ:

Between Rosh Hashanah and Yom Kippur, conclude:

(בָּרוּךְ אַתָּה יהוה הַמֶּלֶךְ הַקָּדוֹשׁ:)

Nekadesh et shimeḥa ba'olam keshem shemakdishim oto bishmey marom kakatuv al yad nevi'eḥa: vekara zeh el zeh ve'amar:
Kadosh kadosh kadosh adonay tzeva'ot melo ḥol ha'aretz kevodo. Le'umatam baruḥ yomeru:
Baruḥ kevod adonay mimekomo. Uvdivrey kodsheḥa katuv leymor: Yimloḥ adonay le'olam elohayiḥ tziyon ledor vador halleluyah.
Ledor vador nagid godleḥa ulnetzaḥ netzaḥim
kedushateḥa nakdish veshivḥaḥa eloheynu mipinu lo yamush le'olam va'ed ki el meleḥ gadol vekadosh atah.
Baruḥ atah adonay ha'el hakadosh.
(Baruḥ atah adonay hameleḥ hakadosh.)

The traditional Amidah *continues on page 227. For the abbreviated* Amidah *continue on page 107.*

KAVANAH. You are eternal, the life of all that lives, the love in all that loves. You animate lifeless matter. You are the courage of those who conquer adversity. You are in the health of those who overcome sickness. You are the hope of those who now sleep in the dust. Yet you are more than all these, O master of life and death and salvation. You are holy and those who strive after holiness worship you. M.M.K./M.S.

4. BINAH / UNDERSTANDING

You graciously endow the human being
with the power to know;
you teach a person understanding.
So may you provide us now
with knowledge, understanding, and intelligence.
Blessed are you, THE FOUNT OF WISDOM,
who graciously bestows all knowledge.

5. TESHUVAH / REPENTANCE

Return us, divine Source, to your Torah,
bring us nearer, our sovereign, to your service.
And restore us, in complete return, into your presence.
Blessed are you, RECEPTIVE ONE,
who takes joy in our return.

6. SELIḤAH / FORGIVENESS

Forgive us, our Creator, for we have done wrong.
Deal mercifully with us, our protector, though we have rebelled.
For you are truly kind and merciful.
Blessed are you, ALL-MERCIFUL,
who graciously abounds in power to forgive.

7. GE'ULAH / REDEMPTION

Behold our need, and plead our cause,
and speedily redeem us, as your name demands,
for you are called a powerful redeemer.
Blessed are you, ALMIGHTY ONE,
redeemer of the people Israel. ↩

ד 4 בִּינָה

אַתָּה חוֹנֵן לְאָדָם דַּעַת וּמְלַמֵּד לֶאֱנוֹשׁ בִּינָה:
חָנֵּנוּ מֵאִתְּךָ דֵּעָה בִּינָה וְהַשְׂכֵּל. בָּרוּךְ אַתָּה יהוה חוֹנֵן הַדָּעַת:

ה 5 תְּשׁוּבָה

הֲשִׁיבֵנוּ מְקוֹרֵנוּ לְתוֹרָתֶךָ: וְקָרְבֵנוּ עֲטַרְתֵּנוּ לַעֲבוֹדָתֶךָ. וְהַחֲזִירֵנוּ
בִּתְשׁוּבָה שְׁלֵמָה לְפָנֶיךָ: בָּרוּךְ אַתָּה יהוה הָרוֹצֶה בִּתְשׁוּבָה:

ו 6 סְלִיחָה

סְלַח־לָנוּ אָבִינוּ כִּי חָטָאנוּ: מְחַל־לָנוּ מַלְכֵּנוּ כִּי פָשָׁעְנוּ: כִּי מוֹחֵל
וְסוֹלֵחַ אָתָּה: בָּרוּךְ אַתָּה יהוה חַנּוּן הַמַּרְבֶּה לִסְלוֹחַ:

ז 7 גְּאֻלָּה

רְאֵה בְעָנְיֵנוּ וְרִיבָה רִיבֵנוּ וּגְאָלֵנוּ מְהֵרָה לְמַעַן שְׁמֶךָ: כִּי גוֹאֵל חָזָק
אָתָּה: בָּרוּךְ אַתָּה יהוה גּוֹאֵל יִשְׂרָאֵל: ←

NOTE. The fifth blessing of the weekday *Amidah* focuses on the call to *teshuvah*—return to the path of Torah and the divine presence. Like the High Holy Day liturgy, this blessing invokes the imagery of kingship. This imagery is male and hierarchical which is problematical for many contemporary Jews. Even more difficult for some is the image of an external God pronouncing individual judgments. This contradicts our sense of the divinity within ourselves tht we strive to keep in our awareness and to bring into harmony with our lives. These difficulties have led to emendation of the traditional wording. אבינו / Our Father has been replaced by מְקוֹרֵנוּ / Divine Source, and מלכנו / Our King has been replaced by עֲטַרְתֵּנוּ / literally, Our Crown, but here translated figuratively as "our sovereign." Compare the alternative and interpretive vesions of *Avinu Malkeynu*, pages 136-143.

D.A.T / J.B.

The truth is that our belief in God is not based upon God's self-revelation but on our discovery of God. According to the modern way of thinking and speaking, it is more correct to say that we discover God than to say that God reveals the divine self to us.

M.M.K. (Adapted)

8. REFU'AH / HEALING

Heal us, NURTURING ONE, so that we may be healed;
help us to restore ourselves into a state of health,
and bring upon us complete cure of all our ailments.

Optional prayer for one who is ill:

(May it be your will, COMPASSIONATE ONE, my God,
God of my ancestors,
that you quickly send forth thorough healing,
a healing of the body and a healing of the spirit,
to the one who ails,

for a female:

to __________ daughter of __________

for a male:

to __________ son of __________
among all others of the people Israel who are ailing.)
And remove from us all suffering and grief,
For you are a sovereign divine power
and a faithful and compassionate healer.
Blessed are you, RESTORER OF LIFE,
who heals the sick among the people Israel.

9. BIRKAT HASHANIM / BLESSING FOR ABUNDANCE

Grant blessing over us, ABUNDANT ONE,
upon this year, and all its forms of produce;
let it be a year of good.

From December 4 till Pesaḥ say:
And grant us dew and rain,
for blessing

From Pesaḥ till December 4 say:
And give blessing

on the earth, and satisfy us with your goodness,
and give blessing to this year
as in the good years of the past.
Blessed are you, ALL-BOUNTIFUL,
who gives blessing to the years. ↩

8 ח רְפוּאָה

רְפָאֵנוּ יהוה וְנֵרָפֵא הוֹשִׁיעֵנוּ וְנִוָּשֵׁעָה וְהַעֲלֵה רְפוּאָה שְׁלֵמָה לְכָל מַכּוֹתֵינוּ

Optional prayer for one who is ill:

(יְהִי רָצוֹן מִלְּפָנֶיךָ יהוה אֱלֹהַי וֵאלֹהֵי אֲבוֹתַי וְאִמּוֹתַי שֶׁתִּשְׁלַח מְהֵרָה רְפוּאָה שְׁלֵמָה מִן הַשָּׁמַיִם רְפוּאַת הַנֶּפֶשׁ וּרְפוּאַת הַגּוּף

לַחוֹלָה _ בַּת _ *for a female:*

לַחוֹלֶה ____ בֶּן ____ *for a male:*

בְּתוֹךְ שְׁאָר חוֹלֵי יִשְׂרָאֵל.)

וְהָסֵר מִמֶּנּוּ יָגוֹן וַאֲנָחָה כִּי אֵל מֶלֶךְ רוֹפֵא נֶאֱמָן וְרַחֲמָן אָתָּה: בָּרוּךְ אַתָּה יהוה רוֹפֵא חוֹלֵי עַמּוֹ יִשְׂרָאֵל:

9 ט בִּרְכַּת הַשָּׁנִים

בָּרֵךְ עָלֵינוּ יהוה אֱלֹהֵינוּ אֶת הַשָּׁנָה הַזֹּאת וְאֶת כָּל מִינֵי תְבוּאָתָהּ לְטוֹבָה

From Pesaḥ till December 4 say:

וְתֵן בְּרָכָה

From December 4 till Pesaḥ say:

וְתֵן טַל וּמָטָר לִבְרָכָה

עַל פְּנֵי הָאֲדָמָה וְשַׂבְּעֵנוּ מִטּוּבֶךָ וּבָרֵךְ שְׁנָתֵנוּ כַּשָּׁנִים הַטּוֹבוֹת: בָּרוּךְ אַתָּה יהוה מְבָרֵךְ הַשָּׁנִים: ←

COMMENTARY. As a God of lovingkindness, God not only teaches us how to conduct ourselves so as to elicit the best in each other, but also calls upon the transgressor to repent. When human beings repent, God forgives, and by forgiveness enables individuals to use their own powers as God would have them do. M.M.K./M.S.

NOTE. Our hope for rain in its season, which sustains crops throughout the year, is expressed in a subtle change of words. "Provide blessing," which is used most of the year, becomes "provide dew and rain for a blessing." Pesaḥ marks the beginning of the spring grain-planting season in Israel. The rabbis used the sun calendar date of December 4 for this prayer for rain to adjust to agricultural conditions in Babylonia. In following their lead, we recognize the need to adjust Jewish practice in response to local climactic, cultural, and political conditions. D.A.T.

10. KIBUTZ GALUYOT / INGATHERING OF THE JEWISH PEOPLE

Sound the great shofar for our freedom,
raise up the banner for the gathering-in of those in exile,
and gather us together from the earth's four corners.
Blessed are you, REDEEMING ONE,
who gathers Israel's dispossessed.

11. DIN / RESTORING JUSTICE

Restore our judges, as of old,
our counselors, as in the beginning,
and remove from us all suffering and grief.
Rule over us, OUR SOVEREIGN, you alone,
with love and with compassion.
Help us achieve justice through the rule of law.

Blessed are you, WISE ONE,
the sovereign who loves righteousness and justice.

Between Rosh Hashanah and Yom Kippur, conclude:

(Blessed are you, ENTHRONED IN MAJESTY,
the sovereign, the source of all just law.)

12. BIRKAT HAMINIM / OVERCOMING DIVISIONS

Let all who speak and act unjustly
find no hope for ill intentions.
Let all wickedness be lost.
Blessed are you, JUST ONE,
who subdues the evildoers. ↩

טו 15 קִבּוּץ גָּלֻיּוֹת

תְּקַע בְּשׁוֹפָר גָּדוֹל לְחֵרוּתֵֽנוּ וְשָׂא נֵס לְקַבֵּץ גָּלֻיּוֹתֵֽינוּ וְקַבְּצֵֽנוּ יַֽחַד מֵאַרְבַּע כַּנְפוֹת הָאָֽרֶץ: בָּרוּךְ אַתָּה יהוה מְקַבֵּץ נִדְחֵי עַמּוֹ יִשְׂרָאֵל:

יא 11 דִּין

הָשִֽׁיבָה שׁוֹפְטֵֽינוּ כְּבָרִאשׁוֹנָה וְיוֹעֲצֵֽינוּ כְּבַתְּחִלָּה וְהָסֵר מִמֶּֽנּוּ יָגוֹן וַאֲנָחָה וּמְלוֹךְ עָלֵֽינוּ אַתָּה יהוה לְבַדְּךָ בְּחֶֽסֶד וּבְרַחֲמִים וְצַדְּקֵֽנוּ בַּמִּשְׁפָּט: בָּרוּךְ אַתָּה יהוה מֶֽלֶךְ אוֹהֵב צְדָקָה וּמִשְׁפָּט:

Between Rosh Hashanah and Yom Kippur conclude:

(בָּרוּךְ אַתָּה יהוה הַמֶּֽלֶךְ הַמִּשְׁפָּט:)

יב 12 בִּרְכַּת הַמִּינִים

וְלַמַּלְשִׁינִים אַל תְּהִי תִקְוָה וְכָל הָרִשְׁעָה כְּרֶֽגַע תֹּאבֵד: בָּרוּךְ אַתָּה יהוה מַכְנִֽיעַ זֵדִים: ←

13. TZADIKIM / COMPASSION FOR THE RIGHTEOUS

For the righteous, and for the pious,
and for the elders of your people, the house of Israel,
and for the remnant of their scholars,
and for the righteous who have chosen to be Jews,
let your compassion be aroused, DEAR ONE, our God,
and give proper recompense to all
who truly have found shelter in your name,
and give us a portion in their midst,
that we may never be ashamed,
for in you we place our trust.
Blessed are you, THE SOURCE OF TRUST,
support and stronghold for the righteous.

14. BINYAN YERUSHALAYIM / REBUILDING JERUSALEM

And to Jerusalem, your city,
may you turn with mercy,
and come home to dwell there,
as you have promised.
And rebuild the city, soon and in our days,
with everlasting peace.
Blessed are you, THE GOD OF ZION,
builder of Jerusalem.

15. YESHU'AH / SALVATION

May you speedily redeem your people Israel,
and raise their stronghold with your help,
for we await with hope throughout our days
the coming of your help.
Blessed are you, THE GOD OF ISRAEL,
who plants the stronghold of your help. ↵

יג 13 צַדִּיקִים

עַל הַצַּדִּיקִים וְעַל הַחֲסִידִים וְעַל זִקְנֵי עַמְּךָ בֵּית יִשְׂרָאֵל וְעַל פְּלֵיטַת סוֹפְרֵיהֶם וְעַל גֵּרֵי הַצֶּדֶק וְעָלֵינוּ יֶהֱמוּ נָא רַחֲמֶיךָ יהוה אֱלֹהֵינוּ וְתֵן שָׂכָר טוֹב לְכֹל הַבּוֹטְחִים בְּשִׁמְךָ בֶּאֱמֶת וְשִׂים חֶלְקֵנוּ עִמָּהֶם וּלְעוֹלָם לֹא נֵבוֹשׁ כִּי בְךָ בָּטָחְנוּ: בָּרוּךְ אַתָּה יהוה מִשְׁעָן וּמִבְטָח לַצַּדִּיקִים:

יד 14 בִּנְיַן יְרוּשָׁלָיִם

וְלִירוּשָׁלַיִם עִירְךָ בְּרַחֲמִים תָּשׁוּב וְתִשְׁכּוֹן בְּתוֹכָהּ כַּאֲשֶׁר דִּבַּרְתָּ וּבְנֵה אוֹתָהּ בְּקָרוֹב בְּיָמֵינוּ בִּנְיַן שָׁלוֹם: בָּרוּךְ אַתָּה יהוה בּוֹנֵה יְרוּשָׁלָיִם:

טו 15 יְשׁוּעָה

אֶת עַמְּךָ יִשְׂרָאֵל מְהֵרָה תִּגְאַל וְקַרְנוֹ תָּרוּם בִּישׁוּעָתֶךָ כִּי לִישׁוּעָתְךָ קִוִּינוּ כָּל הַיּוֹם: בָּרוּךְ אַתָּה יהוה מַצְמִיחַ יְשׁוּעָה: ←

NOTE. The fourteenth blessing of the *Amidah* focuses on the rebuilding of Jerusalem. For centuries the rebuilding of Jerusalem has stood for an end to Jewish suffering and a return to Jewish sovereignty, as well as for the mythic end of days in which Jerusalem would become all that generations of longing Jews could imagine. For us, the rebuilding of Jerusalem signifies a world at peace where all human need is fulfilled. D.A.T.

16. KABBALAT TEFILAH / ACCEPTING PRAYER

Hear our voice, ATTENTIVE ONE, our God,
have mercy and compassion for us,
and accept our prayer
with kindness and with favor,
for you are the God who harkens
to the words of prayer and supplication.
Do not turn us from your presence empty-handed.
For you are one who listens
to the prayer of your people Israel
with compassion.

At this point in the Amidah, *it is customary to add personal petitions for healing or safety, for successfully earning a living and for other hopes and needs. For* Tefilat Hadereḥ / *the Traveler's Prayer, see page 174.*

Optional prayer for parnasah / *sustenance and well-being:*

(You are THE PROVIDER, God who feeds, supports, and sustains all creatures, from the mighty horned oxen to the tiny new-hatched nestlings. May you grant me proper sustenance, supply to me and to my household nourishment, forestalling any state of need. Provide in pleasure, not in pain, in willingness, not in begrudging, in honor, not in shame, for life and for well-being, from the flow of blessing and prosperity, from the flow of blessing from above, so that I may better do your will, and occupy myself with your Torah and uphold your mitzvot. Give me freedom from dependence upon others, that this verse of Scripture might apply to me, as well: "Providing with an open hand, you satisfy the wishes of all life." And also what is written: "Cast yourself upon THE BOUNTIFUL, and God will be your sustenance.") ↩

פותח...רצון / Providing with...of all life (Psalms 145:16).

השלך על...יכלכלך / Cast yourself...your sustenance (Psalms 55:23).

טז 16 קַבָּלַת תְּפִלָּה

שְׁמַע קוֹלֵנוּ יהוה אֱלֹהֵינוּ חוּס וְרַחֵם עָלֵינוּ וְקַבֵּל בְּרַחֲמִים וּבְרָצוֹן
אֶת תְּפִלָּתֵנוּ כִּי אֵל שׁוֹמֵעַ תְּפִלּוֹת וְתַחֲנוּנִים אָתָּה: וּמִלְּפָנֶיךָ מַלְכֵּנוּ
רֵיקָם אַל תְּשִׁיבֵנוּ כִּי אַתָּה שׁוֹמֵעַ תְּפִלַּת עַמְּךָ יִשְׂרָאֵל בְּרַחֲמִים:

At this point in the Amidah, *it is customary to add personal petitions for healing or safety, for successfully earning a living and for other hopes and needs. For* Tefilat Hadereḥ / *The Traveler's Prayer, see page 175.*

Optional prayer for parnasah / *sustenance and well-being:*

(אַתָּה הוּא יהוה הָאֱלֹהִים הַזָּן וּמְפַרְנֵס וּמְכַלְכֵּל הַטְרִיפֵנִי לֶחֶם חֻקִּי
וְהַמְצֵא לִי וּלְכָל בְּנֵי בֵיתִי מְזוֹנוֹתַי קוֹדֶם שֶׁאֶצְטָרֵךְ לָהֶם בְּנַחַת וְלֹא
בְּצַעַר בְּהֶתֵּר וְלֹא בְאִסּוּר בְּכָבוֹד וְלֹא בְבִזָּיוֹן לְחַיִּים וּלְשָׁלוֹם מִשֶּׁפַע
בְּרָכָה וְהַצְלָחָה וּמִשֶּׁפַע בְּרָכָה עֶלְיוֹנָה כְּדֵי שֶׁאוּכַל לַעֲשׂוֹת רְצוֹנֶךָ
וְלַעֲסֹק בְּתוֹרָתֶךָ וּלְקַיֵּם מִצְוֹתֶיךָ: וְאַל תַּצְרִיכֵנִי לִידֵי מַתְּנַת בָּשָׂר
וָדָם: וִיקֻיַּם בִּי מִקְרָא שֶׁכָּתוּב: פּוֹתֵחַ אֶת יָדֶךָ וּמַשְׂבִּיעַ לְכָל חַי רָצוֹן:
וְכָתוּב הַשְׁלֵךְ עַל יהוה יְהָבְךָ וְהוּא יְכַלְכְּלֶךָ.) ←

COMMENTARY. This may be the most poignant of all the benedictions of the Amidah. It occurs after we have prayed about so many important things: health, wisdom, community....Yet only here do we finally ask whether or not God hears our prayer. We ask, by way of stating, that God graciously listen to us. What is God that such hearing is possible? If we have moved beyond a simplistic notion of a giant-figure with omniscient ears, what do we have left that hears? Whatever it is, we affirm it! Somehow the injection of our impassioned words and thoughts into the vast process of existence does something. That something is not merely self-clarification and introspection. Something hears. The cosmos bends towards us and takes cognizance. The particulars are wrapped in mystery; the direction and the flow are known. W.S.

Blessed are you, COMPASSIONATE ONE, who listens to the words of prayer.

Both the full Amidah *and the abbreviated* Amidah *continue here.*

17. AVODAH / WORSHIP

Take pleasure, GRACIOUS ONE, our God,
in Israel, your people;
lovingly accept their fervent prayer.
May Israel's worship always be acceptable to you.

On a Rosh Ḥodesh/New Moon or a Festival, add:
(Our God, our ancients' God,
may our prayer arise and come to you,
and be beheld, and be acceptable.
Let it be heard, acted upon, remembered
—the memory of us and all our needs,
the memory of our ancestors,
the memory of messianic hopes,
the memory of Jerusalem your holy city,
and the memory of all your kin, the house of Israel,
all surviving in your presence.
Act for goodness and grace, for love and care,
for life, well-being, and peace, on this day of ↵

וזכרון ימות המשיח / the memory of messianic hopes. We assert our faith in the coming of a messianic age, a time when justice will reign and all humanity will be united in recognition of the one God. Even in our people's darkest hour, this vision of the future strengthened us as we faced both life and death. However distanced we may be from the more naive aspects of belief in the person of messiah, the vision of a transformed future remains our guide, just as we know that this vision will become reality only if our deeds reflect it. A.G.

בָּרוּךְ אַתָּה יהוה שׁוֹמֵעַ תְּפִלָּה׃

Both the full Amidah *and the abbreviated* Amidah *continue here.*

יז עֲבוֹדָה

רְצֵה יהוה אֱלֹהֵֽינוּ בְּעַמְּךָ יִשְׂרָאֵל וְלַֽהַב תְּפִלָּתָם בְּאַהֲבָה תְקַבֵּל בְּרָצוֹן וּתְהִי לְרָצוֹן תָּמִיד עֲבוֹדַת יִשְׂרָאֵל עַמֶּֽךָ׃

On a Rosh Hodesh/New Moon or a Festival, add:

(אֱלֹהֵֽינוּ וֵאלֹהֵי אֲבוֹתֵֽינוּ וְאִמּוֹתֵֽינוּ יַעֲלֶה וְיָבוֹא וְיַגִּֽיעַ וְיֵרָאֶה וְיֵרָצֶה וְיִשָּׁמַע וְיִפָּקֵד וְיִזָּכֵר זִכְרוֹנֵֽנוּ וּפִקְדוֹנֵֽנוּ וְזִכְרוֹן אֲבוֹתֵֽינוּ וְאִמּוֹתֵֽינוּ וְזִכְרוֹן יְמוֹת הַמָּשִֽׁיחַ וְזִכְרוֹן יְרוּשָׁלַֽיִם עִיר קָדְשֶֽׁךָ וְזִכְרוֹן כָּל עַמְּךָ בֵּית יִשְׂרָאֵל לְפָנֶֽיךָ לִפְלֵיטָה וּלְטוֹבָה לְחֵן וּלְחֶֽסֶד וּלְרַחֲמִים לְחַיִּים וּלְשָׁלוֹם בְּיוֹם ←

ולהב תפלתם. The external mouthing of words alone cannot move us. It is the inward flame of devotion that brings our prayer close to God. Indeed, as the Hebrew phrasing vividly conveys, a passionate longing for godliness can exist among those unable to express that feeling in words. The phrase *lahav tefilatam*, "the flame of Israel's prayer," recalls that feeling of *hitlahavut*: the "in-burning" flame of passionate devotion. To attain *hitlahavut* in prayer is to soar with the rapturous ecstasy of divine communion, to access the infinite and be aflame with the nearness of God.

A.G./M.P.

On Rosh Ḥodesh: the new moon.
On Pesaḥ: the festival of matzot.
On Sukkot: the festival of sukkot.

Remember us this day, ALL-KNOWING ONE, our God, for goodness. Favor us this day with blessing. Preserve us this day for life. With your redeeming, nurturing word, be kind and generous. Act tenderly on our behalf, and grant us victory over all our trials. Truly, our eyes are turned toward you, for you are a providing God; gracious and merciful are you.)

And may our eyes behold your homecoming, with merciful intent, to Zion. Blessed are you, THE FAITHFUL ONE, who brings your presence home to Zion.

18. HODA'AH / THANKS

We give thanks to you, that you are THE ALL-MERCIFUL, our God, God of our ancestors, today and always. A firm, enduring source of life, a shield to us in time of trial, you are ever there, from age to age. We acknowledge you, declare your praise, and thank you for our lives entrusted to your hand, our souls placed in your care, for your miracles that greet us every day, and for your wonders and the good things that are with us every hour, morning, noon, and night. Good One, whose kindness never stops, Kind One, whose loving acts have never failed—always have we placed our hope in you. ↩

KAVANAH. So long as the Jewish people is linked in communion with the eternal, it can look forward to an eternal life for itself. M.M.K. (Adapted)

KAVANAH. Gratitude is the overwhelming experience of the person of faith. Faith stimulates gratitude, and the practice of gratitude expands faith. We experience thankfulness when we know that our lives are safe within God's protection. We trust that the future is assured. We need not consume our days in fear and anxiety. We are released. We can marvel at the daily wonders. S.P.W.

ראֹשׁ הַחֹֽדֶשׁ הַזֶּה	*On Rosh Hodesh:*
חַג הַמַּצּוֹת הַזֶּה	*On Pesah:*
חַג הַסֻּכּוֹת הַזֶּה	*On Sukkot:*

זָכְרֵֽנוּ יהוה אֱלֹהֵֽינוּ בּוֹ לְטוֹבָה: וּפָקְדֵֽנוּ בוֹ לִבְרָכָה וְהוֹשִׁיעֵֽנוּ בוֹ לְחַיִּים: וּבִדְבַר יְשׁוּעָה וְרַחֲמִים חוּס וְחָנֵּֽנוּ וְרַחֵם עָלֵֽינוּ וְהוֹשִׁיעֵֽנוּ כִּי אֵלֶֽיךָ עֵינֵֽינוּ כִּי אֵל מֶֽלֶךְ חַנּוּן וְרַחוּם אָֽתָּה:)

וְתֶחֱזֶֽינָה עֵינֵֽינוּ בְּשׁוּבְךָ לְצִיּוֹן בְּרַחֲמִים: בָּרוּךְ אַתָּה יהוה הַמַּחֲזִיר שְׁכִינָתוֹ לְצִיּוֹן:

יח 18 הוֹדָאָה

מוֹדִים אֲנַֽחְנוּ לָךְ שָׁאַתָּה הוּא יהוה אֱלֹהֵֽינוּ וֵאלֹהֵי אֲבוֹתֵֽינוּ וְאִמּוֹתֵֽינוּ לְעוֹלָם וָעֶד צוּר חַיֵּֽינוּ מָגֵן יִשְׁעֵֽנוּ אַתָּה הוּא לְדוֹר וָדוֹר: נוֹדֶה לְּךָ וּנְסַפֵּר תְּהִלָּתֶֽךָ עַל חַיֵּֽינוּ הַמְּסוּרִים בְּיָדֶֽךָ וְעַל נִשְׁמוֹתֵֽינוּ הַפְּקוּדוֹת לָךְ וְעַל נִסֶּֽיךָ שֶׁבְּכָל יוֹם עִמָּֽנוּ וְעַל נִפְלְאוֹתֶֽיךָ וְטוֹבוֹתֶֽיךָ שֶׁבְּכָל־עֵת עֶֽרֶב וָבֹֽקֶר וְצָהֳרָֽיִם: הַטּוֹב כִּי לֹא כָלוּ רַחֲמֶֽיךָ וְהַמְרַחֵם כִּי לֹא תַֽמּוּ חֲסָדֶֽיךָ מֵעוֹלָם קִוִּֽינוּ לָךְ: ←

DERASH. The insights of wonder must be constantly kept alive. Since there is a need for daily wonder, there is a need for daily worship. The sense of the "miracles which are daily with us," the sense of the "continual marvels," is the source of prayer. There is no worship, no music, no love, if we take for granted the blessings or defeats of living...The profound and perpetual awareness of the wonder of being has become a part of the religious consciousness of the Jew. A.J.H.

(*On Ḥanukah add:* For the miracles, for the redemption, for heroic acts, for saving deeds, for consolations, all of which you have enacted for our ancestors at this time of year in days gone by—as in the days of Matthew, son of Yoḥanan, Hasmonean High Priest, and Matthew's sons: a wicked Hellenistic government arose against your people Israel, forcing them to shun your Torah and to leave off from the laws your will ordained. And you, in your abundant mercy, stood up for Israel in their hour of distress. You pressed their claim, exacted justice for them. You delivered armed might to the weak, the many to the power of the few, the wicked to the power of the just, the vicious to the power of those occupied with your Torah. You made known your name that day, and made it holy in your world. And for your people Israel, you enacted great deliverance, as in our own time. Afterward, your children came into your Temple's inner room. They cleared your sanctuary, purified your holy place, kindled lights inside your holy courtyards, and established these eight days of Ḥanukah, for giving thanks and praise to your great name.) ↵

On Ḥanukah add:

(עַל הַנִּסִּים וְעַל הַפֻּרְקָן וְעַל הַגְּבוּרוֹת וְעַל הַתְּשׁוּעוֹת וְעַל הַנֶּחָמוֹת שֶׁעָשִׂיתָ לַאֲבוֹתֵינוּ וְאִמּוֹתֵינוּ בַּיָּמִים הָהֵם בַּזְּמַן הַזֶּה: בִּימֵי מַתִּתְיָהוּ בֶּן יוֹחָנָן כֹּהֵן גָּדוֹל חַשְׁמוֹנַאי וּבָנָיו כְּשֶׁעָמְדָה מַלְכוּת יָוָן הָרְשָׁעָה עַל עַמְּךָ יִשְׂרָאֵל לְהַשְׁכִּיחָם תּוֹרָתֶךָ וּלְהַעֲבִירָם מֵחֻקֵּי רְצוֹנֶךָ וְאַתָּה בְּרַחֲמֶיךָ הָרַבִּים עָמַדְתָּ לָהֶם בְּעֵת צָרָתָם רַבְתָּ אֶת רִיבָם דַּנְתָּ אֶת דִּינָם מָסַרְתָּ גִּבּוֹרִים בְּיַד חַלָּשִׁים וְרַבִּים בְּיַד מְעַטִּים וּרְשָׁעִים בְּיַד צַדִּיקִים וְזֵדִים בְּיַד עוֹסְקֵי תוֹרָתֶךָ: וּלְךָ עָשִׂיתָ שֵׁם גָּדוֹל וְקָדוֹשׁ בְּעוֹלָמֶךָ וּלְעַמְּךָ יִשְׂרָאֵל עָשִׂיתָ תְּשׁוּעָה גְדוֹלָה וּפֻרְקָן כְּהַיּוֹם הַזֶּה: וְאַחַר כֵּן בָּאוּ בָנֶיךָ לִדְבִיר בֵּיתֶךָ וּפִנּוּ אֶת הֵיכָלֶךָ וְטִהֲרוּ אֶת מִקְדָּשֶׁךָ וְהִדְלִיקוּ נֵרוֹת בְּחַצְרוֹת קָדְשֶׁךָ וְקָבְעוּ שְׁמוֹנַת יְמֵי חֲנֻכָּה אֵלּוּ לְהוֹדוֹת וּלְהַלֵּל לְשִׁמְךָ הַגָּדוֹל:) ←

(*On Purim, add:* For the miracles, and for deliverance,
and for the mighty deeds, and for the saving acts,
and for the consolations
you enacted for our ancestors
In ancient times, and in our own time.

In the days of Mordechai and Esther
in Shushan, the mighty capital [of Persia],
when the wicked Haman rose against them,
seeking to destroy, to kill, and to eradicate
all Jews, the young and old alike,
in a single day,
the thirteenth of the twelfth month,
that is, the month of Adar,
and take as plunder all they owned.

But you, in your abundant mercies,
thwarted his conspiracy, destroyed his plan.
And to the Jews came light and happiness,
and joy and glory.)

For all these things, let your name be blessed,
and raised in honor always, sovereign of ours, forever.

(*Between Rosh Hashanah and Yom Kippur add:* And write down for a good life all the people of your covenant.)

Let all of life acknowledge you!
May all beings praise your name in truth, O God,
our rescue and our aid.
Blessed are you, THE GRACIOUS ONE,
whose name is good, and to whom all thanks are due. ↩

On Purim add:

(עַל הַנִּסִּים וְעַל הַפֻּרְקָן וְעַל הַגְּבוּרוֹת וְעַל הַתְּשׁוּעוֹת וְעַל הַנֶּחָמוֹת
שֶׁעָשִׂיתָ לַאֲבוֹתֵינוּ וְאִמּוֹתֵינוּ בַּיָּמִים הָהֵם בַּזְּמַן הַזֶּה:

בִּימֵי מָרְדְּכַי וְאֶסְתֵּר בְּשׁוּשַׁן הַבִּירָה כְּשֶׁעָמַד עֲלֵיהֶם הָמָן הָרָשָׁע:
בִּקֵּשׁ לְהַשְׁמִיד לַהֲרוֹג וּלְאַבֵּד אֶת כָּל הַיְּהוּדִים מִנַּעַר וְעַד זָקֵן בְּיוֹם
אֶחָד בִּשְׁלוֹשָׁה עָשָׂר לְחֹדֶשׁ שְׁנֵים עָשָׂר הוּא חֹדֶשׁ אֲדָר וּשְׁלָלָם לָבוֹז:
וְאַתָּה בְּרַחֲמֶיךָ הָרַבִּים הֵפַרְתָּ אֶת עֲצָתוֹ וְקִלְקַלְתָּ אֶת מַחֲשַׁבְתּוֹ
לַיְּהוּדִים הָיְתָה אוֹרָה וְשִׂמְחָה וְשָׂשׂוֹן וִיקָר.)

וְעַל כֻּלָּם יִתְבָּרַךְ וְיִתְרוֹמַם שִׁמְךָ מַלְכֵּנוּ תָּמִיד לְעוֹלָם וָעֶד:

Between Rosh Hashanah and Yom Kippur add:

(וּכְתֹב לְחַיִּים טוֹבִים כָּל־בְּנֵי בְרִיתֶךָ:)

וְכֹל הַחַיִּים יוֹדוּךָ סֶּלָה וִיהַלְלוּ אֶת שִׁמְךָ בֶּאֱמֶת הָאֵל יְשׁוּעָתֵנוּ
וְעֶזְרָתֵנוּ סֶלָה: בָּרוּךְ אַתָּה יהוה הַטּוֹב שִׁמְךָ וּלְךָ נָאֶה לְהוֹדוֹת: ←

This prayer helps us to get in touch with our gratitude for the extraordinary yet often overlooked daily workings of the world, and through them to recognize the insignificance of our own roles, to feel humble. In becoming aware of our smallness, we become able to grasp our relatedness to the All. This in turn makes it possible to overcome the loneliness of claiming we have all the answers and the anxiety of always needing to be in control. At these moments the pain of our unfulfilled needs is swept away in the wondrous goodness we feel in the world about us. We give thanks. S.P.W

19. BIRKAT HASHALOM / PEACE BLESSING

Grant abundant peace eternally for Israel, your people. For you are the sovereign source of all peace. So, may it be a good thing in your eyes to bless your people Israel, and all who dwell on earth, in every time and hour, with your peace.

(*Between Rosh Hashanah and Yom Kippur, add:* In the book of life, blessing, peace, and proper sustenance, may we be remembered and inscribed, we and all your people, the house of Israel, for a good life and for peace.)

Blessed are you, COMPASSIONATE ONE, maker of peace.

The Amidah *traditionally concludes with bowing and taking three steps back.*

ואת כל יושבי תבל / all who dwell on earth. According to the sages, every Amidah must conclude with a prayer for peace and an acknowledgment of God as the power that makes for peace. Inclusion of the words "and all who dwell on earth" proclaims that Israel desires the blessing of peace, not for itself alone, but for all humanity. S.S.

עושה השלום / maker of peace. This ancient version of the prayer for peace in its most universal form was assigned in the traditional liturgy to the ten days of *teshuvah*. During the year the text read, "who blesses your people Israel with peace." In our times, when life has been transformed by the constant threat of global destruction, the need of the hour calls for the more universal form of the prayer throughout the year. A.G.

KAVANAH. God is shalom, God's name is shalom, everything is held together by shalom. Zohar

My God, you are *salam* peace.
Peace comes from you goes back to you.
Let us live in peace and with peace.
You are great and generous. Sidi Sheikh Muhammad Al Jemal

19 בִּרְכַּת הַשָּׁלוֹם

שָׁלוֹם רָב עַל יִשְׂרָאֵל עַמְּךָ תָּשִׂים לְעוֹלָם: כִּי אַתָּה הוּא מֶֽלֶךְ אָדוֹן
לְכָל הַשָּׁלוֹם: וְטוֹב בְּעֵינֶֽיךָ לְבָרֵךְ אֶת עַמְּךָ יִשְׂרָאֵל וְאֶת כָּל־יוֹשְׁבֵי
תֵבֵל בְּכָל עֵת וּבְכָל שָׁעָה בִּשְׁלוֹמֶֽךָ:

Between Rosh Hashanah and Yom Kippur, add:

(בְּסֵֽפֶר חַיִּים בְּרָכָה וְשָׁלוֹם וּפַרְנָסָה טוֹבָה נִזָּכֵר וְנִכָּתֵב לְפָנֶֽיךָ אֲנַֽחְנוּ
וְכָל עַמְּךָ בֵּית יִשְׂרָאֵל לְחַיִּים טוֹבִים וּלְשָׁלוֹם:)

בָּרוּךְ אַתָּה יהוה עוֹשֵׂה הַשָּׁלוֹם:

Shalom rav al yisra'el ameḥa tasim le'olam.
Ki atah hu meleḥ adon leḥol hashalom.
Vetov be'eyneḥa levareḥ et ameḥa yisra'el
ve'et kol yoshvey tevel
beḥol et uvḥol sha'ah bishlomeḥa.

Between Rosh Hashanah and Yom Kippur, add:

(Besefer ḥayim beraḥah veshalom ufarnasah tovah
nizaḥer venikatev lefaneḥa
anaḥnu veḥol ameḥa beyt yisra'el
leḥayim tovim ulshalom.)

Baruḥ atah adonay osey hashalom.

The Amidah *traditionally concludes with bowing and taking three steps back.*

KAVANAH. Enable us, God, to behold meaning in the chaos of life about us and purpose in the chaos of life within us. Deliver us from the sense of futility in our strivings toward the light and the truth. Give us strength to ride safely through the maelstrom of petty cares and anxieties. May we behold things in their proper proportions and see life in its wholeness and its holiness.

M.M.K./M.S.

ELOHAY NETZOR / A CONCLUDING MEDITATION

Dear God, protect my tongue from evil,
and my lips from telling lies.
May I turn away from evil
and do what is good in your sight.
Let me be counted among those who seek peace.
May my words of prayer
and my heart's meditation be seen favorably,
BELOVED ONE my rock and my redeemer.
May the one who creates harmony above
make peace
for us and for all Israel,
and for all who dwell on earth.
And say: Amen.

On fast days and during the days between Rosh Hashanah and Yom Kippur, continue with Avinu Malkenu, *or alternatives, pages 136-143.*
On other days, some congregations continue with Taḥanun, *page 424.*

COMMENTARY. The Talmud lists examples of twelve personal meditations that could follow the Amidah. If this one does not speak to you, compose your own, or stand or sit in silent meditation. L.W.K.

NOTE. Like the opening verse of the Amidah, this prayer employs the singular and deals with the power of words. But here the concern is for words between people, not for those directed to God. Some people find it easier to talk to God than to talk to others. L.W.K.

KAVANAH. Sin is the failure to live up to the best that is in us. It means that our souls are not attuned to the divine—that we have betrayed God. M.M.K./M.S.

יהיו...וגואלי / May...redeemer (Psalm 19:15).

אֱלֹהַי נְצוֹר

אֱלֹהַי נְצוֹר לְשׁוֹנִי מֵרָע
וּשְׂפָתַי מִדַּבֵּר מִרְמָה:

יְהִי רָצוֹן שֶׁאָסוּר מֵרָע
וְהַטּוֹב בְּעֵינֶיךָ אֶעֱשֶׂה
יְהִי חֶלְקִי עִם מְבַקְשֵׁי שָׁלוֹם וְרוֹדְפָיו:

יִהְיוּ לְרָצוֹן אִמְרֵי פִי
וְהֶגְיוֹן לִבִּי לְפָנֶיךָ
יהוה צוּרִי וְגוֹאֲלִי:

עֹשֶׂה שָׁלוֹם בִּמְרוֹמָיו
הוּא יַעֲשֶׂה שָׁלוֹם
עָלֵינוּ וְעַל כָּל יִשְׂרָאֵל
וְאִמְרוּ אָמֵן:

Yihyu leratzon imrey fi
vehegyon libi lefaneḥa
adonay tzuri vego'ali.
Oseh shalom bimromav
hu ya'aseh shalom
aleynu ve'al kol yisra'el
ve'al kol yoshvey tevel
ve'imru amen.

On fast days and during the days between Rosh Hashanah and Yom Kippur, continue with Avinu Malkenu *or alternatives, pages 136-143.*
On other days, some congregations continue with Taḥanun, *page 425.*

KADDISH TITKABAL /
KADDISH FOR COMPLETION OF PRAYER

Reader: Let God's name be made great and holy in the world that was created as God willed. May God complete the holy realm in your own lifetime, in your days, and in the days of all the house of Israel, quickly and soon. And say: Amen.

Congregation: May God's great name be blessed forever and as long as worlds endure.

Reader: May it be blessed, and praised, and glorified, and held in honor, viewed with awe, embellished, and revered; and may the blessed name of holiness be hailed, though it be higher (*Between Rosh Hashanah and Yom Kippur, add:* by far) than all the blessings, songs, praises, and consolations that we utter in this world. And say: Amen.

And may the prayer and supplication of the whole house of Israel be acceptable to their creator in the heavens. And say: Amen.

May Heaven grant a universal peace, and life for us, and for all Israel. And say: Amen.

May the one who creates harmony above make peace for us and for all Israel, and for all who dwell on earth. And say: Amen.

NOTE. Kaddish Titkabal concludes the section of the service containing an Amidah / silent prayer. It therefore contains a request for the acceptance of prayer, which is omitted in the Mourner's Kaddish that follows *Aleynu*. D.A.T.

קַדִּישׁ תִּתְקַבַּל

יִתְגַּדַּל וְיִתְקַדַּשׁ שְׁמֵהּ רַבָּא בְּעָלְמָא דִּי בְרָא כִרְעוּתֵהּ וְיַמְלִיךְ מַלְכוּתֵהּ בְּחַיֵּיכוֹן וּבְיוֹמֵיכוֹן וּבְחַיֵּי דְכָל בֵּית יִשְׂרָאֵל בַּעֲגָלָא וּבִזְמַן קָרִיב וְאִמְרוּ אָמֵן:

יְהֵא שְׁמֵהּ רַבָּא מְבָרַךְ לְעָלַם וּלְעָלְמֵי עָלְמַיָּא:

יִתְבָּרַךְ וְיִשְׁתַּבַּח וְיִתְפָּאַר וְיִתְרוֹמַם וְיִתְנַשֵּׂא וְיִתְהַדַּר וְיִתְעַלֶּה וְיִתְהַלַּל שְׁמֵהּ דְּקֻדְשָׁא בְּרִיךְ הוּא

לְעֵֽלָּא (*Between Rosh Hashanah and Yom Kippur, add:* לְעֵֽלָּא) מִן כָּל בִּרְכָתָא וְשִׁירָתָא תֻּשְׁבְּחָתָא וְנֶחֱמָתָא דַּאֲמִירָן בְּעָלְמָא וְאִמְרוּ אָמֵן:

תִּתְקַבַּל צְלוֹתְהוֹן וּבָעוּתְהוֹן דְּכָל בֵּית יִשְׂרָאֵל קֳדָם אֲבוּהוֹן דִּי בִשְׁמַיָּא וְאִמְרוּ אָמֵן:

יְהֵא שְׁלָמָא רַבָּא מִן שְׁמַיָּא וְחַיִּים עָלֵֽינוּ וְעַל כָּל יִשְׂרָאֵל וְאִמְרוּ אָמֵן:

עוֹשֶׂה שָׁלוֹם בִּמְרוֹמָיו הוּא יַעֲשֶׂה שָׁלוֹם עָלֵֽינוּ וְעַל כָּל יִשְׂרָאֵל וְעַל כָּל יוֹשְׁבֵי תֵבֵל וְאִמְרוּ אָמֵן:

Yehey shemey raba mevaraḥ le'alam ulalmey almaya.

Oseh shalom bimromav hu ya'aseh shalom aleynu ve'al kol yisra'el ve'al kol yoshvey tevel ve'imru amen.

ALEYNU

We rise for Aleynu. *It is customary to bow at "bend the knee." For an alternative version* *see page 332.* *Choose one of the following:*

It is up to us to offer praises to the Source of all,
to declare the greatness of the author of Creation,
who gave us teachings of truth
and planted eternal life within us.

It is up to us to offer praises to the Source of all,
to declare the greatness of the author of Creation,
who created heaven's heights and spread out its expanse,
who laid the earth's foundation and brought forth its offspring,
giving life to all its peoples,
the breath of life to all who walk about.

COMMENTARY. This siddur offers several versions of the *Aleynu*. The first, which appeared in the 1945 Reconstructionist siddur, emphasizes that the gift of God's Torah or teaching demands our committed response. The second version, based on Isaiah 42:5 and fit into the *Aleynu* by Rabbi Max D. Klein, emphasizes that our obligation to God flows from our role as part of Creation. The traditional *Aleynu* that appears below the line has troubled Reconstructionist Jews because it implies the inferiority of other faiths and peoples. D.A.T.

COMMENTARY. The theme of *Aleynu* is the anticipation of God's universal rulership. Originally, this glorious hymn introduced the "Rulership" section of the Rosh Hashanah liturgy. Because of its lofty language and message, *Aleynu* was soon added to every worship service. The Reconstructionist version of *Aleynu* shifts the focus from a concern with the specialness of the Jewish people to an emphasis on the unique Torah perspective that enables Israel to help spread God's presence through the universe. This shift eliminates an opportunity for supporting Jewish triumphalism, in favor of stressing the importance of Torah in Jewish living. S.S.

עָלֵינוּ

We rise for Aleynu. *It is customary to bow at* "korim"*. For an alternative version see page 332. Choose one of the following.*

עָלֵינוּ לְשַׁבֵּחַ לַאֲדוֹן הַכֹּל
לָתֵת גְּדֻלָּה לְיוֹצֵר בְּרֵאשִׁית
שֶׁנָּתַן לָנוּ תּוֹרַת אֱמֶת
וְחַיֵּי עוֹלָם נָטַע בְּתוֹכֵנוּ׃

Aleynu leshabe'aḥ la'adon hakol
latet gedulah leyotzer bereyshit
shenatan lanu torat emet
veḥayey olam nata betoḫenu.

Continue on page 253.

עָלֵינוּ לְשַׁבֵּחַ לַאֲדוֹן הַכֹּל
לָתֵת גְּדֻלָּה לְיוֹצֵר בְּרֵאשִׁית
בּוֹרֵא הַשָּׁמַיִם וְנוֹטֵיהֶם
רֹקַע הָאָרֶץ וְצֶאֱצָאֶיהָ
נֹתֵן נְשָׁמָה לָעָם עָלֶיהָ
וְרוּחַ לַהֹלְכִים בָּהּ׃

Aleynu leshabe'aḥ la'adon hakol
latet gedulah leyotzer bereyshit
bore hashamayim venoteyhem
roka ha'aretz vetze'etza'eha
noten neshamah la'am aleha
veru'aḥ laholeḥim ba.

Continue on page 253.

עָלֵינוּ לְשַׁבֵּחַ לַאֲדוֹן הַכֹּל לָתֵת גְּדֻלָּה לְיוֹצֵר בְּרֵאשִׁית שֶׁלֹּא עָשָׂנוּ כְּגוֹיֵי הָאֲרָצוֹת וְלֹא שָׂמָנוּ כְּמִשְׁפְּחוֹת הָאֲדָמָה שֶׁלֹּא שָׂם חֶלְקֵנוּ כָּהֶם וְגוֹרָלֵנוּ כְּכָל הֲמוֹנָם׃

It is up to us to offer praises to the Source of all, to declare the greatness of the author of Creation, who has made us different from the other nations of the earth, and situated us in quite a different spot, and made our daily lot another kind from theirs, and given us a destiny uncommon in this world.

And so, we bend the knee and bow,
acknowledging the sovereign who rules
above all those who rule, the blessed Holy One,
who stretched out the heavens and founded the earth,
whose realm embraces heaven's heights,
whose mighty presence stalks celestial ramparts.
This is our God; there is none else besides,
as it is written in the Torah:
"You shall know this day, and bring it home
inside your heart, that THE SUPREME ONE is God
in the heavens above and on the earth below.
There is no other God." ↩

DERASH. Every person and people that feel they have something to live for, and that are bent on living that life in righteousness, are true witnesses of God. M.M.K.

KAVANAH. As the hand held before the eye hides the tallest mountain, so this small earthly life hides from our gaze the vast radiance and secrets of which the world is full, and if we can take life from before our eyes, as one takes away one's hand, we will see the great radiance within the world. M.B. (Adapted)

וידעת...עוד / You...other God (Deuteronomy 4:39).

וַאֲנַֽחְנוּ כּוֹרְעִים וּמִשְׁתַּחֲוִים וּמוֹדִים לִפְנֵי מֶֽלֶךְ מַלְכֵי הַמְּלָכִים הַקָּדוֹשׁ בָּרוּךְ הוּא:
שֶׁהוּא נוֹטֶה שָׁמַֽיִם וְיוֹסֵד אָֽרֶץ וּמוֹשַׁב יְקָרוֹ בַּשָּׁמַֽיִם מִמַּֽעַל וּשְׁכִינַת עֻזּוֹ בְּגָבְהֵי מְרוֹמִים: הוּא אֱלֹהֵֽינוּ אֵין עוֹד: אֱמֶת מַלְכֵּֽנוּ אֶֽפֶס זוּלָתוֹ כַּכָּתוּב בְּתוֹרָתוֹ: וְיָדַעְתָּ הַיּוֹם וַהֲשֵׁבֹתָ אֶל לְבָבֶֽךָ כִּי יהוה הוּא הָאֱלֹהִים בַּשָּׁמַֽיִם מִמַּֽעַל וְעַל הָאָֽרֶץ מִתָּֽחַת אֵין עוֹד: ←

Va'anaḥnu korim umishtaḥavim umodim
lifney meleḥ malḥey hamelaḥim hakadosh baruḥ hu.
Shehu noteh shamayim veyosed aretz umoshav yekaro
bashamayim mima'al
ush-ḥinat uzo begovhey meromim.
Hu eloheynu eyn od.
Emet malkenu efes zulato kakatuv betorato.
Veyadata hayom vahashevota el levaveḥa
ki adonay hu ha'elohim bashamayim mima'al ve'al ha'aretz
mitaḥat eyn od.

And so, we put our hope in you,
THE EMINENCE, our God,
that soon we may behold
the full splendor of your might,
and see idolatry vanish from the earth,
and all material gods be swept away,
and the power of your rule repair the world,
and all creatures of flesh call on your name,
and all the wicked of the earth turn back to you.
Let all who dwell upon the globe perceive and know
that to you each knee must bend, each tongue swear oath,
and let them give the glory of your name its precious due.
Let all of them take upon themselves your rule.
Reign over them, soon and for always.
For this is all your realm, throughout all worlds, across all time—
as it is written in your Torah:
"THE ETERNAL ONE will reign now and forever."

And it is written:
"THE EVERLASTING ONE will reign
as sovereign over all the earth.
On that day shall THE MANY-NAMED be one,
God's name be one!"

KAVANAH. A world of God callers is a world of truth and peace, a world where lust for power, greed, and envy—the idols of pride—is uprooted from the individual and group psyche. S.P.W.

עַל כֵּן נְקַוֶּה לְךָ יהוה אֱלֹהֵינוּ לִרְאוֹת מְהֵרָה בְּתִפְאֶרֶת עֻזֶּךָ לְהַעֲבִיר גִּלּוּלִים מִן הָאָרֶץ וְהָאֱלִילִים כָּרוֹת יִכָּרֵתוּן לְתַקֵּן עוֹלָם בְּמַלְכוּת שַׁדַּי: וְכָל בְּנֵי בָשָׂר יִקְרְאוּ בִשְׁמֶךָ: לְהַפְנוֹת אֵלֶיךָ כָּל רִשְׁעֵי אָרֶץ: יַכִּירוּ וְיֵדְעוּ כָּל יוֹשְׁבֵי תֵבֵל כִּי לְךָ תִּכְרַע כָּל בֶּרֶךְ תִּשָּׁבַע כָּל־לָשׁוֹן: לְפָנֶיךָ יהוה אֱלֹהֵינוּ יִכְרְעוּ וְיִפֹּלוּ וְלִכְבוֹד שִׁמְךָ יְקָר יִתֵּנוּ וִיקַבְּלוּ כֻלָּם אֶת עֹל מַלְכוּתֶךָ וְתִמְלֹךְ עֲלֵיהֶם מְהֵרָה לְעוֹלָם וָעֶד: כִּי הַמַּלְכוּת שֶׁלְּךָ הִיא וּלְעוֹלְמֵי עַד תִּמְלֹךְ בְּכָבוֹד כַּכָּתוּב בְּתוֹרָתֶךָ: יהוה יִמְלֹךְ לְעֹלָם וָעֶד: וְנֶאֱמַר: וְהָיָה יהוה לְמֶלֶךְ עַל כָּל הָאָרֶץ בַּיּוֹם הַהוּא יִהְיֶה יהוה אֶחָד וּשְׁמוֹ אֶחָד:

Kakatuv betorateḥa: Adonay yimloḥ le'olam va'ed.
Vene'emar: Vehayah adonay lemeleḥ al kol ha'aretz.
Bayom hahu yihyeh adonay eḥad ushmo eḥad.

DERASH. When senseless hatred reigns on earth and people hide their faces from one another, then heaven is forced to hide its face. But when love comes to rule the earth and people reveal their faces to one another, then the splendor of God will be revealed. M.B. (Adapted)

DERASH. It is not the seeking after God that divides but the claim to have found God and to have discovered the only proper way of obeying God and communing with God. M.M.K. (Adapted)

יהוה...ועד / THE ETERNAL ONE...forever (Exodus 15:18).

והיה...אחד / THE EVERLASTING ONE...one (Zechariah 14:9).

Readings suitable for a house of mourning may be added here. *See pages 490-532.*

INTRODUCTION TO THE MOURNERS' KADDISH

In reciting the Kaddish we affirm our awareness of holiness in our world. Much of our experience of divine goodness, grace and love has come to us through those whose lives have touched our own. (Today we remember....) We invoke the transcendent power of love and caring as we sanctify God's name.

KADDISH YATOM / MOURNERS' KADDISH

It is customary for mourners, and those observing Yahrzeit, *to stand for Kaddish. In some congregations everyone rises.*

Reader: Let God's name be made great and holy in the world that was created as God willed. May God complete the holy realm in your own lifetime, in your days, and in the days of all the house of Israel, quickly and soon. And say: Amen.

Congregation: May God's great name be blessed, forever and as long as worlds endure.

Reader: May it be blessed, and praised, and glorified, and held in honor, viewed with awe, embellished, and revered; and may the blessed name of holiness be hailed, though it be higher (*Between Rosh Hashanah and Yom Kippur, add:* by far) than all the blessings, songs, praises and consolations that we utter in this world. And say: Amen.

May Heaven grant a universal peace, and life for us, and for all Israel. And say: Amen.

May the one who creates harmony above, make peace for us and for all Israel, and for all who dwell on earth. And say: Amen.

NOTE. Congregations usually mention the names of congregants and their relatives who have died in the previous week before reciting the Mourner's Kaddish. In many congregations a *Yahrzeit* list is read as well. In more informal settings the leader sometimes invites those present to speak the names of those they wish to be remembered. D.A.T.

Readings suitable for a house of mourning may be added here. See pages 490-532.

קַדִּישׁ יָתוֹם

It is customary for mourners, and those observing Yahrzeit, *to stand for Kaddish. In some congregations everyone rises.*

יִתְגַּדַּל וְיִתְקַדַּשׁ שְׁמֵהּ רַבָּא בְּעָלְמָא דִּי בְרָא כִרְעוּתֵהּ וְיַמְלִיךְ
מַלְכוּתֵהּ בְּחַיֵּיכוֹן וּבְיוֹמֵיכוֹן וּבְחַיֵּי דְכָל בֵּית יִשְׂרָאֵל בַּעֲגָלָא וּבִזְמַן
קָרִיב וְאִמְרוּ אָמֵן:

יְהֵא שְׁמֵהּ רַבָּא מְבָרַךְ לְעָלַם וּלְעָלְמֵי עָלְמַיָּא:

יִתְבָּרַךְ וְיִשְׁתַּבַּח וְיִתְפָּאַר וְיִתְרוֹמַם וְיִתְנַשֵּׂא וְיִתְהַדַּר וְיִתְעַלֶּה
וְיִתְהַלַּל שְׁמֵהּ דְּקֻדְשָׁא בְּרִיךְ הוּא
לְעֵֽלָּא (*Between Rosh Hashanah and Yom Kippur, add:* לְעֵֽלָּא) מִן כָּל בִּרְכָתָא
וְשִׁירָתָא תֻּשְׁבְּחָתָא וְנֶחֱמָתָא דַּאֲמִירָן בְּעָלְמָא וְאִמְרוּ אָמֵן:

יְהֵא שְׁלָמָא רַבָּא מִן שְׁמַיָּא וְחַיִּים עָלֵֽינוּ וְעַל כָּל יִשְׂרָאֵל וְאִמְרוּ אָמֵן:

עוֹשֶׂה שָׁלוֹם בִּמְרוֹמָיו הוּא יַעֲשֶׂה שָׁלוֹם עָלֵֽינוּ וְעַל כָּל יִשְׂרָאֵל וְעַל
כָּל יוֹשְׁבֵי תֵבֵל וְאִמְרוּ אָמֵן:

Reader: Yitgadal veyitkadash shemey raba
be'alma di vera ḥirutey veyamliḥ malḥutey
beḥayeyḥon uvyomeyḥon uvḥayey deḥol beyt yisra'el
ba'agala uvizman kariv ve'imru amen.

Congregation: Yehey shemey raba mevaraḥ le'alam ulalmey almaya.

Reader: Yitbaraḥ veyishtabaḥ veyitpa'ar veyitromam
veyitnasey veyit-hadar veyitaleh veyit-halal
shemey dekudsha beriḥ hu
le'ela (*Between Rosh Hashanah and Yom Kippur, add:* le'ela) min kol birḥata
veshirata tushbeḥata veneḥemata da'amiran be'alma
ve'imru amen.

Yehey shelama raba min shemaya veḥayim aleynu ve'al kol
yisra'el ve'imru amen.

Oseh shalom bimromav hu ya'aseh shalom aleynu ve'al kol
yisra'el ve'al kol yoshvey tevel ve'imru amen.

מַעֲרִיב

MA'ARIV/ EVENING SERVICE

God is compassionate,
forgiving human error
and refusing to destroy,
ready to refrain from anger
and unwilling to awaken wrath.
Extend your help, REDEEMING ONE!
Give answer, sovereign one,
whenever we may call.

When a minyan is present, the Bareḥu *is said. The congregation rises and faces the ark. It is customary to bow.*

Bless THE INFINITE, the blessed One!

Blessed is THE INFINITE, the blessed One, now and forever.

KAVANAH. Public worship aids us by liberating personality from the confining walls of the individual ego. Imprisoned in self, we easily fall prey to morbid brooding. Interference with career, personal disappointment and disillusionment, hurts to vanity, the fear of death—all these tend so to dominate our attention that our minds move in a fixed and narrow system of ideas, which we detest but from which we see no escape. With a whole wide world of boundless opportunities about us, we permit our minds, as it were, to pace up and down within the narrow cell of their ego-prisons. But participation in public worship breaks through the prison of the ego and lets in the light and air of the world. Instead of living but one small and petty life, we now share the multitudinous life of our people. Against the wider horizons that now open to our ken, personal cares do not loom so large. Life becomes infinitely more meaningful and worthwhile when we become aware, through our participation in public worship, of a common life that transcends our individual selves. M.M.K. (Adapted)

מַעֲרִיב

וְהוּא רַחוּם יְכַפֵּר עָוֹן וְלֹא יַשְׁחִית וְהִרְבָּה
לְהָשִׁיב אַפּוֹ וְלֹא יָעִיר כָּל חֲמָתוֹ: יהוה הוֹשִׁיעָה
הַמֶּלֶךְ יַעֲנֵנוּ בְיוֹם קָרְאֵנוּ:

When a minyan is present, the Bareḥu *is said. The congregation rises and faces the ark. It is customary to bow.*

בָּרְכוּ אֶת יהוה הַמְבֹרָךְ:
בָּרוּךְ יהוה הַמְבֹרָךְ לְעוֹלָם וָעֶד:

Bareḥu et adonay hamvoraḥ.
Baruḥ adonay hamvoraḥ le'olam va'ed.

KAVANAH. When we worship in public we know our life is part of a larger life, a wave of an ocean of being—the first-hand experience of that larger life which is God. M.M.K.

COMMENTARY. The evening service begins with ברכו / *Bareḥu*, the call to prayer. It introduces the *Shema* and its blessings, which are then followed by the *Amidah* (Silent Prayer), and the *Aleynu*. The ברכו / *Bareḥu* calls us together for worship by asking that we return blessing to God, who is the source of all blessing. We become a community by sharing this acknowledgment. D.A.T.

ASHER BIDVARO / GOD IN NATURE

For additional readings see pages 433-434.

TRADITIONAL VERSION

Blessed are you, ETERNAL ONE, our God, sovereign of all worlds, by whose word the evenings fall. In wisdom you open heaven's gates. With divine discernment you make seasons change, causing the times to come and go, and ordering the stars on their appointed paths through heaven's dome, all according to your will. Creator of the day and night, who rolls back light before the dark, and dark before the light, who makes day pass away and brings on night, dividing between day and night: The Leader of the Multitudes of Heaven is your name! Living and enduring God, rule over us, now and always. Blessed are you, ALMIGHTY ONE, who makes the evenings fall.

DERASH. When we are about to say: "Blessed are you, our God, sovereign of all worlds," and prepare to utter the first word "blessed," we should do so with all our strength, so that we will have no strength left to say, "are you." And this is the meaning of the verse in the Scriptures: "But they that wait for God shall exchange their strength." What we are really saying is: "Source of life, I am giving you all the strength that is within me in that very first word; now will you, in exchange, give me an abundance of new strength, so that I can go on with my prayer." M.B. (Adapted)

אשר בדברו מעריב ערבים / by whose word the evenings fall. The word plays a central role in the Jewish imagination. Our liturgy fantasizes that God brings on evening each night by saying "Evening!" Thus we repeat each day the original act of Creation that took place by means of the divine word. It is only because we affirm a God who so values language that we feel ourselves able to use words in prayer. Our word, perhaps like God's, gives expression to a depth that goes beyond language, but that can be shared only though the symbolic power of speech. A.G.

אֲשֶׁר בִּדְבָרוֹ

בָּרוּךְ אַתָּה יהוה אֱלֹהֵינוּ מֶלֶךְ הָעוֹלָם אֲשֶׁר בִּדְבָרוֹ מַעֲרִיב עֲרָבִים
בְּחָכְמָה פּוֹתֵחַ שְׁעָרִים וּבִתְבוּנָה מְשַׁנֶּה עִתִּים וּמַחֲלִיף אֶת הַזְּמַנִּים
וּמְסַדֵּר אֶת־הַכּוֹכָבִים בְּמִשְׁמְרוֹתֵיהֶם בָּרָקִיעַ כִּרְצוֹנוֹ: בּוֹרֵא יוֹם
וָלָיְלָה גּוֹלֵל אוֹר מִפְּנֵי חֹשֶׁךְ וְחֹשֶׁךְ מִפְּנֵי אוֹר: *וּמַעֲבִיר יוֹם וּמֵבִיא
לָיְלָה וּמַבְדִּיל בֵּין יוֹם וּבֵין לָיְלָה יהוה צְבָאוֹת שְׁמוֹ: אֵל חַי וְקַיָּם
תָּמִיד יִמְלֹךְ עָלֵינוּ לְעוֹלָם וָעֶד: בָּרוּךְ אַתָּה יהוה הַמַּעֲרִיב עֲרָבִים:

El ḥay vekayam tamid yimloḥ aleynu le'olam va'ed.
Baruḥ atah adonay hama'ariv aravim.

אור, חושך, אור / light, dark, light. The words roll into each other just as day rolls into night. They are not separate realms. They mix together. God rules both light and darkness. בין / *beyn:* between. Similar to בינה / *binah* and תבונה / *tevunah:* understanding. Wisdom is the ability to distinguish between things, to make sense out of confusion. L.W.K.

COMMENTARY. The two *beraḥot* which precede the Shema set the stage for its evening recitation. The first *beraḥah* praises God for the wonders of creation that are visible at twilight: the shifting pattern of the stars, the rhythm of the seasons, the regular passage from day to night. All of these are a nightly reminder of the unchanging plan of creation.

The second *beraḥah* praises God, whose instruction is a special token of love for Israel. Israel responds by meditating upon God's teaching "day and night," "when we lie down and when we rise." This phrasing recalls the preceding *beraḥah*, adding Israel's study of Torah to the natural order: The sun sets, the stars shine, and Israel studies—as regularly as day and night. The phrase "when we lie down and when we rise" anticipates the Shema, which follows. This interplay between the *beraḥot* and the Shema suggests that the Shema is Israel's morning and evening Torah study. At the same time, it is Israel's declaration of the oneness of the power that makes for the natural order and for learning, for creation and human creativity. S.S.

INTERPRETIVE VERSION: ASHER BIDVARO

Praised are you, God, ruler of the universe, who has ordained the rhythm of life. The day with its light calls to activity and exertion. But when the day wanes, when, with the setting of the sun, colors fade, we cease from our labors and welcome the tranquility of the night. The subdued light of the moon and stars, the darkness and the stillness about us invite rest and repose. Trustfully we yield to the quiet of sleep, for we know that, while we are unaware of what goes on within and around us, our powers of body and mind are renewed. Therefore, at this evening hour, we seek composure of spirit. We give thanks for the day and its tasks and for the night and its rest. Praised are you, God, who brings on the evening.

1945 Reconstructionist Prayer Book (Adapted)

KAVANAH. The שמע / Shema is wrapped in אהבה / *ahavah* / love. The blessing preceding the Shema concludes, "who loves your people Israel." This prayer begins "ואהבת / *ve'ahavta*, And you must love יהוה!" First you are loved, then you respond with love. Love is central to Jewish life. Love means commitment and limitations—Torah and mitzvot. That is so both in our relationships with each other and in our relationship with God.

L.W.K.

INTERPRETIVE VERSION: AHAVAT OLAM

We are loved by an unending love.
We are embraced by arms that find us
even when we are hidden from ourselves.

We are touched by fingers that soothe us
even when we are too proud for soothing.
We are counseled by voices that guide us
even when we are too embittered to hear.
We are loved by an unending love.

We are supported by hands that uplift us
even in the midst of a fall.
We are urged on by eyes that meet us
even when we are too weak for meeting.
We are loved by an unending love.

Embraced, touched, soothed, and counseled...
ours are the arms, the fingers, the voices;
ours are the hands, the eyes, the smiles;
We are loved by an unending love.

Blessed are you, BELOVED ONE, who loves your people Israel.

Rami M. Shapiro (Adapted)

AHAVAT OLAM / GOD'S LOVE IN TORAH

With everlasting love, you love the house of Israel. Torah and mitzvot, laws and justice you have taught us. And so, DEAR ONE, our God, when we lie down and when we rise, we reflect upon your laws; we take pleasure in your Torah's words and your mitzvot, now and always. Truly, they are our life, our length of days. On them we meditate by day and night. Your love will never depart from us as long as worlds endure. Blessed are you, BELOVED ONE, who loves your people Israel.

Many contemporary Jews are reciting *beraḥot*/blessings in ways that reflect their theological outlooks and ethical concerns. At any place where a blessing occurs in the liturgy, the following elements can be combined to create alternative formulas for *beraḥot*. This can be done by selecting one phrase from each group to form the introductory clause.

I	Baruḥ atah adonay	בָּרוּךְ אַתָּה יהוה	Blessed are you Adonay
	Beruḥah at yah	בְּרוּכָה אַתְּ יָהּ	Blessed are you Yah
	Nevareḥ et	נְבָרֵךְ אֶת	Let us bless
II	eloheynu	אֱלֹהֵינוּ	our God
	hasheḥinah	הַשְּׁכִינָה	Sheḥinah
	eyn haḥayim	עֵין הַחַיִּים	Source of Life
III	meleḥ ha'olam	מֶלֶךְ הָעוֹלָם	Sovereign of all worlds
	ḥey ha'olamim	חֵי הָעוֹלָמִים	Life of all the worlds
	ruaḥ ha'olam	רוּחַ הָעוֹלָם	Spirit of the world

אַהֲבַת עוֹלָם

אַהֲבַת עוֹלָם בֵּית יִשְׂרָאֵל עַמְּךָ אָהָבְתָּ: תּוֹרָה וּמִצְוֹת חֻקִּים וּמִשְׁפָּטִים
אוֹתָנוּ לִמַּדְתָּ: עַל כֵּן יהוה אֱלֹהֵינוּ בְּשָׁכְבֵנוּ וּבְקוּמֵנוּ נָשִׂיחַ בְּחֻקֶּיךָ
וְנִשְׂמַח בְּדִבְרֵי תוֹרָתֶךָ וּבְמִצְוֹתֶיךָ לְעוֹלָם וָעֶד כִּי הֵם חַיֵּינוּ וְאֹרֶךְ
יָמֵינוּ וּבָהֶם נֶהְגֶּה יוֹמָם וָלָיְלָה: וְאַהֲבָתְךָ לֹא תָסוּר מִמֶּנּוּ לְעוֹלָמִים:
בָּרוּךְ אַתָּה יהוה אוֹהֵב עַמּוֹ יִשְׂרָאֵל:

Ahavat olam beyt yisra'el ameḥa ahavta.
Torah umitzvot ḥukim umishpatim otanu limadeta.
Al ken adonay eloheynu beshoḥvenu uvkumenu nasi'aḥ beḥukeḥa
venismaḥ bedivrey torateḥa uvmitzvoteḥa le'olam va'ed
ki hem ḥayeynu ve'oreḥ yameynu
uvahem nehgeh yomam valaylah.
Ve'ahavateḥa lo tasur mimenu le'olamim.
Baruḥ atah adonay ohev amo yisra'el.

ואהבתך לא תסור. Our text follows the Sephardic version, in the declarative mode ("Your love will never depart from us.") rather than the imperative ("Never remove your love from us!"). Divine love is unconditional. It is available to every one of us when we fashion our lives into channels to receive and share it. The Jewish people together experience that eternal love as reflected in our love for the study of Torah—a wisdom lovingly received, shared, and passed on enriched by each generation. A.G.

DERASH. The term Sheḥinah implies that God is not aloof from human life with all its defeats and triumphs. God is in the very midst of life. The rabbis say that when people suffer for their sins, the Sheḥinah cries out. The Sheḥinah thus moves from Israel to all humanity. M.M.K./M.S.

שמע ישראל יהוה אלהינו יהוה אחד

SHEMA

Listen, Israel: THE ETERNAL is our God,
THE ETERNAL ONE alone!

Blessed be the name and glory of God's realm, forever!

And you must love THE ONE, your God, with your whole heart, with every breath, with all you have. Take these words that I command you now to heart. Teach them intently to your children. Speak them when you sit inside your house or walk upon the road, when you lie down and when you rise. And bind them as a sign upon your hand, and keep them visible before your eyes. Inscribe them on the doorposts of your house and on your gates. ↵

שמע...ובשעריך / Listen...gates (Deuteronomy 6:4-9).

DERASH. The Shema is called *kabbalat ol malḥut shamayim.* We "receive upon ourselves the yoke of the sovereignty of Heaven." To proclaim God as ours and as one is to acknowledge fealty to the divine will—and the Shema is a time to listen. We listen in order to discover God's will.

D.A.T.

ואהבת את יהוה / love יהוה your God. Abbaye said, "Let the love of God be spread through your activities. If a person studies and helps others to do so, if one's business dealings are decent and trustworthy—what do people say? 'Happy is the one who studied Torah, and the one who teaches Torah! Have you seen the one who studied Torah? How beautiful! What a fine person!' Thus, the Torah says, 'You are my servant Israel; I will be glorified by you'" (Isaiah 49:3). TALMUD YOMA 86a

KAVANAH. The moment we transcend our own egos and identify ourselves with one other person we are on the way toward God. God is thus the reality experienced as we-consciousness, in the same way as the self or soul is the reality experienced as I- or self-consciousness. M.M.K.

שְׁמַע

שְׁמַע יִשְׂרָאֵל יהוה אֱלֹהֵינוּ יהוה אֶחָד:

בָּרוּךְ שֵׁם כְּבוֹד מַלְכוּתוֹ לְעוֹלָם וָעֶד:

וְאָהַבְתָּ אֵת יהוה אֱלֹהֶיךָ בְּכָל־לְבָבְךָ וּבְכָל־נַפְשְׁךָ וּבְכָל־מְאֹדֶךָ:
וְהָיוּ הַדְּבָרִים הָאֵלֶּה אֲשֶׁר אָנֹכִי מְצַוְּךָ הַיּוֹם עַל־לְבָבֶךָ:
וְשִׁנַּנְתָּם לְבָנֶיךָ וְדִבַּרְתָּ בָּם בְּשִׁבְתְּךָ בְּבֵיתֶךָ וּבְלֶכְתְּךָ בַדֶּרֶךְ
וּבְשָׁכְבְּךָ וּבְקוּמֶךָ: וּקְשַׁרְתָּם לְאוֹת עַל־יָדֶךָ וְהָיוּ לְטֹטָפֹת בֵּין
עֵינֶיךָ: וּכְתַבְתָּם עַל־מְזֻזוֹת בֵּיתֶךָ וּבִשְׁעָרֶיךָ: ←

Shema yisra'el adonay eloheynu adonay eḥad.
Baruḥ shem kevod malḥuto le'olam va'ed.

Ve'ahavta et adonay eloheḥa
beḥol levaveḥa uvḥol nafsheḥa uvḥol me'odeḥa.
Vehayu hadevarim ha'eleh asher anoḥi metzaveḥa hayom al levaveḥa.
Veshinantam levaneḥa vedibarta bam
beshivteḥa beveyteḥa uvleḥteḥa vadereḥ uvshoḥbeḥa uvkumeḥa.
Ukshartam le'ot al yadeḥa vehayu letotafot beyn eyneḥa.
Uḥtavtam al mezuzot beyteḥa uvishareḥa.

לבבך / *levaveḥa* / your heart. The לב / *lev* / heart, was seen as the source of emotions and intellect. Feelings and reason are complementary partners, not conflicting parts, of the human psyche. The double ב of לבב teaches that a love of God must contain all dualities (e.g. the good and bad in you). L.W.K.

טטפת בין עיניך. *Totafot* might have been pendants or forehead markings. The Torah text sees *totafot* as reminders of the divine will. The English translation captures this figurative meaning of a visible reminder of the mitzvot. D.A.T.

For the second paragraph of the Shema, read either the version below or the biblical selection beginning on page 274, then continue with the third paragraph, page 276.

BIBLICAL SELECTION I

It came to pass, and will again,
that if you truly listen
to the voice of THE ETERNAL ONE, your God,
being sure to do whatever has been asked of you today,
THE ONE, your God, will make of you a model
for all nations of the earth,
and there will come upon you all these blessings,
as you listen to the call of THE ABUNDANT ONE, your God:
Blessed be you in the city,
blessed be you upon the field.
Blessed be the fruit of your womb,
the fruit of your land, the fruit of your cattle,
the calving of your oxen, and the lambing of your sheep.
Blessed be your basket and your kneading-trough.
Blessed be you when you come home,
and blessed be you when you go forth.
See, I have placed in front of you today
both life and good, both death and ill,
commanding you today to love THE BOUNDLESS ONE, your God,
to walk in ways I have ordained,
keeping the commandments, laws, and judgments,
so that you survive and multiply.
THE BOUNTIFUL, your God, will bless you
on the land you are about to enter and inherit. ↩

For the second paragraph of the Shema, read either the version below or the biblical selection beginning on page 275 then continue with the third paragraph, page 277.

BIBLICAL SELECTION I

וְהָיָה אִם־שָׁמוֹעַ תִּשְׁמַע בְּקוֹל יהוה אֱלֹהֶיךָ לִשְׁמֹר לַעֲשׂוֹת אֶת־
כָּל־מִצְוֹתָיו אֲשֶׁר אָנֹכִי מְצַוְּךָ הַיּוֹם וּנְתָנְךָ יהוה אֱלֹהֶיךָ עֶלְיוֹן
עַל כָּל־גּוֹיֵי הָאָרֶץ: וּבָאוּ עָלֶיךָ כָּל־הַבְּרָכוֹת הָאֵלֶּה וְהִשִּׂיגֻךָ
כִּי תִשְׁמַע בְּקוֹל יהוה אֱלֹהֶיךָ: בָּרוּךְ אַתָּה בָּעִיר וּבָרוּךְ אַתָּה
בַּשָּׂדֶה: בָּרוּךְ פְּרִי־בִטְנְךָ וּפְרִי אַדְמָתְךָ וּפְרִי בְהֶמְתֶּךָ שְׁגַר
אֲלָפֶיךָ וְעַשְׁתְּרוֹת צֹאנֶךָ: בָּרוּךְ טַנְאֲךָ וּמִשְׁאַרְתֶּךָ: בָּרוּךְ אַתָּה
בְּבֹאֶךָ וּבָרוּךְ אַתָּה בְּצֵאתֶךָ: ←

רְאֵה נָתַתִּי לְפָנֶיךָ הַיּוֹם אֶת־הַחַיִּים וְאֶת־הַטּוֹב וְאֶת־הַמָּוֶת וְאֶת־
הָרָע: אֲשֶׁר אָנֹכִי מְצַוְּךָ הַיּוֹם לְאַהֲבָה אֶת־יהוה אֱלֹהֶיךָ לָלֶכֶת
בִּדְרָכָיו וְלִשְׁמֹר מִצְוֹתָיו וְחֻקֹּתָיו וּמִשְׁפָּטָיו וְחָיִיתָ וְרָבִיתָ וּבֵרַכְךָ
יהוה אֱלֹהֶיךָ בָּאָרֶץ אֲשֶׁר־אַתָּה בָא־שָׁמָּה לְרִשְׁתָּהּ: וְאִם־יִפְנֶה ←

But if your heart should turn away,
and you not heed, and go astray,
and you submit to other gods and serve them,
I declare to you today that you shall be
destroyed completely; you shall not live out
a great expanse of days upon the land
that you now cross the Jordan to possess.

I call as witnesses concerning you
both heaven and earth, both life and death,
that I have placed in front of you
a blessing and a curse.
Choose life, that you may live,
you and your seed!

Continue on page 276

COMMENTARY. The traditional wording found in Biblical Selection II presents detailed bountiful or devastating consequences of Israel's collective relationship to the mitzvot. That biblical section (Deuteronomy 11:13-21) offers a supernatural theology that many contemporary Jews find difficult. The first part of the biblical section on this page (Deuteronomy 28:1-6, 30:15-19) was included in the 1945 Reconstructionist Siddur. It begins by encouraging observance in the same language, but concentrates on the positive ways in which observance of mitzvot focuses our attention on God's presence as perceived through productivity and the pursuit of abundant life. The second part was first used in the Israeli Progressive movement Siddur, *Ha-avodah Shebalev.* S.S.

KAVANAH. The doctrine of the unity of God calls for the integration of all life's purposes into a consistent pattern of thought and conduct. M.M.K.

DERASH. God is the assumption that there is enough in the world to meet our needs but not to meet our greed for power and pleasure.
M.M.K. (Adapted)

לְבָבְךָ וְלֹא תִשְׁמָע וְנִדַּחְתָּ וְהִשְׁתַּחֲוִיתָ לֵאלֹהִים אֲחֵרִים
וַעֲבַדְתָּם: הִגַּדְתִּי לָכֶם הַיּוֹם כִּי אָבֹד תֹּאבֵדוּן לֹא־תַאֲרִיכֻן יָמִים
עַל־הָאֲדָמָה אֲשֶׁר אַתָּה עֹבֵר אֶת־הַיַּרְדֵּן לָבוֹא שָׁמָּה לְרִשְׁתָּהּ:
הַעִדֹתִי בָכֶם הַיּוֹם אֶת־הַשָּׁמַיִם וְאֶת־הָאָרֶץ הַחַיִּים וְהַמָּוֶת נָתַתִּי
לְפָנֶיךָ הַבְּרָכָה וְהַקְּלָלָה וּבָחַרְתָּ בַּחַיִּים לְמַעַן תִּחְיֶה אַתָּה וְזַרְעֶךָ:

Continue on page 277.

COMMENTARY. The statement of God's oneness unifies not only the context of the Shema but the text as well—three scriptural paragraphs specified in the Mishnah (a second century codification of Jewish law). The powerful declaration of God's unity fuses the responsibility to love God and to study God's teachings (first paragraph) with the lesson that their fulfillment confirms God's presence (second and third paragraphs). Hence, the unity of God as idea and presence. S.S.

In the handwritten scroll of the Torah
The word "Shema" of "*Shema Yisra'el*"
Ends with an oversized *ayin*,
And the word "*Eḥad*"
Ends with an oversized *dalet*.
Taken together
These two letters
Spell "*Ed*," meaning "witness."
    Whenever we recite the Shema
    We bear witness
    To our awareness
    Of God's presence. H.M.

BIBLICAL SELECTION II

And if you truly listen to my bidding, as I bid you now—loving THE FOUNT OF LIFE, your God, and serving God with all your heart, with every breath—then I will give you rain upon your land in its appointed time, the early rain and later rain, so you may gather in your corn, your wine and oil. And I will give you grass upon your field to feed your animals, and you will eat and be content. Beware, then, lest your heart be led astray, and you go off and worship other gods, and you submit to them, so that the anger of THE MIGHTY ONE should burn against you, and seal up the heavens so no rain would fall, so that the ground would not give forth her produce, and you be forced to leave the good land I am giving you.

So place these words upon your heart, into your lifebreath. Bind them as a sign upon your hand, and let them rest before your eyes. Teach them to your children, speaking of them when you sit at home, and when you walk upon the road, when you lie down, and when you rise, inscribe them on the doorposts of your house and on your gates—so that your days and your children's days be many on the land THE FAITHFUL ONE promised to give your ancestors, as long as heaven rests above the earth. ↩

DERASH. The traditional second paragraph of the Shema (Deuteronomy 11:13-21) offers an account of the natural process by which the blessings of God themselves lead to pride, self-satisfaction, and ingratitude on the part of those who receive them. Ironically, the more we are blessed, so it seems, the less grateful and aware of blessing we become. It is when we are most sated, Scripture warns us, that we should be most careful. Fullness can lead to ingratitude, and ingratitude to idolatry—primarily in the form of worship of our own accomplishments. Then, indeed, "the heavens might close up and no rain fall." For, once we begin to worship our achievements, we will never find satisfaction. A.G.

BIBLICAL SELECTION II

וְהָיָה אִם־שָׁמֹעַ תִּשְׁמְעוּ אֶל־מִצְוֹתַי אֲשֶׁר אָנֹכִי מְצַוֶּה
אֶתְכֶם הַיּוֹם לְאַהֲבָה אֶת־יְהוָה אֱלֹהֵיכֶם וּלְעָבְדוֹ בְּכָל־לְבַבְכֶם
וּבְכָל־נַפְשְׁכֶם: וְנָתַתִּי מְטַר־אַרְצְכֶם בְּעִתּוֹ יוֹרֶה וּמַלְקוֹשׁ
וְאָסַפְתָּ דְגָנֶךָ וְתִירֹשְׁךָ וְיִצְהָרֶךָ: וְנָתַתִּי עֵשֶׂב בְּשָׂדְךָ לִבְהֶמְתֶּךָ
וְאָכַלְתָּ וְשָׂבָעְתָּ: הִשָּׁמְרוּ לָכֶם פֶּן־יִפְתֶּה לְבַבְכֶם וְסַרְתֶּם
וַעֲבַדְתֶּם אֱלֹהִים אֲחֵרִים וְהִשְׁתַּחֲוִיתֶם לָהֶם: וְחָרָה אַף־יְהוָה
בָּכֶם וְעָצַר אֶת־הַשָּׁמַיִם וְלֹא־יִהְיֶה מָטָר וְהָאֲדָמָה לֹא תִתֵּן אֶת־
יְבוּלָהּ וַאֲבַדְתֶּם מְהֵרָה מֵעַל הָאָרֶץ הַטֹּבָה אֲשֶׁר יְהוָה נֹתֵן לָכֶם:

וְשַׂמְתֶּם אֶת־דְּבָרַי אֵלֶּה עַל־לְבַבְכֶם וְעַל־נַפְשְׁכֶם וּקְשַׁרְתֶּם אֹתָם
לְאוֹת עַל־יֶדְכֶם וְהָיוּ לְטוֹטָפֹת בֵּין עֵינֵיכֶם: וְלִמַּדְתֶּם אֹתָם אֶת־
בְּנֵיכֶם לְדַבֵּר בָּם בְּשִׁבְתְּךָ בְּבֵיתֶךָ וּבְלֶכְתְּךָ בַדֶּרֶךְ וּבְשָׁכְבְּךָ
וּבְקוּמֶךָ: וּכְתַבְתָּם עַל־מְזוּזוֹת בֵּיתֶךָ וּבִשְׁעָרֶיךָ: לְמַעַן יִרְבּוּ
יְמֵיכֶם וִימֵי בְנֵיכֶם עַל הָאֲדָמָה אֲשֶׁר נִשְׁבַּע יְהוָה לַאֲבֹתֵיכֶם
לָתֵת לָהֶם כִּימֵי הַשָּׁמַיִם עַל־הָאָרֶץ: ←

DERASH. This warning against idolatry has ecological significance. If we continue to pollute the environment—and thus display contempt for the integrity of God's creation—pure rain will cease to fall, and the ground will cease to give forth its produce.

M.L.

THE BOUNDLESS ONE told Moses: Speak to the Israelites—tell them to make themselves *tzitzit* upon the corners of their clothes, throughout their generations. Have them place upon the corner *tzitzit* a twine of royal blue. This is your *tzitzit.* Look at it and remember all the mitzvot of the ETERNAL ONE. And do them, so you won't go off after the lusts of your heart or after what catches your eye, so that you remember to do all my mitzvot and be holy for your God. I am THE FAITHFUL ONE, your God, who brought you from Mitzrayim to be for you a God. I am THE INFINITE, your God.

ויאמר יהוה...אלהיכם / THE BOUNDLESS ONE...God (Numbers 15:37-41).

COMMENTARY. In the ancient Near East, free people wore fringes, or *tzitzit,* on the hems of their everyday clothes. Since only free people wore *tzitzit,* they were a form of identification. Business transactions were sealed by kissing the *tzitzit.*

The mitzvah of *tzitzit* is based on that ancient sign of freedom. The fringes remind us that we voluntarily follow the way of God, who freed us from Egyptian slavery. It is, literally, a string tied around our finger.

Today, many Jews who recite the Shema during the morning service gather the four corners of their *tallitot* (prayer shawls), hold the *tzitzit,* and kiss them at each mention of the word ציצית / *tzitzit.* This custom shows that we take these words seriously like a legal contract. L.W.K.

מצרים / *Mitzrayim* was the escaping Hebrews', not the Egyptians', name for the land of Egypt: perhaps a slave-term, and probably not of Semitic origin, it has associations with the root צרר, to be in distress, constricted, in anguish, or in dire straits. This word powerfully evokes the choking oppression of slavery. As the psalmist wrote: מן המצר קראתי יה / From the depths I called to Yah. M.P.

Transliteration can be found on page 91.

וַיֹּאמֶר יהוה אֶל־מֹשֶׁה לֵּאמֹר׃ דַּבֵּר אֶל־בְּנֵי יִשְׂרָאֵל וְאָמַרְתָּ
אֲלֵהֶם וְעָשׂוּ לָהֶם צִיצִת עַל־כַּנְפֵי בִגְדֵיהֶם לְדֹרֹתָם וְנָתְנוּ עַל־
צִיצִת הַכָּנָף פְּתִיל תְּכֵלֶת׃ וְהָיָה לָכֶם לְצִיצִת וּרְאִיתֶם אֹתוֹ
וּזְכַרְתֶּם אֶת־כָּל־מִצְוֹת יהוה וַעֲשִׂיתֶם אֹתָם וְלֹא תָתוּרוּ אַחֲרֵי
לְבַבְכֶם וְאַחֲרֵי עֵינֵיכֶם אֲשֶׁר־אַתֶּם זֹנִים אַחֲרֵיהֶם׃ לְמַעַן תִּזְכְּרוּ
וַעֲשִׂיתֶם אֶת־כָּל־מִצְוֹתָי וִהְיִיתֶם קְדֹשִׁים לֵאלֹהֵיכֶם׃ אֲנִי יהוה
אֱלֹהֵיכֶם אֲשֶׁר הוֹצֵאתִי אֶתְכֶם מֵאֶרֶץ מִצְרַיִם לִהְיוֹת לָכֶם
לֵאלֹהִים אֲנִי יהוה אֱלֹהֵיכֶם׃ יהוה אֱלֹהֵיכֶם **אֱמֶת**

כל מצות יהוה / all the mitzvot of THE ETERNAL ONE. **כל**, all, as many as possible. According to rabbinic tradition, there are 613 mitzvot in the Torah. A combination of gematria (Jewish numerology) and ritual macrame "proves" that **ציצית** / *tzitzit* equals all 613 mitzvot combined: צ = 90, י = 10, צ = 90, י = 10, ת = 400; all together = 600. Each *tzitzit* has 8 strands (per corner) and 5 knots; 8 + 5 = 13; 13 + 600 = 613. L.W.K.

אחרי עיניכם / after what catches your eye, that is, the physical and material temptations you see. The Baal Shem Tov had a method for dealing with distractions, especially sexual ones. If you can't get that person out of your thoughts, remember that beauty is a reflection of God's image. Redirect that energy towards God. L.W.K.

תכלת is Sidon blue, which is obtained from a shellfish. Sidon or royal blue is associated with majesty—even today the British queen wears a blue sash. The Jews were so oppressed at the time of Bar Koḥbah that indigo, a vegetable dye, replaced Sidon blue on their *tzitzit.* The Romans banned the blue fringe because of its symbolism. During the nineteenth century the Radnizer *ḥasidim* reintroduced its use. Now other Jews have also begun to use it. The long *teḥelet* thread intertwined with short white ones is a complex and powerful image that hints at the interplay between majesty and subject within our own hearts. E.M.

EMET VE'EMUNAH / REDEMPTION

Our faith and truth rest on all this, which is binding upon us:
That THE BOUNDLESS ONE alone is our divinity
and that no divinity exists but One;
that we are Israel, community of God;
that it is God who saves us from the hand
of governments, the very palm of tyrants;
who enacts great deeds without measure,
and wondrous deeds beyond all count;
who puts our souls amid the living,
and who keeps our feet from giving way;
who breaks apart the schemes of those who hate us,
confounds the thoughts of any bearing us ill-will;
that it is God who made miracles for us in Egypt,
signs and wonders in Ham's children's land.
From one generation to the next, God is our guarantor,
and even on a day that turned to night,
God stayed with us when death's deep shadow fell.

COMMENTARY. Two beautiful *beraḥot* complete the liturgical framework of the Shema in the evening service. The first of these is called *Ge'ulah*—"Redemption." Recalling the Exodus from Egypt, it thematically echoes the third paragraph of the Shema. Moreover, it identifies the sovereign God, named in the Shema's credo, as the power that freed Israel from slavery. Its vivid, here-and-now recollection of the escape from Egyptian bondage invites and challenges Israel to claim the redemption as a personal experience in each generation and to hear echoes of that ancient triumph over tyranny in each modern-day struggle for freedom, in every attempt to move toward the messianic future. S.S.

אֱמֶת וֶאֱמוּנָה

אֱמֶת וֶאֱמוּנָה כׇּל זֹאת וְקַיָּם עָלֵינוּ
כִּי הוּא יהוה אֱלֹהֵינוּ וְאֵין זוּלָתוֹ
וַאֲנַחְנוּ יִשְׂרָאֵל עַמּוֹ׃
הַפּוֹדֵנוּ מִיַּד מְלָכִים
הַגּוֹאֲלֵנוּ מִכַּף עָרִיצִים
הָעוֹשֶׂה גְדוֹלוֹת אֵין חֵקֶר
וְנִפְלָאוֹת אֵין מִסְפָּר׃
הַשָּׂם נַפְשֵׁנוּ בַּחַיִּים
וְלֹא נָתַן לַמּוֹט רַגְלֵנוּ׃
הַמֵּפֵר עֲצַת אוֹיְבֵינוּ
וְהַמְקַלְקֵל מַחְשְׁבוֹת שׂוֹנְאֵינוּ׃
הָעוֹשֶׂה לָּנוּ נִסִּים בְּמִצְרַיִם
אוֹתוֹת וּמוֹפְתִים בְּאַדְמַת בְּנֵי חָם׃
מִדּוֹר לְדוֹר הוּא גוֹאֲלֵנוּ׃
וּבַיּוֹם שֶׁהָפַךְ לְלַיְלָה
עִמָּנוּ הָיָה בְּגֵיא צַלְמָוֶת׃ ←

COMMENTARY. The blessing immediately following the Shema deals with the theme of divine redemption. The present text, a rewritten version, includes reference to the Holocaust, from which there was no redemption, and the return to Zion, a fulfillment of Israel's ancient dream. The same divine spirit that gave Israel the courage to seek freedom from Egypt in ancient times inspired those who fought for Israel's freedom in our own day. At the same time, this version omits those portions of the text that glory in the enemy's fall or see in God a force for vengeance. All humans are God's beloved children, as were the Egyptians who drowned at the sea.

A.G.

And even in our age of orphans and survivors,
God's loving acts have not abandoned us,
and God has brought together our scattered kin
from the distant corners of the earth.
As then, so now,
God brings the people Israel forth
from every place of menace, to a lasting freedom.
God is the one who brought the Israelites
through a divided Sea of Reeds.
There, they beheld divine might;
they praised and thanked the Name,
and willingly accepted for themselves
God's rule.

Moses, Miriam, and all the Israelites
broke out in song, abundant in their joy,
and, all as one, they said: ↩

DERASH. Rabbi Judah said: [At the sea] each tribe said to the other, "You go into the sea first!" As they stood there bickering, Naḥshon ben Aminadav jumped into the water. Meanwhile Moses was praying. God said to him, "My friend is drowning—and you pray!" "What can I do?" Moses asked. [God responded as it says in the text,] "Speak to the people of Israel and tell them to go! Raise your staff..." TALMUD SOTAH 37a

NOTE. Biblical references include Job 9:10, Psalm 66:9.

גַּם בְּדוֹר יְתוֹמִים
לֹא עֲזָבוּנוּ חֲסָדָיו
וַיְקַבֵּץ נִדָּחֵינוּ מִקְצוֹת תֵּבֵל:
כְּאָז גַּם עַתָּה
מוֹצִיא אֶת עַמּוֹ יִשְׂרָאֵל
מִכַּף כָּל אוֹיְבָיו
לְחֵרוּת עוֹלָם:
הַמַּעֲבִיר בָּנָיו בֵּין גִּזְרֵי יַם סוּף
שָׁם רָאוּ אֶת גְּבוּרָתוֹ
שַׁבְּחוּ וְהוֹדוּ לִשְׁמוֹ
וּמַלְכוּתוֹ בְּרָצוֹן קִבְּלוּ עֲלֵיהֶם:

מֹשֶׁה וּמִרְיָם וּבְנֵי יִשְׂרָאֵל לְךָ עָנוּ שִׁירָה בְּשִׂמְחָה רַבָּה וְאָמְרוּ כֻלָּם:←

Mosheh umiriam uvney yisra'el leḥa anu shirah besimḥah rabah ve'ameru ḥulam.

"Who among the mighty can compare
to you, WISE ONE?
Who can compare to you,
adorned in holiness,
awesome in praises,
acting wondrously!"

Your children saw you in your majesty,
splitting the sea in front of Moses.
"This is my God!" they cried, and said:

"THE HOLY ONE will reign forever!"
And it was said:

"Yes, THE REDEEMING ONE has rescued Jacob,
saved him
from a power
stronger than his own!"

Blessed are you, THE GUARDIAN, Israel's redeeming power!

When our ancestors
beheld these truths
they proclaimed:
Among all the gods
we can name,
who can compare to the
One Beyond Naming?
Among all the quantities
we can label, number,
mark and measure,
which compares to the
Mystery
at the Heart of Reality?

R.M.S.

מִי־כָמֹכָה בָּאֵלִים יהוה מִי כָּמֹכָה נֶאְדָּר בַּקֹּדֶשׁ
נוֹרָא תְהִלֹּת עֹשֵׂה פֶלֶא׃
מַלְכוּתְךָ רָאוּ בָנֶיךָ בּוֹקֵעַ יָם לִפְנֵי מֹשֶׁה זֶה אֵלִי עָנוּ וְאָמְרוּ׃
יהוה יִמְלֹךְ לְעֹלָם וָעֶד׃
וְנֶאֱמַר׃ כִּי פָדָה יהוה אֶת־יַעֲקֹב וּגְאָלוֹ מִיַּד חָזָק מִמֶּנּוּ׃ בָּרוּךְ אַתָּה
יהוה גָּאַל יִשְׂרָאֵל׃

Mi ḥamoḥah ba'elim adonay.
Mi kamoḥah nedar bakodesh
nora tehilot osey feleh.
Malḥuteḥa ra'u vaneḥa boke'a yam lifney mosheh.
Zeh eli anu ve'ameru.
Adonay yimloḥ le'olam va'ed.
Vene'emar ki fadah adonay et ya'akov ugalo miyad ḥazak mimenu.
Baruḥ atah adonay ga'al yisra'el.

בוקע ים לפני משה. This siddur reinstates reference to the splitting of the sea as a sign of God's redeeming power. The earlier Reconstructionist prayerbook omitted that reference because of its emphasis on supernatural intervention. As myth, however, the ancient tale of wonder underscores the sense of daily miracle in our lives. Even those of us who cannot affirm a God who intervenes in the natural process, and thus cannot accept the literal meaning of the tale, can appreciate its human message. According to the midrash, the sea did not split until one Israelite, Naḥshon ben Aminadav, had the courage to walk upright into the water. Perhaps it was the divine spirit in Naḥshon, rather than the magic of Moses's wand, that caused the sea to split.
A.G.

NOTE. Biblical references include Exodus 15:11, 18 and Jeremiah 31:11.

who ever guards the people Israel
and all who dwell on earth.

HASHKIVENU / DIVINE HELP

For commentary, see pages 286-287.

Help us to lie down, DEAR ONE, our God, in peace, and let us rise again, our sovereign, to life. Spread over us the shelter of your peace. Decree for us a worthy daily lot, and redeem us for the sake of your great name. Protect us and keep from us enemies, illness, sword, famine, and sorrow. Enfold us in the wings of your protection, for you are our redeeming guardian. Truly, a sovereign, gracious and compassionate God are you. Guard our going forth each day for life and peace, now and always. Spread over us the shelter of your peace.

Blessed are you, COMPASSIONATE ONE, who ever guards the people Israel, and all who dwell on earth.

Blessed are you,
Compassionate One,

הַשְׁכִּיבֵֽנוּ

Transliteration and commentary follow on pages 286-287.

הַשְׁכִּיבֵֽנוּ יהוה אֱלֹהֵֽינוּ לְשָׁלוֹם וְהַעֲמִידֵֽנוּ מַלְכֵּֽנוּ לְחַיִּים וּפְרוֹשׂ
עָלֵֽינוּ סֻכַּת שְׁלוֹמֶֽךָ: וְתַקְּנֵֽנוּ בְּעֵצָה טוֹבָה מִלְּפָנֶֽיךָ וְהוֹשִׁיעֵֽנוּ לְמַֽעַן
שְׁמֶֽךָ: וְהָגֵן בַּעֲדֵֽנוּ וְהָסֵר מֵעָלֵֽינוּ אוֹיֵב דֶּֽבֶר וְחֶֽרֶב וְרָעָב וְיָגוֹן: וּבְצֵל
כְּנָפֶֽיךָ תַּסְתִּירֵֽנוּ כִּי אֵל שׁוֹמְרֵֽנוּ וּמַצִּילֵֽנוּ אָֽתָּה כִּי אֵל מֶֽלֶךְ חַנּוּן
וְרַחוּם אָֽתָּה: וּשְׁמוֹר צֵאתֵֽנוּ וּבוֹאֵֽנוּ לְחַיִּים וּלְשָׁלוֹם מֵעַתָּה וְעַד עוֹלָם:
וּפְרוֹשׂ עָלֵֽינוּ סֻכַּת שְׁלוֹמֶֽךָ:

בָּרוּךְ אַתָּה יהוה שׁוֹמֵר עַם יִשְׂרָאֵל וְכָל יוֹשְׁבֵי תֵבֵל לָעַד:

COMMENTARY. *Hashkivenu*—"Help us to lie down [in peace]"—is the final prescribed part of the Shema. It recalls the Shema by expressing the hope that we will "lie down...in peace" and "rise again...to life." An extension of *Emet Ve'emunah, Hashkivenu* joins the vivid recollection of past redemption to a prayer for present protection and future peace. By calling God "guardian" and "protector" but also "redeemer," Israel recognizes new dimensions of the power that makes for freedom. This blessing is unique to the evening service. Perhaps responding to the cold, dark uncertainty of night, we invoke God's dwelling of peace. S.S.

KAVANAH. Enable us, God, to behold meaning in the chaos of life about us and purpose in the chaos of life within us. Deliver us from the sense of futility in our strivings toward the light and the truth. Give us strength to ride safely through the maelstrom of petty cares and anxieties. May we behold things in their proper proportions and see life in its wholeness and its holiness. M.M.K./M.S.

COMMENTARY. The traditional text of this prayer includes the phrase, *haser satan milfanenu ume-aḥarenu*. Some commentators interpret *satan* as "spiritual harmony," but the phrase is omitted here because of its literal reference to a prosecuting angel. The blessing at the end of *Hashkivenu* has been expanded to include our hope that divine protection will be extended to all peoples. D.A.T.

KAVANAH. As we enter the dark of evening, we face the unknown. Earlier, in *Asher Bidvaro* (the Creation section immediately following *Bareḥu*), we affirmed the power that transforms night into day and day into night. Now we call for protection from the shadows that lengthen around us—shadows of fear and guilt, the uncharted future, the ever pursuing past. We ask that the shadows of God's wings envelop us with love and mercy. The unknown night, like the unknown tomorrow, can only be met with faith in the power of infinite compassion to care for us. S.P.W.

Hashkivenu adonay eloheynu leshalom veha'amidenu malkenu leḥayim ufros aleynu sukkat shelomeḥa. Vetakenenu ve'etzah tovah milefaneḥa vehoshi'enu lema'an shemeḥa. Vehagen ba'adeynu vehaser me'aleynu oyev dever veḥerev vera'av veyagon. Uvetzel kenafeḥa tastirenu ki el shomrenu umatzilenu atah ki el meleḥ ḥanun veraḥum atah. Ushmor tzeytenu uvo'enu leḥayim ulshalom me'atah ve'ad olam. Ufros aleynu sukkat shelomeḥa. Baruḥ atah adonay shomer am yisra'el veḥol yoshvey tevel la'ad.

When fears multiply
And danger threatens;
When sickness comes,
When death confronts us—
It is God's blessing of shalom
That sustains us
And upholds us.

Lightening our burden,
Dispelling our worry,
Restoring our strength,
Renewing our hope—
Reviving us.

H.M.

ALL SOULS ARE IN GOD'S KEEPING

Blessed is THE ANCIENT ONE by day,
and blessed is THE LIVING ONE by night.
Blessed is THE GUARDIAN when we lie down,
and blessed is THE FOUNT OF LIFE when we arise.
For in your hands are placed the souls of all the living
and the dead,
in divine hands, the soul of every living thing,
the spirit of each being's flesh.
In your hands I entrust my spirit,
you who have redeemed me, FAITHFUL ONE,
the God of truth.
Our God on high,
make one your name,
sustain your realm continually,
and rule over us, forever and eternally.
Let our eyes behold, our hearts rejoice,
our spirits be uplifted by your redemptive power.
Let the promise told to Zion be made real:
"Your God is sovereign!
THE ETERNAL ONE has reigned,
THE ETERNAL ONE now reigns,
THE ETERNAL ONE shall reign
forever and eternally!"
For all of the created realm is yours,
throughout all worlds, across all time,
for we have no sovereign but you.
Blessed are you, ETERNAL ONE,
you who reign in glory,
may you rule forever over us,
and over all that you have made.

בָּרוּךְ יהוה בַּיּוֹם: בָּרוּךְ יהוה בַּלָּֽיְלָה: בָּרוּךְ יהוה בְּשָׁכְבֵֽנוּ: בָּרוּךְ יהוה בְּקוּמֵֽנוּ: כִּי בְיָדְךָ נַפְשׁוֹת הַחַיִּים וְהַמֵּתִים: אֲשֶׁר בְּיָדוֹ נֶֽפֶשׁ כָּל־חָי וְרֽוּחַ כָּל־בְּשַׂר־אִישׁ וְאִשָּׁה: בְּיָדְךָ אַפְקִיד רוּחִי פָּדִֽיתָה אוֹתִי יהוה אֵל אֱמֶת: אֱלֹהֵֽינוּ שֶׁבַּשָּׁמַֽיִם יַחֵד שִׁמְךָ וְקַיֵּם מַלְכוּתְךָ תָּמִיד וּמְלוֹךְ עָלֵֽינוּ לְעוֹלָם וָעֶד:

יִרְאוּ עֵינֵֽינוּ וְיִשְׂמַח לִבֵּֽנוּ וְתָגֵל נַפְשֵֽׁנוּ בִּישׁוּעָתְךָ בֶּאֱמֶת בֶּאֱמֹר לְצִיּוֹן מָלַךְ אֱלֹהָֽיִךְ: יהוה מֶֽלֶךְ יהוה מָלָךְ יהוה יִמְלֹךְ לְעוֹלָם וָעֶד: כִּי הַמַּלְכוּת שֶׁלְּךָ הִיא וּלְעוֹלְמֵי עַד תִּמְלֹךְ בְּכָבוֹד כִּי אֵין לָנוּ מֶֽלֶךְ אֶלָּא אָֽתָּה. בָּרוּךְ אַתָּה יהוה הַמֶּֽלֶךְ בִּכְבוֹדוֹ תָּמִיד יִמְלוֹךְ עָלֵֽינוּ לְעוֹלָם וָעֶד וְעַל כָּל מַעֲשָׂיו:

ḤATZI KADDISH / SHORT KADDISH

Reader: Let God's name be made great and holy in the world that was created as God willed. May God complete the holy realm in your own lifetime, in your days, and in the days of all the house of Israel, quickly and soon. And say: Amen.

Congregation: May God's great name be blessed, forever and as long as worlds endure.

Reader: May it be blessed, and praised, and glorified, and held in honor, viewed with awe, embellished, and revered; and may the blessed name of holiness be hailed, though it be higher (*Between Rosh Hashanah and Yom Kippur, add:* by far) than all the blessings, songs, praises, and consolations that we utter in this world. And say: Amen.

חֲצִי קַדִּישׁ

יִתְגַּדַּל וְיִתְקַדַּשׁ שְׁמֵהּ רַבָּא בְּעָלְמָא דִּי בְרָא כִרְעוּתֵהּ וְיַמְלִיךְ מַלְכוּתֵהּ בְּחַיֵּיכוֹן וּבְיוֹמֵיכוֹן וּבְחַיֵּי דְכָל בֵּית יִשְׂרָאֵל בַּעֲגָלָא וּבִזְמַן קָרִיב וְאִמְרוּ אָמֵן:

יְהֵא שְׁמֵהּ רַבָּא מְבָרַךְ לְעָלַם וּלְעָלְמֵי עָלְמַיָּא:

יִתְבָּרַךְ וְיִשְׁתַּבַּח וְיִתְפָּאַר וְיִתְרוֹמַם וְיִתְנַשֵּׂא וְיִתְהַדַּר וְיִתְעַלֶּה וְיִתְהַלַּל שְׁמֵהּ דְּקֻדְשָׁא בְּרִיךְ הוּא

לְעֵֽלָּא (*Between Rosh Hashanah and Yom Kippur, add:* לְעֵֽלָּא) מִן כָּל בִּרְכָתָא וְשִׁירָתָא תֻּשְׁבְּחָתָא וְנֶחֱמָתָא דַּאֲמִירָן בְּעָלְמָא וְאִמְרוּ אָמֵן:

Reader: Yitgadal veyitkadash shemey raba
be'alma di vera ḥirutey veyamliḥ malḥutey
beḥayeyḥon uvyomeyḥon uvḥayey deḥol beyt yisra'el
ba'agala uvizman kariv ve'imru amen.

Congregation: Yehey shemey raba mevaraḥ le'alam ulalmey almaya.

Reader: Yitbaraḥ veyishtabaḥ veyitpa'ar veyitromam
veyitnasey veyit-hadar veyitaleh veyit-halal
shemey dekudsha beriḥ hu
le'e̱la (*Between Rosh Hashanah and Yom Kippur, add:* le'ela) min kol birḥata
veshirata tushbeḥata veneḥemata da'amiran be'alma
ve'imru amen.

INTRODUCTIONS TO THE AMIDAH

Standing here in Abraham's desert
Affirming: one God.

Moving in the old spaces
Warmed by our ancestors' embrace.

Standing here in Sarah's tent
Laughing: new life.

Moving in the old spaces
Renewed by our ancestors' hope.

Standing here in my place
Listening to our voices: yearning.

Moving in my own spaces
Translating the silence.

Sandy Eisenberg Sasso

* *

Dear God,
Open the blocked passageways to you,
The congealed places.

Roll away the heavy stone from the well as your servant Jacob did when he beheld his beloved Rachel.

Help us open the doors of trust that have been jammed with hurt and rejection.

As you open the blossoms in spring,
Even as you open the heavens in storm,
Open us—to feel your great, awesome, wonderful presence.

Sheila Peltz Weinberg

KAVANAH. Prayer is communion. To commune with God is to put oneself in touch with the source of cosmic energy. M.M.K.

I will be ever aware of the SOURCE OF LIFE's presence.
In loyalty you sustain the living, nurturing the life of each living thing, upholding those who fall, healing the sick.
May my words of prayer and my heart's meditation be seen favorably, God, my rock and my redeemer
יהוה
שויתי יהוה לנגדי תמיד
How precious is your love, O God,
when earthborn find the shelter of your wings
Guard our going forth each day for life and peace.
spread over us your shelter of peace.
השכיבנו יהוה אלהינו לשלום והעמידנו מלכנו לחיים
ברוך אתה יהוה מחיה כל חי
Blessed are you, THE FOUNT OF LIFE, who gives and renews life.
כי עמך מקור חיים באורך נראה אור
For with you is the Fountain of all life; in your Light do we behold all light.
על מי מנוחות ינהלני נפשי ישובב
You are with me, God Your power and support are there to comfort me.
כי אתה עמדי שבטך ומשענתך המה ינחמני
ברוך אתה בצאתך
ברוך אתה בבאך
For it is a tree of life
עץ חיים היא למחזיקים בה
©Betsy Platkin Teutsch

AMIDAH

The traditional Amidah *follows here. The* Sheviti *meditation begins on page 132. A guided meditation begins on page 128. The* Amidah *is traditionally recited while standing, beginning with three short steps forward and bowing, left and right, a reminder of our entry into the divine presence.*

Open my lips, BELOVED ONE,
and let my mouth declare your praise.

1. AVOT VE'IMOT / ANCESTORS

Blessed are you, ANCIENT ONE, our God, God of our ancestors,

God of Abraham	God of Sarah
God of Isaac	God of Rebekah
God of Jacob	God of Rachel
	and God of Leah; ↩

DERASH. Acknowledging our ancestors reminds us that what we are is shaped by who they were. Just as an acorn is shaped by the oak that preceded it and yet gives birth to a tree uniquely its own, so we are shaped by our ancestors yet give rise to a Judaism all our own. R.M.S.

COMMENTARY. The *Amidah* or "standing prayer" is also called "*Hatefilah* / The Prayer," because of its centrality in every one of the daily services. The *Amidah* in its weekday form is also known as the "*Shemoneh Esrey* / The Eighteen (benedictions)." This name dates from a very early period; nineteen blessings have been included for the last 2000 years. Most liturgy scholars agree that the weekday *Amidah* is structured as a prayer for the arrival of messianic times. The thirteen middle blessings of the weekday *Amidah* are petitions for success and wellbeing that reflect the concerns that occupy our daily circumstances. The *Amidah* always concludes with a prayer for completeness and peace, uniting workday concerns with messianic hope. D.A.T. / R.S.

אדוני...תהלתך / Open...praise (Psalm 51:17).

עֲמִידָה

The traditional Amidah *follows here. The* Sheviti *meditation begins on page 132. A guided meditation begins on page 128. The* Amidah *is traditionally recited while standing, beginning with three short steps forward and bowing, left and right, a reminder of our entry into the divine presence.*

אֲדֹנָי שְׂפָתַי תִּפְתָּח וּפִי יַגִּיד תְּהִלָּתֶךָ:

א 1 אָבוֹת וְאִמּוֹת

בָּרוּךְ אַתָּה יהוה אֱלֹהֵינוּ וֵאלֹהֵי אֲבוֹתֵינוּ וְאִמּוֹתֵינוּ

אֱלֹהֵי אַבְרָהָם	אֱלֹהֵי שָׂרָה
אֱלֹהֵי יִצְחָק	אֱלֹהֵי רִבְקָה
אֱלֹהֵי יַעֲקֹב	אֱלֹהֵי רָחֵל
	וֵאלֹהֵי לֵאָה: ←

Adonay sefatay tiftaḥ ufi yagid tehilateḥa.
Baruḥ atah adonay eloheynu veylohey avoteynu ve'imoteynu

elohey avraham	elohey sarah
elohey yitzḥak	elohey rivkah
elohey ya'akov	elohey raḥel
	veylohey le'ah ↩

COMMENTARY. Throughout the centuries the pursuit of meaningful communal prayer has led to variations in the *Amidah*. These variations reflect the attitudes and beliefs of different prayer communities. In the ongoing pursuit of meaningful prayer for a Reconstructionist prayer community, changes have been introduced into this *Amidah*, most notably in the first two *beraḥot*. The first *beraḥah* has been expanded to include the matriarchs along with the patriarchs as exemplars of God's presence in human lives. By concentrating on examples of healing forces and life-sustaining rains, the second *beraḥah* acknowledges God as the power that sustains life. The traditional emphasis on God's ability to resurrect the dead has been replaced here by a celebration of God as the power that sustains all life.

S.S.

great, heroic, awesome God, supreme divinity,
imparting deeds of kindness, begetter of all;
mindful of the loyalty of Israel's ancestors,
bringing, with love, redemption to their children's children
for the sake of the divine name.

Between Rosh Hashanah and Yom Kippur, add:

(Remember us for life,
sovereign, who wishes us to live,
and write us in the Book of Life,
for your sake, ever-living God.)

Regal One, our help, salvation, and protector:
Blessed are you, KIND ONE,
the shield of Abraham and help of Sarah. ↵

NOTE. The Amidah is made up of three sections. The first and last remain the same for all services, but the central portion differs, containing thirteen blessings on weekdays, and only one on Shabbat and Festivals. The central section on weekdays contains petitions or requests. These workday concerns are set aside on Shabbat and Festivals, when the focus shifts to the joy and holiness of the day. J.B.

COMMENTARY. This version of the first *beraḥah* in the Amidah includes the matriarchs as well as the patriarchs. The phrase "help of Sarah," *ezrat Sarah*, comes from a Hebrew root (עזר) which can mean either "save" or "be strong." This parallels the meaning of *magen* / shield. The biblical text says that Abraham experienced God as a shield and that Sarah experienced God as a helper. Their experience and the example of their lives can enrich our own. Just as Abraham and Sarah found the strength to face the unknown physical and spiritual dangers of their journey, so we seek to find the courage and inspiration to meet the challenges of our own time. R.S.

הָאֵל הַגָּדוֹל הַגִּבּוֹר וְהַנּוֹרָא אֵל עֶלְיוֹן גּוֹמֵל חֲסָדִים טוֹבִים וְקוֹנֵה הַכֹּל וְזוֹכֵר חַסְדֵי אָבוֹת וְאִמּוֹת וּמֵבִיא גְאֻלָּה לִבְנֵי בְנֵיהֶם לְמַעַן שְׁמוֹ בְּאַהֲבָה:

Ha'el hagadol hagibor vehanora el elyon gomel ḥasadim tovim vekoney hakol vezoḥer ḥasdey avot ve'imot umevi ge'ulah livney veneyhem lema'an shemo be'ahavah.

Between Rosh Hashanah and Yom Kippur, add:

(זָכְרֵנוּ לְחַיִּים מֶלֶךְ חָפֵץ בַּחַיִּים וְכָתְבֵנוּ בְּסֵפֶר הַחַיִּים לְמַעַנְךָ אֱלֹהִים חַיִּים:)

(Zoḥrenu leḥayim meleḥ ḥafetz baḥayim veḥotvenu besefer haḥayim lema'aneḥa elohim ḥayim.)

מֶלֶךְ עוֹזֵר וּמוֹשִׁיעַ וּמָגֵן: בָּרוּךְ אַתָּה יהוה מָגֵן אַבְרָהָם וְעֶזְרַת שָׂרָה: ←

Meleḥ ozer umoshi'a umagen. Baruḥ atah adonay magen avraham ve'ezrat sarah. ↩

KAVANAH. God is experienced as עוזר / helper, every time our thought of God furnishes us an escape from the sense of frustration and supplies us with a feeling of permanence in the midst of universal flux.

M.M.K./M.S.

COMMENTARY. A.J. Heschel has said, "The term, 'God of Abraham, Isaac and Jacob' is semantically different from a term such as 'the God of truth, goodness, and beauty.' Abraham, Isaac and Jacob do not signify ideas, principles or abstract values. Nor do they stand for teachers or thinkers, and the term is not to be understood like that of 'the God of Kant, Hegel, and Schelling.' Abraham, Isaac, and Jacob are not principles to be comprehended but lives to be continued. The life of one who joins the covenant of Abraham continues the life of Abraham. For the present is not apart from the past. 'Abraham is still standing before God' (Genesis 18:22). Abraham endures forever. We are Abraham, Isaac, and Jacob." In this same spirit, we are also Sarah and Rebekah, Rachel and Leah. L.W.K.

2. GEVUROT / DIVINE POWER

You are forever powerful, ALMIGHTY ONE,
abundant in your saving acts.

In summer: You send down the dew.

In winter: You cause the wind to blow and the rain to fall.

In loyalty you sustain the living, nurturing the life of every living thing, upholding those who fall, healing the sick, freeing the captive, and remaining faithful to all life held dormant in the earth. Who can compare to you, almighty God, who can resemble you, the source of life and death, who makes salvation grow?

(*Between Rosh Hashanah and Yom Kippur, add:* Who can compare to you, source of all mercy, remembering all creatures mercifully, decreeing life!)

Faithful are you in giving life to every living thing. Blessed are you, THE FOUNT OF LIFE, who gives and renews life.

מוריד הטל/משיב הרוח. We acknowledge the presence of God in the natural rhythms of passing seasons. Our awareness of wind, rain, and dew as daily miracles also serves to remind us that the purity of these gifts, so vital for our survival, must be maintained by human watchfulness. In thanking God for air and water, we assert our commitment to preserving them as sources of life and protecting them from life-destroying pollution. The mention of rain or dew follows the two-season climate of *Eretz Yisra'el*; summer extends from the first day of Pesaḥ until Shemeni Atzeret, and winter until the following Pesaḥ. A.G.

כל חי / every living thing, gives and renews life. The traditional siddur affirms מחיה המתים / revival of the dead. We substitute כל חי, demonstrating an understanding that all of life is rooted in the world's divine order and avoiding affirmation of life after death. We cannot know what happens to us after we die, but we can, by our thought and action, affirm the possibility of this-worldly salvation. D.A.T.

גְּבוּרוֹת

אַתָּה גִּבּוֹר לְעוֹלָם אֲדֹנָי רַב לְהוֹשִׁיעַ:

In summer: מוֹרִיד הַטָּל:

In winter: מַשִּׁיב הָרוּחַ וּמוֹרִיד הַגָּשֶׁם:

Atah gibor le'olam adonay rav lehoshi'a.
In summer: Morid hatal.
In winter: Mashiv haru'aḥ umorid hagashem.

מְכַלְכֵּל חַיִּים בְּחֶסֶד מְחַיֵּה כָּל חַי בְּרַחֲמִים רַבִּים סוֹמֵךְ נוֹפְלִים וְרוֹפֵא חוֹלִים וּמַתִּיר אֲסוּרִים וּמְקַיֵּם אֱמוּנָתוֹ לִישֵׁנֵי עָפָר: מִי כָמוֹךָ בַּעַל גְּבוּרוֹת וּמִי דּוֹמֶה לָּךְ מֶלֶךְ מֵמִית וּמְחַיֶּה וּמַצְמִיחַ יְשׁוּעָה:

Meḥalkel ḥayim beḥesed meḥayey kol ḥay beraḥamim rabim someḥ noflim verofey ḥolim umatir asurim umkayem emunato lisheney afar. Mi ḥamoḥa ba'al gevurot umi domeh laḥ meleḥ memit umḥayeh umatzmi'aḥ yeshu'ah.

Between Rosh Hashanah and Yom Kippur, add:

(מִי כָמוֹךָ אַב הָרַחֲמִים זוֹכֵר יְצוּרָיו לְחַיִּים בְּרַחֲמִים:)

(Mi ḥamoḥa av haraḥamim zoḥer yetzurav leḥayim beraḥamim.)

וְנֶאֱמָן אַתָּה לְהַחֲיוֹת כָּל חָי: בָּרוּךְ אַתָּה יהוה מְחַיֵּה כָּל חָי: ←

Vene'eman atah lehaḥayot kol ḥay. Baruḥ atah adonay meḥayey kol ḥay. ↵

3. KEDUSHAT HASHEM / HALLOWING GOD'S NAME

Holy are you. Your name is holy. And all holy beings hail you each day. Blessed are you, THE AWESOME ONE, the holy God.

(*Between Rosh Hashanah and Yom Kippur, conclude:* the holy sovereign.)

For the abbreviated Amidah, continue on page 106.

4. BINAH / INSIGHT

You graciously endow the human being
with the power to know;

At the conclusion of Shabbat or a festival say:

(You have given us knowledge of your Torah and taught us to do your will. HOLY ONE, our God, you have divided between the holy and the ordinary, between daylight and dark, between the seventh day and the first six days of Creation. Our creator, our sovereign, grant that the coming days bring us peace. Free us from all wrongdoing, and purify us from all moral flaw that we may cling to you in awe.)

you teach a person understanding.
So may you provide us now
with knowledge, understanding, and intelligence.
Blessed are you, THE FOUNT OF WISDOM
who graciously bestows all knowledge.

DERASH. We ask God to remove the impurities that have collected in our minds so that we might be truthful enough to serve God. What are these impurities, these false coverings? They are the myth of isolation, the denial of interrelatedness, the prideful pretense that we are alone and abandoned in the cosmos. S.P.W.

DERASH. The creation of the world is not completed so long as we have not fulfilled our creative function in it. M.M.K.

3 קְדֻשַּׁת הַשֵּׁם

אַתָּה קָדוֹשׁ וְשִׁמְךָ קָדוֹשׁ וּקְדוֹשִׁים בְּכָל יוֹם יְהַלְלֽוּךָ סֶּֽלָה: בָּרוּךְ
אַתָּה יהוה הָאֵל הַקָּדוֹשׁ:

(*Between Rosh Hashanah and Yom Kippur, conclude:* הַמֶּֽלֶךְ הַקָּדוֹשׁ)

For the abbreviated Amidah, continue on page 107.

4 בִּינָה

אַתָּה חוֹנֵן לְאָדָם דַּֽעַת וּמְלַמֵּד לֶאֱנוֹשׁ בִּינָה:

At the conclusion of Shabbat or a festival say:

(אַתָּה חוֹנַנְתָּֽנוּ לְמַדַּע תּוֹרָתֶךָ וַתְּלַמְּדֵֽנוּ לַעֲשׂוֹת חֻקֵּי רְצוֹנֶֽךָ וַתַּבְדֵּל
יהוה אֱלֹהֵֽינוּ בֵּין קֹֽדֶשׁ לְחוֹל בֵּין אוֹר לְחֹשֶׁךְ בֵּין יוֹם הַשְּׁבִיעִי לְשֵׁשֶׁת
יְמֵי הַמַּעֲשֶׂה: אָבִֽינוּ מַלְכֵּֽנוּ הָחֵל עָלֵֽינוּ הַיָּמִים הַבָּאִים לִקְרָאתֵֽנוּ
לְשָׁלוֹם חֲשׂוּכִים מִכָּל־חֵטְא וּמְנֻקִּים מִכָּל־עָוֹן וּמְדֻבָּקִים בְּיִרְאָתֶֽךָ.)

חָנֵּֽנוּ מֵאִתְּךָ דֵּעָה בִּינָה וְהַשְׂכֵּל: בָּרוּךְ אַתָּה יהוה חוֹנֵן הַדָּֽעַת: ←

COMMENTARY. One of the most distinguished words in the Bible is the word *kadosh*, a word which more than any other is representative of the mystery and the majesty of the divine. Now what was the first holy object in the history of the world? Was it a mountain? Was it an altar?

It is indeed a unique occasion at which the word *kadosh* is used for the first time: in the book of Genesis, at the end of the story of creation. How extremely significant is the fact that it is applied to time. "And God blessed the seventh day and made it *kadosh*." There is no reference in the record of creation to any object in space that would be endowed with the quality of *kedushah*, holiness.

A.J.H.

5. TESHUVAH / REPENTANCE

Return us, divine source, to your Torah,
bring us nearer, our sovereign, to your service.
And restore us, in complete return, into your presence.
Blessed are you, RECEPTIVE ONE,
who takes joy in our return.

6. SELIḤAH / FORGIVENESS

Forgive us, our Creator, for we have done wrong.
Deal mercifully with us, our protector, though we have rebelled.
you are truly kind and merciful.
Blessed are you, ALL-MERCIFUL,
who graciously abounds in power to forgive.

7. GE'ULAH / REDEMPTION

Behold our need, and plead our cause,
and speedily redeem us, as your name demands,
for you are called a powerful redeemer.
Blessed are you, ALMIGHTY ONE,
redeemer of the people Israel. ↵

The truth is that our belief in God is not based upon God's self-revelation but on our discovery of God. According to the modern way of thinking and speaking, it is more correct to say that we discover God than to say that God reveals the divine self to us. M.M.K. (Adapted)

ה 5 תְּשׁוּבָה

הֲשִׁיבֵנוּ מְקוֹרֵנוּ לְתוֹרָתֶךָ: וְקָרְבֵנוּ עֲטַרְתֵּנוּ לַעֲבוֹדָתֶךָ. וְהַחֲזִירֵנוּ בִּתְשׁוּבָה שְׁלֵמָה לְפָנֶיךָ: בָּרוּךְ אַתָּה יהוה הָרוֹצֶה בִּתְשׁוּבָה:

ו 6 סְלִיחָה

סְלַח־לָנוּ אָבִינוּ כִּי חָטָאנוּ: מְחַל־לָנוּ מַלְכֵּנוּ כִּי פָשָׁעְנוּ: כִּי מוֹחֵל וְסוֹלֵחַ אָתָּה: בָּרוּךְ אַתָּה יהוה: חַנּוּן הַמַּרְבֶּה לִסְלוֹחַ:

ז 7 גְּאֻלָּה

רְאֵה בְעָנְיֵנוּ וְרִיבָה רִיבֵנוּ וּגְאָלֵנוּ מְהֵרָה לְמַעַן שְׁמֶךָ: כִּי גוֹאֵל חָזָק אָתָּה: בָּרוּךְ אַתָּה יהוה גוֹאֵל יִשְׂרָאֵל: ←

Note. The fifth blessing of the weekday *Amidah* focuses on the call to *teshuvah* – return to the path of Torah and the divine presence. Like the High Holy Day liturgy, this blessing invokes the imagery of kingship. This imagery is male and hierarchical, which is problematical for many contemporary Jews. Even more difficult for some is the image of an external God pronouncing individual judgments. This contradicts our sense of the divinity within ourselves that we strive to keep in our awareness and to bring into harmony with our lives. These difficulties have led to emendation of the traditional wording. אבינו / Our father has been replaced by מקורנו / divine source, and מלכנו / our king has been replaced by עטרתנו / our crown, here translated figuratively as "our sovereign." Compare the alternative and interpretive versions of *Avinu Malkenu*, pages 136-143.

D.A.T./J.B.

8. REFU'AH / HEALING

Heal us, NURTURING ONE, so that we may be healed,
help us to restore ourselves to a state of health,
and bring upon us complete cure of all our ailments.

Optional prayer for one who is ill:

(May it be your will, COMPASSIONATE ONE, our God,
God of our ancestors,
that you quickly send forth thorough healing,
a healing of the body and a healing of the spirit,
to the one who ails,

for a female:

to __________ daughter of __________

for a male:

to __________ son of __________
among all others of the people Israel who are ailing.)
And remove from us all suffering and grief.
For you are a sovereign divine power
and a faithful and compassionate healer.
Blessed are you, RESTORER OF ALL LIFE,
who heals the sick among the people Israel.

9. BIRKAT HASHANIM / BLESSING FOR ABUNDANCE

Grant blessing over us, ABUNDANT ONE,
upon this year, and all its forms of produce;
let it be a year of good.

From December 4th till Pesaḥ say:

And grant us dew and rain,
for blessing

From Pesaḥ till December 4th say:

And give blessing

on earth, and satisfy us with your goodness,
and give blessing to this year
as in the good years of the past.
Blessed are you, ALL BOUNTIFUL,
who gives blessing to the years. ⮐

8 רְפוּאָה

רְפָאֵנוּ יהוה וְנֵרָפֵא הוֹשִׁיעֵנוּ וְנִוָּשֵׁעָה וְהַעֲלֵה רְפוּאָה שְׁלֵמָה לְכָל מַכּוֹתֵינוּ:

Optional prayer for one who is ill:

(יְהִי רָצוֹן מִלְּפָנֶיךָ יהוה אֱלֹהֵינוּ וֵאלֹהֵי אֲבוֹתֵינוּ וְאִמּוֹתֵינוּ שֶׁתִּשְׁלַח מְהֵרָה רְפוּאָה שְׁלֵמָה מִן הַשָּׁמַיִם רְפוּאַת הַנֶּפֶשׁ וּרְפוּאַת הַגּוּף

for a female: לַחוֹלָה ____ בַּת ____

for a male: לַחוֹלֶה ____ בֶּן ____

בְּתוֹךְ שְׁאָר חוֹלֵי יִשְׂרָאֵל:)

וְהָסֵר מִמֶּנּוּ יָגוֹן וַאֲנָחָה כִּי אֵל מֶלֶךְ רוֹפֵא נֶאֱמָן וְרַחֲמָן אָתָּה: בָּרוּךְ אַתָּה יהוה רוֹפֵא חוֹלֵי עַמּוֹ יִשְׂרָאֵל:

9 בִּרְכַּת הַשָּׁנִים

בָּרֵךְ עָלֵינוּ יהוה אֱלֹהֵינוּ אֶת הַשָּׁנָה הַזֹּאת וְאֶת כָּל מִינֵי תְבוּאָתָהּ לְטוֹבָה

From Pesaḥ till December 4th say:

וְתֵן בְּרָכָה

From December 4th till Pesaḥ say:

וְתֵן טַל וּמָטָר לִבְרָכָה

עַל פְּנֵי הָאֲדָמָה וְשַׂבְּעֵנוּ מִטּוּבֶךָ וּבָרֵךְ שְׁנָתֵנוּ כַּשָּׁנִים הַטּוֹבוֹת: בָּרוּךְ אַתָּה יהוה מְבָרֵךְ הַשָּׁנִים: ←

COMMENTARY. As a God of lovingkindness, God not only teaches us how to conduct ourselves so as to elicit the best in each other, but also calls upon the transgressor to repent. When human beings repent, God forgives, and by forgiveness enables individuals to use their own powers as God would have them do. M.M.K./M.S.

NOTE. Our hope for rain in its season, which sustains crops throughout the year, is expressed in a subtle change of words. "Provide blessing," which is used most of the year becomes "provide dew and rain for a blessing." Pesaḥ marks the beginning of the spring grain planting season in Israel. The rabbis used the sun calendar date of December 4 for this prayer for rain to adjust to agricultural conditions in Babylonia. In following their lead, we recognize the need to adjust Jewish practice in response to local climactic, cultural, and political conditions. D.A.T.

10. KIBUTZ GALUYOT / INGATHERING OF THE JEWISH PEOPLE

Sound the great shofar for our freedom,
raise up the banner for the gathering-in of those in exile,
and gather us together from the earth's four corners.
Blessed are you, REDEEMING ONE,
who gathers Israel's dispossessed.

11. DIN / RESTORING JUSTICE

Restore our judges, as of old,
our counselors, as in the beginning,
and remove from us all suffering and grief.
Rule over us, OUR SOVEREIGN, you alone,
with love and with compassion.
Help us achieve justice through the rule of law.

Blessed are you, WISE ONE,
the sovereign who loves righteousness and justice.

Between Rosh Hashanah and Yom Kippur, conclude:

(Blessed are you, ENTHRONED IN MAJESTY,
the sovereign, the source of all just law.)

12. BIRKAT HAMINIM / OVERCOMING DIVISIONS

Let all who speak and act unjustly
find no hope for ill intentions.
Let all wickedness be lost.
Blessed are you, JUST ONE,
who subdues the evildoers. ↩

10 קִבּוּץ גָּלֻיּוֹת

תְּקַע בְּשׁוֹפָר גָּדוֹל לְחֵרוּתֵֽנוּ וְשָׂא נֵס לְקַבֵּץ גָּלֻיּוֹתֵֽינוּ וְקַבְּצֵֽנוּ יַֽחַד מֵאַרְבַּע כַּנְפוֹת הָאָֽרֶץ: בָּרוּךְ אַתָּה יהוה מְקַבֵּץ נִדְחֵי עַמּוֹ יִשְׂרָאֵל:

11 דִּין

הָשִֽׁיבָה שׁוֹפְטֵֽינוּ כְּבָרִאשׁוֹנָה וְיוֹעֲצֵֽינוּ כְּבַתְּחִלָּה וְהָסֵר מִמֶּֽנּוּ יָגוֹן וַאֲנָחָה וּמְלוֹךְ עָלֵֽינוּ אַתָּה יהוה לְבַדְּךָ בְּחֶֽסֶד וּבְרַחֲמִים וְצַדְּקֵֽנוּ בַּמִּשְׁפָּט: בָּרוּךְ אַתָּה יהוה מֶֽלֶךְ אוֹהֵב צְדָקָה וּמִשְׁפָּט:

Between Rosh Hashanah and Yom Kippur, conclude:

(בָּרוּךְ אַתָּה יהוה הַמֶּֽלֶךְ הַמִּשְׁפָּט:)

12 בִּרְכַּת הַמִּינִים

וְלַמַּלְשִׁינִים אַל תְּהִי תִקְוָה וְכָל הָרִשְׁעָה כְּרֶֽגַע תֹּאבֵד: בָּרוּךְ אַתָּה יהוה מַכְנִֽיעַ זֵדִים: ←

13. TZADIKIM / COMPASSION FOR THE RIGHTEOUS

For the righteous, and for the pious,
and for the elders of your people, the house of Israel,
and for the remnant of their scholars,
and for the righteous who have chosen to be Jews,
let your compassion be aroused, DEAR ONE, our God,
and give proper recompense to all
who truly have found shelter in your name,
and give us a portion in their midst,
that we may never be ashamed,
for in you we place our trust.
Blessed are you, THE SOURCE OF TRUST,
support and stronghold for the righteous.

14. BINYAN YERUSHALAYIM / REBUILDING JERUSALEM

And to Jerusalem, your city,
may you turn with mercy,
and come home to dwell there,
as you have promised.
And rebuild the city, soon and in our days,
with everlasting peace.
Blessed are you, THE GOD OF ZION,
builder of Jerusalem.

15. YESHU'AH / SALVATION

May you speedily redeem your people Israel,
and raise their stronghold with your help,
for we await with hope throughout our days
the coming of your help.
Blessed are you, THE GOD OF ISRAEL,
who plants the stronghold of your help. ↩

יג 13 צַדִּיקִים

עַל הַצַּדִּיקִים וְעַל הַחֲסִידִים וְעַל זִקְנֵי עַמְּךָ בֵּית יִשְׂרָאֵל וְעַל פְּלֵיטַת
סוֹפְרֵיהֶם וְעַל גֵּרֵי הַצֶּדֶק וְעָלֵינוּ יֶהֱמוּ נָא רַחֲמֶיךָ יהוה אֱלֹהֵינוּ וְתֵן
שָׂכָר טוֹב לְכֹל הַבּוֹטְחִים בְּשִׁמְךָ בֶּאֱמֶת וְשִׂים חֶלְקֵנוּ עִמָּהֶם וּלְעוֹלָם
לֹא נֵבוֹשׁ כִּי בְךָ בָּטָחְנוּ: בָּרוּךְ אַתָּה יהוה מִשְׁעָן וּמִבְטָח לַצַּדִּיקִים:

יד 14 בִּנְיַן יְרוּשָׁלַיִם

וְלִירוּשָׁלַיִם עִירְךָ בְּרַחֲמִים תָּשׁוּב וְתִשְׁכּוֹן בְּתוֹכָהּ כַּאֲשֶׁר דִּבַּרְתָּ וּבְנֵה
אוֹתָהּ בְּקָרוֹב בְּיָמֵינוּ בִּנְיַן שָׁלוֹם: בָּרוּךְ אַתָּה יהוה בּוֹנֵה יְרוּשָׁלָיִם:

טו 15 יְשׁוּעָה

אֶת עַמְּךָ יִשְׂרָאֵל מְהֵרָה תִּגְאַל וְקַרְנוֹ תָּרוּם בִּישׁוּעָתֶךָ כִּי לִישׁוּעָתְךָ
קִוִּינוּ כָּל הַיּוֹם: בָּרוּךְ אַתָּה יהוה מַצְמִיחַ קֶרֶן יְשׁוּעָה:

NOTE. The fourteenth blessing of the *Amidah* focuses on the rebuilding of Jerusalem. For centuries the rebuilding of Jerusalem has stood for an end to Jewish suffering and a return to Jewish sovereignty, as well as for the mythic end of days in which Jerusalem would become all that generations of longing Jews could imagine. For us, the rebuilding of Jerusalem signifies a world at peace and in which all human need is fulfilled. D.A.T.

16. KABBALAT TEFILAH / ACCEPTING PRAYER

Hear our voice, ATTENTIVE ONE, our God,
have mercy and compassion for us,
and accept our prayer
with kindness and with favor,
for you are the God who harkens
to the words of prayer and supplication.
Do not turn us from your presence empty-handed.
For you are one who listens
to the prayer of your people Israel
with compassion.

Blessed are you, COMPASSIONATE ONE, who listens to the words of prayer. ↩

At this point in the Amidah it is customary to add personal petitions for healing or safety, for successfully earning a living, and for other hopes and needs. For Tefilat Haderekh */ The Travelers' prayer, see page 174. For* Parnasah */ Sustenance and well being, see page 234.*

שמע קולנו / Hear our voice. After all these specific requests and petitions why do we still ask God to hear our prayers? Don't we assume God has been listening to our voice all along? All prayer is about opening. The *Shema Kolenu* / Hear our voice indicates how wide and expansive we have become. No longer is content expressed. It is pure compassion—pure opening alone that we seek. Our innermost hopes have been expressed through the specific litany of needs—now our voice rises from the tender core of our beings. We are one with all Israel whose cries have been heard in love. We cannot return empty. The opening itself is the filling. S.P.W.

16 קַבָּלַת תְּפִלָּה

שְׁמַע קוֹלֵנוּ יהוה אֱלֹהֵינוּ חוּס וְרַחֵם עָלֵינוּ וְקַבֵּל בְּרַחֲמִים וּבְרָצוֹן
אֶת תְּפִלָּתֵנוּ כִּי אֵל שׁוֹמֵעַ תְּפִלּוֹת וְתַחֲנוּנִים אָתָּה: וּמִלְּפָנֶיךָ מַלְכֵּנוּ
רֵיקָם אַל תְּשִׁיבֵנוּ כִּי אַתָּה שׁוֹמֵעַ תְּפִלַּת עַמְּךָ יִשְׂרָאֵל בְּרַחֲמִים:
בָּרוּךְ אַתָּה יהוה שׁוֹמֵעַ תְּפִלָּה: ←

At this point in the Amidah it is customary to add personal petitions for healing or safety, for successfully earning a living, and for other hopes and needs. *For* Tefilat Hadereh̩ */ The Travelers' prayer, see page 175. For* Parnasah */ Sustenance and well being, see page 235.*

COMMENTARY. This may be the most poignant of all the benedictions of the Amidah. It occurs after we have prayed about so many important things: health, wisdom, community...Yet only here do we finally ask whether or not God hears our prayer. We ask, by way of stating, that God graciously listen to us. What is God that such hearing is possible? If we have moved beyond a simplistic notion of a giant-figure with omniscient ears, what do we have left that hears? Whatever it is, we affirm it! Somehow the injection of our impassioned words and thoughts into the vast process of existence does something. That something is not merely self-clarification and introspection. Something hears. The cosmos bends towards us and takes cognizance. The particulars are wrapped in mystery; the direction and the flow are known. W.S.

פותח...רצון / Providing with...of all life (Psalm 145:16).
השלך על...יכלכלך / Cast yourself...our sustenance (Psalm 55:23).

Both the full Amidah *and the abbreviated* Amidah *continue here.*

17. AVODAH / WORSHIP

Take pleasure, GRACIOUS ONE, our God, in Israel your people; lovingly accept their fervent prayer. May Israel's worship always be acceptable to you.

On a Rosh Ḥodesh / New Moon or Festival add:

(Our God, our ancients' God, may our prayer arise and come to you, and be beheld, and be acceptable. Let it be heard, acted upon, remembered—the memory of us and all our needs, the memory of our ancestors, the memory of messianic hopes, the memory of Jerusalem your holy city, and the memory of all your kin, the house of Israel, all surviving in your presence. Act for goodness and grace, for love and care, for life, well-being, and peace, on this day of

On Rosh Ḥodesh: the new moon.
On Pesaḥ: the festival of matzot.
On Sukkot: the festival of sukkot. ↩

KAVANAH. Prayer itself is the divinity. — Pinḥas of Koretz

וזכרון ימות המשיח. We assert our faith in the coming of a messianic age, a time when justice will reign and all humanity will be united in recognition of the one God. Even in our people's darkest hour, this vision of the future strengthened us as we faced both life and death. However distanced we may be from the more naive aspects of belief in the person of the messiah, the vision of a transformed future remains our guide, just as we know that the vision will become reality only if our deeds reflect it. — A.G.

Both the full Amidah *and the abbreviated* Amidah *continue here.*

עֲבוֹדָה

רְצֵה יהוה אֱלֹהֵינוּ בְּעַמְּךָ יִשְׂרָאֵל וְלַהַב תְּפִלָּתָם בְּאַהֲבָה תְּקַבֵּל בְּרָצוֹן וּתְהִי לְרָצוֹן תָּמִיד עֲבוֹדַת יִשְׂרָאֵל עַמֶּךָ׃

On a Rosh Ḥodesh / *New Moon or Festival, add:*

(אֱלֹהֵינוּ וֵאלֹהֵי אֲבוֹתֵינוּ וְאִמּוֹתֵינוּ יַעֲלֶה וְיָבוֹא וְיַגִּיעַ וְיֵרָאֶה וְיֵרָצֶה וְיִשָּׁמַע וְיִפָּקֵד וְיִזָּכֵר זִכְרוֹנֵנוּ וּפִקְדוֹנֵנוּ וְזִכְרוֹן אֲבוֹתֵינוּ וְאִמּוֹתֵינוּ וְזִכְרוֹן יְמוֹת הַמָּשִׁיחַ וְזִכְרוֹן יְרוּשָׁלַיִם עִיר קָדְשֶׁךָ וְזִכְרוֹן כָּל עַמְּךָ בֵּית יִשְׂרָאֵל לְפָנֶיךָ לִפְלֵיטָה וּלְטוֹבָה לְחֵן וּלְחֶסֶד וּלְרַחֲמִים לְחַיִּים וּלְשָׁלוֹם בְּיוֹם

רֹאשׁ הַחֹדֶשׁ הַזֶּה	*On Rosh Ḥodesh:*
חַג הַמַּצּוֹת הַזֶּה	*On Pesaḥ*
חַג הַסֻּכּוֹת הַזֶּה	← *On Sukkot:*

ולהב תפלתם. The external mouthing of words alone cannot move us. It is the inward flame of devotion that brings our prayer close to God. Indeed, as the Hebrew phrasing vividly conveys, a passionate longing for godliness can exist among those unable to express that feeling in words. The phrase *lahav tefilatam*, "the flame of Israel's prayer," recalls that feeling of *hitlahavut*: the "in-burning" flame of passionate devotion. To attain *hitlahavut* in prayer is to soar with the rapturous ecstasy of divine communion, to access the infinite and be aflame with the nearness of God.

A.G. / M.P.

Remember us this day, ALL-KNOWING ONE, our God, for goodness. Favor us this day with blessing. Preserve us this day for life. With your redeeming, nurturing word, be kind and generous. Act tenderly on our behalf, and grant us victory over all our trials. Truly, our eyes are turned toward you, for you are a providing God, gracious and merciful are you.)

And may our eyes behold your homecoming, with merciful intent, to Zion. Blessed are you, THE FAITHFUL ONE, who brings your presence home to Zion.

18. HODA'AH / THANKS

We give thanks to you that you are THE ALL-MERCIFUL, our God, God of our ancestors, today and always. A firm, enduring source of life, a shield to us in time of trial, you are ever there, from age to age. We acknowledge you, declare your praise, and thank you for our lives entrusted to your hand, our souls placed in your care, for your miracles that greet us every day, and for your wonders and the good things that are with us every hour, morning, noon, and night. Good One, whose kindness never stops, Kind One, whose loving acts have never failed—always have we placed our hope in you. ↩

KAVANAH. Gratitude is the overwhelming experience of the person of faith. Faith stimulates gratitude, and the practice of gratitude expands faith. We experience thankfulness when we know that our lives are safe within God's protection. We trust that the future is assured. We need not consume our days in fear and anxiety. We are released. We can marvel at the daily wonders. S.P.W.

זָכְרֵנוּ יהוה אֱלֹהֵינוּ בּוֹ לְטוֹבָה: וּפָקְדֵנוּ לִבְרָכָה וְהוֹשִׁיעֵנוּ בוֹ לְחַיִּים:
וּבִדְבַר יְשׁוּעָה וְרַחֲמִים חוּס וְחָנֵּנוּ וְרַחֵם עָלֵינוּ וְהוֹשִׁיעֵנוּ כִּי אֵלֶיךָ
עֵינֵינוּ כִּי אֵל מֶלֶךְ חַנּוּן וְרַחוּם אָתָּה:)

וְתֶחֱזֶינָה עֵינֵינוּ בְּשׁוּבְךָ לְצִיּוֹן בְּרַחֲמִים: בָּרוּךְ אַתָּה יהוה הַמַּחֲזִיר
שְׁכִינָתוֹ לְצִיּוֹן:

יח 18 הוֹדָאָה

מוֹדִים אֲנַחְנוּ לָךְ שָׁאַתָּה הוּא יהוה אֱלֹהֵינוּ וֵאלֹהֵי אֲבוֹתֵינוּ
וְאִמּוֹתֵינוּ לְעוֹלָם וָעֶד צוּר חַיֵּינוּ מָגֵן יִשְׁעֵנוּ אַתָּה הוּא לְדוֹר וָדוֹר:
נוֹדֶה לְּךָ וּנְסַפֵּר תְּהִלָּתֶךָ עַל חַיֵּינוּ הַמְּסוּרִים בְּיָדֶךָ וְעַל נִשְׁמוֹתֵינוּ
הַפְּקוּדוֹת לָךְ וְעַל נִסֶּיךָ שֶׁבְּכָל יוֹם עִמָּנוּ וְעַל נִפְלְאוֹתֶיךָ וְטוֹבוֹתֶיךָ
שֶׁבְּכָל־עֵת עֶרֶב וָבֹקֶר וְצָהֳרָיִם: הַטּוֹב כִּי לֹא כָלוּ רַחֲמֶיךָ וְהַמְרַחֵם
כִּי לֹא תַמּוּ חֲסָדֶיךָ מֵעוֹלָם קִוִּינוּ לָךְ: ←

KAVANAH. So long as the Jewish people is linked in communion with the eternal, it can look forward to an eternal life for itself. M.M.K. (Adapted)

DERASH. The insights of wonder must be constantly kept alive. Since there is a need for daily wonder, there is a need for daily worship. The sense of the "miracles which are daily with us," the sense of the "continual marvels," is the source of prayer. There is no worship, no music, no love, if we take for granted the blessings or defeats of living....The profound and perpetual awareness of the wonder of being has become a part of the religious consciousness of the Jew. A.J.H.

(*On Ḥanukah add:* For the miracles, for the redemption, for heroic acts, for saving deeds, for consolations, all of which you have enacted for our ancestors at this time of year in days gone by—as in the days of Matthew, son of Yoḥanan, Hasmonean High Priest, and Matthew's sons: a wicked Hellenistic government arose against your people Israel, forcing them to shun your Torah and to leave off from the laws your will ordained. And you, in your abundant mercy, stood up for Israel in their hour of distress. You pressed their claim, exacted justice for them. You delivered armed might to the weak, the many to the power of the few, the wicked to the power of the just, the vicious to the power of those occupied with your Torah. You made known your name that day, and made it holy in your world. And for your people Israel you enacted great deliverance, as in our own time. Afterward, your children came into your Temple's inner room. They cleared your sanctuary, purified your holy place, kindled lights inside your holy courtyards, and established these eight days of Ḥanukah, for giving thanks and praise to your great name.) ↵

On Ḥanukah add:

(עַל הַנִּסִּים וְעַל הַפֻּרְקָן וְעַל הַגְּבוּרוֹת וְעַל הַתְּשׁוּעוֹת וְעַל הַנֶּחָמוֹת
שֶׁעָשִׂיתָ לַאֲבוֹתֵינוּ וְאִמּוֹתֵינוּ בַּיָּמִים הָהֵם בַּזְּמַן הַזֶּה: בִּימֵי מַתִּתְיָהוּ
בֶּן יוֹחָנָן כֹּהֵן גָּדוֹל חַשְׁמוֹנַאי וּבָנָיו כְּשֶׁעָמְדָה מַלְכוּת יָוָן הָרְשָׁעָה
עַל עַמְּךָ יִשְׂרָאֵל לְהַשְׁכִּיחָם תּוֹרָתֶךָ וּלְהַעֲבִירָם מֵחֻקֵּי רְצוֹנֶךָ וְאַתָּה
בְּרַחֲמֶיךָ הָרַבִּים עָמַדְתָּ לָהֶם בְּעֵת צָרָתָם רַבְתָּ אֶת רִיבָם דַּנְתָּ אֶת
דִּינָם מָסַרְתָּ גִּבּוֹרִים בְּיַד חַלָּשִׁים וְרַבִּים בְּיַד מְעַטִּים וּרְשָׁעִים בְּיַד
צַדִּיקִים וְזֵדִים בְּיַד עוֹסְקֵי תוֹרָתֶךָ: וּלְךָ עָשִׂיתָ שֵׁם גָּדוֹל וְקָדוֹשׁ
בְּעוֹלָמֶךָ וּלְעַמְּךָ יִשְׂרָאֵל עָשִׂיתָ תְּשׁוּעָה גְדוֹלָה וּפֻרְקָן כְּהַיּוֹם הַזֶּה:
וְאַחַר כֵּן בָּאוּ בָנֶיךָ לִדְבִיר בֵּיתֶךָ וּפִנּוּ אֶת הֵיכָלֶךָ וְטִהֲרוּ אֶת מִקְדָּשֶׁךָ
וְהִדְלִיקוּ נֵרוֹת בְּחַצְרוֹת קָדְשֶׁךָ וְקָבְעוּ שְׁמוֹנַת יְמֵי חֲנֻכָּה אֵלּוּ
לְהוֹדוֹת וּלְהַלֵּל לְשִׁמְךָ הַגָּדוֹל:) ←

(*On Purim, add:* For the miracles, and for deliverance,
and for the mighty deeds, and for the saving acts,
and for the consolations
you enacted for our ancestors
in ancient times, and in our own time.

In the days of Mordechai and Esther
in Shushan, the mighty capital [of Persia],
when the wicked Haman rose against them,
seeking to destroy, to kill, and to eradicate
all Jews, the young and old alike,
in a single day,
the thirteenth of the twelfth month,
that is, the month of Adar,
and take as plunder all they owned.

But you, in your abundant mercies,
thwarted his conspiracy, destroyed his plan.
And to the Jews came light and happiness,
and joy and glory.)

For all these things, let your name be blessed and raised in honor always, sovereign of ours, forever.

(*Between Rosh Hashanah and Yom Kippur, add:* And write down for a good life all the people of your covenant.)

Let all of life acknowledge you! May all beings praise your name in truth, O God, our rescue and our aid. Blessed are you, THE GRACIOUS ONE, whose name is good, to whom all thanks are due. ↩

ליהודים...ויקר / to the Jews...glory (Esther 8:16).

On Purim add:

(עַל הַנִּסִּים וְעַל הַפֻּרְקָן וְעַל הַגְּבוּרוֹת וְעַל הַתְּשׁוּעוֹת וְעַל הַנֶּחָמוֹת שֶׁעָשִׂיתָ לַאֲבוֹתֵינוּ וְאִמּוֹתֵינוּ בַּיָּמִים הָהֵם בַּזְּמַן הַזֶּה:

בִּימֵי מָרְדְּכַי וְאֶסְתֵּר בְּשׁוּשַׁן הַבִּירָה כְּשֶׁעָמַד עֲלֵיהֶם הָמָן הָרָשָׁע: בִּקֵּשׁ לְהַשְׁמִיד לַהֲרוֹג וּלְאַבֵּד אֶת כָּל הַיְּהוּדִים מִנַּעַר וְעַד זָקֵן בְּיוֹם אֶחָד בִּשְׁלוֹשָׁה עָשָׂר לְחֹדֶשׁ שְׁנֵים עָשָׂר הוּא חֹדֶשׁ אֲדָר וּשְׁלָלָם לָבוֹז: וְאַתָּה בְּרַחֲמֶיךָ הָרַבִּים הֵפַרְתָּ אֶת עֲצָתוֹ וְקִלְקַלְתָּ אֶת מַחֲשַׁבְתּוֹ לַיְּהוּדִים הָיְתָה אוֹרָה וְשִׂמְחָה וְשָׂשׂוֹן וִיקָר:)

וְעַל כֻּלָּם יִתְבָּרַךְ וְיִתְרוֹמַם שִׁמְךָ מַלְכֵּנוּ תָּמִיד לְעוֹלָם וָעֶד:

Between Rosh Hashanah and Yom Kippur, add:

(וּכְתֹב לְחַיִּים טוֹבִים כָּל־בְּנֵי בְרִיתֶךָ:)

וְכֹל הַחַיִּים יוֹדוּךָ סֶּלָה וִיהַלְלוּ אֶת שִׁמְךָ בֶּאֱמֶת הָאֵל יְשׁוּעָתֵנוּ וְעֶזְרָתֵנוּ סֶלָה: בָּרוּךְ אַתָּה יהוה הַטּוֹב שִׁמְךָ וּלְךָ נָאֶה לְהוֹדוֹת: ←

KAVANAH. This prayer helps us to get in touch with our gratitude for the extraordinary yet often overlooked daily workings of the world, and through them to recognize the insignificance of our own roles, to feel humble. In becoming aware of our smallness, we become able to grasp our relatedness to the All. This in turn makes it possible to overcome the loneliness of claiming we have all the answers and the anxiety of always needing to be in control. At these moments the pain of our unfulfilled needs is swept away in the wondrous goodness we feel in the world about us. We give thanks.

S.P.W.

19. BIRKAT HASHALOM / BLESSING FOR PEACE

Grant abundant peace eternally for Israel, your people. For you are the sovereign source of all peace. So, may it be a good thing in your eyes to bless your people Israel, and all who dwell on earth, in every time and hour, with your peace.

(*Between Rosh Hashanah and Yom Kippur, add:* In the book of life, blessing, peace, and proper sustenance, may we be remembered and inscribed, we and all your people, the house of Israel, for a good life and for peace.)

Blessed are you, COMPASSIONATE ONE, maker of peace.

The Amidah *traditionally concludes with bowing and taking three steps back.*

ואת כל יושבי תבל. According to the sages, every *Amidah* must conclude with a prayer for peace and an acknowledgment of God as the power that makes for peace. Inclusion of the words "and all who dwell on earth" proclaims that Israel desires the blessing of peace, not for itself alone, but for all humanity. S.S.

עושה השלום / Maker of peace. This ancient version of the prayer for peace in its most universal form was assigned in the traditional liturgy to the ten days of *teshuvah*. During the year the text read, "who blesses your people Israel with peace." In our time, when life has been transformed by the constant threat of global destruction, the need of the hour calls for the more universal form of the prayer throughout the year. A.G.

KAVANAH. God is shalom. God's name is shalom, everything is held together by shalom. Zohar

My God, you are *salam* peace.
Peace comes from you, goes back to you.
Let us live in peace and with peace.
You are great and generous. Sidi Sheikh Muhammad Al Jemal

19 בִּרְכַּת הַשָּׁלוֹם

שָׁלוֹם רָב עַל יִשְׂרָאֵל עַמְּךָ תָּשִׂים לְעוֹלָם: כִּי אַתָּה הוּא מֶֽלֶךְ אָדוֹן לְכָל הַשָּׁלוֹם: וְטוֹב בְּעֵינֶֽיךָ לְבָרֵךְ אֶת עַמְּךָ יִשְׂרָאֵל וְאֶת כָּל־יוֹשְׁבֵי תֵבֵל בְּכָל עֵת וּבְכָל שָׁעָה בִּשְׁלוֹמֶֽךָ:

Between Rosh Hashanah and Yom Kippur, add:

(בְּסֵֽפֶר חַיִּים בְּרָכָה וְשָׁלוֹם וּפַרְנָסָה טוֹבָה נִזָּכֵר וְנִכָּתֵב לְפָנֶֽיךָ אֲנַֽחְנוּ וְכָל עַמְּךָ בֵּית יִשְׂרָאֵל לְחַיִּים טוֹבִים וּלְשָׁלוֹם:)

בָּרוּךְ אַתָּה יהוה עוֹשֵׂה הַשָּׁלוֹם:

Shalom rav al yisra'el ameḥa tasim le'olam.
Ki atah hu meleḥ adon leḥol hashalom.
Vetov be'eyneḥa levareḥ et ameḥa yisra'el
ve'et kol yoshvey tevel
beḥol et uvḥol sha'ah bishlomeḥa.

Between Rosh Hashanah and Yom Kippur, add:

(Besefer ḥayim beraḥah veshalom ufarnasah tovah nizaḥer venikatev lefaneḥa
anaḥnu veḥol ameḥa beyt yisra'el
leḥayim tovim ulshalom.)

Baruḥ atah adonay osey hashalom.

The Amidah traditionally concludes with bowing and taking three steps back.

RIBONO SHEL OLAM / CONCLUDING MEDITATION

Sovereign of the universe,
fulfill my heart's petitions for the good.
Let me be worthy to perform your will with a whole heart.
Deliver me from the inclination to do evil,
and give me my portion in your Torah.
May I merit, with all Israel, your people,
that your Presence dwell upon us.
Make evident among us
the spirit of wisdom and understanding,
the spirit of counsel and strength,
the spirit of knowledge and the awe of THE CREATOR.
May divine love surround the one
who trusts in THE ETERNAL.

May my words of prayer, and my heart's meditation
be seen favorably, PRECIOUS ONE,
my rock, my champion.

May the one who creates harmony above
make peace for us and for all Israel,
and for all who dwell on earth.
And say: Amen.

On fast days and during the days between Rosh Hashanah and Yom Kippur, continue with Avinu Malkenu, *pages 136-143.*

רִבּוֹנוֹ שֶׁל עוֹלָם

רִבּוֹנוֹ שֶׁל עוֹלָם מַלֵּא מִשְׁאֲלוֹת לִבִּי לְטוֹבָה וְזַכֵּנִי לַעֲשׂוֹת רְצוֹנְךָ
בְּלֵבָב שָׁלֵם: מַלְּטֵנִי מִיֵּצֶר הָרָע וְתֵן חֶלְקִי בְּתוֹרָתֶךָ: זַכֵּינִי עִם כָּל
יִשְׂרָאֵל עַמֶּךָ שֶׁתַּשְׁרֶה שְׁכִינָתְךָ עָלֵינוּ וְהוֹפַע עָלֵינוּ רוּחַ חָכְמָה
וּבִינָה רוּחַ עֵצָה וּגְבוּרָה רוּחַ דַּעַת וְיִרְאַת יהוה:
וְהַבּוֹטֵחַ בַּיהוה חֶסֶד יְסוֹבְבֶנּוּ.
יִהְיוּ לְרָצוֹן אִמְרֵי פִי וְהֶגְיוֹן לִבִּי לְפָנֶיךָ יהוה צוּרִי וְגוֹאֲלִי:
עוֹשֶׂה שָׁלוֹם בִּמְרוֹמָיו הוּא יַעֲשֶׂה שָׁלוֹם עָלֵינוּ וְעַל כָּל יִשְׂרָאֵל וְעַל
כָּל יוֹשְׁבֵי תֵבֵל וְאִמְרוּ אָמֵן:

On fast days and during the days between Rosh Hashanah and Yom Kippur, continue with Avinu Malkenu, *pages 136-143.*

שכינתך / *sheḥinateḥa* / your Presence. This term is one of the most frequent ways of speaking of God in rabbinic and mystical tradition. The term derives from Exodus 25:8: "And I shall dwell in their midst" (*veshaḥanti betoḥam*). God's Presence coming to dwell in the Tabernacle was believed to be the normal outcome of the priestly sacrificial labors. When Israel's Second Temple was destroyed, the belief arose that God continues to dwell among Israelites during study and prayer. "If two sit and there are words of Torah between them, the Sheḥinah dwells with them. (*Pirkey Avot* 3:3).

J.R.

יהיו...וגואלי / May...champion (Psalm 19:15).

KADDISH TITKABAL / KADDISH FOR THE COMPLETION OF PRAYER

Reader: Let God's name be made great and holy in the world that was created as God willed. May God complete the holy realm in your own lifetime, in your days, and in the days of all the house of Israel, quickly and soon. And say: Amen.

Congregation: May God's great name be blessed forever and as long as worlds endure.

Reader: May it be blessed, and praised, and glorified, and held in honor, viewed with awe, embellished, and revered; and may the blessed name of holiness be hailed, though it be higher (*Between Rosh Hashanah and Yom Kippur, add:* by far) than all the blessings, songs, praises, and consolations that we utter in this world. And say: Amen.

And may the prayer and supplication of the whole house of Israel be acceptable to their creator in the heavens. And say: Amen.

May Heaven grant a universal peace, and life for us, and for all Israel. And say: Amen.

May the one who creates harmony above make peace for us and for all Israel, and for all who dwell on earth. And say: Amen.

NOTE. Kaddish Titkabal concludes the section of the service containing an *Amidah* / silent prayer. It therefore contains a request for the acceptance of prayer, which is omitted in the Mourners' Kaddish that follows *Aleynu*. D.A.T.

קַדִּישׁ תִּתְקַבַּל

יִתְגַּדַּל וְיִתְקַדַּשׁ שְׁמֵהּ רַבָּא בְּעָלְמָא דִּי בְרָא כִרְעוּתֵהּ וְיַמְלִיךְ מַלְכוּתֵהּ בְּחַיֵּיכוֹן וּבְיוֹמֵיכוֹן וּבְחַיֵּי דְכָל בֵּית יִשְׂרָאֵל בַּעֲגָלָא וּבִזְמַן קָרִיב וְאִמְרוּ אָמֵן:

יְהֵא שְׁמֵהּ רַבָּא מְבָרַךְ לְעָלַם וּלְעָלְמֵי עָלְמַיָּא:

יִתְבָּרַךְ וְיִשְׁתַּבַּח וְיִתְפָּאַר וְיִתְרוֹמַם וְיִתְנַשֵּׂא וְיִתְהַדַּר וְיִתְעַלֶּה וְיִתְהַלַּל שְׁמֵהּ דְּקֻדְשָׁא בְּרִיךְ הוּא

לְעֵֽלָּא (*Between Rosh Hashanah and Yom Kippur, add:* לְעֵֽלָּא) מִן כָּל בִּרְכָתָא וְשִׁירָתָא תֻּשְׁבְּחָתָא וְנֶחֱמָתָא דַּאֲמִירָן בְּעָלְמָא וְאִמְרוּ אָמֵן:

תִּתְקַבַּל צְלוֹתְהוֹן וּבָעוּתְהוֹן דְּכָל בֵּית יִשְׂרָאֵל קֳדָם אֲבוּהוֹן דִּי בִשְׁמַיָּא וְאִמְרוּ אָמֵן:

יְהֵא שְׁלָמָא רַבָּא מִן שְׁמַיָּא וְחַיִּים עָלֵֽינוּ וְעַל כָּל יִשְׂרָאֵל וְאִמְרוּ אָמֵן:

עוֹשֶׂה שָׁלוֹם בִּמְרוֹמָיו הוּא יַעֲשֶׂה שָׁלוֹם עָלֵֽינוּ וְעַל כָּל יִשְׂרָאֵל וְעַל כָּל יוֹשְׁבֵי תֵבֵל וְאִמְרוּ אָמֵן:

Yehey shemey raba mevaraḥ le'alam ulalmey almaya.
Oseh shalom bimromav hu ya'aseh shalom aleynu ve'al kol yisra'el ve'al kol yoshvey tevel ve'imru amen.

KAVANAH. Adding the rabbinic phrase "*ve'al kol yoshvey tevel*" (and for all who dwell on earth) logically completes the concentric circles of our aspirations—our care starts with our minyan, extends to the entire Jewish people, and radiates outward from there to all who share our planet.

D.A.T.

From the second day of Pesaḥ *until* Shavuot *the counting of the* Omer, *pages 414-423, is inserted here. On Saturday evening, in public worship, Havdalah, pages 350-357, is recited here. On Purim, turn to page 388 for the blessings preceding the Megillah reading. On Tisha Be'Av the book of* אֵיכָה */ Eyḥah/Lamentations and other readings are added here. For readings see pages 472-477.*

ALEYNU

We rise for Aleynu. *It is customary to bow at "bend the knee." For an alternative version see page 332. Choose one of the following:*

It is up to us to offer praises to the Source of all,
to declare the greatness of the author of Creation,
who gave to us teachings of truth
and planted eternal life within us.

It is up to us to offer praises to the Source of all,
to declare the greatness of the author of Creation,
who created heaven's heights and spread out its expanse,
who laid the earth's foundation and brought forth its offspring,
giving life to all its peoples,
the breath of life to all who walk about.

COMMENTARY. This siddur offers several versions of the *Aleynu*. The first, which appeared in the 1945 Reconstructionist siddur, emphasizes that the gift of God's Torah or teaching demands our committed response. The second version, based on Isaiah 42:5 and fit into the *Aleynu* by Rabbi Max D. Klein, emphasizes that our obligation to God flows from our role as part of Creation. The traditional *Aleynu* that appears below the line has troubled Reconstructionist Jews because it implies the inferiority of other faiths and peoples. D.A.T.

COMMENTARY. The theme of *Aleynu* is the anticipation of God's universal rulership. Originally, this glorious hymn introduced the "Rulership" section of the Rosh Hashanah liturgy. Because of its lofty language and message, *Aleynu* was soon added to every worship service. The Reconstructionist version of *Aleynu* shifts the focus from a concern with the specialness of the Jewish people to an emphasis on the unique Torah perspective that enables Israel to help spread God's presence through the universe. This shift eliminates an opportunity for Jewish triumphalism, in favor of stressing the importance of Torah in Jewish living. S.S.

From the second day of Pesaḥ *until* Shavuot *the counting of the* Omer, *pages 414-423, is inserted here. In public worship on Saturday evening, Havdalah, pages 350-357, is recited here. On Purim, turn to page 389 for the blessings preceding the Megillah reading. On Tisha Be'Av the book of* אֵיכָה */ Eyḥah/Lamentations and other readings are added here. For readings see pages 472-477.*

עָלֵינוּ

We rise for Aleynu. *It is customary to bow at* korim. *Choose one of the following.*

עָלֵינוּ לְשַׁבֵּחַ לַאֲדוֹן הַכֹּל
לָתֵת גְּדֻלָּה לְיוֹצֵר בְּרֵאשִׁית
שֶׁנָּתַן לָנוּ תּוֹרַת אֱמֶת
וְחַיֵּי עוֹלָם נָטַע בְּתוֹכֵנוּ: ←

Aleynu leshabe'aḥ la'adon hakol
latet gedulah leyotzer bereyshit
shenatan lanu torat emet
veḥayey olam nata betoḥenu.

Continue on page 329.

עָלֵינוּ לְשַׁבֵּחַ לַאֲדוֹן הַכֹּל
לָתֵת גְּדֻלָּה לְיוֹצֵר בְּרֵאשִׁית
בּוֹרֵא הַשָּׁמַיִם וְנוֹטֵיהֶם
רֹקַע הָאָרֶץ וְצֶאֱצָאֶיהָ
נֹתֵן נְשָׁמָה לָעָם עָלֶיהָ
וְרוּחַ לַהֹלְכִים בָּהּ: ←

Aleynu leshabe'aḥ la'adon hakol
latet gedulah leyotzer bereyshit.
bore hashamayim venoteyhem
roka ha'aretz vetze'etza'eha
noten neshamah la'am aleha
veru'aḥ laholeḥim ba.

Continue on page 329.

עָלֵינוּ לְשַׁבֵּחַ לַאֲדוֹן הַכֹּל לָתֵת גְּדֻלָּה
לְיוֹצֵר בְּרֵאשִׁית שֶׁלֹּא עָשָׂנוּ כְּגוֹיֵי
הָאֲרָצוֹת וְלֹא שָׂמָנוּ כְּמִשְׁפְּחוֹת הָאֲדָמָה
שֶׁלֹּא שָׂם חֶלְקֵנוּ כָּהֶם וְגוֹרָלֵנוּ כְּכָל
הֲמוֹנָם:

It is up to us to offer praises to the Source of all, to declare the greatness of the author of Creation, who has made us different from the other nations of the earth, and situated us in quite a different spot, and made our daily lot another kind from theirs, and given us a destiny uncommon in his world.

And so, we bend the knee and bow,
acknowledging the sovereign who rules
above all those who rule, the blessed Holy One,
who stretched out the heavens and founded the earth,
whose realm embraces heaven's heights,
whose mighty presence stalks celestial ramparts.
This is our God; there is none else besides,
as it is written in the Torah:
"You shall know this day, and bring it home
inside your heart, that THE SUPREME ONE is God
in the heavens above and on the earth below.
There is no other God." ↩

DERASH. Every person and people that feel they have something to live for, and that are bent on living that life in righteousness, are true witnesses of God. M.M.K.

KAVANAH. As the hand held before the eye hides the tallest mountain, so this small earthly life hides from our gaze the vast radiance and secrets of which the world is full, and if we can take life from before our eyes, as one takes away one's hand, we will see the great radiance within the world. M.B. (Adapted)

וידעת...עוד / You...other God (Deuteronomy 4:39).

וַאֲנַ֫חְנוּ כּוֹרְעִים וּמִשְׁתַּחֲוִים וּמוֹדִים לִפְנֵי מֶ֫לֶךְ מַלְכֵי הַמְּלָכִים הַקָּדוֹשׁ בָּרוּךְ הוּא:
שֶׁהוּא נוֹטֶה שָׁמַ֫יִם וְיוֹסֵד אָ֫רֶץ וּמוֹשַׁב יְקָרוֹ בַּשָּׁמַ֫יִם מִמַּ֫עַל וּשְׁכִינַת עֻזּוֹ בְּגָבְהֵי מְרוֹמִים: הוּא אֱלֹהֵ֫ינוּ אֵין עוֹד: אֱמֶת מַלְכֵּ֫נוּ אֶ֫פֶס זוּלָתוֹ כַּכָּתוּב בְּתוֹרָתוֹ: וְיָדַעְתָּ הַיּוֹם וַהֲשֵׁבֹתָ אֶל לְבָבֶ֫ךָ כִּי יהוה הוּא הָאֱלֹהִים בַּשָּׁמַ֫יִם מִמַּ֫עַל וְעַל הָאָ֫רֶץ מִתָּ֫חַת אֵין עוֹד: ←

Va'anaḥnu korim umishtaḥavim umodim
lifney meleḥ malḥey hamelaḥim hakadosh baruḥ hu.
Shehu noteh shamayim veyosed aretz umoshav yekaro
bashamayim mima'al
ush-ḥinat uzo begovhey meromim.
Hu eloheynu eyn od.
Emet malkenu efes zulato kakatuv betorato.
Veyadata hayom vahashevota el levaveḥa
ki adonay hu ha'elohim bashamayim mima'al ve'al ha'aretz
mitaḥat eyn od.

And so, we put our hope in you,
THE EMINENCE, our God,
that soon we may behold
the full splendor of your might,
and see idolatry vanish from the earth,
and all material gods be swept away,
and the power of your rule repair the world,
and all creatures of flesh call on your name,
and all the wicked of the earth turn back to you.
Let all who dwell upon the globe perceive and know
that to you each knee must bend, each tongue swear oath,
and let them give the glory of your name its precious due.
Let all of them take upon themselves your rule.
Reign over them, soon and for always.
For this is all your realm, throughout all worlds, across all time—
as it is written in your Torah:
"THE ETERNAL ONE will reign now and forever."

And it is written:
"THE EVERLASTING ONE will reign
as sovereign over all the earth.
On that day shall THE MANY-NAMED be one,
God's name be one!"

KAVANAH. A world of God callers is a world of truth and peace, a world where lust for power, greed, and envy—the idols of pride—is uprooted from the individual and group psyche. S.P.W.

עַל כֵּן נְקַוֶּה לְךָ יהוה אֱלֹהֵינוּ לִרְאוֹת מְהֵרָה בְּתִפְאֶרֶת עֻזֶּךָ לְהַעֲבִיר
גִּלּוּלִים מִן הָאָרֶץ וְהָאֱלִילִים כָּרוֹת יִכָּרֵתוּן לְתַקֵּן עוֹלָם בְּמַלְכוּת
שַׁדַּי: וְכָל בְּנֵי בָשָׂר יִקְרְאוּ בִשְׁמֶךָ: לְהַפְנוֹת אֵלֶיךָ כָּל רִשְׁעֵי אָרֶץ:
יַכִּירוּ וְיֵדְעוּ כָּל יוֹשְׁבֵי תֵבֵל כִּי לְךָ תִּכְרַע כָּל בֶּרֶךְ תִּשָּׁבַע כָּל־לָשׁוֹן:
לְפָנֶיךָ יהוה אֱלֹהֵינוּ יִכְרְעוּ וְיִפֹּלוּ וְלִכְבוֹד שִׁמְךָ יְקָר יִתֵּנוּ וִיקַבְּלוּ
כֻלָּם אֶת עֹל מַלְכוּתֶךָ וְתִמְלֹךְ עֲלֵיהֶם מְהֵרָה לְעוֹלָם וָעֶד: כִּי
הַמַּלְכוּת שֶׁלְּךָ הִיא וּלְעוֹלְמֵי עַד תִּמְלֹךְ בְּכָבוֹד כַּכָּתוּב בְּתוֹרָתֶךָ:
יהוה יִמְלֹךְ לְעֹלָם וָעֶד: וְנֶאֱמַר: וְהָיָה יהוה לְמֶלֶךְ עַל כָּל הָאָרֶץ
בַּיּוֹם הַהוּא יִהְיֶה יהוה אֶחָד וּשְׁמוֹ אֶחָד:

Kakatuv betorateḥa: Adonay yimloḥ le'olam va'ed.
Vene'emar: Vehayah adonay lemeleḥ al kol ha'aretz.
Bayom hahu yihyeh adonay eḥad ushmo eḥad.

DERASH. When senseless hatred reigns on earth and people hide their faces from one another, then heaven is forced to hide its face. But when love comes to rule the earth and people reveal their faces to one another, then the splendor of God will be revealed. M.B. (Adapted)

DERASH. It is not the seeking after God that divides but the claim to have found God and to have discovered the only proper way of obeying God and communing with God. M.M.K./M.S.

יהוה...ועד / THE ETERNAL ONE...forever (Exodus 15:18).

והיה...אחד / THE EVERLASTING ONE...one (Zechariah 14:9).

ALEYNU / ALTERNATIVE VERSIONS

It is up to us
to hallow Creation,
to respond to Life
with the fullness of our lives.
It is up to us
to meet the World,
to embrace the Whole
even as we wrestle
with its parts.
It is up to us
to repair the World
and to bind our lives to the Truth.

Therefore we bend the knee
and shake off the stiffness that keeps us
from the subtle
graces of Life
and the supple
gestures of Love.
With reverence
and thanksgiving
we accept our destiny
and set for ourselves
the task of redemption.

Rami M. Shapiro

And then all that has divided us will merge
And then compassion will be wedded to power
And then softness will come to a world that is harsh and unkind
And then both men and women will be gentle
And then both women and men will be strong
And then no person will be subject to another's will
And then all will be rich and free and varied
And then the greed of some will give way to the needs of many
And then all will share equally in the Earth's abundance
And then all will care for the sick and the weak and the old
And then all will nourish the young
And then all will cherish life's creatures
And then all will live in harmony with each other and the Earth
And then everywhere will be called Eden once again.

Judy Chicago

Readings appropriate to a house of mourning may be added at this point. For a selection of readings, *see pages 490 to 532.*

INTRODUCTION TO THE MOURNERS' KADDISH

In reciting the Kaddish we affirm our awareness of holiness in our world. Much of our experience of divine goodness, grace and love has come to us through those whose lives have touched our own. (Today we remember...) We invoke the transcendent power of love and caring as we sanctify God's name.

It is customary for mourners, and those observing Yahrzeit, to stand for Kaddish. In some congregations everyone rises.

THE MOURNERS' KADDISH

Reader: Let God's name be made great and holy in the world that was created as God willed. May God complete the holy realm in your own lifetime, in your days, and in the days of all the house of Israel, quickly and soon. And say: Amen.

Congregation: May God's great name be blessed, forever and as long as worlds endure.

Reader: May it be blessed, and praised, and glorified, and held in honor, viewed with awe, embellished, and revered; and may the blessed name of holiness be hailed, though it be higher (*Between Rosh Hashanah and Yom Kippur, add:* by far) than all the blessings, songs, praises, and consolations that we utter in this world. And say: Amen.

May Heaven grant a universal peace, and life for us, and for all Israel. And say: Amen.

May the one who creates harmony above, make peace for us and for all Israel, and for all who dwell on earth. And say: Amen.

Love is not changed by Death,
And nothing is lost and all in the end is harvest.

Edith Sitwell

Readings appropriate to a house of mourning may be added at this point. For a selection of readings, see pages 431 to 532.

קַדִּישׁ יָתוֹם

It is customary for mourners, and those observing Yahrzeit, to stand for Kaddish. In some congregations everyone rises.

יִתְגַּדַּל וְיִתְקַדַּשׁ שְׁמֵהּ רַבָּא בְּעָלְמָא דִּי בְרָא כִרְעוּתֵהּ וְיַמְלִיךְ
מַלְכוּתֵהּ בְּחַיֵּיכוֹן וּבְיוֹמֵיכוֹן וּבְחַיֵּי דְכָל בֵּית יִשְׂרָאֵל בַּעֲגָלָא וּבִזְמַן
קָרִיב וְאִמְרוּ אָמֵן:
יְהֵא שְׁמֵהּ רַבָּא מְבָרַךְ לְעָלַם וּלְעָלְמֵי עָלְמַיָּא:
יִתְבָּרַךְ וְיִשְׁתַּבַּח וְיִתְפָּאַר וְיִתְרוֹמַם וְיִתְנַשֵּׂא וְיִתְהַדַּר וְיִתְעַלֶּה
וְיִתְהַלַּל שְׁמֵהּ דְּקֻדְשָׁא בְּרִיךְ הוּא
לְעֵֽלָּא (*Between Rosh Hashanah and Yom Kippur, add:* לְעֵֽלָּא) מִן כָּל בִּרְכָתָא
וְשִׁירָתָא תֻּשְׁבְּחָתָא וְנֶחֱמָתָא דַּאֲמִירָן בְּעָלְמָא וְאִמְרוּ אָמֵן:
יְהֵא שְׁלָמָא רַבָּא מִן שְׁמַיָּא וְחַיִּים עָלֵֽינוּ וְעַל כָּל יִשְׂרָאֵל וְאִמְרוּ אָמֵן:
עוֹשֶׂה שָׁלוֹם בִּמְרוֹמָיו הוּא יַעֲשֶׂה שָׁלוֹם עָלֵֽינוּ וְעַל כָּל יִשְׂרָאֵל וְעַל
כָּל יוֹשְׁבֵי תֵבֵל וְאִמְרוּ אָמֵן:

Reader: Yitgadal veyitkadash shemey raba
be'alma di vera ḥirutey veyamliḥ malḥutey
beḥayeyḥon uvyomeyḥon uvḥayey deḥol beyt yisra'el
ba'agala uvizman kariv ve'imru amen.

Congregation: Yehey shemey raba mevaraḥ le'alam ulalmey almaya.

Reader: Yitbaraḥ veyishtabaḥ veyitpa'ar veyitromam
veyitnasey veyit-hadar veyitaleh veyit-halal
shemey dekudsha beriḥ hu
le'ela (*Between Rosh Hashanah and Yom Kippur, add:* le'ela) min kol birḥata
veshirata tushbeḥata veneḥemata da'amiran be'alma
ve'imru amen.

Yehey shelama raba min shemaya veḥayim aleynu ve'al kol
yisra'el ve'imru amen.
Oseh shalom bimromav hu ya'aseh shalom aleynu ve'al kol
yisra'el ve'al kol yoshvey tevel ve'imru amen.

The following psalm is traditionally recited at this point each morning and evening from Rosh Ḥodesh Elul *through* Hoshanah Rabah.

[A psalm] of David.
THE ETERNAL is my light and my salvation; whom, then, should I fear?
THE ALMIGHTY is my living source of strength; before whom should I tremble?

When evildoers approach to eat my flesh, when tormenters and enemies come after me,
see how they stumble; see how they tumble down!

Should a force encamp against me, my heart shall have no fear;
should a war arise against me, in one thing I shall trust,

one thing have I asked of GOD, one goal do I pursue: to dwell in THE ETERNAL's house throughout my days,
to know the bliss of THE SUBLIME, to visit in God's temple.

Truly, in a day of trouble, I am nestled in God's shelter, hidden in the recess of God's tent.
God sets me high upon a rock. ↩

KAVANAH. Throughout history it has been true that sometimes good people suffer through no fault of their own. The psalmist is not so naive as to be unaware of this reality. How can there be shelter in the midst of swarming enemies? With physical protection unlikely, the shelter invoked here provides not physical but spiritual succor. The psalmist seeks the calm and bliss that come from an awareness of the divine made manifest in the workings of the human heart. With this sense of a greatness that transcends physical peril, enemies' violence causes no fear, and slanderers can do little damage. Living directed to the divine gives us the power not to avoid mortal danger, but to transcend our fear of it. D.A.T.

The following psalm is traditionally recited at this point each morning and evening from Rosh Ḥodesh Elul *through* Hoshanah Rabah.

לְדָוִד

יהוה אוֹרִי וְיִשְׁעִי מִמִּי אִירָא:
יהוה מָעוֹז חַיַּי מִמִּי אֶפְחָד:
בִּקְרֹב עָלַי מְרֵעִים לֶאֱכֹל אֶת בְּשָׂרִי
צָרַי וְאֹיְבַי לִי הֵמָּה כָּשְׁלוּ וְנָפָלוּ:
אִם תַּחֲנֶה עָלַי מַחֲנֶה לֹא יִירָא לִבִּי
אִם תָּקוּם עָלַי מִלְחָמָה בְּזֹאת אֲנִי בוֹטֵחַ:
אַחַת שָׁאַלְתִּי מֵאֵת יהוה אוֹתָהּ אֲבַקֵּשׁ שִׁבְתִּי בְּבֵית יהוה כָּל יְמֵי
חַיַּי לַחֲזוֹת בְּנֹעַם יהוה וּלְבַקֵּר בְּהֵיכָלוֹ:
כִּי יִצְפְּנֵנִי בְּסֻכּוֹ בְּיוֹם רָעָה יַסְתִּרֵנִי בְּסֵתֶר אָהֳלוֹ בְּצוּר יְרוֹמְמֵנִי: ←

Aḥat sha'alti me'et adonay otah avakesh shivti beveyt adonay kol yemey ḥayay laḥazot beno'am adonay ulevaker beheyḥalo.

COMMENTARY. We say this psalm every day from the first of *Elul* through *Hoshanah Rabah*. The rabbis doubtless chose it to accompany us through every phase of the fall holiday season because it encompasses such a range of powerful emotions. Identifying with the experience of the speaker can help us to be in touch with our fears of abandonment, our need for security, our yearning for joyful religious experience, our need for guidance from God, or our steadying commitment to never lose hope. Above all, we experience the psalmist's vulnerability. Feeling that it is possible to be hidden and secure within God's presence, the speaker also knows, by contrast, the terrible fear that God can hide the divine countenance and seem utterly unavailable. The psalm delicately balances these two kinds of hiddenness, as it tries to find a metaphoric "level path," the right way of walking in a difficult, dangerous world. The psalm ends by urging that we seek our God, clinging to hope in the return of God's presence. H.L.

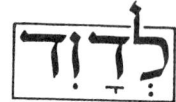

And now, my head is raised in triumph on my foes around me,
and I offer sacrifice in celebration in God's tent.
I offer song and melody to MY REDEEMER.

Hear me, PRECIOUS ONE, I call aloud;
be gracious to me, answer me!

To you my heart cries out, to you my face is turned,
your presence, GRACIOUS ONE, I seek.

Hide not your face from me: do not, in anger, turn away your servant.
You have been my help, don't shun me now; do not abandon me, my God who saves!

For my father and my mother have abandoned me,
but THE LIVING ONE shall take me in.

Teach me your way, WISE ONE, and guide me in a just path as I meet my foes.
Don't place me at the mercy of my enemies, for slanderers arise against me, and they fume in violence.

Were it not for my belief that I'll behold GOD's goodness in the Land of Life...
Hope, then, for THE ETERNAL ONE; strengthen your heart with courage, and have hope in THE ETERNAL.

Psalm 27

וְעַתָּה יָרוּם רֹאשִׁי עַל אֹיְבַי סְבִיבוֹתַי וְאֶזְבְּחָה בְאָהֳלוֹ זִבְחֵי תְרוּעָה
אָשִׁירָה וַאֲזַמְּרָה לַיהוה:
שְׁמַע יהוה קוֹלִי אֶקְרָא וְחָנֵּנִי וַעֲנֵנִי:
לְךָ אָמַר לִבִּי בַּקְּשׁוּ פָנָי אֶת פָּנֶיךָ יהוה אֲבַקֵּשׁ:
אַל תַּסְתֵּר פָּנֶיךָ מִמֶּנִּי אַל תַּט בְּאַף עַבְדֶּךָ עֶזְרָתִי הָיִיתָ אַל תִּטְּשֵׁנִי
וְאַל תַּעַזְבֵנִי אֱלֹהֵי יִשְׁעִי:
כִּי אָבִי וְאִמִּי עֲזָבוּנִי וַיהוה יַאַסְפֵנִי:
הוֹרֵנִי יהוה דַּרְכֶּךָ וּנְחֵנִי בְּאֹרַח מִישׁוֹר לְמַעַן שׁוֹרְרָי:
אַל תִּתְּנֵנִי בְּנֶפֶשׁ צָרָי כִּי קָמוּ בִי עֵדֵי שֶׁקֶר וִיפֵחַ חָמָס:
*לוּלֵא הֶאֱמַנְתִּי לִרְאוֹת בְּטוּב יהוה בְּאֶרֶץ חַיִּים:
קַוֵּה אֶל יהוה חֲזַק וְיַאֲמֵץ לִבֶּךָ וְקַוֵּה אֶל יהוה:

KAVANAH. This psalm speaks of evildoers, but also refers to our illness, pain, the trials and tribulations we all suffer, and our concerns and worries with living. The plane on which we focus our everyday consciousness keeps us in touch with all the things that go wrong in our lives—both small and large. This psalm urges an awareness of a different plane, one where we focus on the eternal instead of the everyday. Here we are nutured by spiritual connection. Here we gain perspective on the whirl of activity that dominates our everyday lives. Here we find the strength and goodness that can sustain us in our daily tasks. D.A.T.

This psalm is often read by mourners.

A Psalm of David
THE ETERNAL is my shepherd; I shall never be in need.
Amid the choicest grasses does God set me down.
God leads me by the calmest waters,
and restores my soul.
God takes me along paths of righteousness,
in keeping with the honor of God's name.
Even should I wander in a valley of the darkest shadows,
I will fear no evil.
You are with me, God. Your power and support
  are there to comfort me.
You set in front of me a table
in the presence of my enemies.
You anoint my head with oil; my cup is overflowing.
Surely, good and loving-kindness will pursue me
  all the days of my life,
and I shall come to dwell inside the house
  of THE ETERNAL for a length of days.

Psalm 23

COMMENTARY. This psalm offers comfort to mourners, but not to them alone. Its images of pastoral quiet and abundant nourishment speak to all who seek a spiritual oasis in the midst of daily struggle. The psalm's speaker is fully reconciled with the divine; therefore, with the calmest of voices, the psalmist can lead us gently but firmly along the path toward faithfulness. H.L.

This psalm is often read by mourners.

מִזְמוֹר לְדָוִד
יהוה רֹעִי לֹא אֶחְסָר׃ בִּנְאוֹת דֶּשֶׁא יַרְבִּיצֵנִי
עַל־מֵי מְנֻחוֹת יְנַהֲלֵנִי׃ נַפְשִׁי יְשׁוֹבֵב
יַנְחֵנִי בְמַעְגְּלֵי־צֶדֶק לְמַעַן שְׁמוֹ׃
גַּם כִּי־אֵלֵךְ בְּגֵיא צַלְמָוֶת לֹא־אִירָא רָע
כִּי־אַתָּה עִמָּדִי שִׁבְטְךָ וּמִשְׁעַנְתֶּךָ הֵמָּה יְנַחֲמֻנִי׃
תַּעֲרֹךְ לְפָנַי שֻׁלְחָן נֶגֶד צֹרְרָי
דִּשַּׁנְתָּ בַשֶּׁמֶן רֹאשִׁי כּוֹסִי רְוָיָה׃
אַךְ טוֹב וָחֶסֶד יִרְדְּפוּנִי כָּל־יְמֵי חַיָּי
וְשַׁבְתִּי בְּבֵית־יהוה לְאֹרֶךְ יָמִים׃

Mizmor ledavid
adonay ro'i lo eḥsar. Binot deshe yarbitzeni
al mey menuḥot yenahaleni. Nafshi yeshovev
yanḥeni vemageley tzedek lema'an shemo.
Gam ki eleḥ begey tzalmavet lo ira ra
ki atah imadi shivteḥa umishanteḥa hemah
yenaḥamuni.
Ta'aroḥ lefanay shulḥan neged tzoreray
dishanta vashemen roshi kosi revayah.
Aḥ tov vaḥesed yirdefuni kol yemey ḥayay
veshavti beveyt adonay le'oreḥ yamim.

The psalm is often sung at the third meal of Shabbat. This meal is associated with the messianic transformation from a world of injustice and suffering to righteousness and peace. The melodies to which it is sung at this time evoke both joyous anticipation and soulful yearning. H.L.

Yigdal / Great is...can be found on page 206.

ADON OLAM / CROWN OF ALL TIME

This translation can be sung to the same melody as the Hebrew.

Crown of all time, the one who reigned
before all mortal shape was made,
and when God's will brought forth all things
then was the name supreme proclaimed.

And after everything is gone,
yet One alone, awesome, will reign.
God was, and is, and will remain,
in splendid balance, over all.

And God is One, no second is,
none can compare, or share God's place.
Without beginning, without end,
God's is all might and royal grace.

This is my God, my help who lives,
refuge from pain in time of trial,
my banner, and my place to fly,
my cup's portion when, dry, I cry.

To God's kind hand I pledge my soul
each time I sleep, again to wake,
and with my soul, this body, here.
Yah's love is mine; I shall not fear.

KAVANAH. God is that aspect of reality which elicits from us the best that is in us and enables us to bear the worst that can befall us. M.M.K.

Yigdal / Great is...can be found on page 207.

אֲדוֹן עוֹלָם

אֲדוֹן עוֹלָם אֲשֶׁר מָלַךְ בְּטֶרֶם כָּל יְצִיר נִבְרָא:
לְעֵת נַעֲשָׂה בְחֶפְצוֹ כֹּל אֲזַי מֶלֶךְ שְׁמוֹ נִקְרָא:

וְאַחֲרֵי כִּכְלוֹת הַכֹּל לְבַדּוֹ יִמְלֹךְ נוֹרָא:
וְהוּא הָיָה וְהוּא הֹוֶה וְהוּא יִהְיֶה בְּתִפְאָרָה:

וְהוּא אֶחָד וְאֵין שֵׁנִי לְהַמְשִׁיל לוֹ לְהַחְבִּירָה:
בְּלִי רֵאשִׁית בְּלִי תַכְלִית וְלוֹ הָעֹז וְהַמִּשְׂרָה:

וְהוּא אֵלִי וְחַי גּוֹאֲלִי וְצוּר חֶבְלִי בְּעֵת צָרָה:
וְהוּא נִסִּי וּמָנוֹס לִי מְנָת כּוֹסִי בְּיוֹם אֶקְרָא:

בְּיָדוֹ אַפְקִיד רוּחִי בְּעֵת אִישַׁן וְאָעִירָה:
וְעִם רוּחִי גְּוִיָּתִי יהוה לִי וְלֹא אִירָא:

Adon olam asher malaḥ, beterem kol yetzir nivra.
Le'et na'asah veḥeftzo kol, azay meleḥ shemo nikra.
Ve'aḥarey kiḥlot hakol, levado yimloḥ nora.
Vehu hayah vehu hoveh, vehu yihyeh betifarah.
Vehu eḥad ve'eyn sheni, lehamshil lo lehaḥbirah.
Beli reshit beli taḥlit, velo ha'oz vehamisrah.
Vehu eli veḥay go'ali, vetzur ḥevli be'et tzarah.
Vehu nisi umanos li, menat kosi beyom ekra.
Beyado afkid ruḥi, be'et ishan ve'a'irah.
Ve'im ruḥi geviyati, adonay li velo ira.

NOTE. *Adon Olam*, like *Yigdal*, states principles of Jewish faith. It is frequently attributed to Solomon ibn Gabirol, a medieval Sephardic poet.

J.B.

שלום
Shalom
עלינו
for us
ועל כל ישראל
and for all Israel
ועל כל יושבי תבל
and for all who dwell on earth

KERIAT SHEMA SHE'AL HAMITAH / THE BEDTIME SHEMA

Behold, I now forgive whoever has provoked my anger or annoyance,
whoever has done wrong to me,
whether to my body or my spirit,
or to my honor, or to all that may belong to me,
whether willingly, or inadvertently, or by design,
whether by speech or deed—
let no one suffer punishment on my account.

Blessed are you, ETERNAL ONE, our God,
the sovereign of all worlds,
who makes the weight of sleep to fall upon my eyes,
and slumber on my eyelids.
May it be your will, ETERNAL GUARDIAN, my God,
and God of my ancestors,
that you help me to lie down in peace,
and to arise in peace,
and do not let my thoughts make me afraid,
nor my bad dreams, nor my preoccupations.
May my bed be safely guarded in your presence,
and may you give light to my eyes lest I should sleep without awakening,
for you are giver of the light of living to the pupil of the eye.
Blessed are you, ETERNAL LAMP,
who gives light to the world in all its glory.

קְרִיאַת שְׁמַע שֶׁעַל הַמִּטָּה

הֲרֵינִי מוֹחֵל לְכָל מִי שֶׁהִכְעִיס וְהִקְנִיט אוֹתִי אוֹ שֶׁחָטָא כְּנֶגְדִּי בֵּין בְּגוּפִי בֵּין בְּמָמוֹנִי בֵּין בִּכְבוֹדִי בֵּין בְּכָל אֲשֶׁר לִי בֵּין בְּאֹנֶס בֵּין בְּרָצוֹן בֵּין בְּשׁוֹגֵג בֵּין בְּמֵזִיד בֵּין בְּדִבּוּר בֵּין בְּמַעֲשֶׂה וְלֹא יֵעָנֵשׁ שׁוּם אָדָם בְּסִבָּתִי:

בָּרוּךְ אַתָּה יהוה אֱלֹהֵינוּ מֶלֶךְ הָעוֹלָם הַמַּפִּיל חֶבְלֵי שֵׁנָה עַל עֵינַי וּתְנוּמָה עַל עַפְעַפָּי: וִיהִי רָצוֹן מִלְּפָנֶיךָ יהוה אֱלֹהַי וֵאלֹהֵי אֲבוֹתַי שֶׁתַּשְׁכִּיבֵנִי לְשָׁלוֹם וְתַעֲמִידֵנִי לְשָׁלוֹם וְאַל יְבַהֲלוּנִי רַעְיוֹנַי וַחֲלוֹמוֹת רָעִים וְהִרְהוּרִים רָעִים וּתְהִי מִטָּתִי שְׁלֵמָה לְפָנֶיךָ: וְהָאֵר עֵינַי פֶּן אִישַׁן הַמָּוֶת כִּי אַתָּה הַמֵּאִיר לְאִישׁוֹן בַּת עָיִן: בָּרוּךְ אַתָּה יהוה הַמֵּאִיר לָעוֹלָם כֻּלּוֹ בִּכְבוֹדוֹ.

NOTE. Before the development of the full *Ma'ariv* evening service, the biblical commandment to recite the Shema "when lying down" was fulfilled at night by reciting the Shema at bedtime. This version was retained separately, partly because it was seen as protection against the dangers of the night (Beraḥot 5a). For contemporary Jews it provides an opportunity for releasing the angers and frustrations of the day and rediscovering the pools of tranquility within. This tranquility gives way to trust as we move towards sleep. D.A.T.

שמע ישראל יהוה אלהינו יהוה אחד

Listen, Israel: יהוה our God, יהוה is One!

Blessed be the glory of the Sovereign Name forever.

And you must love THE ONE your God, with your whole heart, with every breath, with all you have. Take these words that I command you now to heart. Teach them intently to your children; speak them when sitting in your house and walking on the road, when lying down and getting up. Bind them as a sign upon your hand, and keep them visible before your eyes. Write them on the doorposts of your house and on your gates.

Let our divine protector's pleasure be upon us, and the labor of our hands, make it secure, the labor of our hands ensure!

Help us to lie down, DEAR ONE, our God, in peace,
and let us rise again, our sovereign, to life.
Spread over us the shelter of your peace.
Decree for us a worthy daily lot,
and redeem us for the sake of your great name,
protecting us,
removing from our midst
all enmity, disease, and violence,
all suffering and hunger,
and enfold us in the wings of your protection.
For you are our redeeming guardian.
Truly, a sovereign, gracious, and compassionate God are you.
Please guard us when we go forth and when we return,
ensuring life and peace, both now and always.

"I lie down, I sleep, and I awake,
knowing THE ETERNAL ONE is my support."

שְׁמַע יִשְׂרָאֵל יהוה אֱלֹהֵינוּ יהוה אֶחָד׃

Shema yisra'el adonay eloheynu adonay eḥad.

בָּרוּךְ שֵׁם כְּבוֹד מַלְכוּתוֹ לְעוֹלָם וָעֶד׃

וְאָהַבְתָּ אֵת יהוה אֱלֹהֶיךָ בְּכָל־לְבָבְךָ וּבְכָל־נַפְשְׁךָ וּבְכָל־מְאֹדֶךָ׃ וְהָיוּ הַדְּבָרִים הָאֵלֶּה אֲשֶׁר אָנֹכִי מְצַוְּךָ הַיּוֹם עַל־לְבָבֶךָ׃ וְשִׁנַּנְתָּם לְבָנֶיךָ וְדִבַּרְתָּ בָּם בְּשִׁבְתְּךָ בְּבֵיתֶךָ וּבְלֶכְתְּךָ בַדֶּרֶךְ וּבְשָׁכְבְּךָ וּבְקוּמֶךָ׃ וּקְשַׁרְתָּם לְאוֹת עַל־יָדֶךָ וְהָיוּ לְטֹטָפֹת בֵּין עֵינֶיךָ׃ וּכְתַבְתָּם עַל־מְזֻזוֹת בֵּיתֶךָ וּבִשְׁעָרֶיךָ׃

וִיהִי נֹעַם אֲדֹנָי אֱלֹהֵינוּ עָלֵינוּ וּמַעֲשֵׂה יָדֵינוּ כּוֹנְנָה עָלֵינוּ וּמַעֲשֵׂה יָדֵינוּ כּוֹנְנֵהוּ׃

הַשְׁכִּיבֵנוּ יהוה אֱלֹהֵינוּ לְשָׁלוֹם וְהַעֲמִידֵנוּ מַלְכֵּנוּ לְחַיִּים וּפְרֹשׂ עָלֵינוּ סֻכַּת שְׁלוֹמֶךָ וְתַקְּנֵנוּ בְּעֵצָה טוֹבָה מִלְּפָנֶיךָ וְהוֹשִׁיעֵנוּ לְמַעַן שְׁמֶךָ׃ וְהָגֵן בַּעֲדֵנוּ וְהָסֵר מֵעָלֵינוּ אוֹיֵב דֶּבֶר וְחֶרֶב וְרָעָב וְיָגוֹן וּבְצֵל כְּנָפֶיךָ תַּסְתִּירֵנוּ׃ כִּי אֵל שׁוֹמְרֵנוּ וּמַצִּילֵנוּ אָתָּה כִּי אֵל מֶלֶךְ חַנּוּן וְרַחוּם אָתָּה׃ וּשְׁמֹר צֵאתֵנוּ וּבוֹאֵנוּ לְחַיִּים וּלְשָׁלוֹם מֵעַתָּה וְעַד עוֹלָם.

אֲנִי שָׁכַבְתִּי וָאִישָׁנָה הֱקִיצוֹתִי כִּי יהוה יִסְמְכֵנִי.

ויהי נעם...עלינו / Let our...ensure! (Psalm 90:17).
אני...יסמכני / I lie...support (Psalm 3:6).

HAVDALAH

At the end of Shabbat, a Havdalah *candle is lit. A full cup of wine and spices are near at hand, and the lights are dimmed.*
At the end of a festival, and at the start of Ḥol Hamo'ed, *the candle and spices are omitted if it is not Saturday night. On a Saturday night when Sunday is a holiday,* Havdalah *becomes a section of the festival Kiddush (see,* Kol Haneshamah: Shabbat & Festivals*).*

Elijah the prophet, come speedily to us hailing messianic days. Miriam the prophet will dance with us at the waters of redemption.

NOTE. Traditionally *Havdalah* is said after three stars appear in the sky on Saturday evening, making Shabbat about twenty-five hours long. In families that observe this tradition, younger children relish the task of finding stars.

Some sing "*Eliyahu Hanavi*" at the beginning of *Havdalah*, and some at the end. We have put it before *Havdalah* to set a mood of contemplation. This order builds toward the mood of jubilance expressed in the song "*Hamavdil.*"

Havdalah is recited not only on Shabbat but also at the conclusion of Festivals. When Festivals end at times other than Saturday nights, *Havdalah* includes only two blessings—over wine and over separation. D.A.T.

COMMENTARY. As Shabbat fades, our people's centuries-old yearning for redemption is voiced through song. When we sing the traditional "Eliyahu Hanavi," we recall the saving message and leadership of Elijah the Prophet, harbinger of the messianic age. The contemporary lyrics of "*Miriam Hanevi'ah*" parallel the traditional, offering an inspiring leadership model. Midrash tells us that Miriam helped to bolster the Israelite women's courage in taking the risk of fleeing Egypt toward freedom. A prophet in her own right, Miriam led our people in a celebration and dance after we "took the plunge" to freedom at the Reed Sea (Exodus 15:20-21). As we strive for תיקון עולם / repair of the world and as we pray for the coming of the messianic age, both Elijah and Miriam are inspiring prophetic figures who model leadership traits that may help to strengthen us on our journey toward redemption. L.B.

הַבְדָּלָה

אֵלִיָּהוּ הַנָּבִיא אֵלִיָּהוּ הַתִּשְׁבִּי אֵלִיָּהוּ הַגִּלְעָדִי׃
בִּמְהֵרָה בְיָמֵינוּ יָבֹא אֵלֵינוּ עִם מָשִׁיחַ בֶּן דָּוִד׃

Eliyahu hanavi, Eliyahu hatishbi, Eliyahu hagiladi.
Bimherah veyameynu yavo eleynu, im mashi'aḥ ben David.

מִרְיָם הַנְּבִיאָה עֹז וְזִמְרָה בְּיָדָהּ
מִרְיָם תִּרְקֹד אִתָּנוּ לְהַגְדִּיל זִמְרַת עוֹלָם
מִרְיָם תִּרְקֹד אִתָּנוּ לְתַקֵּן אֶת־הָעוֹלָם׃
בִּמְהֵרָה בְיָמֵינוּ הִיא תְּבִיאֵנוּ
אֶל מֵי הַיְשׁוּעָה׃

Leila Gal Berner

Miriam hanevi'ah oz vezimrah beyadah.
Miriam tirkod itanu lehagdil zimrat olam.
Miriam tirkod itanu letaken et ha'olam.
Bimherah veyameynu hi tevi'enu
el mey hayeshu'a.

This paragraph is omitted when Havdalah *is recited in the synagogue.*

The wine cup is raised.

Behold, my God of help,
in whom I trust, and tremble not.
Truly, my strength and melody is YAH, THE ONE,
who is for me the source of help.
So draw, in joy, the waters
from the Fount of Help.
All help belongs to you.
Upon your people is your blessing. Let it happen!
With us is THE GREAT ONE of the Multitudes of Heaven,
stronghold for us, the God of Jacob. Be it so!
O, GREAT ONE of the Multitudes of Heaven,
happy is the human being who trusts in you!
REDEEMING ONE, extend your help.
Our sovereign, answer us whenever we may call.
The Jews of old had light,
and happiness, and joy, and love—
may it be so for us!
My Cup of Help I raise,
and in THE OMNIPRESENT's name
I call.

This paragraph is omitted when Havdalah *is recited in the synagogue.*

The wine cup is raised.

הִנֵּה אֵל יְשׁוּעָתִי אֶבְטַח וְלֹא אֶפְחָד כִּי עָזִּי וְזִמְרָת יָהּ יהוה וַיְהִי לִי
לִישׁוּעָה: וּשְׁאַבְתֶּם מַֽיִם בְּשָׂשׂוֹן מִמַּעַיְנֵי הַיְשׁוּעָה: לַיהוה הַיְשׁוּעָה
עַל עַמְּךָ בִרְכָתֶֽךָ סֶּֽלָה: יהוה צְבָאוֹת עִמָּֽנוּ מִשְׂגָּב לָֽנוּ אֱלֹהֵי יַעֲקֹב
סֶֽלָה: יהוה צְבָאוֹת אַשְׁרֵי אָדָם בֹּטֵֽחַ בָּךְ: יהוה הוֹשִֽׁיעָה הַמֶּֽלֶךְ יַעֲנֵֽנוּ
בְיוֹם קָרְאֵֽנוּ: לַיְּהוּדִים הָיְתָה אוֹרָה וְשִׂמְחָה וְשָׂשׂוֹן וִיקָר: כֵּן תִּהְיֶה
לָֽנוּ: כּוֹס יְשׁוּעוֹת אֶשָּׂא וּבְשֵׁם יהוה אֶקְרָא:

Hiney el yeshu'ati evtaḥ velo efḥad ki ozi vezimrat yah adonay vayhi li lishu'ah. Ushavtem mayim besason mima'ayney hayshu'ah. Ladonay hayshu'ah al ameḥa birḥateḥa selah. Adonay tzeva'ot imanu misgav lanu elohey ya'akov selah. Adonay tzeva'ot ashrey adam bote'aḥ baḥ. Adonay hoshi'ah hameleḥ ya'anenu veyom korenu. Layehudim hayetah orah vesimḥah vesason vikar. Ken tihyeh lanu. Kos yeshu'ot esa uvshem adonay ekra.

Biblical references include Isaiah 12:2-3; Psalms 3:9, 46:12, 84:13, 20:10; Esther 8:16; Psalm 116:13.

KAVANAH. Tradition has it that the *neshamah yeterah* / additional soul we receive at the beginning of Shabbat stays with us until *Havdalah*, when it departs. We do not want to lose that additional bit of soul, and therefore linger and relish the fading embers of the day. D.A.T.

With the permission of this company:
Blessed are you, THE BOUNDLESS ONE, our God, the sovereign of all worlds, who created the fruit of the vine.

It is the custom in some families for everyone to take a sip of the wine here. Others wait until after the final beraḥah / *blessing.*

Blessed are you, REVIVER our God, the sovereign of all worlds, who creates various spices.

After the blessing is said, the leader smells the spices and passes them on.

Blessed are you, THE RADIANCE, our God, the sovereign of all worlds, who creates the light of fire.

After reciting the blessing over fire, participants hold their hands before the candle flame so that their fingers look radiant in its light and then cast shadows on their palms. Then the following blessing is said.

Blessed are you, THE MANY-NAMED, our God, the sovereign of all worlds, who separates between holy and ordinary, light and dark, the seventh day and the six days of work. Blessed are you, THE INDIVISIBLE who separates the holy from the ordinary.

The candle is now extinguished. Some families do this by immersing it in wine from the cup. Lights are turned on, and we continue in lively song.

COMMENTARY. While lighting candles marks both the beginning and the end of Shabbat, the *Havdalah* candle has a meaning different from that of the *Erev Shabbat* candles. Lighting this new fire signals commencement of the work week because fire is so often an instrument of labor. Every *beraḥah* / blessing must correlate to an event or action so that it is not in vain. We "use" the candlelight here to cast a shadow on our palms by lifting our curled fingers toward the light.

A time of transitions, *Havdalah* lends itself to comment about life cycle transitions as well. It is a wonderful place to insert parents' hopes for a bar / bat mitzvah at the transition from childhood to adolescence. *Brit* ceremonies for new-born girls can easily be created around *Havdalah*. Weddings, new jobs, beginning of school and graduation are some of the occasions when people might want to add personal words to *Havdalah*.

D.A.T.

סַבְרֵי חֲבֵרַי:
בָּרוּךְ אַתָּה יהוה אֱלֹהֵינוּ מֶלֶךְ הָעוֹלָם בּוֹרֵא פְּרִי הַגָּפֶן:

Savrey ḥaveray.
Baruḥ atah adonay eloheynu meleḥ ha'olam borey peri hagafen.

It is the custom in some families for everyone to take a sip of the wine here. Others wait until after the final beraḥah / *blessing.*

בָּרוּךְ אַתָּה יהוה אֱלֹהֵינוּ מֶלֶךְ הָעוֹלָם בּוֹרֵא מִינֵי בְשָׂמִים:

Baruḥ atah adonay eloheynu meleḥ ha'olam borey miney vesamim.

After the blessing is said, the leader smells the spices and passes them on.

בָּרוּךְ אַתָּה יהוה אֱלֹהֵינוּ מֶלֶךְ הָעוֹלָם בּוֹרֵא מְאוֹרֵי הָאֵשׁ:

Baruḥ atah adonay eloheynu meleḥ ha'olam borey me'orey ha'esh.

After reciting the blessing over fire, participants hold their hands before the candle flame so that their fingers look radiant in its light and then cast shadows on their palms. Then the following blessing is said.

בָּרוּךְ אַתָּה יהוה אֱלֹהֵינוּ מֶלֶךְ הָעוֹלָם הַמַּבְדִּיל בֵּין קֹדֶשׁ לְחֹל בֵּין אוֹר לְחֹשֶׁךְ בֵּין יוֹם הַשְּׁבִיעִי לְשֵׁשֶׁת יְמֵי הַמַּעֲשֶׂה: בָּרוּךְ אַתָּה יהוה הַמַּבְדִּיל בֵּין קֹדֶשׁ לְחֹל:

Baruḥ atah adonay eloheynu meleḥ ha'olam hamavdil beyn kodesh leḥol beyn or leḥosheḥ beyn yom hashevi'i lesheshet yemey hama'aseh. Baruḥ atah adonay hamavdil beyn kodesh leḥol.

The candle is now extinguished. Some families do this by immersing it in wine from the cup. Lights are turned on, and we continue in lively song.

COMMENTARY. Just as we greet Shabbat with blessing, we usher it out with blessing. Candlelight and wine mark these borders. Thus we attempt to bring the flavor and insight of Shabbat into the everyday. At *Havdalah* there is the addition of spices, as if to revive our spirits flagging at the loss of Shabbat and to bear the sweet savor of Shabbat into the week. D.A.T.

HAMAVDIL / THE ONE WHO DIVIDES

This translation can be sung to the same melody as Shavu'a Tov.

May the one who divides
  between holy and plain,
forgive our sins,
  and ease our pain.
Posterity and plenty
  add to our gain,
like seashore sands,
  like stars at night.

The day moves on
  like palm tree's shade,
I call to God
  who charts the way.
The watchman says,
  "The morn has come,
and soon the night,
  yes, soon the night."

Your justice strong
  as Mount Tabor,
My sins forgive,
  my faults ignore.
Let me be pure,
  like long before,
My blemish fade
  like passing night.

NOTE. Composed by Rabbi Isaac ibn Ghayat, who lived in eleventh-century Spain, for the conclusion of Yom Kippur, *Hamavdil* hails the divine power that allows us forgiveness, renewed vigor and redemption. A.G.

אמר...לילה / The watchman...night (Isaiah 21:12).
כיום...בלילה / Let...night (Psalm 90:4).

הַמַּבְדִּיל

הַמַּבְדִּיל בֵּין קֹֽדֶשׁ לְחֹל חַטֹּאתֵֽינוּ הוּא יִמְחֹל
זַרְעֵֽנוּ וְכַסְפֵּֽנוּ יַרְבֶּה כַּחוֹל וְכַכּוֹכָבִים בַּלָּֽיְלָה:
יוֹם פָּנָה כְּצֵל תֹּֽמֶר אֶקְרָא לָאֵל עָלַי גֹּמֵר
אָמַר שׁוֹמֵר אָתָא בֹֽקֶר וְגַם לָֽיְלָה:
צִדְקָתְךָ כְּהַר תָּבוֹר עַל חֲטָאַי עָבֹר תַּעֲבֹר
כְּיוֹם אֶתְמוֹל כִּי יַעֲבֹר וְאַשְׁמוּרָה בַלָּֽיְלָה:

Hamavdil beyn kodesh leḥol
Ḥatoteynu hu yimḥol
Zarenu veḥaspenu yarbeh kaḥol
Veḥakoḥavim balaylah.

Yom panah ketzel tomer
Ekra la'el alay gomer
Amar shomer ata voker vegam laylah.

Tzidkateḥa kehar tavor
Al ḥata'ay avor ta'avor
Keyom etmol ki ya'avor
Ve'ashmurah valaylah.

שָׁבֽוּעַ טוֹב. / Shavu'a tov. / Have a good week.
אַ גוטע וואָך. / A gute voch. / A good week.

SHAVU'A TOV!

NETILAT LULAV / WAVING THE LULAV

The blessing over the lulav *and* etrog *is recited on Sukkot immediately after the* Shaḥarit Amidah. *The* lulav *is held in the right hand, the* etrog *in the left. The blessing is recited with the stem of the* etrog *held up and with the two hands together. Then the* etrog *is turned right side up, arms are extended, and the* lulav *and* etrog *are shaken in all four directions as well as up and down. This is done each day of Sukkot except for Shabbat.*

Here I stand, ready in body and mind to fulfill the mitzvah of the Four Species of the Tree, as it is written in the Torah: "You shall take up for yourselves upon the first day [of Sukkot] the ornamental fruit, the fronds of date palms, sprig of myrtle tree, and willows of the stream." And as I wave them, may a wealth of blessings and of holy thoughts pour forth upon me. May you bring us near to you in perfect oneness, and spread over us the shelter of your peace, and may the pleasure of THE MERCIFUL, our God, dwell over us. And may you make secure for us the labor of our hands, the labor of our hands ensure. Blessed is THE ONE, eternally. Amen! Amen!

Blessed are you, ABUNDANT ONE, our God, the sovereign of all worlds, who has made us holy with your mitzvot, and commanded us to take and wave the *lulav.*

On the first day that the lulav *is shaken each year, add:*

Blessed are you, ETERNAL ONE, our God, the sovereign of all worlds, who gave us life, and kept us strong, and brought us to this time.

Continue with Hallel, *page 360.*

Biblical references include Leviticus 23:40; Psalms 90:17, 89:53.

COMMENTARY. *Lulav* literally means "palm branch," but by custom we call the Sukkot cluster of palm, myrtle, and water willow by the name *lulav* because of the palm branch's prominence.

We shake the *lulav* in all four directions as well as up and down to indicate that the divine presence knows no barriers of time or space.

Traditionally, blessing precedes action. After the blessing the *etrog* is returned to its natural position with the stem down. So are we challenged to find the natural balance in our lives. D.A.T.

נְטִילַת לוּלָב

The blessing over the lulav *and* etrog *is recited on Sukkot immediately after the* Shaḥarit Amidah. *The* lulav *is held in the right hand, the* etrog *in the left. The blessing is recited with the stem of the* etrog *held up and with the two hands together. Then the* etrog *is turned right side up, arms are extended, and the* lulav *and* etrog *are shaken in all four directions as well as up and down. This is done each day of Sukkot except for Shabbat.*

הִנְנִי מוּכָן וּמְזֻמָּן לְקַיֵּם מִצְוַת אַרְבָּעָה מִינִים כַּכָּתוּב בַּתּוֹרָה: וּלְקַחְתֶּם לָכֶם בַּיּוֹם הָרִאשׁוֹן פְּרִי עֵץ הָדָר כַּפֹּת תְּמָרִים וַעֲנַף עֵץ עָבֹת וְעַרְבֵי נָֽחַל: וּבְנַעֲנוּעִי אוֹתָם יַשְׁפִּֽיעַ עָלַי שֶֽׁפַע בְּרָכוֹת וּמַחֲשָׁבוֹת קְדוֹשׁוֹת וְקָרְבֵֽנוּ אֵלֶֽיךָ בְּיִחוּד שָׁלֵם וּפְרוֹשׂ עָלֵֽינוּ סֻכַּת שְׁלוֹמֶֽךָ: וִיהִי נֹֽעַם יהוה אֱלֹהֵֽינוּ עָלֵֽינוּ וּמַעֲשֵׂה יָדֵֽינוּ כּוֹנְנָה עָלֵֽינוּ וּמַעֲשֵׂה יָדֵֽינוּ כּוֹנְנֵֽהוּ: בָּרוּךְ יהוה לְעוֹלָם אָמֵן וְאָמֵן:

בָּרוּךְ אַתָּה יהוה אֱלֹהֵֽינוּ מֶֽלֶךְ הָעוֹלָם אֲשֶׁר קִדְּשָֽׁנוּ בְּמִצְוֹתָיו וְצִוָּֽנוּ עַל נְטִילַת לוּלָב:

Baruḥ atah adonay eloheynu meleḥ ha'olam asher kideshanu bemitzvotav vetzivanu al netilat lulav.

On the first day that the lulav *is shaken each year, add:*

בָּרוּךְ אַתָּה יהוה אֱלֹהֵֽינוּ מֶֽלֶךְ הָעוֹלָם
שֶׁהֶחֱיָֽנוּ וְקִיְּמָֽנוּ וְהִגִּיעָֽנוּ לַזְּמַן הַזֶּה:

Baruḥ atah adonay eloheynu meleḥ ha'olam sheheḥeyanu vekiyemanu vehigi'anu lazeman hazeh.

Continue with Hallel, *page 361.*

DERASH. The willow has no smell or taste; the myrtle has smell but not taste; the palm, taste but not smell; the *etrog*, both smell and taste. In the *lulav* all are united, each is necessary; even the lowliest is required to bring out the worth of all.

The sight and smell of these four species help us celebrate the bounteous diversity of nature and remind us that we are responsible for preserving the conditions that make their growth possible. Human life requires the flourishing of trees: the divine presence in the interdependence of species.

We hold these diverse species together as a reminder that the diversity in the world comprises the elements of its unity. So can we discover the unity in human life.

D.A.T.

HALLEL / PSALMS OF PRAISE

Hallel is recited in its full form during Shaḥarit on Shavuot, Sukkot, Shemini Atzeret / Simḥat Torah, Ḥanukah, Yom Ha'atzma'ut and the first two days of Pesaḥ. It is recited in a somewhat shortened form (half Hallel) on Rosh Ḥodesh and the last six days of Pesaḥ. When Hallel is recited on Sukkot (except on Shabbat) the lulav *and the* etrog *are held. When the verses* הודו ליהוה כי טוב / Hodu ladonay ki tov *and* אנא יהוה הושיעה נא / Ana adonay hoshi'ah na *are recited, the* lulav *is shaken in the six directions.*

Blessed are you, REDEEMING ONE, our God, the sovereign of all worlds, who has made us holy with your commandments, and commanded us to recite the Hallel.

COMMENTARY. Hallel, meaning "praise," consists of six ancient prayer-poems, Psalms 113-118, which have been used in Jewish worship since antiquity. Joyous melodies for the chanting of these songs highlight the theme of deliverance. They are enclosed by two blessings that signify our intention to praise God. Hallel is chanted on the joyous pilgrimage festivals, of Pesaḥ, Shavuot, and Sukkot, on Ḥanukah and on Rosh Ḥodesh, the minor holiday of the New Moon. Since the founding of the State of Israel, Hallel has also been recited on Israel's Independence Day. The joyous mood of Hallel is considered inappropriate for Rosh Hashanah and Yom Kippur, with their awesome themes. On Purim, the reading of the Megillah is thought to take the place of Hallel. H.L.

הַלֵּל

Hallel is recited in its full form during Shaḥarit on Shavuot, Sukkot, Shemini Atzeret / Simḥat Torah, Ḥanukah, Yom Ha'atzma'ut and the first two days of Pesaḥ. It is recited in a somewhat shortened form (half Hallel) on Rosh Ḥodesh and the last six days of Pesaḥ. When Hallel is recited on Sukkot (except on Shabbat) the lulav *and the* etrog *are held. When the verses* הודו ליהוה כי טוב / Hodu ladonay ki tov *and* אנא יהוה הושיעה נא / Ana adonay hoshi'ah na *are recited, the* lulav *is shaken in the six directions.*

בָּרוּךְ אַתָּה יהוה אֱלֹהֵֽינוּ מֶֽלֶךְ הָעוֹלָם אֲשֶׁר קִדְּשָֽׁנוּ בְּמִצְוֹתָיו וְצִוָּֽנוּ לִקְרֹא אֶת הַהַלֵּל׃ ←

Baruḥ atah adonay eloheynu meleḥ ha'olam asher kideshanu bemitzvotav vetzivanu likro et hahalel.

COMMENTARY. More than any other series of Jewish prayers, chanting the Hallel psalms marks the cycles of the Jewish year. We sing Hallel at each new moon (when the Jewish month begins), and on each day of the three pilgrimage festivals. Just as the singing of Hallel reminds us of the inevitable return of joyous times, so does its theme of one "delivered from the ropes of death" (Psalm 116) or released "from my distress" (Psalm 118) remind us even when we are in the midst of pain, sorrow, and despair that joyous moments will surely return. R.S.

NOTE. In addition to the traditional times, it is modern Israeli and Zionist practice to say Hallel on the 5th of Iyar (Israel Independence Day). Some also say the Hallel on the 28th of Iyar (Jerusalem Day). E.M.

Halleluyah! Cry praise, all you who serve THE OMNIPRESENT,
praise the name of THE ETERNAL!

Let the name of THE INCOMPARABLE be blessed,
henceforth and for eternity!

From east to west, sunrise to sunset,
hailed in every place: the name of GOD!

Raised up above all nations is THE SOVEREIGN ONE,
above even the heavens is God's glory!

Who is like THE BOUNDLESS ONE, our God?
Enthroned on high,

who gazes down on all,
in heaven and on earth,

who raises from the dust the poor,
from ash-heaps lifts aloft the needy,

placing them beside the privileged,
together with the privileged of the nation,

turning the childless household
into a home rejoicing in its children
Halleluyah! ↩

Psalm 113

הַלְלוּיָהּ

הַלְלוּ עַבְדֵי יהוה   הַלְלוּ אֶת־שֵׁם יהוה:
יְהִי שֵׁם יהוה מְבֹרָךְ   מֵעַתָּה וְעַד־עוֹלָם:

מִמִּזְרַח־שֶׁמֶשׁ עַד־מְבוֹאוֹ   מְהֻלָּל שֵׁם יהוה:

רָם עַל־כָּל־גּוֹיִם יהוה   עַל הַשָּׁמַיִם כְּבוֹדוֹ:

מִי כַּיהוה אֱלֹהֵינוּ   הַמַּגְבִּיהִי לָשָׁבֶת:

הַמַּשְׁפִּילִי לִרְאוֹת   בַּשָּׁמַיִם וּבָאָרֶץ:

מְקִימִי מֵעָפָר דָּל   מֵאַשְׁפֹּת יָרִים אֶבְיוֹן:

*לְהוֹשִׁיבִי עִם־נְדִיבִים   עִם נְדִיבֵי עַמּוֹ:

מוֹשִׁיבִי עֲקֶרֶת הַבַּיִת   אֵם־הַבָּנִים שְׂמֵחָה

הַלְלוּיָהּ ←

When Israel went forth out of Egypt,
House of Jacob from the people of a foreign tongue,

Judah became God's holy place,
Israel became God's seat of rule.

The Sea beheld and fled,
the Jordan turned, reversed its flow.

The mountains danced about like rams,
the hills, like flocks of lambs.

What's wrong with you, O Sea, that you should flee?
And you, O Jordan, that you turn around?

You mountains, why do you rejoice like rams,
you hills, like flocks of lambs?

Tremble, earth, before the mighty one,
before the God of Jacob,

who turns the rock into a pool of water,
the flint into a bubbling fount! ↩

Psalm 114

KAVANAH. Why does Hallel contain psalms written both in the first person singular and in the plural? To help us keep alive both a personal relationship to God and a collective one. We cannot legitimately say, "We praise you," unless each of us is included in the we. Otherwise, the ritual of collective praise becomes an empty formality, not a true expression of community. H.L.

COMMENTARY. This psalm juxtaposes two crossings of water—that of the Reed Sea and, forty years later, of the Jordan. The repetition of the final miracle of the Exodus at the time of the initial entry to Canaan connects those two events and suggests that the second is the fulfillment of the first. H.L.

בְּצֵאת יִשְׂרָאֵל מִמִּצְרָיִם בֵּית יַעֲקֹב מֵעַם לֹעֵז׃

הָיְתָה יְהוּדָה לְקׇדְשׁוֹ יִשְׂרָאֵל מַמְשְׁלוֹתָיו׃

הַיָּם רָאָה וַיָּנֹס הַיַּרְדֵּן יִסֹּב לְאָחוֹר׃

הֶהָרִים רָקְדוּ כְאֵילִים גְּבָעוֹת כִּבְנֵי־צֹאן׃

מַה־לְּךָ הַיָּם כִּי תָנוּס הַיַּרְדֵּן תִּסֹּב לְאָחוֹר׃

הֶהָרִים תִּרְקְדוּ כְאֵילִים גְּבָעוֹת כִּבְנֵי־צֹאן׃

מִלִּפְנֵי אָדוֹן חוּלִי אָרֶץ מִלִּפְנֵי אֱלוֹהַּ יַעֲקֹב׃

הַהֹפְכִי הַצּוּר אֲגַם־מָיִם חַלָּמִישׁ לְמַעְיְנוֹ־מָיִם׃ ←

Betzeyt yisra'el mimitzrayim beyt ya'akov me'am lo'ez.
Hayetah yehudah lekodsho yisra'el mamshelotav.
Hayam ra'ah vayanos hayarden yisov le'aḥor.
Heharim rakedu ḥe'eylim geva'ot kivney tzon.
Ma leḥa hayam ki tanus hayarden tisov le'aḥor.
Heharim tirkedu ḥe'eylim geva'ot kivney tzon.
Milifney adon ḥuli aretz milifney eloha ya'akov.
Hahofḥi hatzur agam mayim ḥalamish lemayno mayim. ←

COMMENTARY. This psalm juxtaposes a number of moments when the course of nature was said to have been disrupted on behalf of Israel. According to tradition, when the Israelites left Egypt and when they entered Canaan, waters parted before the travelling host. In the desert, rocks were made to give forth water so the Israelites could drink. In the poet's imagination, the mountains responded to these moments of redemption with their own rhythmic dance. Nature in the poem is neither fixed nor immutable. The psalm reminds us that nature is more fluid than we might think, and like history open to surprising transformations. H.L.

On Rosh Ḥodesh and the last six days of Pesaḥ, omit the following:

Not for us, ETERNAL ONE; no, not for us,
but for your name: Bring forth a glorious event,
attesting to your love and to your truth!

Why should unbelievers say, "Where is their God?"

when our God is over us, and doing all according to desire!

Their preoccupations are with silverwork and gold,
with works of human hands.

They have a mouth, but they can't speak.
They have eyes, but they can't see.
They have ears, but they can't hear. ↩

עצביהם / Their preoccupations. Many translators have followed earlier commentators in rendering **עצביהם** as "their fingers." The goal of these commentators was to emphasize the foolishness of idolators. A careful grammatical examination of the text indicates that while the traditional translation may have been emotionally satisfying to downtrodden generations, its exaggerated emphasis on the worthlessness of idols does not exist in the original text. Preoccupation with "silver and gold" still prevents many of us from keeping in sight the sources of transcendent value in our lives. D.A.T.

פה להם / They have a mouth...This passage calls to mind others in Scripture, such as Deuteronomy 4:28, Psalm 135:15-18, and Isaiah 44:9-20, that debunk idolatry as the worship of inanimate objects. The verses here remarkably establish an equivalence between the idol itself, its maker, and its worshipper: all three are "lifeless," in body or in spirit. Only worship of the Creator of all life can put us in touch with the mystery of life, thus enabling us to sense and to affirm our aliveness. J.R.

On Rosh Ḥodesh and the last six days of Pesaḥ, omit the following.

לֹא לָנוּ יהוה לֹא לָנוּ כִּי־לְשִׁמְךָ תֵּן כָּבוֹד
עַל־חַסְדְּךָ עַל־אֲמִתֶּךָ׃
לָמָּה יֹאמְרוּ הַגּוֹיִם אַיֵּה־נָא אֱלֹהֵיהֶם׃
וֵאלֹהֵינוּ בַשָּׁמָיִם כֹּל אֲשֶׁר־חָפֵץ עָשָׂה׃
עֲצַבֵּיהֶם כֶּסֶף וְזָהָב מַעֲשֵׂה יְדֵי אָדָם׃
פֶּה־לָהֶם וְלֹא יְדַבֵּרוּ עֵינַיִם לָהֶם וְלֹא יִרְאוּ׃ ←

Lo lanu adonay lo lanu ki leshimeḥa ten kavod al ḥasdeḥa al amiteḥa.
Lamah yomeru hagoyim ayey-na eloheyhem.
Veyloheynu vashamayim kol asher ḥafetz asah.
Atzabeyhem kesef vezahav ma'asey yedey adam.
Peh lahem velo yedaberu eynayim lahem velo yiru.

DERASH. According to legend it was on the second day after going forth from Egypt that the Israelites crossed the sea in triumph and the Egyptians drowned. The midrash says that when the angels celebrated this victory, God cried out, "My children have drowned in the sea!" Throughout our history, Jews have shortened Hallel on the last six days of Pesaḥ as a reminder that our joy must be dimmed in the face of any sorrow—even the losses of our enemies. D.A.T.

They have a nose, but they can't smell.
They have their hands, but they can't feel.
They have their feet, but they can't walk.
They have nothing in their throats to say.

All that they make is just like them,
and all who trust in them.

Let Israel trust in THE ETERNAL ONE,
who is their help and sheltering place.
Let the House of Aaron trust in THE COMPASSIONATE,
who is their help and sheltering place.
Let all who fear THE MIGHTY ONE trust in THE FOUNT OF LIFE,
who is their help and sheltering place.

Psalm 115:1-11

אָזְנַיִם לָהֶם וְלֹא יִשְׁמָעוּ אַף לָהֶם וְלֹא יְרִיחוּן׃

יְדֵיהֶם וְלֹא יְמִישׁוּן רַגְלֵיהֶם וְלֹא יְהַלֵּכוּ

לֹא יֶהְגּוּ בִּגְרוֹנָם׃

כְּמוֹהֶם יִהְיוּ עֹשֵׂיהֶם כֹּל אֲשֶׁר־בֹּטֵחַ בָּהֶם׃

יִשְׂרָאֵל בְּטַח בַּיהוה עֶזְרָם וּמָגִנָּם הוּא׃

*בֵּית אַהֲרֹן בִּטְחוּ בַיהוה עֶזְרָם וּמָגִנָּם הוּא׃

יִרְאֵי יהוה בִּטְחוּ בַיהוה עֶזְרָם וּמָגִנָּם הוּא׃ ←

Oznayim lahem velo yishma'u af lahem velo yeriḥun.
Yedeyhem velo yemishun ragleyhem velo yehaleḥu lo yegu bigronam.
Kemohem yiyu oseyhem kol asher bote'aḥ bahem.
Yisra'el betaḥ badonay ezram umaginam hu.
Beyt aharon biteḥu badonay ezram umaginam hu.
Yirey adonay biteḥu badonay ezram umaginam hu.

THE REDEEMING ONE who has remembered us will bless us all—

will bless the House of Israel,
will bless the House of Aaron,
will bless the ones in awe of THE DIVINE,
young and old alike.

THE ABUNDANT ONE will add to you,
to you and to your children.
Blessed are you to your CREATOR,
to the maker of the heavens and the earth.
The skies are heaven, they belong to GOD,
the earth God gave for human life.
The dead cannot say "Halleluyah,"
none who have descended into stillness.
But we, the living, bless Yah's name,
today and forever, Halleluyah! ↩

Psalm 115:12-19

COMMENTARY. This psalm calls on Israel, the House of Aaron, and those "who fear" to trust in God. The psalmist looks forward to God's blessing flowing upon those same three groups of people. Rashi comments that "all who fear THE MIGHTY ONE" indicates the converts who have chosen Judaism. Franz Rosenzweig interprets Psalm 115 as a comment on all people who trust in God and keep up a never-ending song of praise. This psalm, claims Rosenzweig, expresses our hope for a world redeemed from division.
H.L.

יהוה זְכָרָ֫נוּ יְבָרֵךְ

יְבָרֵךְ אֶת־בֵּית יִשְׂרָאֵל יְבָרֵךְ אֶת־בֵּית אַהֲרֹן:

יְבָרֵךְ יִרְאֵי יהוה הַקְּטַנִּים עִם־הַגְּדֹלִים:

יֹסֵף יהוה עֲלֵיכֶם עֲלֵיכֶם וְעַל־בְּנֵיכֶם:

בְּרוּכִים אַתֶּם לַיהוה עֹשֵׂה שָׁמַ֫יִם וָאָ֫רֶץ:

הַשָּׁמַ֫יִם שָׁמַ֫יִם לַיהוה וְהָאָ֫רֶץ נָתַן לִבְנֵי־אָדָם:

לֹא הַמֵּתִים יְהַלְלוּ־יָהּ וְלֹא כָּל־יֹרְדֵי דוּמָה:

וַאֲנַ֫חְנוּ נְבָרֵךְ יָהּ מֵעַתָּה וְעַד־עוֹלָם הַלְלוּיָהּ:

Adonay zeḥaranu yevareḥ.
Yevareḥ et beyt yisra'el yevareḥ et beyt aharon.
Yevareḥ yirey adonay haketanim im hagedolim.
Yosef adonay aleyḥem aleyḥem ve'al beneyḥem.
Beruḥim atem ladonay oseh shamayim va'aretz.
Hashamayim shamayim ladonay veha'aretz natan livney adam.
Lo hametim yehalelu yah velo kol yordey dumah.
Va'anaḥnu nevareḥ yah me'atah ve'ad olam
Halleluyah.

On Rosh Ḥodesh and the last six days of Pesaḥ omit the following:

My love abounds, for GOD has heard
my voice, my plea for help.
God turns an ear to me,
while, in my days of trial, I call out.
The ropes of death have wrapped around me,
and in my trials Sheol itself has found me,
while I find pain and suffering.

And in the name of THE REDEEMER I call out:
"I pray, ETERNAL ONE, deliver me!"

Gracious is THE FOUNT OF MERCY, truly just.
Our God is one who acts in tenderness.
THE COMPASSIONATE protects those wandering in confusion,
I who feel so destitute, I, too, receive God's help.
Return, my soul, to your tranquility,
for THE REDEEMER has been generous with you!

Truly, you released my soul from death,
my eye from tears, my foot from stumbling!

I walk about before THE OMNIPRESENT,
to the world of life I have returned.

I am full of faith! For once I cried,
"How very desolate am I!"

Once, in my alarm, I said,
"How false is everyone!" ↩

Psalm 116:1-11

COMMENTARY. Even though the speaker has been saved from death, his or her soul remains troubled: "Return, my soul, to your tranquility." Under the speaker's song of thanksgiving, lies a profound feeling of human vulnerability. H.L.

On Rosh Ḥodesh and the last six days of Pesaḥ omit the following:

אָהַבְתִּי כִּי־יִשְׁמַע יהוה אֶת־קוֹלִי תַּחֲנוּנָי׃

כִּי־הִטָּה אָזְנוֹ לִי וּבְיָמַי אֶקְרָא׃

אֲפָפוּנִי חֶבְלֵי־מָוֶת וּמְצָרֵי שְׁאוֹל מְצָאוּנִי

צָרָה וְיָגוֹן אֶמְצָא׃

וּבְשֵׁם־יהוה אֶקְרָא אָנָּה יהוה מַלְּטָה נַפְשִׁי׃

חַנּוּן יהוה וְצַדִּיק וֵאלֹהֵינוּ מְרַחֵם׃

שֹׁמֵר פְּתָאיִם יהוה דַּלּוֹתִי וְלִי יְהוֹשִׁיעַ׃

שׁוּבִי נַפְשִׁי לִמְנוּחָיְכִי כִּי יהוה גָּמַל עָלָיְכִי׃

כִּי חִלַּצְתָּ נַפְשִׁי מִמָּוֶת אֶת־עֵינִי מִן־דִּמְעָה

אֶת־רַגְלִי מִדֶּחִי׃

אֶתְהַלֵּךְ לִפְנֵי יהוה בְּאַרְצוֹת הַחַיִּים׃

*הֶאֱמַנְתִּי כִּי אֲדַבֵּר אֲנִי עָנִיתִי מְאֹד׃

אֲנִי אָמַרְתִּי בְחָפְזִי כָּל־הָאָדָם כֹּזֵב׃ ←

Ahavti ki yishma adonay et koli taḥanunay,
Ki hitah ozno li uvyamay ekra.
Afafuni ḥevley mavet umetzarey she'ol metza'uni tzarah veyagon emtza.
Uveshem adonay ekra ana adonay maletah nafshi.
Ḥanun adonay vetzadik veyloheynu meraḥem.
Shomer peta'im adonay daloti veli yehoshi'a.
Shuvi nafshi limnuḥayḥi ki adonay gamal alayḥi.
Ki ḥilatzeta nafshi mimavet et eyni min dima et ragli mideḥi.
Et'haleyḥ lifney adonay be'artzot haḥayim.
He'emanti ki adaber ani aniti me'od.
Ani amarti veḥofzi kol ha'adam kozev.

And now, what shall I give back to GOD?—
for all God's bounties are upon me!

Salvation's cup I raise,
and in the name of THE ETERNAL, I call out.

My vow to THE REDEEMER I repay—
here, I pray, before all those assembled here!

THE MERCIFUL does not regard as trivial
the death of those who care for God.

Now, ABUNDANT ONE, I am your servant.

I, your servant, child of your servant,
I whose fetters you have opened up.

To you I make my offering of thanks,
and in the name of THE REDEEMER I call out.
My vow to THE ETERNAL I repay—
here, I pray, before all those assembled here
in courtyards of the House of GOD,
amid Jerusalem's most hallowed inner halls:
Halleluyah! ↩

Psalm 116:12-19

מָה־אָשִׁיב לַיהוה כָּל־תַּגְמוּלוֹהִי עָלָי׃

כּוֹס־יְשׁוּעוֹת אֶשָּׂא וּבְשֵׁם יהוה אֶקְרָא׃

נְדָרַי לַיהוה אֲשַׁלֵּם נֶגְדָה־נָּא לְכָל־עַמּוֹ׃

יָקָר בְּעֵינֵי יהוה הַמָּוְתָה לַחֲסִידָיו׃

אָנָּה יהוה כִּי־אֲנִי עַבְדֶּךָ

אֲנִי־עַבְדְּךָ בֶּן־אֲמָתֶךָ פִּתַּחְתָּ לְמוֹסֵרָי׃

לְךָ־אֶזְבַּח זֶבַח תּוֹדָה וּבְשֵׁם יהוה אֶקְרָא׃

*נְדָרַי לַיהוה אֲשַׁלֵּם נֶגְדָה־נָּא לְכָל־עַמּוֹ׃

בְּחַצְרוֹת בֵּית יהוה בְּתוֹכֵכִי יְרוּשָׁלָםִ

הַלְלוּיָהּ׃

Mah ashiv ladonay kol tagmulohi alay.
Kos yeshu'ot esa uveshem adonay ekra.
Nedaray ladonay ashalem negdah-na leḥol amo.
Yakar be'eynay adonay hamavtah laḥasidav.
Ana adonay ki ani avdeḥa
Ani avdeḥa ben amateḥa pitaḥta lemoseray.
Leḥa ezbaḥ zevaḥ todah uveshem adonay ekra.
Nedaray ladonay ashalem negdah-na leḥol amo.
Beḥatzrot beyt adonay betoḥeḥi yerushala'im halleluyah.

Praise THE OMNIPRESENT, all you nations,
all peoples, sing the praise of God!
For God's love overpowers us,
the truth of THE ETERNAL is forever.
Halleluyah!

Psalm 117

Give thanks to THE ETERNAL, who is good,
whose love is everlasting!

Let Israelites declare today,
God's love is everlasting!

Let the House of Aaron say,
God's love is everlasting!

Let those in awe of GOD declare,
God's love is everlasting!

Psalm 118:1-4

COMMENTARY. It is striking that the shortest psalm in the Book of Psalms is also the most universal. Jewish universalism is rooted, the psalm testifies, in Jewish particularism. Because we know God through the divine relationship to the people Israel, we urge all other nations to come to a similar awareness of God. We urge them to do what we do in Hallel, to praise the Eternal. H.L.

הַלְלוּ אֶת־יהוה כָּל־גּוֹיִם שַׁבְּחוּהוּ כָּל־הָאֻמִּים

כִּי גָבַר עָלֵינוּ חַסְדּוֹ וֶאֱמֶת־יהוה לְעוֹלָם

הַלְלוּיָהּ

Halelu et adonay kol goyim
shabeḥuhu kol ha'umim
Ki gavar aleynu ḥasdo
ve'emet adonay le'olam
Halleluyah.

הוֹדוּ לַיהוה כִּי טוֹב כִּי לְעוֹלָם חַסְדּוֹ:

יֹאמַר נָא יִשְׂרָאֵל כִּי לְעוֹלָם חַסְדּוֹ:

יֹאמְרוּ נָא בֵית אַהֲרֹן כִּי לְעוֹלָם חַסְדּוֹ:

יֹאמְרוּ נָא יִרְאֵי יהוה כִּי לְעוֹלָם חַסְדּוֹ: ←

Hodu ladonay ki tov Ki le'olam ḥasdo.
Yomar na yisra'el Ki le'olam ḥasdo.
Yomru na veyt aharon Ki le'olam ḥasdo.
Yomru na yirey adonay Ki le'olam ḥasdo. ↩

From my distress, I cried out: "Yah!"
Yah answered, bringing great release.

The One is with me; I shall have no fear.
What can a human being do to me?

The One is with me, bringing help.
I gaze triumphantly upon my foes.

To trust in The Invincible is good,
and surer than a trust in human power.

To trust in The Invisible is good,
and surer than a trust in human benefactors.

All nations have surrounded me,
but with God's name I cut them off.

They surrounded me; yes, they surrounded me,
but with God's name I cut them off.

They surrounded me like swarming bees.
Like a brushfire, they were quenched,
and with God's name I cut them off.

You pushed me down, pushed me to fall,
but The Redeemer has brought help to me.

My strength, my song, is Yah,
who was for me a source of help. ↩

Commentary. From my distress, I cried out: "Yah!" The divine name "Yah," a shortened form of the name YHWH, occurs frequently in biblical poetry, and, unlike the unvocalized Tetragrammaton (whose pronunciation is considered taboo), is pronounced as written. It also appears in the common psalmodic exclamation "Halleluyah!" (literally, "Praise Yah!") and is frequently an element in Hebrew personal names—for example, Isaiah (Hebrew *Yeshayahu*, "Yah's help"), Uriah ("Yah's light"), Nehemiah ("Yah's consolation"). J.R.

מִן־הַמֵּצַר קָרָֽאתִי יָּהּ עָנָֽנִי בַמֶּרְחָב יָהּ׃

יהוה לִי לֹא אִירָא   מַה־יַּעֲשֶׂה לִי אָדָם׃

יהוה לִי בְּעֹזְרָי   וַאֲנִי אֶרְאֶה בְשֹׂנְאָי׃

טוֹב לַחֲסוֹת בַּיהוה   מִבְּטֹחַ בָּאָדָם׃

טוֹב לַחֲסוֹת בַּיהוה   מִבְּטֹחַ בִּנְדִיבִים׃

כָּל־גּוֹיִם סְבָבֽוּנִי   בְּשֵׁם יהוה כִּי אֲמִילַם׃

סַבּֽוּנִי גַם־סְבָבֽוּנִי   בְּשֵׁם יהוה כִּי אֲמִילַם׃

סַבּֽוּנִי כִדְבוֹרִים דֹּעֲכוּ כְּאֵשׁ קוֹצִים

בְּשֵׁם יהוה כִּי אֲמִילַם׃

דַּחֹה דְחִיתַֽנִי לִנְפֹּל   וַיהוה עֲזָרָֽנִי׃

עָזִּי וְזִמְרָת יָהּ   וַֽיְהִי־לִי לִישׁוּעָה׃ ←

Min hametzar karati yah anani vamerḥav yah.
Adonay li lo ira ma ya'aseh li adam.
Adonay li be'ozray va'ani ereh vesonay.
Tov laḥasot badonay mibeto'aḥ ba'adam.
Tov laḥasot badonay mibeto'aḥ bindivim.
Kol goyim sevavuni beshem adonay ki amilam.
Sabuni gam sevavuni beshem adonay ki amilam.
Sabuni ḥidvorim do'aḥu ke'esh kotzim
beshem adonay ki amilam.
Daḥo deḥitani linpol vadonay azarani.
Ozi vezimrat yah vayhi li lishu'ah. ↩

The sound of song rejoicing in God's help
resounds amid the tents of all the just:
"THE MIGHTY ONE's right hand delivers strength!
THE MIGHTY ONE's right hand is lifted up,
THE MIGHTY ONE's right hand delivers strength!"

I shall not die, but I shall live,
and I shall tell the acts of Yah.

I truly have been tried by Yah,
but I was never given up to die.

Open to me, O you gateways of justice,
Yes, let me come in, and give thanks unto Yah!

This is the gateway to ONE EVERLASTING,
let all who are righteous come in. ↩

COMMENTARY. *Rosh pinah* not only refers to the cornerstone but to the keystone. The psalmist is pointing out that we must see that every nation, every person has a place among God's wonders. It was a common occurrence for the workers building a wall to reject a stone for the foundation because its sides were not straight. The architect would know that among these rejects with slanted sides could be found one perfectly shaped to be the exalted central stone of the arch. E.M.

COMMENTARY. פתחו לי שערי-צדק / Open to me, O you gateways of justice. These words suggest several different meanings. Open up the gates of righteousness *for* me—either because I am one of the righteous and deserve to gain entrance or because I hope to receive charity through the righteousness of others. Or perhaps, "open up the gates of righteousness *to* me," that I too may learn to open up my heart, thus becoming one of the righteous.

The welcoming gesture of opening the gates leads to greater justice in our world. Those who pass through the gates of righteousness and open them to others enter God's gateway to sing Yah's praises among a community of the righteous. R.S.

קוֹל רִנָּה וִישׁוּעָה   בְּאָהֳלֵי צַדִּיקִים

יְמִין יהוה עֹשָׂה חָיִל: יְמִין יהוה רוֹמֵמָה

יְמִין יהוה עֹשָׂה חָיִל:

לֹא אָמוּת כִּי־אֶחְיֶה   וַאֲסַפֵּר מַעֲשֵׂי יָהּ:

יַסֹּר יִסְּרַנִּי יָּהּ   וְלַמָּוֶת לֹא נְתָנָנִי:

פִּתְחוּ־לִי שַׁעֲרֵי־צֶדֶק   אָבֹא־בָם אוֹדֶה יָהּ:

זֶה־הַשַּׁעַר לַיהוה   צַדִּיקִים יָבֹאוּ בוֹ: ←

Kol rinah vishu'ah be'oholey tzadikim
yemin adonay osah ḥayil. Yemin adonay romemah
yemin adonay osah ḥayil.
Lo amut ki eḥyeh va'asaper ma'asey yah.
Yasor yiserani yah velamavet lo netanani.
Pitḥu li sha'arey tzedek avo vam odeh yah.
Zeh hasha'ar ladonay tzadikim yavo'u vo.

I give thanks to you, for you have answered me,
and have been to me a source of help.

The stone rejected by the builders,
has become this place's founding stone.

From THE BOUNTIFUL this thing has come,
something wonderful, before our very eyes.

This very day, THE MIGHTY ONE has acted.
Let us celebrate it, and express our joy.

I pray, ABUNDANT ONE, send us your help!

I pray, ABUNDANT ONE, send us your help!

I pray, ABUNDANT ONE, help us prevail!

I pray, ABUNDANT ONE, help us prevail! ↩

Each verse is chanted twice:

אוֹדְךָ כִּי עֲנִיתָֽנִי וַתְּהִי־לִי לִישׁוּעָה׃

אֶֽבֶן מָאֲסוּ הַבּוֹנִים הָיְתָה לְרֹאשׁ פִּנָּה׃

מֵאֵת יהוה הָיְתָה זֹּאת הִיא נִפְלָאת בְּעֵינֵֽינוּ׃

זֶה־הַיּוֹם עָשָׂה יהוה נָגִֽילָה וְנִשְׂמְחָה בוֹ׃ ←

Each verse is chanted twice:

Odeḥa ki anitani vatehi li lishu'ah.
Even ma'asu habonim hayetah lerosh pinah.
Me'et adonay hayetah zot hi niflat be'eyneynu.
Zeh hayom asah adonay nagilah venismeḥa vo.

Responsively

אָֽנָּא יהוה הוֹשִֽׁיעָה נָּא
אָֽנָּא יהוה הוֹשִֽׁיעָה נָּא
אָֽנָּא יהוה הַצְלִֽיחָה נָּא
אָֽנָּא יהוה הַצְלִֽיחָה נָּא׃

Ana adonay hoshi'ah na
Ana adonay hoshi'ah na
Ana adonay hatzliḥa na
Ana adonay hatzliḥa na.

Blessed all those who come in THIS ONE's name—
we bless you in the OMNIPRESENT's house.

Divine is THE ETERNAL ONE, who gives us light.

Adorn the festive place with leafy boughs,
up to the corners of the altar shrine.

You are my God; to you I offer thanks—
my God, whom I revere.

Give thanks to THE ETERNAL, who is good,
whose love is everlasting. Psalm 118:5-29

Let all your works give praise to you, MAJESTIC ONE, our God, and all who care for you, all the righteous who enact your will. Let all the House of Israel, your people, with rejoicing offer thanks, and bless, and praise, and magnify, and raise up, and revere, and declare holy, and enthrone your name, our sovereign, for to you all thanks are fitting, and to your name it is so pleasing to sing praise. For from everlasting to everlasting, you are God. Blessed are you, ABUNDANT ONE, the sovereign addressed in every praise.

On Yom Ha'atzma'ut continue with Kaddish Titkabal, page 146, then Aleynu, page 168. On all other holidays, continue with Kaddish Titkabal, page 146, then Torah reading, page 146.

COMMENTARY. The mood of the lines, "I pray, ABUNDANT ONE, send us your help! / I pray, ABUNDANT ONE, help us prevail!" does not correspond with the jubilance of the victory parade dramatized in this psalm. The rest of the psalm is rich with praise; only here do we find the urgency and terseness of petition. This petition reveals the essence of a relationship with God. Just as God's mitzvot speak to us in the imperative, "Do this...don't do this," so we acknowledge the closeness of our relationship by also speaking to God in the imperative: "Send us...help us." If we cannot speak of our most basic needs in prayer, when can we speak of them? H.L.

בָּרוּךְ הַבָּא בְּשֵׁם יהוה　　בֵּרַכְנוּכֶם מִבֵּית יהוה:

אֵל יהוה וַיָּאֶר לָנוּ　　אִסְרוּ־חַג בַּעֲבֹתִים
עַד־קַרְנוֹת הַמִּזְבֵּחַ:

אֵלִי אַתָּה וְאוֹדֶךָּ　　אֱלֹהַי אֲרוֹמְמֶךָּ:

הוֹדוּ לַיהוה כִּי־טוֹב　　כִּי לְעוֹלָם חַסְדּוֹ:

Baruḥ haba beshem adonay
beraḥnuḥem mibeyt adonay.
El adonay vaya'er lanu
isru ḥag ba'avotim ad karnot hamizbe'aḥ.
Eli atah ve'odeka elohay aromemeka.
Hodu ladonay ki tov ki le'olam ḥasdo.

יְהַלְלוּךָ יהוה אֱלֹהֵינוּ כָּל מַעֲשֶׂיךָ וַחֲסִידֶיךָ צַדִּיקִים עוֹשֵׂי רְצוֹנֶךָ וְכָל עַמְּךָ בֵּית יִשְׂרָאֵל בְּרִנָּה יוֹדוּ וִיבָרְכוּ וִישַׁבְּחוּ וִיפָאֲרוּ וִירוֹמְמוּ וְיַעֲרִיצוּ וְיַקְדִּישׁוּ וְיַמְלִיכוּ אֶת שִׁמְךָ מַלְכֵּנוּ *כִּי לְךָ טוֹב לְהוֹדוֹת וּלְשִׁמְךָ נָאֶה לְזַמֵּר כִּי מֵעוֹלָם עַד עוֹלָם אַתָּה אֵל: בָּרוּךְ אַתָּה יהוה מֶלֶךְ מְהֻלָּל בַּתִּשְׁבָּחוֹת:

On Yom Ha'atzma'ut continue with Kaddish Titkabal, page 145, then Aleynu, page 169. On all other holidays, continue with Kaddish Titkabal, page 145, then Torah Reading, page 147.

HADLAKAT NER SHEL ḤANUKAH / ḤANUKAH CANDLELIGHTING

Candles are lit after dark. It is traditional to place the candles in a window where they can be seen from the street. On Friday evening the Ḥanukah candles are lit prior to lighting the Shabbat candles. On Saturday evening they are lit after Havdalah.
When placing candles in the menorah, we start on the right, putting in one candle for each night, plus the shamash / *servant candle. After the blessings are recited, we use the* shamash *to light the other candles from left to right.*

Blessed are you, SOURCE OF LIGHT, our God, the sovereign of all worlds, who has made us holy with your mitzvot, and commanded us to kindle Ḥanukah light.

Blessed are you, THE REDEEMER our God, the sovereign of all worlds, who did miracles for our ancestors in those days at this season.

On the first night of Ḥanukah add:
Blessed are you, ETERNAL ONE our God, the sovereign of all worlds, who gave us life, and kept us strong, and brought us to this time.

MA'OZ TZUR / ROCK OF AGES

This translation can be sung to the same melody as the Hebrew.

Rock of Ages, let our song
Praise your saving power;
You amid the raging foes
Were our shelt'ring tower.
Furious, they assailed us,
But your arm availed us,
And your word
Broke their sword
When our own strength failed us.

Adapted from a translation by Gustav Göttheil

NOTE. Additional songs for Ḥanukah can be found in *Kol Haneshamah: Shirim Uvraḥot.*
J.B.

הַדְלָקַת נֵר שֶׁל חֲנוּכָּה

בָּרוּךְ אַתָּה יהוה אֱלֹהֵינוּ מֶלֶךְ הָעוֹלָם אֲשֶׁר קִדְּשָׁנוּ
בְּמִצְוֹתָיו וְצִוָּנוּ לְהַדְלִיק נֵר שֶׁל חֲנֻכָּה:

Baruḥ atah adonay eloheynu meleḥ ha'olam asher kideshanu bemitzvotav vetzivanu lehadlik ner shel ḥanukah.

בָּרוּךְ אַתָּה יהוה אֱלֹהֵינוּ מֶלֶךְ הָעוֹלָם שֶׁעָשָׂה נִסִּים לַאֲבוֹתֵינוּ בַּיָּמִים
הָהֵם בַּזְּמַן הַזֶּה:

Baruḥ atah adonay eloheynu meleḥ ha'olam she'asah nisim la'avoteynu bayamim hahem bazeman hazeh.

On the first night of Ḥanukah add:

בָּרוּךְ אַתָּה יהוה אֱלֹהֵינוּ מֶלֶךְ הָעוֹלָם
שֶׁהֶחֱיָנוּ וְקִיְּמָנוּ וְהִגִּיעָנוּ לַזְּמַן הַזֶּה:

Baruḥ atah adonay eloheynu meleḥ ha'olam sheheḥeyanu vekiyemanu vehigi'anu lazeman hazeh.

מָעוֹז צוּר

מָעוֹז צוּר יְשׁוּעָתִי לְךָ נָאֶה לְשַׁבֵּחַ:
תִּכּוֹן בֵּית תְּפִלָּתִי וְשָׁם תּוֹדָה נְזַבֵּחַ:
לְעֵת תָּכִין מַטְבֵּחַ מִצָּר הַמְנַבֵּחַ:
אָז אֶגְמוֹר בְּשִׁיר מִזְמוֹר חֲנֻכַּת הַמִּזְבֵּחַ:

יְוָנִים נִקְבְּצוּ עָלַי אֲזַי בִּימֵי חַשְׁמַנִּים:
וּפָרְצוּ חוֹמוֹת מִגְדָּלַי וְטִמְּאוּ כָּל הַשְּׁמָנִים:
וּמִנּוֹתַר קַנְקַנִּים נַעֲשָׂה נֵס לַשּׁוֹשַׁנִּים:
בְּנֵי בִינָה יְמֵי שְׁמוֹנָה קָבְעוּ שִׁיר וּרְנָנִים:

Ma'oz tzur yeshu'ati leḥa na'eh leshabe'aḥ.
Tikon beyt tefilati vesham todah nezabe'aḥ.
Le'et taḥin matbe'aḥ mitzar hamnabe'aḥ.
Az egmor beshir mizmor ḥanukat hamizbe'aḥ.

PURIM

On Purim, the following blessings are said, after which the Megillah *is read:*

Blessed are you, REDEEMING ONE, our God, the sovereign of all worlds, who has made us holy with mitzvot, and has commanded us to read from the Megillah.

Blessed are you, ETERNAL ONE, our God, the sovereign of all worlds, who wrought wonders for our ancestors in former days at this time of year.

Blessed are you ETERNAL ONE, our God, the sovereign of all worlds, who gave us life, and kept us strong, and brought us to this time.

COMMENTARY. On Purim and Ḥanukah special blessings acknowledge נסים / wonders wrought for our ancestors. How do we understand these wonders? Not as acknowledgments of victories at the end of bloody battles, nor as a divine hand interfering to alter the course of history. We cannot help but marvel, however, at the creativity and vigor of a Jewish people that continues to survive. Like Maimonides, we do not expect wonders to overturn the course of nature. Nonetheless, it would be to our detriment to ignore the wonders with which we are surrounded daily or to miss the opportunity to relish them on days when they have been traditionally celebrated by the Jewish people. In celebrating wonders, we remind ourselves of both the power in collective action, and the startling accomplishment that a single determined individual can achieve. D.A.T.

פּוּרִים

On Purim, the following blessings are said, after which the Megillah *is read:*

בָּרוּךְ אַתָּה יהוה אֱלֹהֵינוּ מֶלֶךְ הָעוֹלָם אֲשֶׁר קִדְּשָׁנוּ בְּמִצְוֹתָיו

בָּרוּךְ אַתָּה יהוה אֱלֹהֵינוּ מֶלֶךְ הָעוֹלָם שֶׁעָשָׂה נִסִּים לַאֲבוֹתֵינוּ
וּלְאִמּוֹתֵינוּ בַּיָּמִים הָהֵם בַּזְּמַן הַזֶּה׃

בָּרוּךְ אַתָּה יהוה אֱלֹהֵינוּ מֶלֶךְ הָעוֹלָם
שֶׁהֶחֱיָנוּ וְקִיְּמָנוּ וְהִגִּיעָנוּ לַזְּמַן הַזֶּה׃

Baruḥ atah adonay eloheynu meleḥ ha'olam asher kideshanu bemitzvotav vetzivanu al mikra megillah.

Baruḥ atah adonay eloheynu meleḥ ha'olam she'asah nisim la'avoteynu ule'imoteynu bayamim hahem bazeman hazeh.

Baruḥ atah adonay eloheynu meleḥ ha'olam sheheḥeyanu vekiyemanu vehigi'anu lazeman hazeh.

After reading the Megillah, one or more of the following songs can be sung. Continue Ma'ariv with Aleynu on page 326. Continue Shaḥarit with Returning the Torah on page 164.

SHOSHANAT YA'AKOV / JACOB'S FLOWERING

Behold the flowering of Jacob's strength!
Relive the joy and happiness when all of us beheld
the blue of royal glory worn by Mordechai
in honor of his deeds.

You, O God, were always there
to help your people in their hour of need,
and you shall ever be their hope
as one age passes to the next.

You shall always make it known
that those who hope for you cannot be shamed,
nor shall they ever be disgraced
who find in you their refuge and their trust.

Cursed is Haman,
who has sought my end and my destruction!
Blessed be Mordechai, the Jew,
who triumphs and endures!

After reading the Megillah, one or more of the following songs can be sung. *Continue Ma'ariv with Aleynu on page 327. Continue Shaḥarit with Returning the Torah on page 165.*

שׁוֹשַׁנַּת יַעֲקֹב

שׁוֹשַׁנַּת יַעֲקֹב צָהֲלָה וְשָׂמֵחָה
בִּרְאוֹתָם יַחַד תְּכֵלֶת מָרְדְּכָי:
תְּשׁוּעָתָם הָיִיתָ לָנֶצַח
וְתִקְוָתָם בְּכָל דּוֹר וָדוֹר:
לְהוֹדִיעַ שֶׁכָּל קֹוֶיךָ לֹא יֵבֹשׁוּ
וְלֹא יִכָּלְמוּ לָנֶצַח כָּל הַחוֹסִים בָּךְ.
אָרוּר הָמָן אֲשֶׁר בִּקֵּשׁ לְאַבְּדִי
בָּרוּךְ מָרְדְּכַי הַיְּהוּדִי:

Shoshanat ya'akov tzahalah vesameḥah, birotam yaḥad teḥelet mordeḥay.
Teshu'atam hayita lanetzaḥ vetikvatam beḥol dor vador.
Lehodi'a shekol koveḥa lo yevoshu velo yikalmu lanetzaḥ kol haḥosim baḥ.
Arur haman asher bikesh le'abedi, baruḥ mordeḥay hayehudi.

ḤAG PURIM, ḤAG PURIM / A SONG FOR PURIM

This version may be sung to the same melody as the Hebrew.

Purim feast, a Purim feast,
for all the Jews a mighty feast,
when drinks abound, noisemakers growl,
when song and dance raise joyous howl!

Come, raise a big noise,
rash, rash, rash!
Come, raise a loud noise,
rash, rash, rash!
Come, raise a sharp noise,
rash, rash, rash!
With your *rashanim*!

Purim feast, a Purim feast,
when all exchange their gifts and treats,
delightful tastes and choicest sweets,
the finest cakes and nut-filled eats!

Come, raise a big noise,
rash, rash, rash!
Come, raise a loud noise,
rash, rash, rash!
Come, raise a sharp noise,
rash, rash, rash!
With your *rashanim*!

חַג פּוּרִים

חַג פּוּרִים חַג פּוּרִים —
חַג גָּדוֹל הוּא לַיְּהוּדִים
מַסֵּכוֹת רַעֲשָׁנִים
זְמִירוֹת רִקּוּדִים:

הָבָה נַרְעִישָׁה
רַשׁ רַשׁ רַשׁ:
הָבָה נַרְעִישָׁה
רַשׁ רַשׁ רַשׁ:
הָבָה נַרְעִישָׁה
רַשׁ רַשׁ רַשׁ
בָּרַעֲשָׁנִים:

חַג פּוּרִים חַג פּוּרִים —
זֶה אֶל זֶה שׁוֹלְחִים מָנוֹת!
מַחְמַדִּים מַמְתַּקִּים
תּוּפִינִים מִגְדָּנוֹת:

הָבָה נַרְעִישָׁה
רַשׁ רַשׁ רַשׁ:
הָבָה נַרְעִישָׁה
רַשׁ רַשׁ רַשׁ:
הָבָה נַרְעִישָׁה
רַשׁ רַשׁ רַשׁ
בָּרַעֲשָׁנִים:

Ḥag purim, ḥag purim, ḥag gadol hu layhudim, maseyḥot ra'ashanim zemirot rikudim.

Havah narisha rash rash rash, havah narisha rash rash rash, havah narisha rash rash rash, bara'ashanim.

Ḥag purim, ḥag purim, zeh el zeh sholeḥim manot maḥmadim mamtakim, tofinim migdanot.

Havah narisha rash rash rash, havah narisha rash rash rash, havah narisha rash rash rash, bara'ashanim.

HOSHANOT / PRAYERS FOR REDEMPTION

On Sukkot, the Hoshanot are recited before returning the Torah to the Ark. During Sukkot, each day except Shabbat, the lulav *and* etrog *are held. One or more Torah scrolls are brought to the* bimah */ lectern. The Reader chants the following, repeated by the congregation.*

Hosha na!
For your sake, our God, Hosha na!
For your sake, our Creator, Hosha na!
For your sake, our Redeemer, Hosha na!
For your sake, our Teacher, Hosha na!

Continue with the readings for the appropriate day of Ḥol Hamo'ed *Sukkot.*
For second day, turn to page 396.
For third day, turn to page 398.
For fourth day, turn to page 400.
For fifth day, turn to page 402.
For sixth day, turn to page 404.
For Hoshanah Rabah, turn to page 406.

הוֹשַׁעְנוֹת

On Sukkot, the Hoshanot are recited before returning the Torah to the Ark. During Sukkot, each day except Shabbat, the lulav *and* etrog *are held. One or more Torah scrolls are brought to the* bimah */ lectern. The Reader chants the following, repeated by the congregation.*

הוֹשַׁע נָא:

לְמַעַנְךָ אֱלֹהֵינוּ הוֹשַׁע נָא:
לְמַעַנְךָ בּוֹרְאֵנוּ הוֹשַׁע נָא:
לְמַעַנְךָ גּוֹאֲלֵנוּ הוֹשַׁע נָא:
לְמַעַנְךָ דּוֹרְשֵׁנוּ הוֹשַׁע נָא:

Hosha na.
Lema'anḥa eloheynu hosha na.
Lema'anḥa borenu hosha na.
Lema'anḥa go'alenu hosha na.
Lema'anḥa dorshenu hosha na.

Continue with the readings for the appropriate day of Ḥol Hamo'ed *Sukkot.*
For second day, turn to page 397.
For third day, turn to page 399.
For fourth day, turn to page 401.
For fifth day, turn to page 403.
For sixth day, turn to page 405.
For Hoshanah Rabah, turn to page 407.

It is customary to form a procession for the Hoshanot. The Torah scrolls lead the procession, followed by those carrying lulav *and* etrog, *with others bringing up the rear.*
On the second day of Sukkot recite:

Eretz Yisrael: her
banim (children) and her *bonim* (builders); her
granaries and storage-houses; her
disciples and her benefactors; her
hilltops and her valleys; her
village assemblies and her councils; her
sages and her young people; her
wise and literate; her
toddlers and her nurselings; her
Jewish settlements and towns; her
Knesset and municipalities; her
learned and her studious; her
migrants, visitors and immigrants; her
notables and ministers of state; her
scholars and her artisans; her
entrepreneurs and her merchants; her
pleasant groves and vineyards; her
soldiers and her defenders; her
kibbutzim and moshavim; her
rugged shepherds and her farmers; her
sitting judges and her officiers of law; her
towers and her citadels.
Hosha na!

Redeem your people, bless your inheritance; and nurture them and carry them throughout all time. And may these words with which I supplicate before THE FOUNT OF LIFE be near to THE ETERNAL ONE, our God, by day and night, working justice for God's servant, and justice for the people Israel; a timely prayer that all the peoples of the earth may know that THE ETERNAL ONE is God; there is none else!

The Scroll is returned to the Ark.
Continue with Kaddish Titkabal, page 144.

It is customary to form a procession for the Hoshanot. The Torah scrolls lead the procession, followed by those carrying lulav *and* etrog, *with others bringing up the rear.*
On the second day of Sukkot recite:

אֶ֫רֶץ יִשְׂרָאֵל: בָּנֶ֫יהָ־בּוֹנֶ֫יהָ: גִּנְזֵי אוֹצְרוֹתֶ֫יהָ: דּוֹרְשֶׁ֫יהָ וְעוֹזְרֶ֫יהָ: הָרֶ֫יהָ
וַעֲמָקֶ֫יהָ: וְעִידוֹתֶ֫יהָ וְכִנּוּסֶ֫יהָ: זְקֵנֶ֫יהָ וּצְעִירֶ֫יהָ: חַכְמֵי מִכְלְלוֹתֶ֫יהָ:
טַפֵּי־טִפּוּחֶ֫יהָ: יְשׁוּבֶ֫יהָ וּכְפָרֶ֫יהָ: כְּנֶסְתָּהּ וְעִירִיּוֹתֶ֫יהָ: לוֹמְדֵי תוֹרוֹתֶ֫יהָ:
מְבַקְּרֶ֫יהָ וְעוֹלֶ֫יהָ: נְשִׂיאָהּ וְשָׂרֶ֫יהָ: סוֹפְרֶ֫יהָ וְאָמָּנֶ֫יהָ: עַסְקָנֶ֫יהָ וְסוֹחֲרֶ֫יהָ:
פַּרְדֵּסֶ֫יהָ וּכְרָמֶ֫יהָ: צְבָאוֹתֶ֫יהָ וּמָגִנֶּ֫יהָ: קִבּוּצֶ֫יהָ וּמוֹשָׁבֶ֫יהָ: רוֹעֶ֫יהָ
וְאִכָּרֶ֫יהָ: שׁוֹפְטֶ֫יהָ וְשׁוֹטְרֶ֫יהָ תַּלְפִּיּוֹתֶ֫יהָ וּמִבְצָרֶ֫יהָ: הוֹשַׁע נָא:

הוֹשִׁ֫יעָה אֶת־עַמֶּ֫ךָ וּבָרֵךְ אֶת־נַחֲלָתֶ֫ךָ וּרְעֵם וְנַשְּׂאֵם עַד־הָעוֹלָם: וְיִהְיוּ
דְבָרַי אֵ֫לֶּה אֲשֶׁר הִתְחַנַּ֫נְתִּי לִפְנֵי יהוה קְרֹבִים אֶל־יהוה אֱלֹהֵ֫ינוּ יוֹמָם
וָלָ֫יְלָה לַעֲשׂוֹת מִשְׁפַּט עַבְדּוֹ וּמִשְׁפַּט עַמּוֹ יִשְׂרָאֵל דְּבַר־יוֹם בְּיוֹמוֹ:
לְמַ֫עַן דַּ֫עַת כָּל־עַמֵּי הָאָ֫רֶץ כִּי יהוה הוּא הָאֱלֹהִים אֵין עוֹד:

Hoshi'ah et ameḥa uvareḥ et naḥalateḥa
urem venasem ad ha'olam.

The Scroll is returned to the Ark.
Continue with Kaddish Titkabal, page 145.

NOTE. *Eretz Yisrael* / The Land of Israel. This acrostic prayer presents a fine portrait of Israel's thriving prosperity, as a vision of fulfillment of the traditional prophecies of a rebirth of the Jewish people in the Land. But the final word, "*Hosha na* ("Save us, please!"), stresses the perennial vulnerability of the Land, and the dependence of a reborn Israel on the continued protection and blessing of God. J.R.

NOTE. *banim...bonim.* The source of this play on words is Talmud Beraḥot 64a: "The disciples of the wise increase peace in the world, as it says, 'And all your children shall be learned in THE OMNIPRESENT's ways, and great shall be their peaceful state!' (Isa. 54:13). Do not read *'banayiḥ'* (your children) but *'bonayiḥ'* (your builders)." This marvelously compressed teaching establishes the implicit connection between procreation, transmission of Torah, cultural continuity, human progress, and world peace—a connection that is the fundamental premise of all Jewish learning. J.R.

It is customary to form a procession for the Hoshanot. The Torah scrolls lead the procession, followed by those carrying lulav *and* etrog, *with others bringing up the rear.*
On the third day of Sukkot recite:

Arranging now my plea, I here
beseech you from this place, and,
gaining consciousness of sin through fasts,
declare my quest for you to help me.
Hearken to me and my cry, and
waken to my need, and save me now.
Set me in mind; be merciful, Redeemer.
Help me, Living One; may you delight in it.
Let no more evil happen to me!
May you hurry, God of my salvation,
never failing to redeem; please
set aside my sin and grant forgiveness.
Overlook my wrongdoings, and
please turn toward me with your help. My
stronghold, righteous one, my savior,
come, accept my cry, and
raise the horn of my salvation,
sheltering Almighty One, redeemer, hear my cry:
Hosha na!
Turn toward me now, and bring your help!
Hosha na!

Redeem your people, bless your inheritance; and nurture them and carry them throughout all time. And may these words with which I supplicate before THE FOUNT OF LIFE be near to THE ETERNAL ONE, our God, by day and night, working justice for God's servant, and justice for the people Israel; a timely prayer that all the peoples of the earth may know that THE ETERNAL ONE is God; there is none else!

The Scroll is returned to the Ark.
Continue with Kaddish Titkabal, page 144.

It is customary to form a procession for the Hoshanot. The Torah scrolls lead the procession, followed by those carrying lulav *and* etrog, *with others bringing up the rear.*
On the third day of Sukkot recite:

הוֹשַׁע נָא: אֶעֱרוֹךְ שׁוּעִי: בְּבֵית שַׁוְעִי: גִּלִּיתִי בַצּוֹם פִּשְׁעִי: דְּרַשְׁתִּיךָ
בּוֹ לְהוֹשִׁיעִי: הַקְשִׁיבָה לְקוֹל שַׁוְעִי: וְקוּמָה וְהוֹשִׁיעִי: זְכוֹר וְרַחֵם
מוֹשִׁיעִי: חַי כֵּן תְּשַׁעְשְׁעִי: טוֹב בְּאֶנֶק שְׁעִי בַּל עוֹד תַּרְשִׁיעִי: מַהֵר
אֱלֹהֵי יִשְׁעִי: נֶצַח לְהוֹשִׁיעִי שָׂא נָא עֲוֹן רִשְׁעִי: עֲבוֹר עַל פִּשְׁעִי:
פְּנֵה נָא לְהוֹשִׁיעִי: צוּר צַדִּיק מוֹשִׁיעִי: קַבֵּל נָא שַׁוְעִי: רוֹמֵם קֶרֶן
יִשְׁעִי: שַׁדַּי מוֹשִׁיעִי: הוֹשַׁע נָא: תּוֹפִיעַ וְתוֹשִׁיעִי: הוֹשַׁע נָא:

הוֹשִׁיעָה אֶת־עַמֶּךָ וּבָרֵךְ אֶת־נַחֲלָתֶךָ וּרְעֵם וְנַשְּׂאֵם עַד־הָעוֹלָם: וְיִהְיוּ
דְבָרַי אֵלֶּה אֲשֶׁר הִתְחַנַּנְתִּי לִפְנֵי יהוה קְרֹבִים אֶל־יהוה אֱלֹהֵינוּ יוֹמָם
וָלָיְלָה לַעֲשׂוֹת מִשְׁפַּט עַבְדּוֹ וּמִשְׁפַּט עַמּוֹ יִשְׂרָאֵל דְּבַר־יוֹם בְּיוֹמוֹ:
לְמַעַן דַּעַת כָּל־עַמֵּי הָאָרֶץ כִּי יהוה הוּא הָאֱלֹהִים אֵין עוֹד:

Hoshi'ah et ameḥa uvareḥ et naḥalateḥa
urem venasem ad ha'olam.

The Scroll is returned to the Ark.
Continue with Kaddish Titkabal, page 145.

הושיעה...העולם / Redeem...time (Psalm 28:9).
ויהיו...עוד / And...else! (I Kings 8:59-60)

NOTE. Several of the Hoshanot follow an alphabetic acrostic pattern, which this translation preserves. The Hebrew original of this Hoshanah suspends the acrostic pattern for four lines (*tet*, *yod*, *kaf*, and *lamed*), which seem to have been lost or deleted.

J.R.

It is customary to form a procession for the Hoshanot. The Torah scrolls lead the procession, followed by those carrying lulav *and* etrog, *with others bringing up the rear.*
On the fourth day of Sukkot recite:

A people steady as a rampart wall,
bright as sunshine's rays, yet now
gone into exile, and forlorn; the
date-palm's stature is her form.
How often she is slain for you—
very much like altar lambs! And
scattered now among her enemies,
how faithfully she clings to you!
The yoke of service she endures,
your oneness she alone affirms,
conquered and exiled though she may be,
learning your awe-inspiring sanctity.
Maligned and struck upon the cheek,
now she is beaten in the street.
Sorrowful suffering she has borne,
oppressed and troubled, she is
protected by Yah's bounty and redeemed,
still holy as a flock of Temple sheep,
communities of Jacob's line, sealed and
recorded with your sacred Name; now
she cries out to you: "Hosha na!"
Take her now into your care.
Hosha na!

Redeem your people, bless your inheritance; and nurure them and carry them throughout all time. And may these words with which I supplicate before The Fount of Life be near to The Eternal One, our God, by day and night, working justice for God's servant, and justice for the people Israel; a timely prayer that all the peoples of the earth may know that The Eternal One is God; there is none else!

The Scroll is returned to the Ark.
Continue with Kaddish Titkabal, page 144.

It is customary to form a procession for the Hoshanot. The Torah scrolls lead the procession, followed by those carrying lulav *and* etrog, *with others bringing up the rear.*
On the fourth day of Sukkot recite:

הוֹשַׁע נָא: אֹם אֲנִי חוֹמָה: בָּרָה כַּחַמָּה: גּוֹלָה וְסוּרָה: דָּמְתָה לְתָמָר:
הַהֲרוּגָה עָלֶיךָ: וְנֶחֱשֶׁבֶת כְּצֹאן טִבְחָה: זְרוּיָה בֵּין מַכְעִיסֶיהָ: חֲבוּקָה
וּדְבוּקָה בָּךְ: טוֹעֶנֶת עֻלָּךְ: יְחִידָה לְיַחֲדָךְ: כְּבוּשָׁה בַּגּוֹלָה: לוֹמֶדֶת
יִרְאָתָךְ: מְרוּטַת לֶחִי: נְתוּנָה לְמַכִּים: סוֹבֶלֶת סִבְלָךְ: עֲנִיָּה סֹעֲרָה:
פְּדוּיַת טוֹבִיָּה: צֹאן קָדָשִׁים: קְהִלּוֹת יַעֲקֹב: רְשׁוּמִים בִּשְׁמֶךָ שׁוֹאֲגִים
הוֹשַׁע נָא: תְּמוּכִים עָלֶיךָ: הוֹשַׁע נָא:

הוֹשִׁיעָה אֶת־עַמֶּךָ וּבָרֵךְ אֶת־נַחֲלָתֶךָ וּרְעֵם וְנַשְּׂאֵם עַד־הָעוֹלָם: וְיִהְיוּ
דְבָרַי אֵלֶּה אֲשֶׁר הִתְחַנַּנְתִּי לִפְנֵי יהוה קְרֹבִים אֶל־יהוה אֱלֹהֵינוּ יוֹמָם
וָלָיְלָה לַעֲשׂוֹת מִשְׁפַּט עַבְדּוֹ וּמִשְׁפַּט עַמּוֹ יִשְׂרָאֵל דְּבַר־יוֹם בְּיוֹמוֹ:
לְמַעַן דַּעַת כָּל־עַמֵּי הָאָרֶץ כִּי יהוה הוּא הָאֱלֹהִים אֵין עוֹד:

Hoshi'ah et ameḥa uvareḥ et naḥalateḥa
urem venasem ad ha'olam.

The Scroll is returned to the Ark.
Continue with Kaddish Titkabal, page 145.

NOTE. פדוית טוביה / protected by Yah's bounty. Literally, "redeemed by Tobiah," normally understood as an alternative name for Moses. The name may also refer to events of the Apocryphal Book of Tobit, which tells how Tobias, son of Tobit (a descendant of the tribe of Naftali living in Nineveh), rescues his kinswoman, the maiden Sarah, from an evil spell cast by the demon Ashmodai. Freed from the spell, she marries Tobias. Such tales of enchantment and redemption were common in Jewish folklore and legend, and were often read as allegories of the exile and redemption of the people Israel.

J.R.

It is customary to form a procession for the Hoshanot. The Torah scrolls lead the procession, followed by those carrying lulav *and* etrog, *with others bringing up the rear.*
On the fifth day of Sukkot recite:

All-saving God, who promised
by a fourfold oath to save,
grown weary are we in our cries,
despairing of the worth of sighs,
however much our words delight,
with riddles and with fancy's flight,
still we are crying for relief, and
hoping for the end of grief, and
tied to you, awaiting your attention.
Yet we seek to know time's secrets,
kneeling in our cries of prayer, to
learn to understand the prophecies
made long ago, in utterance by you.
Now, you who gives forth saving acts,
secretly numbered in their meanings,
our testimony let them here declare! O,
power of redemption, you are the
Tzaddik (Righteous) for the saved, who
come together in the City of Salvation,
raising up their heartfelt cry,
sounded three hours of the day: Hosha na!
Thus, hurry forth to save us now!
Hosha na!

Redeem your people, bless your inheritance; and nurture them and carry them throughout all time. And may these words with which I supplicate before THE FOUNT OF LIFE be near to THE ETERNAL ONE, our God, by day and night, working justice for God's servant, and justice for the people Israel; a timely prayer that all the peoples of the earth may know that THE ETERNAL ONE is God; there is none else!

The Scroll is returned to the Ark.
Continue with Kaddish Titkabal, page 144.

It is customary to form a procession for the Hoshanot. The Torah scrolls lead the procession, followed by those carrying lulav *and* etrog, *with others bringing up the rear.*
On the fifth day of Sukkot recite:

הוֹשַׁע נָא: אֵל לְמוֹשָׁעוֹת: בְּאַרְבַּע שְׁבוּעוֹת: גָּשִׁים בְּשַׁוְעוֹת: דּוֹפְקֵי
עֶרֶךְ שׁוּעוֹת: הוֹגֵי שַׁעֲשׁוּעוֹת: וְחִידוֹתָם מִשְׁתַּעַשְׁעוֹת: זוֹעֲקִים
לְהַשְׁעוֹת: חוֹכֵי יְשׁוּעוֹת: טְפוּלִים בָּךְ שְׁעוֹת: יוֹדְעֵי בִּין שָׁעוֹת:
כּוֹרְעֶיךָ בְּשַׁוְעוֹת: לְהָבִין שְׁמוּעוֹת: מִפִּיךָ נִשְׁמָעוֹת: נוֹתֵן תְּשׁוּעוֹת:
סְפוּרוֹת מַשְׁמָעוֹת: עֵדוּת מַשְׁמִיעוֹת: פּוֹעֵל יְשׁוּעוֹת: צַדִּיק נוֹשָׁעוֹת:
קִרְיַת תְּשׁוּעוֹת: רֶגֶשׁ תְּשׁוּאוֹת: שָׁלֹשׁ שָׁעוֹת: הוֹשַׁע נָא: תָּחִישׁ
לִתְשׁוּעוֹת: הוֹשַׁע נָא:

הוֹשִׁיעָה אֶת־עַמֶּךָ וּבָרֵךְ אֶת־נַחֲלָתֶךָ וּרְעֵם וְנַשְּׂאֵם עַד־הָעוֹלָם: וְיִהְיוּ
דְבָרַי אֵלֶּה אֲשֶׁר הִתְחַנַּנְתִּי לִפְנֵי יהוה קְרֹבִים אֶל־יהוה אֱלֹהֵינוּ יוֹמָם
וָלָיְלָה לַעֲשׂוֹת מִשְׁפַּט עַבְדּוֹ וּמִשְׁפַּט עַמּוֹ יִשְׂרָאֵל דְּבַר־יוֹם בְּיוֹמוֹ:
לְמַעַן דַּעַת כָּל־עַמֵּי הָאָרֶץ כִּי יהוה הוּא הָאֱלֹהִים אֵין עוֹד:

Hoshi'ah et ameḥa uvareḥ et naḥalateḥa
urem venasem ad ha'olam.

The Scroll is returned to the Ark.
Continue with Kaddish Titkabal, page 145.

NOTE. The extremely condensed and elliptical style of the Hebrew original makes any translation necessarily approximate. The final word of each line in the original plays on the letters *shin* and *ayin*, the principal root letters of the words "*Hosha na*" ("Save us, please!"). J.R.

ספורות משמעות / secretly numbered in their meanings. The Hebrew here ("numbered of meanings") is extremely obscure. It may refer to the four levels of interpretation of the Torah: *peshat* (literal), *derash* (moral), *remez* (allegorical), and *sod* (mystical). Or it may simply say that Scripture's original prophecies of salvation are now, in a time of trouble for the people Israel, as obscure as ciphers (*sefurot*), and demand a new redemption in order to become clear. J.R.

עדות משמיעות / our testimony let them here declare. Literally, "testimony declaring." The poet is perhaps saying that because Scripture's promises of redemption for the Jews have become obscure in a dark time, a new turn of good fortune can make those prophecies a testimony for the *present* era, if God wishes it. J.R.

It is customary to form a procession for the Hoshanot. The Torah scrolls lead the procession, followed by those carrying lulav *and* etrog, *with others bringing up the rear.*
On the sixth day of Sukkot recite:

For the sake of your All-embracing truth,
for the sake of your Binding covenant,
for the sake of your Greatness and your beauty,
for the sake of your Divine decree,
for the sake of your Heavenly splendor,
for the sake of your Wise assembly,
for the sake of your Sign and remembrance,
for the sake of your Heavenly love,
for the sake of your Timeless good,
for the sake of your Indivisibility,
for the sake of your Consoling glory,
for the sake of your Learning's light,
for the sake of your Majestic sovereignty,
for the sake of your Name's victory,
for the sake of your Sublime mystery,
for the sake of your Omnipotence,
for the sake of your Praise eternal,
for the sake of your Complete and utter holiness,
for the sake of your Supernal justice,
for the sake of your Redeeming and abundant love,
for the sake of your Sheḥinah's presence, save us, please,
for the sake of your Thunderous praises, save us please!

Redeem your people, bless your inheritance; and nurture them and carry them throughout all time. And may these words with which I pray before THE FOUNT OF LIFE be near to THE ETERNAL ONE, our God, by day and night, working justice for God's servant, and justice for the people Israel; timely prayer—that all the peoples of the earth may know that THE ETERNAL ONE is God; there is none else!

The Scroll is returned to the Ark.
Continue with Kaddish Titkabal, page 144.

It is customary to form a procession for the Hoshanot. The Torah scrolls lead the procession, followed by those carrying lulav *and* etrog, *with others bringing up the rear.*
On the sixth day of Sukkot recite:

הוֹשַׁע נָא: לְמַֽעַן אֲמִתָּךְ: לְמַֽעַן בְּרִיתָךְ: לְמַֽעַן גָּדְלָךְ וְתִפְאַרְתָּךְ:
לְמַֽעַן דָּתָךְ: לְמַֽעַן הוֹדָךְ: לְמַֽעַן וִעוּדָךְ: לְמַֽעַן זִכְרָךְ: לְמַֽעַן חַסְדָּךְ:
לְמַֽעַן טוּבָךְ: לְמַֽעַן יִחוּדָךְ: לְמַֽעַן כְּבוֹדָךְ: לְמַֽעַן לִמּוּדָךְ: לְמַֽעַן
מַלְכוּתָךְ: לְמַֽעַן נִצְחָךְ: לְמַֽעַן סוֹדָךְ: לְמַֽעַן עֻזָּךְ: לְמַֽעַן פְּאֵרָךְ: לְמַֽעַן
צִדְקָתָךְ: לְמַֽעַן קְדֻשָּׁתָךְ: לְמַֽעַן רַחֲמֶֽיךָ הָרַבִּים: לְמַֽעַן שְׁכִינָתָךְ: הוֹשַׁע
נָא: לְמַֽעַן תְּהִלָּתָךְ: הוֹשַׁע נָא:

הוֹשִֽׁיעָה אֶת־עַמֶּֽךָ וּבָרֵךְ אֶת־נַחֲלָתֶֽךָ וּרְעֵם וְנַשְּׂאֵם עַד־הָעוֹלָם: וְיִהְיוּ
דְבָרַי אֵֽלֶּה אֲשֶׁר הִתְחַנַּֽנְתִּי לִפְנֵי יהוה קְרֹבִים אֶל־יהוה אֱלֹהֵֽינוּ יוֹמָם
וָלָֽיְלָה לַעֲשׂוֹת מִשְׁפַּט עַבְדּוֹ וּמִשְׁפַּט עַמּוֹ יִשְׂרָאֵל דְּבַר־יוֹם בְּיוֹמוֹ:
לְמַֽעַן דַּֽעַת כָּל־עַמֵּי הָאָֽרֶץ כִּי יהוה הוּא הָאֱלֹהִים אֵין עוֹד:

Hoshi'ah et ameḥa uvareḥ et naḥalateḥa
urem venasem ad ha'olam.

The Scroll is returned to the Ark.
Continue with Kaddish Titkabal, page 145.

הושיעה...העולם / Redeem...time (Psalm 28:9).
ויהיו...עוד / And...else (I Kings 8:59-60).

NOTE. An alphabetical acrostic occurs in both the Hebrew and English of למען אמיתך / for the sake of your All-embracing truth, signifying the all-encompassing divine presence. R.S.

It is customary to form a procession for the Hoshanot. The Torah scrolls lead the procession, followed by those carrying lulav *and* etrog, *with others bringing up the rear.*
On Hoshanah Rabah, which is the seventh day of Sukkot, recite the following. A procession circles the room a total of seven times.

For the sake of your All-embracing truth,
for the sake of your Binding covenant,
for the sake of your Greatness and your beauty,
for the sake of your Divine decree,
for the sake of your Heavenly splendor,
for the sake of your Wise assembly,
for the sake of your Sign and remembrance,
for the sake of your Heavenly love,
for the sake of your Timeless good,
for the sake of your Indivisibility,
for the sake of your Consoling glory,
for the sake of your Learning's light,
for the sake of your Majestic sovereignty,
for the sake of your Name's victory,
for the sake of your Sublime mystery,
for the sake of your Omnipotence,
for the sake of your Praise eternal,
for the sake of your Complete and utter holiness,
for the sake of your Supernal justice,
for the sake of your Redeeming and abundant love,
for the sake of your Sheḥinah's presence,
save us, please,
for the sake of your Thunderous praises,
save us please!

It is customary to form a procession for the Hoshanot. The Torah scrolls lead the procession, followed by those carrying lulav *and* etrog, *with others bringing up the rear.*
On Hoshanah Rabah, which is the seventh day of Sukkot, recite the following. A procession circles the room a total of seven times.

הוֹשַׁע נָא: לְמַ֫עַן אֲמִתָּךְ: לְמַ֫עַן בְּרִיתָךְ: לְמַ֫עַן גָּדְלָךְ וְתִפְאַרְתָּךְ:
לְמַ֫עַן דָּתָךְ: לְמַ֫עַן הוֹדָךְ: לְמַ֫עַן וְעוּדָךְ: לְמַ֫עַן זִכְרָךְ: לְמַ֫עַן חַסְדָּךְ:
לְמַ֫עַן טוּבָךְ: לְמַ֫עַן יִחוּדָךְ: לְמַ֫עַן כְּבוֹדָךְ: לְמַ֫עַן לִמּוּדָךְ: לְמַ֫עַן
מַלְכוּתָךְ: לְמַ֫עַן נִצְחָךְ: לְמַ֫עַן סוֹדָךְ: לְמַ֫עַן עֻזָּךְ: לְמַ֫עַן פְּאֵרָךְ: לְמַ֫עַן
צִדְקָתָךְ: לְמַ֫עַן קְדֻשָּׁתָךְ: לְמַ֫עַן רַחֲמֶ֫יךָ הָרַבִּים: לְמַ֫עַן שְׁכִינָתָךְ: הוֹשַׁע
נָא: לְמַ֫עַן תְּהִלָּתָךְ: הוֹשַׁע נָא: ←

NOTE. Hosha na! is a contraction of two Hebrew words meaning "Save, please." This exclamation punctuates the Hoshanot, the prayers for divine help recited on the seventh day of Sukkot, known as Hoshanah Rabah, "the Great Hosha na." The derived English word "hosanna" means an exclamation of praise for God, but the Hebrew term is more plaintive and beseeching in keeping with the solemnity of a holiday that traditionally marks an end to the period of divine judgment that began with Rosh Hashanah.

J.R.

Appoint us for a good name and for praise,
return to us our pledge and our inheritance,
and raise us ever upward in your service.
Plant us firmly like a tree beside a spring,
and save us from all harm and from all sickness,
and surround us with a crown of perfect love,
and lead us beside tranquil waters, please.
Fill us with your wisdom and intelligence,
and clothe us in the garb of strength and greatness.
Crown us with the crown of your perfection,
and keep us on a straight and level path,
and set us firmly in the ways of honesty.
Endow us with your mercy and compassion,
and save us with your great and mighty hand.
Exalt us with the splendor of your praise,
and bring us to the destined End of Days.
Glorify us with salvation and with joy,
and make us strong with rest and with deliverance.
Revive us with your rebuilt City, as of old,
and let us be remembered in the joy of times to come.
  Hosha na!
May the God of Jacob make us powerful and strong.
  Hosha na!

הוֹשַׁע נָא תִּתְּנֵנוּ לְשֵׁם וְלִתְהִלָּה: תְּשִׁיבֵנוּ אֶל־הַחֶבֶל וְאֶל־הַנַּחֲלָה: תְּרוֹמְמֵנוּ לְמַעְלָה לְמָעְלָה: תַּצִּיבֵנוּ כְּעֵץ עַל פַּלְגֵי מַיִם שְׁתוּלָה: תִּפְדֵּנוּ מִכָּל־נֶגַע וּמַחֲלָה: תְּעַטְּרֵנוּ בְּאַהֲבָה כְלוּלָה: תְּנַהֲלֵנוּ עַל־מֵי מְנוּחוֹת סֶלָה: תְּמַלְּאֵנוּ חָכְמָה וְשִׂכְלָה: תַּלְבִּישֵׁנוּ עֹז וּגְדֻלָּה: תַּכְתִּירֵנוּ בְּכֶתֶר כְּלוּלָה: תְּיַשְּׁרֵנוּ בְּאֹרַח סְלוּלָה: תִּטָּעֵנוּ בְּיֹשֶׁר מְסִלָּה: תְּחָנֵּנוּ בְּרַחֲמִים וּבְחֶמְלָה: תּוֹשִׁיעֵנוּ בְּיָדְךָ הַגְּדוֹלָה: תְּהַדְּרֵנוּ בְּזִיו הֲמֻלָּה: תַּגִּיעֵנוּ לְקֵץ הַגְּאֻלָּה: תְּאַדְּרֵנוּ בְּיֶשַׁע וְגִילָה: תְּאַמְּצֵנוּ בְּרֶוַח וְהַצָּלָה: תְּלַבְּבֵנוּ בְּבִנְיַן עִירְךָ כְּבַתְּחִלָּה: תַּזְכִּירֵנוּ בְּשָׂשׂוֹן וְגִילָה: הוֹשַׁע נָא: תְּחַזְּקֵנוּ אֱלֹהֵי יַעֲקֹב סֶלָה: הוֹשַׁע נָא: ←

A people guarded like the pupil of an eye, studying a doctrine that restores the soul, learning in depth the laws of the Shabbat, clinging to the Beloved One upon Shabbat, meditating on the Torah on Shabbat, praising its Creator on Shabbat, "remembering" and "keeping" Shabbat holiness, attaining joy and inspiration on Shabbat, tasting pleasure on Shabbat, forgetting suffering and sorrow on Shabbat, proclaiming honor and delight upon Shabbat, changing clothing and array upon Shabbat, preparing food and drink for the Shabbat, kindling light with blessing on Shabbat, feasting with joyous feasts upon Shabbat, breaking two loaves of bread upon Shabbat, opening the mouth with songs upon Shabbat, rejoicing and being happy with Shabbat delight, sanctifying the holiness of the day upon Shabbat, finding relief and rest upon Shabbat, tranquility and peace in Shabbat rest. May you, [Oh God,] cause this people to inherit "a day that is complete Shabbat!" ↩

אֹם נְצוּרָה כְּבָבַת: בּוֹנֶנֶת בְּדָת נֶפֶשׁ מְשִׁיבַת: גּוֹמֶרֶת הִלְכוֹת שַׁבָּת: דְּבֵקָה בְּדוֹדָהּ בַּשַּׁבָּת: הוֹגָה בַּתּוֹרָה בַּשַּׁבָּת: וּמְשַׁבַּחַת לְבוֹרְאָהּ בַּשַּׁבָּת: זוֹכֶרֶת וְשׁוֹמֶרֶת קְדֻשַּׁת שַׁבָּת: חֶדְוָה וָנֶפֶשׁ מַשִּׂיגָה בַּשַּׁבָּת: טוֹעֶמֶת נְעָמֵי שַׁבָּת: יָגוֹן וְצַעַר שׁוֹכַחַת בַּשַּׁבָּת: כָּבוֹד וָעֹנֶג קוֹרְאָה לַשַּׁבָּת: לְבוּשׁ וּכְסוּת מְחַלֶּפֶת בַּשַּׁבָּת: מַאֲכָל וּמִשְׁתֶּה מְכִינָה לַשַּׁבָּת: נֵר מַדְלִיקָה בִּבְרָכָה בַּשַּׁבָּת: סְעוּדוֹת שִׂמְחָה סוֹעֶדֶת בַּשַּׁבָּת: עַל שְׁתֵּי כִכָּרוֹת בּוֹצַעַת בַּשַּׁבָּת: פּוֹצָה פֶּה בִּזְמִירוֹת בַּשַּׁבָּת: צוֹהֶלֶת וּשְׂמֵחָה בְּעֹנֶג שַׁבָּת: קִדּוּשׁ הַיּוֹם מְקַדֶּשֶׁת בַּשַּׁבָּת: רְוָחָה וַהֲנָחָה מוֹצֵאת בַּשַּׁבָּת: שַׁאֲנַנָּה וּשְׁלֵוָה בִּמְנוּחַת שַׁבָּת: תַּנְחִילֶנָּה יוֹם שֶׁכֻּלּוֹ שַׁבָּת: ←

The Lulav and Etrog are put down, and each person takes a bunch of willow.

A voice proclaims, proclaims and says:
Your promise of redemption comes to fulfillment.
The voice of my beloved, behold, it comes!

Yes, it proclaims, and says:
She is in labor and gives birth! Who is this?
Who has heard of a thing such as this?

Yes, it proclaims, and says:
A blameless one has wrought all these things.
Who has seen such things?

Yes, it proclaims, and says:
Turn toward me, and be redeemed!
Today, if only you will listen to my voice!

Yes, it proclaims, and says:

Reader and congregation three times:

A voice proclaims, proclaims and says...

The willow branches are struck at least three times; some continue until all the leaves fall off.

Redeem your people, bless your inheritance; and nurture them and carry them throughout all time. And may these words with which I supplicate before The Fount of Life be near to The Eternal One, our God, by day and night, working justice for God's servant, and justice for the people Israel; a timely prayer—that all the peoples of the earth may know that The Eternal One is God; there is none else!

Continue with returning of the Torah to the Ark, page 164.

The Lulav and Etrog are put down, and each person takes a bunch of willow.

קוֹל מְבַשֵּׂר מְבַשֵּׂר וְאוֹמֵר:

Kol mevaser mevaser ve'omer.

אֹמֶן יֶשְׁעֲךָ בָּא קוֹל דוֹדִי הִנֵּה זֶה בָּא:

Omen yeshaha ba kol dodi hiney zeh ba.

מְבַשֵּׂר וְאוֹמֵר:

mevaser ve'omer

חָלָה וְיָלְדָה מִי זֹאת מִי־שָׁמַע כָּזֹאת:

מְבַשֵּׂר וְאוֹמֵר:

mevaser ve'omer

טָהוֹר פָּעַל כָּל־אֵלֶּה מִי רָאָה כָּאֵלֶּה:

מְבַשֵּׂר וְאוֹמֵר:

mevaser ve'omer

פְּנוּ־אֵלַי וְהִוָּשְׁעוּ הַיּוֹם אִם־בְּקוֹלִי תִשְׁמָעוּ:

מְבַשֵּׂר וְאוֹמֵר:

mevaser ve'omer

Reader and Congregation three times:

קוֹל מְבַשֵּׂר מְבַשֵּׂר וְאוֹמֵר:

Kol mevaser mevaser ve'omer.

The willow branches are struck at least three times; some continue until all the leaves fall off.

הוֹשִׁיעָה אֶת־עַמֶּךָ וּבָרֵךְ אֶת־נַחֲלָתֶךָ וּרְעֵם וְנַשְּׂאֵם עַד־הָעוֹלָם: וְיִהְיוּ
דְבָרַי אֵלֶּה אֲשֶׁר הִתְחַנַּנְתִּי לִפְנֵי יהוה קְרֹבִים אֶל־יהוה אֱלֹהֵינוּ יוֹמָם
וָלָיְלָה לַעֲשׂוֹת מִשְׁפַּט עַבְדּוֹ וּמִשְׁפַּט עַמּוֹ יִשְׂרָאֵל דְּבַר־יוֹם בְּיוֹמוֹ:
לְמַעַן דַּעַת כָּל־עַמֵּי הָאָרֶץ כִּי יהוה הוּא הָאֱלֹהִים אֵין עוֹד:

Continue with returning of the Torah to the Ark, page 165.

סֵדֶר סְפִירַת הָעֹמֶר

ORDER OF COUNTING THE OMER

From the eve of the Second Day of Pesaḥ through the evening before Shavuot, the days are counted as follows after the evening Amidah:

MEDITATION

On the second day of Pesaḥ in ancient times, our ancestors brought the first sheaf of barley reaped that season as an offering to God. From that day, they began counting the days and weeks to Shavuot, when they would celebrate the beginning of the wheat harvest by offering the loaves made of the first wheat. Even after the Temple was destroyed and offerings were no longer brought, they continued to count the days from Pesaḥ to Shavuot in accordance with the biblical injunction.

וּסְפַרְתֶּם לָכֶם מִמָּחֳרַת הַשַּׁבָּת מִיּוֹם הֲבִיאֲכֶם אֶת־עֹמֶר הַתְּנוּפָה שֶׁבַע שַׁבָּתוֹת תְּמִימֹת תִּהְיֶינָה: עַד מִמָּחֳרַת הַשַּׁבָּת הַשְּׁבִיעִית תִּסְפְּרוּ חֲמִשִּׁים יוֹם וְהִקְרַבְתֶּם מִנְחָה חֲדָשָׁה לַיהוָה:

And you shall count from the day after the Sabbath, from the day that you brought the sheaf of the wave offering; seven full weeks shall they be; continuing fifty days to the day after the seventh Sabbath; then you shall present a cereal offering of new grain to the ETERNAL.

Leviticus 23:15-17

Thus our ancestors linked Pesaḥ and Shavuot as occasions for thanking God for the fruits of the field. So do we thank God for the renewal of life which all nature proclaims at this season.

However, as Pesaḥ and Shavuot acquired historical significance, their linkage through the counting of the intervening days took on new meaning. It connected the idea of freedom, associated with Pesaḥ, with the idea of Torah, associated with Shavuot. It thus proclaimed that:

אֵין לְךָ בֶּן חוֹרִין אֶלָּא מִי שֶׁעוֹסֵק בְּתַלְמוּד תּוֹרָה:

Only one who engages in the study of Torah is truly free.

Before counting the Omer say:

בָּרוּךְ אַתָּה יהוה אֱלֹהֵינוּ מֶלֶךְ הָעוֹלָם אֲשֶׁר קִדְּשָׁנוּ בְּמִצְוֹתָיו וְצִוָּנוּ עַל סְפִירַת הָעֹמֶר:

Baruḥ atah adonay eloheynu meleḥ ha'olam asher kideshanu bemitzvotav vetzivanu al sefirat ha'omer.

Blessed are you, ETERNAL, our God, the sovereign of all worlds, who has made us holy with your mitzvot, and commanded us concerning the counting of the Omer.

אין...תורה / Only...free (Pirkey Avot 6:2).

1. This is the first day of the Omer.

2. This is the second day of the Omer.

3. This is the third day of the Omer.

4. This is the fourth day of the Omer.

5. This is the fifth day of the Omer.

6. This is the sixth day of the Omer.

7. This is the seventh day, making one week of the Omer.

8. This is the eighth day, making one week and one day of the Omer.

9. This is the ninth day, making one week and two days of the Omer.

10. This is the tenth day, making one week and three days of the Omer.

11. This is the eleventh day, making one week and four days of the Omer.

12. This is the twelfth day, making one week and five days of the Omer.

13. This is the thirteenth day, making one week and six days of the Omer.

14. This is the fourteenth day, making two weeks of the Omer.

15. This is the fifteenth day, making two weeks and one day of the Omer.

16. This is the sixteenth day, making two weeks and two days of the Omer.

17. This is the seventeenth day, making two weeks and three days of the Omer.

1. הַיּוֹם יוֹם אֶחָד לָעֹֽמֶר:
2. הַיּוֹם שְׁנֵי יָמִים לָעֹֽמֶר:
3. הַיּוֹם שְׁלֹשָׁה יָמִים לָעֹֽמֶר:
4. הַיּוֹם אַרְבָּעָה יָמִים לָעֹֽמֶר:
5. הַיּוֹם חֲמִשָּׁה יָמִים לָעֹֽמֶר:
6. הַיּוֹם שִׁשָּׁה יָמִים לָעֹֽמֶר:
7. הַיּוֹם שִׁבְעָה יָמִים שֶׁהֵם שָׁבֽוּעַ אֶחָד לָעֹֽמֶר:
8. הַיּוֹם שְׁמוֹנָה יָמִים שֶׁהֵם שָׁבֽוּעַ אֶחָד וְיוֹם אֶחָד לָעֹֽמֶר:
9. הַיּוֹם תִּשְׁעָה יָמִים שֶׁהֵם שָׁבֽוּעַ אֶחָד וּשְׁנֵי יָמִים לָעֹֽמֶר:
10. הַיּוֹם עֲשָׂרָה יָמִים שֶׁהֵם שָׁבֽוּעַ אֶחָד וּשְׁלֹשָׁה יָמִים לָעֹֽמֶר:
11. הַיּוֹם אַחַד־עָשָׂר יוֹם שֶׁהֵם שָׁבֽוּעַ אֶחָד וְאַרְבָּעָה יָמִים לָעֹֽמֶר:
12. הַיּוֹם שְׁנֵים־עָשָׂר יוֹם שֶׁהֵם שָׁבֽוּעַ אֶחָד וַחֲמִשָּׁה יָמִים לָעֹֽמֶר:
13. הַיּוֹם שְׁלֹשָׁה־עָשָׂר יוֹם שֶׁהֵם שָׁבֽוּעַ אֶחָד וְשִׁשָּׁה יָמִים לָעֹֽמֶר:
14. הַיּוֹם אַרְבָּעָה־עָשָׂר יוֹם שֶׁהֵם שְׁנֵי שָׁבוּעוֹת לָעֹֽמֶר:
15. הַיּוֹם חֲמִשָּׁה־עָשָׂר יוֹם שֶׁהֵם שְׁנֵי שָׁבוּעוֹת וְיוֹם אֶחָד לָעֹֽמֶר:
16. הַיּוֹם שִׁשָּׁה־עָשָׂר יוֹם שֶׁהֵם שְׁנֵי שָׁבוּעוֹת וּשְׁנֵי יָמִים לָעֹֽמֶר:
17. הַיּוֹם שִׁבְעָה־עָשָׂר יוֹם שֶׁהֵם שְׁנֵי שָׁבוּעוֹת וּשְׁלֹשָׁה יָמִים לָעֹֽמֶר:

18. This is the eighteenth day, making two weeks and four days of the Omer.

19. This is the nineteenth day, making two weeks and five days of the Omer.

20. This is the twentieth day, making two weeks and six days of the Omer.

21. This is the twenty-first day, making three weeks of the Omer.

22. This is the twenty-second day, making three weeks and one day of the Omer.

23. This is the twenty-third day, making three weeks and two days of the Omer.

24. This is the twenty-fourth day, making three weeks and three days of the Omer.

25. This is the twenty-fifth day, making three weeks and four days of the Omer.

26. This is the twenty-sixth day, making three weeks and five days of the Omer.

27. This is the twenty-seventh day, making three weeks and six days of the Omer.

28. This is the twenty-eighth day, making four weeks of the Omer.

29. This is the twenty-ninth day, making four weeks and one day of the Omer.

18. הַיּוֹם שְׁמוֹנָה־עָשָׂר יוֹם שֶׁהֵם שְׁנֵי שָׁבוּעוֹת וְאַרְבָּעָה יָמִים לָעֹֽמֶר׃

19. הַיּוֹם תִּשְׁעָה־עָשָׂר יוֹם שֶׁהֵם שְׁנֵי שָׁבוּעוֹת וַחֲמִשָּׁה יָמִים לָעֹֽמֶר׃

20. הַיּוֹם עֶשְׂרִים יוֹם שֶׁהֵם שְׁנֵי שָׁבוּעוֹת וְשִׁשָּׁה יָמִים לָעֹֽמֶר׃

21. הַיּוֹם אֶחָד וְעֶשְׂרִים יוֹם שֶׁהֵם שְׁלשָׁה שָׁבוּעוֹת לָעֹֽמֶר׃

22. הַיּוֹם שְׁנַֽיִם וְעֶשְׂרִים יוֹם שֶׁהֵם שְׁלשָׁה שָׁבוּעוֹת וְיוֹם אֶחָד לָעֹֽמֶר׃

23. הַיּוֹם שְׁלשָׁה וְעֶשְׂרִים יוֹם שֶׁהֵם שְׁלשָׁה שָׁבוּעוֹת וּשְׁנֵי יָמִים לָעֹֽמֶר׃

24. הַיּוֹם אַרְבָּעָה וְעֶשְׂרִים יוֹם שֶׁהֵם שְׁלשָׁה שָׁבוּעוֹת וּשְׁלשָׁה יָמִים לָעֹֽמֶר׃

25. הַיּוֹם חֲמִשָּׁה וְעֶשְׂרִים יוֹם שֶׁהֵם שְׁלשָׁה שָׁבוּעוֹת וְאַרְבָּעָה יָמִים לָעֹֽמֶר׃

26. הַיּוֹם שִׁשָּׁה וְעֶשְׂרִים יוֹם שֶׁהֵם שְׁלשָׁה שָׁבוּעוֹת וַחֲמִשָּׁה יָמִים לָעֹֽמֶר׃

27. הַיּוֹם שִׁבְעָה וְעֶשְׂרִים יוֹם שֶׁהֵם שְׁלשָׁה שָׁבוּעוֹת וְשִׁשָּׁה יָמִים לָעֹֽמֶר׃

28. הַיּוֹם שְׁמוֹנָה וְעֶשְׂרִים יוֹם שֶׁהֵם אַרְבָּעָה שָׁבוּעוֹת לָעֹֽמֶר׃

29. הַיּוֹם תִּשְׁעָה וְעֶשְׂרִים יוֹם שֶׁהֵם אַרְבָּעָה שָׁבוּעוֹת וְיוֹם אֶחָד לָעֹֽמֶר׃

30. This is the thirtieth day, making four weeks and two days of the Omer.

31. This is the thirty-first day, making four weeks and three days of the Omer.

32. This is the thirty-second day, making four weeks and four days of the Omer.

33. This is the thirty-third day, making four weeks and five days of the Omer.

34. This is the thirty-fourth day, making four weeks and six days of the Omer.

35. This is the thirty-fifth day, making five weeks of the Omer.

36. This is the thirty-sixth day, making five weeks and one day of the Omer.

37. This is the thirty-seventh day, making five weeks and two days of the Omer.

38. This is the thirty-eighth day, making five weeks and three days of the Omer.

39. This is the thirty-ninth day, making five weeks and four days of the Omer.

40. This is the fortieth day, making five weeks and five days of the Omer.

41. This is the forty-first day, making five weeks and six days of the Omer.

30. הַיּוֹם שְׁלֹשִׁים יוֹם שֶׁהֵם אַרְבָּעָה שָׁבוּעוֹת וּשְׁנֵי יָמִים לָעֽוֹמֶר:

31. הַיּוֹם אֶחָד וּשְׁלֹשִׁים יוֹם שֶׁהֵם אַרְבָּעָה שָׁבוּעוֹת וּשְׁלֹשָׁה יָמִים לָעֽוֹמֶר:

32. הַיּוֹם שְׁנַֽיִם וּשְׁלֹשִׁים יוֹם שֶׁהֵם אַרְבָּעָה שָׁבוּעוֹת וְאַרְבָּעָה יָמִים לָעֽוֹמֶר:

33. הַיּוֹם שְׁלֹשָׁה וּשְׁלֹשִׁים יוֹם שֶׁהֵם אַרְבָּעָה שָׁבוּעוֹת וַחֲמִשָּׁה יָמִים לָעֽוֹמֶר:

34. הַיּוֹם אַרְבָּעָה וּשְׁלֹשִׁים יוֹם שֶׁהֵם אַרְבָּעָה שָׁבוּעוֹת וְשִׁשָּׁה יָמִים לָעֽוֹמֶר:

35. הַיּוֹם חֲמִשָּׁה וּשְׁלֹשִׁים יוֹם שֶׁהֵם חֲמִשָּׁה שָׁבוּעוֹת לָעֽוֹמֶר:

36. הַיּוֹם שִׁשָּׁה וּשְׁלֹשִׁים יוֹם שֶׁהֵם חֲמִשָּׁה שָׁבוּעוֹת וְיוֹם אֶחָד לָעֽוֹמֶר:

37. הַיּוֹם שִׁבְעָה וּשְׁלֹשִׁים יוֹם שֶׁהֵם חֲמִשָּׁה שָׁבוּעוֹת וּשְׁנֵי יָמִים לָעֽוֹמֶר:

38. הַיּוֹם שְׁמוֹנָה וּשְׁלֹשִׁים יוֹם שֶׁהֵם חֲמִשָּׁה שָׁבוּעוֹת וּשְׁלֹשָׁה יָמִים לָעֽוֹמֶר:

39. הַיּוֹם תִּשְׁעָה וּשְׁלֹשִׁים יוֹם שֶׁהֵם חֲמִשָּׁה שָׁבוּעוֹת וְאַרְבָּעָה יָמִים לָעֽוֹמֶר:

40. הַיּוֹם אַרְבָּעִים יוֹם שֶׁהֵם חֲמִשָּׁה שָׁבוּעוֹת וַחֲמִשָּׁה יָמִים לָעֽוֹמֶר:

41. הַיּוֹם אֶחָד וְאַרְבָּעִים יוֹם שֶׁהֵם חֲמִשָּׁה שָׁבוּעוֹת וְשִׁשָּׁה יָמִים לָעֽוֹמֶר:

42. This is the forty-second day, making six weeks of the Omer.

43. This is the forty-third day, making six weeks and one day of the Omer.

44. This is the forty-fourth day, making six weeks and two days of the Omer.

45. This is the forty-fifth day, making six weeks and three days of the Omer.

46. This is the forty-sixth day, making six weeks and four days of the Omer.

47. This is the forty-seventh day, making six weeks and five days of the Omer.

48. This is the forty-eighth day, making six weeks and six days of the Omer.

49. This is the forty-ninth day, making seven weeks of the Omer.

Continue on page 326.

42. הַיּוֹם שְׁנַיִם וְאַרְבָּעִים יוֹם שֶׁהֵם שִׁשָּׁה שָׁבוּעוֹת לָעֹמֶר:

43. הַיּוֹם שְׁלֹשָׁה וְאַרְבָּעִים יוֹם שֶׁהֵם שִׁשָּׁה שָׁבוּעוֹת וְיוֹם אֶחָד לָעֹמֶר:

44. הַיּוֹם אַרְבָּעָה וְאַרְבָּעִים יוֹם שֶׁהֵם שִׁשָּׁה שָׁבוּעוֹת וּשְׁנֵי יָמִים לָעֹמֶר:

45. הַיּוֹם חֲמִשָּׁה וְאַרְבָּעִים יוֹם שֶׁהֵם שִׁשָּׁה שָׁבוּעוֹת וּשְׁלֹשָׁה יָמִים לָעֹמֶר:

46. הַיּוֹם שִׁשָּׁה וְאַרְבָּעִים יוֹם שֶׁהֵם שִׁשָּׁה שָׁבוּעוֹת וְאַרְבָּעָה יָמִים לָעֹמֶר:

47. הַיּוֹם שִׁבְעָה וְאַרְבָּעִים יוֹם שֶׁהֵם שִׁשָּׁה שָׁבוּעוֹת וַחֲמִשָּׁה יָמִים לָעֹמֶר:

48. הַיּוֹם שְׁמוֹנָה וְאַרְבָּעִים יוֹם שֶׁהֵם שִׁשָּׁה שָׁבוּעוֹת וְשִׁשָּׁה יָמִים לָעֹמֶר:

49. הַיּוֹם תִּשְׁעָה וְאַרְבָּעִים יוֹם שֶׁהֵם שִׁבְעָה שָׁבוּעוֹת לָעֹמֶר:

Continue on page 327.

TAḤANUN / SUPPLICATION

O, guardian of Israel,
preserve the remnant of the people Israel,
and let Israel never be destroyed,
they who utter: "Hear, O Israel..."

O, guardian of a unique nation,
preserve the remnant of a unique people,
and let this unique nation never be destroyed,
they who unify your name by saying: "THE ETERNAL is our God,
THE ETERNAL ONE alone!"

O, guardian of a holy nation,
preserve the remnant of a holy people,
and let this holy people never be destroyed,
they who, thrice daily, utter "Holy, holy, holy..."
to the Holy One.

You who take pleasure in compassion and are satisfied with supplications,
take pleasure and satisfaction in this humble generation, for they have no one to help them.
Our creator, our sovereign, be gracious with us and respond to us, for we have no deeds to justify us;
deal with us in righteousness and love, and save us now! ⮐

תַּחֲנוּן

שׁוֹמֵר יִשְׂרָאֵל שְׁמוֹר שְׁאֵרִית יִשְׂרָאֵל וְאַל יֹאבַד יִשְׂרָאֵל הָאוֹמְרִים שְׁמַע יִשְׂרָאֵל:
שׁוֹמֵר גּוֹי אֶחָד שְׁמוֹר שְׁאֵרִית עַם אֶחָד וְאַל יֹאבַד גּוֹי אֶחָד הַמְיַחֲדִים שִׁמְךָ יהוה אֱלֹהֵינוּ יהוה אֶחָד:
שׁוֹמֵר גּוֹי קָדוֹשׁ שְׁמוֹר שְׁאֵרִית עַם קָדוֹשׁ וְאַל יֹאבַד גּוֹי קָדוֹשׁ הַמְשַׁלְּשִׁים בְּשָׁלֹשׁ קְדֻשּׁוֹת לְקָדוֹשׁ:
מִתְרַצֶּה בְּרַחֲמִים וּמִתְפַּיֵּס בְּתַחֲנוּנִים הִתְרַצֵּה וְהִתְפַּיֵּס לְדוֹר עָנִי כִּי אֵין עוֹזֵר: אָבִינוּ מַלְכֵּנוּ חָנֵּנוּ וַעֲנֵנוּ כִּי אֵין בָּנוּ מַעֲשִׂים עֲשֵׂה עִמָּנוּ צְדָקָה וָחֶסֶד וְהוֹשִׁיעֵנוּ: ←

Shomer yisra'el shemor she'eyrit yisra'el ve'al yovad yisra'el ha'omrim shema yisra'el.
Shomer goy eḥad shemor she'erit am eḥad ve'al yovad goy eḥad hameyaḥadim shimeḥa adonay eloheynu adonay eḥad.
Shomer goy kadosh shemor she'erit am kadosh ve'al yovad goy kadosh hameshaleshim beshalosh kedushat lekadosh.

NOTE. It is customary to recite *Taḥanun* sitting with head bowed and resting on one's arm. The head is lifted for *va'anaḥnu lo neyda*, page 427.

J.B.

COMMENTARY. *Taḥanun*, or supplication, is a continuation and intensification of the weekday *Amidah*'s theme of calling on the mercy and compassion of God. The mood of this prayer is somber and intense, seeking acceptance of us as we are, in all our imperfections. This explains the omission of *Taḥanun* on sad occasions, in order not to add to the mood, as well as on holidays.

J.B.

And as for us, we know not what will happen,
but our eyes are turned toward you.
Remember your compassion and your love, ETERNAL ONE,
they are as ancient as the world.
May your lovingkindness be extended over us,
as we have ever placed our hope in you.
And do not hold against us earlier misdeeds,
but let your mercies rush to meet us,
for we sit in desolation.
Be gracious with us and respond to us,
for we are wearied from much plundering.
When angry, do remember to be merciful,
for you know our inner nature.
Do remember us, though we are made of dust,
and save us, and forgive us our wrongdoings,
for the sake of your great name.

Continue with Kaddish Titkabal, page 144 for Shaḥarit or page 248 for Minḥah.

וַאֲנַחְנוּ לֹא נֵדַע מַה נַּעֲשֶׂה כִּי עָלֶיךָ עֵינֵינוּ: זְכֹר רַחֲמֶיךָ יהוה
וַחֲסָדֶיךָ כִּי מֵעוֹלָם הֵמָּה: יְהִי חַסְדְּךָ יהוה עָלֵינוּ כַּאֲשֶׁר יִחַלְנוּ לָךְ:
אַל תִּזְכָּר־לָנוּ עֲוֹנוֹת רִאשׁוֹנִים מַהֵר יְקַדְּמוּנוּ רַחֲמֶיךָ כִּי דַלּוֹנוּ מְאֹד:
חָנֵּנוּ יהוה חָנֵּנוּ כִּי רַב שָׂבַעְנוּ בוּז: בְּרֹגֶז רַחֵם תִּזְכּוֹר: כִּי הוּא יָדַע
יִצְרֵנוּ זָכוּר כִּי עָפָר אֲנָחְנוּ: * עָזְרֵנוּ אֱלֹהֵי יִשְׁעֵנוּ עַל דְּבַר כְּבוֹד
שְׁמֶךָ וְהַצִּילֵנוּ וְכַפֵּר עַל חַטֹּאתֵינוּ לְמַעַן שְׁמֶךָ:

Continue with Kaddish Titkabal, page 145 for Shaḥarit or page 248 for Minḥah.

To be read by the mourner(s) on the morning of the conclusion of Shivah.

As Jewish tradition prescribes *shivah*, a period of intense mourning, so too does it prescribe a moment when *shivah* ends. Today, we walk out the door of the *shivah* house back into engagement with daily concerns. Mourning is far from over, but today we take important steps back into life. At this moment, we ask:

יהוה עֹז לְעַמּוֹ יִתֵּן יהוה יְבָרֵךְ אֶת־עַמּוֹ בַשָּׁלוֹם׃

Adonay oz le'amo yiten, adonay yivareḥ et amo vashalom.

May You, REDEEMING ONE, give strength to your people. May You, ETERNAL ONE, bless your people with peace.

MERCIFUL ONE, grant healing, comfort, and strength to those who mourn the loss of __________ . May his/her memory be a source of blessing in their lives. May they find consolation and peace with each other and return to doing deeds that strengthen the bonds of the living. Amen.

יהוה עז...בשלום / May...peace! (Psalms 29:11).

יהוה נְחֵ֣נִי בְצִדְקָתֶ֣ךָ הַיְשַׁ֖ר לְפָנַ֣י דַּרְכֶּֽךָ׃

Adonay ne<u>h</u>eni vetzidka<u>te</u>ḥa hayeshar lefanay dar<u>ke</u>ḥa.

Guiding One, lead me in your righteousness, make your path straight before me.

It is customary to walk a short distance. Some people circle the block on which they live.

יהוה...דרכך / Guiding...me. (Psalms 5:9).

Jews traditionally observe *shivah*/mourning for a person in one of seven relationships – for a parent, a child, a sibling, or a spouse/partner. One may also undertake mourning for others. *Avelut*/mourning consists of four periods. The first, the period following the death but preceding the funeral, is technically not mourning. This is called *aninut*. The second period is *shivah*, the period of intense mourning that takes place during the week following the funeral. It is called *shivah*/seven because the traditional length of this period is seven days. The third period is *sheloshim*/thirty, which traditionally continues until the thirtieth day following the funeral. Most mourners choose to continue the process of actively mourning for the remainder of the eleven months that make up the "year" of mourning. Jews do not customarily mourn for longer than eleven months. Each year we recall those we have lost on the anniversary of the date of their death (usually the Hebrew calendar date). This is the *yahrtzeit*.

The restrictions on mourners vary through the course of the period of mourning. During *shivah*, traditionally a mourner remains indoors at home, and avoids most normal activities. It is customary to mark the end of *shivah* with a ritual for the conclusion of *shivah*, as presented here.

J.B.

READINGS

PRAYER

Teach me my God, a blessing, a prayer
On the mystery of a withered leaf
On ripened fruit so fair
On the freedom to see, to sense,
To breathe, to know, to hope, to despair.

Teach my lips a blessing, a hymn of praise
As each morning and night
You renew Your days,
Lest my days be as the one before
Lest routine set my ways.

...לַמְּדֵנִי, אֱלֹהַי, בָּרֵךְ וְהִתְפַּלֵּל
עַל סוֹד עָלֶה קָמֵל, עַל נֹגַהּ פְּרִי בָּשֵׁל,
עַל הַחֵרוּת הַזֹּאת: לִרְאוֹת, לָחוּשׁ, לִנְשֹׁם,
לָדַעַת, לְיַחֵל, לְהִכָּשֵׁל:

לַמֵּד אֶת שִׂפְתוֹתַי בְּרָכָה וְשִׁיר הַלֵּל
בְּהִתְחַדֵּשׁ זְמַנְּךָ עִם בֹּקֶר וְעִם לֵיל,
לְבַל יִהְיֶה יוֹמִי הַיּוֹם כִּתְמוֹל שִׁלְשׁוֹם,
לְבַל יִהְיֶה עָלַי יוֹמִי הֶרְגֵּל...

Lea Goldberg (translated by Pnina Peli)

Submit to God

Submit to God, uniquely conscious soul,
And rush to worship God in reverence.
Day and night turn toward your eternal source—
Why pursue vanity and emptiness?
Filled with life you resemble the living God
Who is invisible as you are unseen.
If your Creator be pure and flawless,
Know that you too are perfect and pure.
The Mighty One holds the heavens on one arm,
As you uphold the silent body.
My soul, present your songs to your Rock
Who has not placed your form in the dust.
My limbs, praise your Rock continuously
The one whose name every soul does praise.

שְׁחִי לָאֵל יְחִידָה הַחֲכָמָה
וְרוּצִי לַעֲבֹד אוֹתוֹ בְּאֵימָה:
לְעוֹלָמֵךְ פְּנִי לֵילֵךְ וְיוֹמֵךְ
וְלָמָּה תִרְדְּפִי הֶבֶל וְלָמָּה:
מְשׁוּלָה אַתְּ בְּחַיּוּתֵךְ לְאֵל חַי
אֲשֶׁר נֶעְלָם כְּמוֹ אַתְּ נַעֲלָמָה:
הֲלֹא אִם יוֹצְרֵךְ טָהוֹר וְנָקִי
דְּעִי כִּי כֵן טְהוֹרָה אַתְּ וְתַמָּה:
חֲסִין יִשָּׂא שְׁחָקִים עַל זְרוֹעוֹ
כְּמוֹ תִשְּׂאִי גְוִיָּה נֶאֱלָמָה:
זְמִירוֹת קַדְּמִי נַפְשִׁי לְצוּרֵךְ
אֲשֶׁר לֹא שָׂם דְּמוּתֵךְ בָּאֲדָמָה:
קְרָבַי בָּרֲכוּ תָמִיד לְצוּרְכֶם
אֲשֶׁר לְשְׁמוֹ תְּהַלֵּל כָּל נְשָׁמָה:

Solomon ibn Gabirol (translated by Reena Spicehandler)

NATURE

In Praise
GENESIS 1, 2

Hail the hand that scattered space with stars,
Wrapped whirling world in bright blue blanket, air,
Made worlds within worlds, elements in earth,
Souls within skins, every one a teeming universe,
Every tree a system of semantics, and pushed
Beyond probability to place consciousness
On this cooling crust of burning rock.

Oh praise that hand, mind, heart, soul, power or force
That so inclosed, separated, limited planets, trees, humans
Yet breaks all bounds and borders
To lavish on us light, love, life
This trembling glory.

Ruth Brin

My Thoughts Awaken Me to See You

My thoughts awaken me to see you;
They show me in my heart's eye your deeds;
They teach me to tell your wonders,
  "When I behold your heavens,
  The work your fingers made."

Around its course the disk of heaven walks,
A potter's wheel enwhirling the world;
It has no lips, and yet it tells your glory
To earth, unmoved within its orbit,
  Suspended in the void,
  By cords of your love stayed.

Thither the sun yearns, and there burns,
And of its light some to the moon lends.
While heaven's sphere is spread out like a tent,
With stars blooming on it, a garden,
  Proclaiming how profound
  The plans that you have laid.

יְעִירוּנִי שְׂעִפַּי לַחֲזוֹתֶךָ
וְיַרְאוּנִי בְּעֵין לֵב נוֹרְאוֹתֶיךָ
וְיוֹרוּנִי לְהַגִּיד נִפְלְאוֹתֶיךָ
כִּי אֶרְאֶה שָׁמֶיךָ מַעֲשֵׂה אֶצְבְּעוֹתֶיךָ׃
מִתְהַלֵּךְ עֲלֵי קַו חוּג שָׁמַיִם
וּמְסַבֵּב מְסִבָּתוֹ כְּאָבְנַיִם
וּמְסַפֵּר כְּבוֹדְךָ בְּלִי שְׂפָתַיִם
וְהָאָרֶץ עוֹמֶדֶת בִּנְתַּיִם
וְהִיא תְלוּיָה בְּחַבְלֵי אַהֲבָתֶךָ׃

שָׁם שׁוֹאֵף הַשֶּׁמֶשׁ וְזוֹרֵחַ
וְהוּא אוֹצֵל מֵאוֹרוֹ לְיָרֵחַ
וְהַגַּלְגַּל כְּמוֹ אֹהֶל מוֹתֵחַ
וְכוֹכָבִים עָלָיו כְּגַן פּוֹרֵחַ
לְהוֹדִיעַ עֹמֶק מַחְשְׁבוֹתֶיךָ׃

Moses ibn Ezra (translated by Raymond Sheindlin [Adapted])

SOCIAL ACTION

We Cannot Merely Pray

We cannot merely pray to you O God to end war;
For the world was made in such a way
That we must find our own path of peace
Within ourselves and with our neighbor.

We cannot merely pray to you O God to root out prejudice;
For we already have eyes
With which to see the good in all people
If we would only use them rightly.

We cannot merely pray to you O God to end starvation;
For we already have the resources
With which to feed the entire world
If we would only use them wisely.

We cannot merely pray to you O God to end despair;
For we already have the power
To clear away slums and to give hope
If we would only use our power justly.

We cannot merely pray to you O God to end disease:
For we already have great minds
With which to search out cures and healings
If we would only use them constructively.

Therefore we pray instead
For strength, determination, and will power,
To *do* instead of merely to pray
To *become* instead of merely to wish;
So that our world may be safe,
And so that our lives may be blessed.

Jack Riemer (Adapted)

TORAH STUDY

Somewhere out of time
In the mystery of time
Somewhere between memory and forgetfulness,
Dimly though
I remember how once I stood
at Your mountain trembling
Amid the fire and the thunder.
How I stood there, out of bondage
In a strange land and afraid.
And You loved me and You fed me
And I feasted on Your words.
And, yes, I can remember
How the thunder was my heart
And the fire was my soul.
God, I do remember.
The fire burns in me anew.
And here I am once more
A witness to that timeless moment.
Present now in the light of Your Torah
I am reborn.

Nancy Lee Gossels

All I Got Was Words

When I was a boy and fancy free,	
my folks had no fine clothes for me.	
All I got was words:	
Got tsu danken	(Thank God)
Zoln mir lebn un zeyn gezunt.	(We should live and be well)
When I was wont to travel far,	
They didn't provide for me a car.	
All I got was words:	
Gey gezunt	(Go in health)
Gey palmelekh	(Go slowly)
Hob a gliklekhe rayse.	(Have a good trip)
I wanted to increase my knowledge	
But they couldn't send me to college.	
All I got was words:	
Hob seykhel	(Have common sense)
Zey nisht keyn nar	(Don't be a fool)
Toyreh iz di beste skhoyre.	(Torah is the best merchandise)
The years have flown,	
the world has turned,	
things I've gotten, things I've learned,	
Yet I remember	
Zog dem emes	(Tell the truth)
Gib tsedukeh	(Give *tzedakah*)
Hob rakhmones	(Have compassion)
Zey a mensch!	(Be a mensch!)

Author Unknown

EXODUS

I Shall Sing to the Lord a New Song

I, Miriam, stand at the sea
and turn
to face the desert
stretching endless and
still.
My eyes are dazzled
The sky brilliant blue
Sunburnt sands unyielding white.
My hands turn to dove wings.
My arms
reach
for the sky
and I want to sing
the song rising inside me.
My mouth open
I stop.
Where are the words?
Where the melody?
In a moment of panic
My eyes go blind.
Can I take a step
Without knowing a
Destination?
Will I falter
Will I fall
Will the ground sink away from under me?

The song still unformed—
How can I sing? ↩

To take the first step—
To sing a new song—
Is to close one's eyes
and dive
into unknown waters.
For a moment knowing nothing risking all—
But then to discover

The waters are friendly
The ground is firm.
And the song—
the song rises again.
Out of my mouth
come words lifting the wind.
And I hear
for the first
the song
that has been in my heart
silent
unknown
even to me.

Ruth H. Sohn

ELUL AND TESHUVAH

God, help me through the days of *Elul* to prepare myself for the New Year with its promise of new life for my body and my soul.

Help me face questions I wish to avoid!
Help me accept truths which do not comfort!
I wish to journey to the light, but the path to it is hidden by all the promises I never kept, by the goodness I deserted.
May the words from the past show me the way of return.
I begin the road of repentance. Meet me, God, as I journey on it.

The gates of prayer are sometimes open and sometimes closed, but the gates of repentance are ever open. As the sea is always accessible, so is the hand of the Holy One always open to receive penitents.

אַף שַׁעֲרֵי תְפִלָּה פְּעָמִים פְּתוּחִים פְּעָמִים נְעוּלִים אֲבָל הַיָּם הַזֶּה לְעוֹלָם פָּתוּחַ: כָּךְ יָדוֹ שֶׁל הַקָּדוֹשׁ בָּרוּךְ הוּא לְעוֹלָם פְּתוּחָה לְקַבֵּל שָׁבִים.

Deuteronomy Rabbah

There is no righteous person on earth whose deeds are always good and who does not sin.

כִּי אָדָם אֵין צַדִּיק בָּאָרֶץ אֲשֶׁר יַעֲשֶׂה-טּוֹב וְלֹא יֶחֱטָא:

Ecclesiastes 7:20

NOTE. *Elul*, the month preceding Rosh Hashanah, is a time of contemplation and preparation for the days of awe that are about to come. It is a time of introspection, asking forgiveness of others, doing good deeds, and giving extra *tzedakah*. As a reminder of these tasks, the *Shofar* is sounded at the conclusion of every weekday morning service, and penitential prayers (*Seliḥot*) are recited. The readings given here are meant to aid in the personal reflections that are integral to the season. D.A.T. / J.B.

A king's son had gone astray from his father for a hundred days. His friends said to him: "Return to your father." He said: "I cannot." Then his father sent a message: "Return as far as you can, and I will come to you the rest of the way." So God says, "Return to Me, and I will return to you." (Malachi 3:7).

לבן מלך שהיה רחוק מאביו מהלך מאה יום: אמרו לו אוהביו חזור אצל אביך: אמר להם איני יכול: שלח אביו ואמר לו הלך מה שאתה יכול לפי כחך ואני בא אצלך בשאר הדרך: כך אמר להם הַקדוש ברוך הוא (מלאכי ג) שובו אלי ואשובה אליכם:

Pesikta Rabati

Since the ten days of *teshuvah* are days of good will, let everyone seek to do good deeds the first thing in the morning. Though everyone does *teshuvah* on Rosh Hashanah, that is *teshuvah* in thought alone. Active *teshuvah*, which is impossible on Rosh Hashanah, is needed. This need for active *teshuvah* is filled during those of the ten days of *teshuvah* that are weekdays.

הואיל ועשרת ימי תשובה הם ימי רצון יבקש מיד בבואו מבית הכנסת בשחרית לעשות מצוה במעשה: שבראש השנה הכל עושין תשובה אלא שהיא תשובה במחשבה: וצריכין תשובה במעשה שלא יתכן בראש השנה שהוא יום טוב: לפיכך מתקנין זה בעשרת ימי תשובה שהם ימי חול:

Abraham of Seḥotshov

The zodiac symbol for *Tishrey* is a balance—which is an intimation that all the deeds of humanity are weighed in the balance "to assess every person according to his ways, according to the fruit of her doings" (Jeremiah 17:10).

תשרי מזלו מאזנים: רמז שכל מעשיהם של בני אדם נשקלין במאזנים לתת לאיש כדרכיו וכפרי מעלליו:

Kad Hakemah

Do not say that one does *teshuvah* only for transgressions that involve an act such as whoring, theft, and robbery. Just as one must turn in *teshuvah* from these, so one must search out evil thoughts and turn from anger, hostility, jealousy, mockery, the pursuit of money or honor, and the greed for food—for all these one must turn in *teshuvah*. These iniquities are more serious than those that involve an act, for when one is addicted to them, it is difficult to stop doing them. And thus it is said (Isaiah 55:7): "Let the wicked man forsake his way, and the woman of iniquity her thoughts."

אל תאמר שאין תשובה אלא מעבירות שיש בהן מעשה כגון זנות וגזל וגניבה אלא כשם שצריך אדם לשוב מאלו כך הוא צריך לחפש בדעות רעות שיש לו ולשוב מן הכעס ומן האיבה ומן הקנאה ומן ההתול ומרדיפת הממון והכבוד ומרדיפת המאכלות וכיוצא בהן מן הכל צריך לחזור בתשובה: ואלו העוונות קשים מאותן שיש בהן מעשה שבזמן שהאדם נשקע באלו קשה הוא לפרוש מהם: וכן הוא אומר (ישעיה סה) יעזוב רשע דרכו ואיש און מחשבתיו:

Maimonides, Hilḥot Teshuvah

A tale is told of one who sat in study before the *tzaddik* Rabbi Mordecai of Nadvorna, and before Rosh Hashanah came to obtain permission to leave. The *tzaddik* said to him, "Why are you hurrying?" He replied, "I am leading the service, and I must look into the festival prayer book and put my prayers in order." Said the *tzaddik*, "The prayer book is the same as it was last year. It would be better for you to look into your deeds and put yourself in order."

מעשה באחד שישב אצל הרב הצדיק ר' מרדכי מנדבורנא: קודם ראש השנה בא ליטול רשות להפטר: אמר לו אותו צדיק מפני מה אתה ממהר: אמר לו שליח ציבור אני ואני צריך לעיין במחזור ולהסדיר תפילתי: אמר לו המחזור בעינו עומד כדאשתקד אלא מוטב שתעיין במעשיך ותסדר את עצמך:

Likutey Mahariaḥ

Everyone must prepare with *teshuvah*, prayer and charity for thirty days before we appear in judgment before God on Rosh Hashanah. We each give all our hearts to the service of God. The initials of the words, *Ani Ledodi Vedodi Li* (I am my beloved's and my beloved is mine—Song of Songs 6:3), when read consecutively, spell *Elul*. If Israel longs to turn in complete *teshuvah* to God, then God will accept them in *teshuvah*."

חייב כל אדם להכין עצמו ליום שיכנס למשפט לפני השם בראש השנה שלושים יום קודם בתשובה ותפילה וצדקה: ויתן כל לבו לעבודת השם: ודורשי רשומות אמרו אני לדודי ודודי לי (שיר השירים ג') ראשי תיבות אלול: אם ישראל משתוקקים לשוב בתשובה שלימה לאביהם שבשמים אף הוא יתברך תשוקתו עליהם ומקבלם בתשובה.

Mateh Moshe

Everyone is given free will. Anyone who wishes to turn to the good way and be righteous can do so. Or anyone who wishes to turn to the evil way and be wicked has that power too. Thus it is written in the Torah: "Behold, the man is become as one of us, to know good and evil (Genesis 3:22)." Humanity has become unique in the world. We are the only species that by our own knowledge and reason knows good and evil. We can do whatever we wish. No one can hinder us from doing good or evil.

רשות לכל אדם נתונה אם רצה להטות עצמו לדרך טובה ולהיות צדיק הרשות בידו: ואם רצה להטות עצמו לדרך רעה ולהיות רשע הרשות בידו: הוא שכתוב בתורה (בראשית ג) הן האדם היה כאחד ממנו לדעת טוב ורע: כלומר הן מין זה של אדם היה יחיד בעולם ואין מין שני דומה לו בזה הענין שיהא הוא מעצמו בדעתו ובמחשבתו יודע הטוב והרע ועושה כל מה שהוא חפץ: ואין מי שיעכב בידו מלעשות הטוב או הרע.

Maimonides, Hilḥot Teshuvah

The essence of repentance is bound up more with turning than with response. When response is direct and immediate, the process of repentance cannot continue because it has in a way arrived at its goal; whereas one of its essential components is an increase of tension, the tension of the ongoing experience and of yearning.

Adin Steinsaltz

A man had been wandering about in a forest for several days, not knowing which was the right way out. Suddenly he saw a man approaching him. His heart was filled with joy. "Now I shall certainly find out which is the right way," he thought to himself. When they neared one another, he asked the man, "Brother, tell me which is the right way. I have been wandering about in this forest for several days." The other said, "Brother, I do not know the way out either. For I too have been wandering about here for many, many days. But *this* I can tell you: do not take the way I have been taking, for that will lead you astray. And now let us look for a new way out together."

So it is with us. One thing I can tell you: we should not continue the way we have been going, for that way leads one astray. Now let us look for a new way."

אדם תעה כמה ימים ביער ולא היה יודע איזוהי דרך נכונה: פתאום ראה אדם אחר הולך לקראתו: באה שמחה גדולה בלבו: עתה בוודאי ידע הדרך הנכונה: כיון שפגעו זה בזה שאל אותו אחי אמור לי היכן הדרך הנכונה: זה כמה ימים אני תועה: אמר לו אחי אף אני איני יודע שאף אני תועה כאן כבר ימים הרבה: אלא אומר לך בדרך שהלכתי אני אל תלך אתה שבדרך זו תועים: ועכשיו נחפש דרך חדשה: כן אנחנו: דבר זה אני יכול לומר לכם שבדרך שהלכנו עד עכשיו אין לנו ללכת שבדרך זו תועים: אלא עכשיו נחפש דרך חדשה:

Rabbi Ḥayim of Zans

The Gift of Choice

I came into the world without being asked,
And when the time for dying comes
I shall not be consulted;

But between the boundaries of birth and death
Lies the dominion of Choice:

To be a doer or a dreamer,
To be a lifter or a leaner,
To speak out or remain silent,
To extend a hand in friendship
Or to look the other way;
To feel the sufferings of others
Or to be callous and insensitive.

These are the choices;
It is in the choosing
That my measure as a person
Is determined.

Gertrude Hildreth Housman

There was once a poor countrywoman who had many children. They were always begging for food, but she had none to give them. One day she found an egg. She called her children and said, "Children, children, we've nothing to worry about any more; I've found an egg. And being a provident woman, I'll not eat the egg, but shall ask my neighbor for permission to set it under her setting hen until a chick is hatched. For I am a provident woman! And we'll not eat the chick but will set her on eggs, and the eggs will hatch into chickens. And the chickens in their turn will hatch many eggs, and we'll have many chickens and many eggs. But I'm a provident woman! I'll not eat the chickens and not eat the eggs, but shall sell them and buy a heifer. And I'll not eat the heifer, but shall raise it to a cow, and not eat the cow until it calves. And I'll not eat it then,

either, and we'll have cows and calves. For I'm a provident woman! And I'll sell the cows and the calves and buy a field, and we'll have fields and cows and calves, and we won't need anything any more!" The countrywoman was speaking in this fashion and playing with the egg when it fell out of her hands and broke.

That is how we are. When the Holy Days arrive, people resolve to do *teshuvah*, thinking in their hearts, "I'll do this, and I'll do that." But the days slip by in mere deliberation, and thought doesn't lead to action.

רגיל היה רבינו לומר כפרית אחת עניה: היו לה כמה ילדים: היו מבקשים אוכל ולא היה לה ליתן להם: פעם אחת מצאה ביצה: קראה לילדיה ואמרה ילדים שוב אין לנו לדאוג: ביצה מצאתי ואני הרי בעלת תכלית אני: לא אוכל את הביצה אלא אבקש מן השכן שיניח לי ליתן אותה תחת תרנגולת רובצת על ביצים עד שתצא מן הביצה תרנגולת: הלא בעלת תכלית אני ולא נאכל את התרנגולת אלא אושיב אותה על ביצים ויצאו מהביצים תרנגולות: והתרנגולות אף הן יטילו ביצים הרבה עד שיהיו לנו תרנגולות הרבה וביצים הרבה: ואני בעלת תכלית אני: לא אוכל לא את התרנגולות ולא את הביצים אלא אמכור אותן ואקנה לי עגלה: והעגלה לא אוכל אלא אגדל אותה עד שתעשה פרה: ואת הפרה לא אוכל עד שתלד ולדות: ואף אותם לא נאכל ויהיו לנו פרות ועגלים: הלא בעלת תכלית אני: ואמכור הפרות והעגלים ואקח שדה ויהיו לנו שדות ופרות ועגלים ולא יחסר לנו עוד מאומה: עד שאותה כפרית מדברת כך ומשתעשעת באותה ביצה נפלה הביצה מידיה ונשברה:

כך אנחנו: כשבאים הימים הקדושים כל אדם מקבל עליו לעשות תשובה וחושב בלבו כך אעשה וכך אעשה: אבל הימים עוברים בהרהורי דברים בלבד ואין המחשבה מביאה לידי מעשה:

Folktale

TU BISHVAT

On Tu Bishvat
When spring comes,
An angel descends, ledger in hand,
And records each bud, each twig, each tree,
And all our garden flowers.
From town to town, from village to village,
The angel makes a winged way,
Searching the valleys, inspecting the hills,
Flying over the desert
And returns to heaven.
And when the ledger will be full
Of trees and blossoms and shrubs,
When the desert is turned into a meadow
And all our land is a watered garden,
Messianic days will be with us.

Attributed to Shin Shalom (translator unknown)

YOM HASHO'AH

Legacy

I'm just like other kids
  except I don't have much fun
My mother is like other mothers
  except she has a number on her arm
My father is an ordinary father
  except he screams in his sleep
My family is like other families
  except I have no grandparents
My home is like other homes
  except it's dark inside
My world is like everyone else's
  except there is no peace
I'm just like other Jews
  except Kaddish was the first prayer I learned.

Dana D. Shuster

They

There they were many, O God, so many,
Such vital ones and unafraid,
Such notable ones, with beard and braid—
And talking, in a marvelous strange way.

And under every roof they would sing—
With Torah chant and scripture cymbals—
Such rare songs, proud and boastful:
Of the golden peacock and Elimelekh the king.

But above their heads only the sun in its stare
Saw the raw fury, the killer's cold blade,
How with wild force it descended,
And what massacres were there.

Now they are but a trace of that fury:
An axed forest, a couple of trees. ↩

זיי . . .

זיי זענען דאָרט, אוי, גאָט, געווען אַ סך, אַ סך,
אַזעלכע לעבעדיקע און אַזעלכע בראַווע,
אַזעלכע שטאַלטנע, בערדיקע און קוטשעראַווע —
און מיט אַ ווונדערלעכער אויסטערלישער שפּראַך.

און זינגען פֿלעגן זיי פֿון אונטער יעדן דאַך
אַזעלכע האָפֿערדיקע לידער און טשיקאַווע:
פֿון מלך אלי־מלך און דער שיינער פּאַווע,
מיט מעבֿיר־סדרה־טראָפּ און צימבלען פֿון תּנך.

נאָר איבער זייער קאָפּ — די זון האָט נאָר געזען
די רויע גוואַלד, דעם קאַלטן מעסער בײַם רוצח,
ווי ער איז איבער זיי אַראָפּ, מיט ווילדן כּח,
ווי ער איז איבער זיי אַראָפּ, מיט ווילדן כּח,

און ס׳אַראַ מערדערײַ איז דאָרט געווען!
איצט זענען זיי אַ זכר נאָר פֿון יענער גוואַלד:
אַ צוויי־דרײַ ביימער פֿון אַן אויסגעהאַקטן וואַלד.

Mani Leyb (translated from the Yiddish by David G. Roskies and Hillel Schwartz)

Lament for the European Exile

The thin mask of my sleep
Caught fire.
I woke
With my face seared.
I had seen the flames of the sunset,
But this was a new sun,
A red sun
That lit up the night
With a strange, cruel light,
In which I saw the heavens
Swallowing hell,
And the earth spawning out
Living death.

I knew that this sun
Was the blood of my people
Gathering in the sky,
Ripping the darkness
With a flaring cry.
For on the highways of the world
It poured along.
In the world's fields
It watered.
The blood knew no rest.
It rose
And split the night's calm. ↩

The Angel of Death
Said to me:
"Thou art my son.
Today I watched thy birth."
And a new heart
Beat in me.

Weak-voiced,
Jerking in agonies of death.
My flesh
Became dead flesh.
The blood flowed dumb
In my veins.

Can I mourn?
I am an elegy.
Lament?
My mind is lamentation.
Can I rise
With death heavy on my limbs,
Or see
When Nothing hangs at my eyelash?
I will mourn and rise.
Your look will ask in my eyes
Atonement for your blood
At the hands of the world
That shed it.

A. L. Strauss (translated by A.C. Jacobs)

Pledge

(This poem is engraved in the wall of Yad Vashem shrine in Jerusalem.)

By leave of my eyes that watched the bereaving
Add cry after cry to my crushed heart's burden,
By leave of my trust that taught me forgiving
Till the pall of days that seared beyond pardon,
I have sworn an oath: to remember each grieving,
To remember, never to harden.

Nothing, till ten generations give way,
Till soothed is the rankling, annulled each pain,
Till the rods that punished are purged away.
I vow that the dark wrath pass not in vain.
I vow that at dawn I never more stray.
Lest now I learn nothing, again.

נֶדֶר

עַל דַּעַת עֵינַי שֶׁרָאוּ אֶת הַשְּׁכוֹל
וְעָמְסוּ זְעָקוֹת עַל לִבִּי הַשָּׁחוּחַ,
עַל דַּעַת רַחֲמַי שֶׁהוֹרוּנִי לִמְחֹל,
עַד בָּאוּ יָמִים שֶׁאָיְמוּ מִלְּסַלֹּחַ,
נָדַרְתִּי הַנֶּדֶר: לִזְכֹּר אֶת הַכֹּל,
לִזְכֹּר — וְדָבָר לֹא לִשְׁכֹּחַ.

דָּבָר לֹא לִשְׁכֹּחַ — עַד דּוֹר עֲשִׂירִי,
עַד שֹׁךְ עֶלְבּוֹנַי, עַד כֻּלָּם, עַד כְּלָהֵם,
עֲדֵי יִכְלוּ כָּל שִׁבְטֵי מוּסָרִי.
קוֹנָם אִם לָרִיק יַעֲבֹר לֵיל הַזָּעַם,
קוֹנָם אִם לַבֹּקֶר אֶחְזוֹר לְסוּרִי
וּמְאוּם לֹא אֶלְמַד גַּם הַפָּעַם:

Abraham Shlonsky

Chorus of the Rescued

We, the rescued,
From whose hollow bones death had begun to whittle his flutes,
And on whose sinews he had already stroked his bow—
Our bodies continue to lament
With their mutilated music.
We, the rescued,
The nooses wound for our necks still dangle
before us in the blue air—
Hourglasses still fill with our dripping blood.
We, the rescued,
The worms of fear still feed on us.
Our constellation is buried in dust.
We, the rescued,
Beg you:
Show us your sun, but gradually.
Lead us from star to star, step by step.
Be gentle when you teach us to live again.
Lest the song of a bird,
Or a pail being filled at the well,
Let our badly sealed pain burst forth again
and carry us away—
We beg you:
Do not show us an angry dog, not yet—
It could be, it could be
That we will dissolve into dust—
Dissolve into dust before your eyes.
For what binds our fabric together?
We whose breath vacated us,
Whose soul fled to Him out of that midnight
Long before our bodies were rescued
Into the ark of the moment. ↵

We, the rescued,
We press your hand
We look into your eye—
But all that binds us together now is leave-taking,
The leave-taking in the dust
Binds us together with you.

Nelly Sachs (translated from the German by Michael Roloff)

Jewish Partisan Song

Never say that there is only death for you
Though leaden skies may be concealing days of blue—
Because the hour we have hungered for is near;
Beneath our tread the earth shall tremble: We are here!

From land of palm-tree to the far-off land of snow
We shall be coming with our torment and our woe,
And everywhere our blood has sunk into the earth
Shall our bravery, our vigor blossom forth!

We'll have the morning sun to set our day aglow,
And all our yesterdays shall vanish with the foe,
And if the time is long before the sun appears,
Then let this song go like a signal through the years.

This song was written with our blood, and not with lead;
It's not a song that birds sing overhead,
It was a people, among toppling barricades,
That sang this song of ours with pistols and grenades.

So never say that there is only death for you.
Leaden skies may be concealing days of blue—
Yet the hour we have hungered for is near;
Beneath our tread the earth shall tremble: We are here!

פּאַרטיזאַנער־הימען

זאָג ניט קיין מאָל, אַז דו גייסט דעם לעצטן ורעג,
ווען הימלען בלײַענע פֿאַרשטעלן בלאָע טעג.
קומען וועט נאָך אונדזער אויסגעבענקטע שעה,
עס וועט אַ פּויק טאָן אונדזער טראָט: "מיר זײַנען דאָ!"

פֿון גרינעם פּאַלמענלאַנד ביז לאַנד פֿון ווײַסן שניי
מיר קומען אָן מיט אונדזער פּײַן, מיט אונדזער וויי,
און וווּ געפֿאַלן איז אַ שפּריץ פֿון אונדזער בלוט,
שפּראָצן וועט דאָרט אונדזער גבֿורה, אונדזער מוט.

עס וועט די מאָרגנזון באַגילדן אונדז דעם הײַנט,
און דער נעכטן וועט פֿאַרשווינדן מיטן פֿײַנד.

נאָר אויב פֿאַרזאַמען וועט די זון אין דעם קאַיאָר,
ווי אַ פּאַראָל זאָל גיין דאָס ליד פֿון דור צו דור!

געשריבן איז דאָס ליד מיט בלוט און ניט מיט בלײַ.
ס'איז ניט קיין לידל פֿון אַ פֿויגל אויף דער פֿרײַ —
דאָס האָט אַ פֿאָלק צעווישן פֿאַלנדיקע ווענט
דאָס ליד געזונגען מיט נאַגאַנעס אין די הענט.

טאָ זאָג ניט קיין מאָל, אַז דו גייסט דעם לעצטן וועג,
ווען הימלען בלײַענע פֿאַרשטעלן בלאָע טעג.
קומען וועט נאָך אונדזער אויסגעבענקטע שעה,
עס וועט אַ פּויק טאָן אונדזער טראָט: "מיר זײַנען דאָ!"

Hirsh Glik (translated by Aaron Kramer)

YOM HA'ATZMA'UT

To Touch Hands in Peace

We pray for Israel,
Both the mystic ideal of our ancestors' dreams,
And the living miracle, here and now,
Built of heart, muscle, and steel.

May she endure and guard her soul,
Surviving the relentless, age-old hatreds,
The cynical concealment of diplomatic deceit,
And the rumblings that warn of war.

May Israel continue to be the temple that magnetizes
The loving eyes of Jews in all corners:

The Jew in a land of affluence and relative peace
Who forgets the glory and pain of his being,
And the Jew in a land of oppression whose bloodied fist
Beats in anguish and pride
Against the cage of his enslavement.

May Israel yet embrace her homeless, her own,
And bind the ingathered into one people.

May those who yearn for a society built on human concern
Find the vision of the prophets realized in her.
May her readiness to defend
Never diminish her search for peace.

May we always dare to hope
That in our day the antagonisms will end,
That all the displaced, Arab and Jew, will be rooted again,
That within Israel and across her borders
All God's children will touch hands in peace.

Nachum Waldman

Let us stand silent in memory of our dearly beloved sons and daughters who gave their lives for the liberation of our homeland and the security of our people.

They gave all they had. They poured out their lifeblood for the freedom of Israel, even as the living waters quench the thirst of the arid soil.

Not in monuments of stones or trees shall be preserved their memory, but in the reverence and pride which will, until the end of time, fill the hearts of our people when their memory is recalled.

Our hearts are filled to overflowing with praise and thanksgiving to the Rock of Israel. But let us not delude ourselves that our work is finished. We are still at the beginning.

The road stretching ahead is long and hard, and there are still many obstacles in our way....The sword is still girded round our loins; let us not boast as men who have taken it off.

On our festive day, let us review in joy and thanksgiving the mighty deeds of the past and let us resolve to apply ourselves with all our might and all our heart to the new efforts of the future.

David Ben Gurion

The power of THE HOLY SPIRIT was upon me,
and it bore me forth upon the breath of THE ETERNAL,
and it set me down amid a certain valley,
which was filled with bones.
It carried me above the bones, around and around,
and there I saw that they were many on the valley's ground,
and they were very dry.
It said to me: "Oh, human being, shall these bones yet live?"
And I replied: "ALMIGHTY ONE, you alone can know."
And it said to me, "Call out in prophecy upon these bones,
and say to them: You dry bones,
hearken to the word of THE REDEEMING ONE!
Thus says the power of THE OMNIPRESENT to these bones:
Behold, I breathe my spirit into you, and you shall live,
and I shall give you sinews, and shall grow upon you flesh,
and I shall cover you with skin, and place within you breath,
and you shall live,
and you shall know
that I am THE ETERNAL ONE!"

And I prophesied as I had been commanded,
and as I called out there arose a sound,
behold, it was a sound of tumult,
and the bones began to come together, each to each.
And while I watched, behold, they took on flesh and sinews,
and from above a covering of skin was placed upon them,
though they had no breath within them.

And the spirit said to me: "Call out in prophecy,
call to the wind, and prophesy, Oh human being,
and tell the wind: Thus says the power of THE OMNIPRESENT,
From all four directions, come, Oh wind,
blow through the bodies of these slain ones,
let them come to life!" ↩

And I prophesied as I had been commanded,
and the wind entered their bodies and they came to life,
and stood upon their feet,
a great and mighty multitude.

And the spirit said to me: "Oh human being,
these bones are the entire House of Israel—
they who have said, 'Our bones have withered,
and our hope is lost, our life has been cut off!'
Therefore, call out in prophecy and say to them:
Thus says the power of THE OMNIPRESENT:
Behold, I am opening your graves,
and I shall raise you up from where you lie,
my people, and shall bring you to the land of Israel,
and you shall know that I am THE ETERNAL ONE,
I who open up your graves
and raise you up, my people, from your place of burial!
I place my spirit into you, and you shall live,
and I shall set you down upon your native ground,
that you may know that I, THE OMNIPRESENT ONE,
have spoken and have acted!
Thus says THE ETERNAL ONE."

הָיְתָה עָלַי יַד־יהוה וַיּוֹצִאֵנִי בְרוּחַ יהוה וַיְנִיחֵנִי בְּתוֹךְ הַבִּקְעָה וְהִיא
מְלֵאָה עֲצָמוֹת: וְהֶעֱבִירַנִי עֲלֵיהֶם סָבִיב סָבִיב וְהִנֵּה רַבּוֹת מְאֹד
עַל־פְּנֵי הַבִּקְעָה וְהִנֵּה יְבֵשׁוֹת מְאֹד: וַיֹּאמֶר אֵלַי בֶּן־אָדָם הֲתִחְיֶינָה
הָעֲצָמוֹת הָאֵלֶּה וָאֹמַר אֲדֹנָי יהוה אַתָּה יָדָעְתָּ: וַיֹּאמֶר אֵלַי הִנָּבֵא
עַל־הָעֲצָמוֹת הָאֵלֶּה וְאָמַרְתָּ אֲלֵיהֶם הָעֲצָמוֹת הַיְבֵשׁוֹת שִׁמְעוּ
דְּבַר־יהוה: כֹּה אָמַר אֲדֹנָי יהוה לָעֲצָמוֹת הָאֵלֶּה הִנֵּה אֲנִי מֵבִיא בָכֶם
רוּחַ וִחְיִיתֶם: וְנָתַתִּי עֲלֵיכֶם גִּידִים וְהַעֲלֵתִי עֲלֵיכֶם בָּשָׂר וְקָרַמְתִּי
עֲלֵיכֶם עוֹר וְנָתַתִּי בָכֶם רוּחַ וִחְיִיתֶם וִידַעְתֶּם כִּי־אֲנִי יהוה: וְנִבֵּאתִי
כַּאֲשֶׁר צֻוֵּיתִי וַיְהִי־קוֹל כְּהִנָּבְאִי וְהִנֵּה־רַעַשׁ וַתִּקְרְבוּ עֲצָמוֹת עֶצֶם ←

אֶל־עַצְמוֹ: וְרָאִיתִי וְהִנֵּה־עֲלֵיהֶם גִּידִים וּבָשָׂר עָלָה וַיִּקְרַם עֲלֵיהֶם
גִּידִים וּבָשָׂר עָלָה וַיִּקְרַם עֲלֵיהֶם עוֹד מִלְמָעְלָה וְרוּחַ אֵין בָּהֶם:
וַיֹּאמֶר אֵלַי הִנָּבֵא אֶל־הָרוּחַ הִנָּבֵא בֶן־אָדָם וְאָמַרְתָּ אֶל־הָרוּחַ כֹּה־אָמַר
אֲדֹנָי יהוה מֵאַרְבַּע רוּחוֹת בֹּאִי הָרוּחַ וּפְחִי בַּהֲרוּגִים הָאֵלֶּה וְיִחְיוּ:
וְהִנַּבֵּאתִי כַּאֲשֶׁר צִוָּנִי וַתָּבוֹא בָהֶם הָרוּחַ וַיִּחְיוּ וַיַּעַמְדוּ עַל־רַגְלֵיהֶם
חַיִל גָּדוֹל מְאֹד מְאֹד: וַיֹּאמֶר אֵלַי בֶּן־אָדָם הָעֲצָמוֹת הָאֵלֶּה כָּל־בֵּית
יִשְׂרָאֵל הֵמָּה הִנֵּה אֹמְרִים יָבְשׁוּ עַצְמוֹתֵינוּ וְאָבְדָה תִקְוָתֵנוּ נִגְזַרְנוּ
לָנוּ: לָכֵן הִנָּבֵא וְאָמַרְתָּ אֲלֵיהֶם כֹּה־אָמַר אֲדֹנָי יהוה הִנֵּה אֲנִי פֹתֵחַ
אֶת־קִבְרוֹתֵיכֶם וְהַעֲלֵיתִי אֶתְכֶם מִקִּבְרוֹתֵיכֶם עַמִּי וְהֵבֵאתִי אֶתְכֶם
אֶל־אַדְמַת יִשְׂרָאֵל: וִידַעְתֶּם כִּי־אֲנִי יהוה בְּפִתְחִי אֶת־קִבְרוֹתֵיכֶם
וּבְהַעֲלוֹתִי אֶתְכֶם מִקִּבְרוֹתֵיכֶם עַמִּי: וְנָתַתִּי רוּחִי בָּכֶם וִחְיִיתֶם
וְהִנַּחְתִּי אֶתְכֶם עַל־אַדְמַתְכֶם וִידַעְתֶּם כִּי אֲנִי יהוה דִּבַּרְתִּי וְעָשִׂיתִי
נְאֻם־יהוה:

Ezekiel 37:1-14 (translated by Joel Rosenberg)

Sisu et Yerushalayim

Rejoice in Jerusalem, be happy with her, all who love her.

Upon your walls, City of David, I have placed watchmen day and night.

Do not fear, my servant Jacob, for those who hate you will flee from you.

Look around and see everything, gather and come to her.

Your people shall all be righteous forever and inherit the land. ↩

שִׂישׂוּ אֶת יְרוּשָׁלַיִם

שִׂישׂוּ אֶת יְרוּשָׁלַ֫יִם גִּילוּ בָהּ
גִּילוּ בָהּ כָּל אוֹהֲבֶ֫יהָ כָּל אוֹהֲבֶיהָ:

עַל חוֹמוֹתַ֫יִךְ עִיר דָּוִד הִפְקַ֫דְתִּי שׁוֹמְרִים
כָּל הַיּוֹם וְכָל הַלַּ֫יְלָה:

אַל תִּירָא וְאַל תֵּחַת עַבְדִּי יַעֲקֹב
כִּי יָפוּצוּ מְשַׂנְאֶ֫יךָ מִפָּנֶ֫יךָ. שִׂישׂוּ...

שְׂאִי סָבִיב עֵינַ֫יִךְ וּרְאִי כֻּלָּם
נִקְבְּצוּ וּבָאוּ לָךְ. שִׂישׂוּ...

וְעַמֵּךְ כֻּלָּם צַדִּיקִים
לְעוֹלָם יִירְשׁוּ אָ֫רֶץ. שִׂישׂוּ...

Sisu et yerushalayim gilu vah
Gilu vah kol ohavehah kol ohavehah.
Al ḥomotayiḥ ir david hifkadeti shomrim
Kol hayom ve ḥol halaylah.
Al tirah ve'al teyḥat avdi ya'akov
Ki yafutzu mesaneḥa mipaneḥa.
Se'i saviv eynayiḥ uri ḥulam
Nikbetzu uva'u laḥ
Ve'ameḥ kulam tzadikim le'olam yirshu aretz.

Translated by David A. Teutsch

Jerusalem, Jerusalem (Jerusalem of Gold)

This translation can be sung to the same melody as the Hebrew.

The olive trees that stand in silence
Up on the hills of time,
To hear the voices of the city
As bells of evening chime.

The Shofar sounding from the Temple
To call the world to prayer,
The shepherd pauses in the valley
And peace is everywhere.

The water well for those who thirsted,
The ancient market square,
Your golden sun that lights the future
For people everywhere.
How many songs,
How many stories,
The stony hills recall.
Around her heart my city carries
A lonely ancient wall.

And far away beyond the desert
A thousand suns will glow.
We shall be going to the Jordan,
By way of Jericho.
My simple voice cannot acclaim thee,
Too weak the words I choose,
Jerusalem, if I forget thee,
May my right hand its cunning lose.

Jerusalem, Jerusalem,
Forever young, yet forever old,
My heart will sing your songs of glory, Jerusalem.
Jerusalem, Jerusalem,
Oh, city with a heart of gold,
My heart will sing your songs of glory, Jerusalem. ↩

יְרוּשָׁלַיִם שֶׁל זָהָב

אֲוִיר הָרִים צָלוּל כַּיַּיִן וְרֵיחַ אֳרָנִים
נִשָּׂא בְּרוּחַ הָעַרְבַּיִם עִם קוֹל פַּעֲמוֹנִים.
וּבְתַרְדֵּמַת אִילָן וָאֶבֶן שְׁבוּיָה בַּחֲלוֹמָהּ
הָעִיר אֲשֶׁר בָּדָד יוֹשֶׁבֶת וּבְלִבָּהּ חוֹמָה.

יְרוּשָׁלַיִם שֶׁל זָהָב וְשֶׁל נְחֹשֶׁת וְשֶׁל אוֹר
הֲלֹא לְכָל שִׁירַיִךְ אֲנִי כִּנּוֹר.

חָזַרְנוּ אֶל בּוֹרוֹת הַמַּיִם לַשּׁוּק וְלַכִּכָּר
שׁוֹפָר קוֹרֵא בְּהַר־הַבַּיִת בָּעִיר הָעַתִּיקָה
וּבַמְּעָרוֹת אֲשֶׁר בַּסֶּלַע אַלְפֵי שְׁמָשׁוֹת זוֹרְחוֹת
וְשׁוּב נֵרֵד אֶל יַם־הַמֶּלַח בְּדֶרֶךְ יְרִיחוֹ.

יְרוּשָׁלַיִם שֶׁל זָהָב וְשֶׁל נְחֹשֶׁת וְשֶׁל אוֹר
הֲלֹא לְכָל שִׁירַיִךְ אֲנִי כִּנּוֹר.

אַךְ בְּבוֹאִי הַיּוֹם לָשִׁיר לָךְ וְלָךְ לִקְשׁוֹר כְּתָרִים
קָטֹנְתִּי מִצְּעִיר בָּנַיִךְ וּמֵאַחֲרוֹן הַמְשׁוֹרְרִים
כִּי שְׁמֵךְ צוֹרֵב אֶת הַשְּׂפָתַיִם כִּנְשִׁיקַת שָׂרָף
אִם אֶשְׁכָּחֵךְ יְרוּשָׁלַיִם אֲשֶׁר כֻּלָּהּ זָהָב.

יְרוּשָׁלַיִם שֶׁל זָהָב וְשֶׁל נְחֹשֶׁת וְשֶׁל אוֹר
הֲלֹא לְכָל שִׁירַיִךְ אֲנִי כִּנּוֹר. ←

Avir harim tzalul kayayin verey'aḥ oranim
nisa beru'aḥ ha'arbayim im kol pa'amonim.
Uvtardemat ilan va'even shevuyah baḥalomah
ha'ir asher badad yoshevet uvlibah ḥomah.

Yerushalayim shel zahav veshel neḥoshet veshel or
halo leḥol shirayiḥ ani kinor.

Ḥazarnu el borot hamayim lashuk velakikar
shofar korey behar habayit ba'ir ha'atikah
uvame'arot asher basela alfey shemashot zorḥot
veshuv nered el yam hamelaḥ bedereḥ yeriḥo.

Yerushalayim shel zahav veshel neḥoshet veshel or
halo leḥol shirayiḥ ani kinor.

Aḥ bevo'i hayom lashir laḥ velaḥ likshor ketarim
katonti mitze'ir banayiḥ ume'aḥaron hameshorerim
ki shemeḥ tzorev et hasefatayim kinshikat saraf
im eshkaḥeḥ yerushalayim asher kulah zahav.

Yerushalayim shel zahav veshel neḥoshet veshel or
halo leḥol shirayiḥ ani kinor.

Naomi Shemer (translated by Norman Newell)

Ode to Zion

Zion, ask now of the welfare of your captive ones abroad,
who ask of yours, who are the remnant of your brood.

From west, and east, from north and south: Shalom!
From near and far, from every side, accept our wish of peace.

I howl like jackals when I weep for all your woes,
but when I dream of your captivity's return, I am a vessel for
your songs.

My heart yearns sorely for Bethel and Peniel,
for Maḥanaim, and for all the meeting places of the ones whom
you have purified.

There, the One Who Dwells Within abides with you,
and your Creator opens up your gates to face the gates on
high.

I would choose, for pouring out my soul, that place
where the divine breath once was poured into your prophets.

You are the royal house, you are the seat of the Eternal.
How can it be that the unworthy sit where once your noble ones
had reigned?

Would that it were given me to roam in places where
divinity appeared before your seers and your messengers!

Would that wings were made for me to wander far aloft,
to lay the pieces of my cloven heart amid your mountain clefts!

I'd fall, my face touching your ground, taking great pleasure
from your stones, and paying tender homage to your dust.

I'd pass among your forests and your vineyards, and I'd stand
upon your Gilead's crest, behold in wonderment your heights of
Abarim. ↩

All souls that live breathe something of your land, its flowing myrrh,
its soil's grains, its rivers' honeyed taste.

Yet how can I take pleasure now to see
the predatory dogs tear at your lion cubs?

Zion, the completion of all beauty, you still are bound up with your ancient love and grace:
to you are bound the souls of all your friends,

those who rejoice when you are well, who are in pain
when you are desolate, and who shed tears over your broken state.

And from the pit of their captivity, they breathe your air:
and wherever they may be, they bow in prayer toward your gates.

The glitter of idolatry shall fade and pass away;
your splendor is eternal, and your crown for all the ages.

And you whom God desired for a dwelling place, happy are they
whom God brings near to you, to dwell within your courts!

Happy those who wait, and come to see the rising
of your light—on them may your dawn break!

May they enjoy the bounty of your favor, and rejoice
at your rejoicing, as you come back to the dawning of your ancient youth. ↩

שאפים נגדך ומשתחוים / they breathe your air. Literally, "they aspire toward you." The Hebrew verb, like the English word "aspire," is based on a root meaning "to breathe." J.R.

צִיּוֹן הֲלֹא תִשְׁאֲלִי לִשְׁלוֹם אֲסִירָיִךְ
דּוֹרְשֵׁי שְׁלוֹמֵךְ וְהֵם יֶתֶר עֲדָרָיִךְ:

מִיָּם וּמִזְרָח וּמִצָּפוֹן וְתֵימָן שְׁלוֹם
רָחוֹק וְקָרוֹב שְׂאִי מִכָּל־עֲבָרָיִךְ:

לִבְכּוֹת עֱנוּתֵךְ אֲנִי תַנִּים וְעֵת אֶחֱלֹם
שִׁיבַת שְׁבוּתֵךְ אֲנִי כִנּוֹר לְשִׁירָיִךְ:

לִבִּי לְבֵית־אֵל וְלִפְנִיאֵל מְאֹד יֶהֱמֶה
וּלְמַחֲנַיִם וְכָל־פִּגְעֵי טְהוֹרָיִךְ:

שָׁם הַשְּׁכִינָה שְׁכֵנָה־לָךְ וְהַיּוֹצְרֵךְ
פָּתַח לְמוּל שַׁעֲרֵי שַׁחַק שְׁעָרָיִךְ:

אֶבְחַר לְנַפְשִׁי לְהִשְׁתַּפֵּךְ בְּמָקוֹם אֲשֶׁר
רוּחַ־אֱלֹהִים שְׁפוּכָה עַל־בְּחִירָיִךְ:

אַתְּ בֵּית־מְלוּכָה וְאַתְּ כִּסֵּא אֲדֹנָי וְאֵיךְ
יָשְׁבוּ עֲבָדִים עֲלֵי כִסְאוֹת גְּבִירָיִךְ:

מִי יִתְּנֵנִי מְשׁוֹטֵט בַּמְּקוֹמוֹת אֲשֶׁר
נִגְלוּ אֱלֹהִים לְחֹזַיִךְ וְצִירָיִךְ:

מִי יַעֲשֶׂה־לִּי כְנָפַיִם וְאַרְחִיק נְדֹד
אָנִיד לְבִתְרֵי לְבָבִי בֵּין בְּתָרָיִךְ:

אֶפֹּל לְאַפַּי עֲלֵי אַרְצֵךְ וְאֶרְצֶה אֲבָנַיִךְ
מְאֹד וַאֲחֹנֵן אֶת־עֲפָרָיִךְ:

אֶעֱבֹר בְּיַעְרֵךְ וְכַרְמִלֵּךְ וְאֶעֱמֹד בְּגִלְעָדֵךְ
וְאֶשְׁתּוֹמְמָה אֶל־הַר עֲבָרָיִךְ. ←

חַיֵּי נְשָׁמוֹת אֲוִיר אַרְצֵךְ וּמִמָּר־דְּרוֹר
אֲבְקַת עֲפָרֵךְ וְנֹפֶת צוּף נְהָרָיִךְ׃

אֵיךְ יֶעֱרַב לִי אֲכֹל וּשְׁתוֹת בְּעֵת אֶחֱזֶה
כִּי יִסְחֲבוּ הַכְּלָבִים אֶת־כְּפִירָיִךְ׃

צִיּוֹן כְּלִילַת יֳפִי אַהֲבָה וְחֵן תִּקְשְׁרִי
מֵאָז וּבָךְ נִקְשְׁרוּ נַפְשׁוֹת חֲבֵרָיִךְ׃

הֵם הַשְּׂמֵחִים לְשַׁלְוָתֵךְ וְהַכֹּאֲבִים
עַל־שׁוֹמֲמוּתֵךְ וּבֹכִים עַל־שְׁבָרָיִךְ׃

מִבּוֹר שְׁבִי שֹׁאֲפִים נֶגְדֵּךְ וּמִשְׁתַּחֲוִים
אִישׁ מִמְּקוֹמוֹ אֱלֵי־נֹכַח שְׁעָרָיִךְ׃

יִשְׁנֶה וְיַחְלֹף כְּלִיל כָּל־מַמְלְכוֹת הָאֱלִיל
חָסְנֵךְ לְעוֹלָם לְדוֹר וָדוֹר נְזָרָיִךְ׃

אִוֵּךְ לְמוֹשָׁב אֱלֹהָיִךְ וְאַשְׁרֵי־אֱנוֹשׁ
יִבְחַר יְקָרֵב וְיִשְׁכֹּן בַּחֲצֵרָיִךְ׃

אַשְׁרֵי מְחַכֶּה וְיַגִּיעַ וְיִרְאֶה עֲלוֹת
אוֹרֵךְ וְיִבָּקְעוּ עָלָיו שְׁחָרָיִךְ׃

לִרְאוֹת בְּטוֹבַת בְּחִירַיִךְ וְלַעְלֹז בְּשִׂמְחָתֵךְ
בְּשׁוּבֵךְ אֱלֵי קַדְמוּת נְעוּרָיִךְ׃

Yehudah Halevi (translated by Joel Rosenberg)

In Germany at the End of World War II

Perhaps for the thousandth time, the Jewish committee in Buchenwald was holding a meeting on the question: Where to? A Polish Jew, a German, a Czech, a Hungarian—each faced the same burning problem: Where should the few surviving Jews of Buchenwald go? How could we ever have believed that at the end of the war the surviving Jews would have no more worries, that everything would be fine! The world, we had thought, would welcome our few survivors with open arms! We, the first victims of the Nazis. They would love us!

Quickly enough, we saw that the world had other things on its mind than Jewish suffering. So where to?

Comrade Posnansky put forth an idea: into our own kibbutz. To build a group of Buchenwald's youth, and find a farm where we could prepare for Palestine. A wonderful idea. There would be no lack of candidates for the kibbutz, for energy was reawakening in the survivors and seeking an outlet.

From that idea sprang Kibbutz Buchenwald.

After several days of coming and going, the Jewish committee in Buchenwald possessed a document from the American Military Government which gave it the right to make use, for a long term, of the township farm of Eggendorf, near Blankenheim.

June 3, 1945—Here we are, the first few comrades, sitting on a truck that is taking us away from Buchenwald. Finally, the Buchenwald chapter is ended. The concrete road takes us away from the barracks, the watchtowers, the SS quarters; on this straight road, which turns neither to right nor to left, we head for our new life. We are all determined to follow this road to a place of our own, a Jewish settlement where we can put our energies into something that will belong only to us, a place where we can live for the future. This road must take us to Palestine.

Members of Kibbutz Buchenwald

Hatikvah

So long as a Jewish soul still lives within a heart,
And so long as an eye gazes longingly to Zion in the far
reaches of the East,
Then the hope is not lost,
The hope of two thousand years,
That we may be a free people in our land,
Land of Zion and Jerusalem.

הַתִּקְוָה

כָּל עוֹד בַּלֵּבָב פְּנִימָה
נֶפֶשׁ יְהוּדִי הוֹמִיָּה
וּלְפַאֲתֵי מִזְרָח קָדִימָה
עַיִן לְצִיּוֹן צוֹפִיָּה
עוֹד לֹא אָבְדָה תִּקְוָתֵנוּ
הַתִּקְוָה מִשְּׁנוֹת אַלְפַּיִם
לִהְיוֹת עַם חָפְשִׁי בְּאַרְצֵנוּ
בְּאֶרֶץ צִיּוֹן וִירוּשָׁלַיִם.

Kol od balevav penimah nefesh yehudi homiyah
Ulfa'atey mizraḥ kadimah ayin letziyon tzofiyah
Od lo avedah tikvatenu hatikvah mishenot alpayim
Lihyot am ḥofshi be'artzenu be'eretz tziyon virushalayim.

Naftali Herz Imber (translated by Judith Kaplan Eisenstein)

TISHA BE'AV

Al Naharot Bavel / At Babel's Rivers

At Babel's rivers,
there we sat, and there we wept,
when we remembered Zion.
There, beside the river's willows,
we hung up our harps,
because our captors there
demanded of us words of song,
and those who mocked us
called for sounds of joy:
"Sing for us one of the songs of Zion!"
How can we sing
a song of ZION'S STRENGTH
upon a foreign soil?

עַל־נַהֲרוֹת בָּבֶל
שָׁם יָשַׁבְנוּ גַּם־בָּכִינוּ
בְּזָכְרֵנוּ אֶת־צִיּוֹן׃
עַל־עֲרָבִים בְּתוֹכָהּ
תָּלִינוּ כִּנּוֹרוֹתֵינוּ׃
כִּי שָׁם שְׁאֵלוּנוּ
שׁוֹבֵינוּ דִּבְרֵי־שִׁיר
וְתוֹלָלֵינוּ שִׂמְחָה
שִׁירוּ לָנוּ מִשִּׁיר צִיּוֹן׃
אֵיךְ נָשִׁיר אֶת־שִׁיר־יהוה
עַל־אַדְמַת נֵכָר׃

If I forget, you O Jerusalem,
may my right hand forget its strength!
Let my tongue cling thickly to my palate,
if I ever fail to keep you in my memory,
if I should ever fail to hold Jerusalem
above my highest joy.

אִם־אֶשְׁכָּחֵךְ יְרוּשָׁלָיִם
תִּשְׁכַּח יְמִינִי׃
תִּדְבַּק לְשׁוֹנִי לְחִכִּי
אִם־לֹא אֶזְכְּרֵכִי
אִם־לֹא אַעֲלֶה אֶת־יְרוּשָׁלַיִם
עַל־רֹאשׁ שִׂמְחָתִי׃

Psalm 136:1-6 (translated by Joel Rosenberg)

Naḥamu, Naḥamu Ami / Comfort Now My People!

"Comfort, comfort now my people!"
shall your God declare.
"Speak to the heart of Jerusalem, call unto her,
that her time of trial is fulfilled,
that her wrongdoing is forgiven,
that she has received from THE ALMIGHTY'S hand
double repayment for her errors."

A voice calls out
amid the wilderness: "Clear out a path,
set down amid the arid waste a highway for our God!
Let every valley be filled up,
let every mountain and every hill be leveled,
let the crooked be made straight,
let all the rough lands be made smooth.
Upon a mountaintop ascend,
you who brings forth Zion's tidings,
make your voice loud and strong,
you who brings tidings to Jerusalem,
raise your voice, and do not be afraid,
declare to Judah's towns:
Here is your God!
Here is your sovereign ETERNAL ONE, who comes in strength,
whose arm brings the authority to reign.
Behold, God brings reward,
God's power is present all around.
As the shepherd nourishes the flock,
God's arm shall gather all the lambs,
and carry them in tender care,
and nurse and guide." ↩

נַחֲמוּ נַחֲמוּ עַמִּי
יֹאמַר אֱלֹהֵיכֶם:
דַּבְּרוּ עַל־לֵב יְרוּשָׁלַיִם וְקִרְאוּ אֵלֶיהָ
כִּי מָלְאָה צְבָאָהּ
כִּי נִרְצָה עֲוֹנָהּ
כִּי לָקְחָה מִיַּד יהוה
כִּפְלַיִם בְּכָל־חַטֹּאתֶיהָ:
קוֹל קוֹרֵא
בַּמִּדְבָּר פַּנּוּ דֶּרֶךְ יהוה
יַשְּׁרוּ בָּעֲרָבָה מְסִלָּה לֵאלֹהֵינוּ:
כָּל־גֶּיא יִנָּשֵׂא
וְכָל־הַר וְגִבְעָה יִשְׁפָּלוּ
וְהָיָה הֶעָקֹב לְמִישׁוֹר
וְהָרְכָסִים לְבִקְעָה:
עַל־הַר־גָּבֹהַּ עֲלִי־לָךְ מְבַשֶּׂרֶת צִיּוֹן
הָרִימִי בַכֹּחַ קוֹלֵךְ מְבַשֶּׂרֶת יְרוּשָׁלָיִם
הָרִימִי אַל־תִּירָאִי
אִמְרִי לְעָרֵי יְהוּדָה
הִנֵּה אֱלֹהֵיכֶם:
הִנֵּה אֲדֹנָי יהוה בְּחָזָק יָבוֹא
וּזְרֹעוֹ מֹשְׁלָה לוֹ
הִנֵּה שְׂכָרוֹ אִתּוֹ
וּפְעֻלָּתוֹ לְפָנָיו:
כְּרֹעֶה עֶדְרוֹ יִרְעֶה
בִּזְרֹעוֹ יְקַבֵּץ טְלָאִים
וּבְחֵיקוֹ יִשָּׂא
עָלוֹת יְנַהֵל:

Isaiah 40:1-5, 9-11 (translated by Joel Rosenberg)

Me'al Pisgat Har-Hatzofim / From Mt. Scopus' Crest

From Mt. Scopus' crest, peace unto you, Jerusalem,
From Mt. Scopus' crest, I bow my face toward you.
A hundred generations I have dreamed of you, of meriting to see your face's light.
Jerusalem, Jerusalem, let your face shine upon your children.
Jerusalem, Jerusalem, I shall rebuild you from your ruins.

From Mt. Scopus' crest, peace unto you, Jerusalem,
Thousands of exiles, from all corners of the earth, turn eyes toward you,
with thousands of blessings, be you blessed, O sovereign holy place, O city of divine rule.
Jerusalem, Jerusalem, I shall not move from here,
Jerusalem, Jerusalem, let redemption come, yes let it come!

מֵעַל־פִּסְגַּת הַר הַצּוֹפִים שָׁלוֹם לָךְ יְרוּשָׁלָיִם.
מֵעַל־פִּסְגַּת הַר הַצּוֹפִים אֶשְׁתַּחֲוֶה לָךְ אַפָּיִם.
מֵאָה דוֹרוֹת חָלַמְתִּי עָלַיִךְ. לִזְכּוֹת לִרְאוֹת בְּאוֹר פָּנָיִךְ:
יְרוּשָׁלַיִם יְרוּשָׁלַיִם הָאִירִי פָּנַיִךְ לִבְנֵךְ.
יְרוּשָׁלַיִם יְרוּשָׁלַיִם מֵחָרְבוֹתַיִךְ אֶבְנֵךְ:

מֵעַל־פִּסְגַּת הַר הַצּוֹפִים שָׁלוֹם לָךְ יְרוּשָׁלָיִם.
אַלְפֵי גוֹלִים מִקְצוֹת כָּל־תֵּבֵל נוֹשְׂאִים אֵלַיִךְ עֵינָיִם.
בְּאַלְפֵי בְרָכוֹת הֲיִי בְרוּכָה מִקְדַּשׁ מֶלֶךְ עִיר מְלוּכָה:
יְרוּשָׁלַיִם יְרוּשָׁלַיִם אֲנִי לֹא אָזוּז מִפֹּה.
יְרוּשָׁלַיִם יְרוּשָׁלַיִם תָּבֹא הַגְּאֻלָּה תָּבֹא:

Avigdor Hame'iri (translation by Joel Rosenberg)

When the Eternal Brought the Captives Back to Zion

When THE REDEEMER brought about Zion's return,
we were like dreamers.
For then our mouths were filled with song,
our tongues with joyous cries. ↩

Then did they say among the nations,
"The God of Israel has done wonderfully for us.
Yes, we are happy now.
Return, Redeemer, all our captive people,
like the rivers in the Negev sands.
May those who sow while shedding tears,
bring in their harvest with a joyous shout.
Now see them weeping as they walk,
the seed-bag carried in their hands;
now hear them come with joyous song,
their harvest bundles borne aloft!

שִׁיר הַמַּעֲלוֹת	Shir hama'alot
בְּשׁוּב יהוה אֶת־שִׁיבַת צִיּוֹן	beshuv adonay et shivat tziyon
הָיִינוּ כְּחֹלְמִים׃	hayinu keḥolmim.
אָז יִמָּלֵא שְׂחוֹק פִּינוּ	Az yimaley seḥok pinu
וּלְשׁוֹנֵנוּ רִנָּה׃	ulshonenu rinah.
אָז יֹאמְרוּ בַגּוֹיִם	Az yomeru vagoyim
הִגְדִּיל יהוה לַעֲשׂוֹת עִם־אֵלֶּה׃	higdil adonay la'asot im eleh.
הִגְדִּיל יהוה לַעֲשׂוֹת עִמָּנוּ	Higdil adonay la'asot imanu
הָיִינוּ שְׂמֵחִים׃	hayinu semeḥim.
שׁוּבָה יהוה אֶת־שְׁבִיתֵנוּ	Shuvah adonay et shevitenu
כַּאֲפִיקִים בַּנֶּגֶב׃	ka'afikim banegev.
הַזֹּרְעִים בְּדִמְעָה	Hazorim bedimah
בְּרִנָּה יִקְצֹרוּ׃	berinah yiktzoru.
הָלוֹךְ יֵלֵךְ וּבָכֹה	Haloḥ yeleḥ uvaḥoh
נֹשֵׂא מֶשֶׁךְ־הַזָּרַע	nosey mesheḥ hazara
בֹּא־יָבֹא בְרִנָּה	bo yavo verinah
נֹשֵׂא אֲלֻמֹּתָיו׃	nosey alumotav.

Psalm 126 (translated by Joel Rosenberg)

Song of Those Who Died in Vain

Sit down and bargain
All you like, grizzled old foxes.
We'll wall you up in a splendid palace
With food, wine, good beds and a good fire
Provided that you discuss, negotiate
For our and your children's lives.
May all the wisdom of the universe
Converge to bless your minds
And guide you in the maze.
But outside in the cold we will be waiting for you,
The army of those who died in vain,
We of the Marne, of Montecassino,
Treblinka, Dresden and Hiroshima.
And with us will be
The leprous and the people with trachoma,
The Disappeared Ones of Buenos Aires,
Dead Cambodians and dying Ethiopians,
The Prague negotiators,
The bled-dry of Calcutta,
The innocents slaughtered in Bologna.
Heaven help you if you come out disagreeing:
You'll be clutched tight in our embrace.
We are invincible because we are the conquered,
Invulnerable because already dead;
We laugh at your missiles.
Sit down and bargain
Until your tongues are dry.
If the havoc and the shame continue
We'll drown you in our putrefaction.

Primo Levi

NEW YEAR'S DAY

Each year should be the best year we have yet lived.
Each year we are more learned in the ways of life.
Each year we are wiser than the year before.
Each year our eyes know better the sights to seek.
Each year our ears listen with a finer tuning.
Every happening is a jewel, wrought about the fancy of time.
All that we understand of the universe is the setting for each sight and sound of day.
The child looks with gladness each year to be one year older.
Should not this welcome pursue us all our years?
The piling of the years is a richness like the piling of gold.
Our years are coins with which we can purchase more wisely at the bazaars of each new season.
Our love is more pliant and patient having been taught by time.
This New Year is one year older than the last.
The earth is more abounding in its growth.
The creatures have moved another step in their unfolding.
Humankind has left us one more year of art for our contemplation.
History is one year more resonant with lessons.
The sunrises are one year more familiar and promising.
The sunsets are one year less fearful, and the peace of the night is one year closer.

Kenneth L. Patton

MARTIN LUTHER KING DAY

Now is the time to make justice a reality for all of God's children...[And] we will not be satisfied until justice rolls down like water and righteousness like a mighty stream....

I say to you today, my friends, even though we face the difficulties of today and tomorrow, I still have a dream. It is a dream deeply rooted in the American dream. I have a dream that one day this nation will rise up and live out the true meaning of its creed: "We hold these truths to be self-evident that all men are created equal...." This is our hope.

With this faith we will be able to hew out of the mountain of despair a stone of hope. With this faith we will be able to transform the jangling discords of our nation into a beautiful symphony of brotherhood. With this faith we will be able to work together, to pray together, to struggle together, to go to jail together, to stand up for freedom together, knowing that we will be free one day....

So, let freedom ring from the prodigious hilltops of New Hampshire. Let freedom ring from the mighty mountains of New York. Let freedom ring from the heightening Alleghenies of Pennsylvania. Let freedom ring from the snowcapped Rockies of Colorado. Let freedom ring from the curvaceous slopes of California. Let freedom ring from Stone Mountain of Georgia; let freedom ring from Lookout Mountain of Tennessee; let freedom ring from every hill and molehill of Mississippi—from every mountainside, let freedom ring.

And when this happens, when we allow freedom to ring, when we let it ring from every village, from every hamlet, from every state and every city, we will be able to speed up that day when all of God's children, black and white, Jew and Gentile, Protestant and Catholic, will be able to join hands and sing in the words of the old Negro spiritual: "Free at last! Free at last! Thank God almighty, we are free at last!"

Martin Luther King, Jr. (on the steps of the Lincoln Memorial August 28, 1963)

PRESIDENTS' DAY

Most governments have been based practically on the denial of the equal rights...ours began by affirming those rights. They said, some...are too ignorant and vicious to share in government. Possibly so, said we; and by your system you would always keep them ignorant and vicious. We proposed to give all a chance; and we expected the weak to grow stronger; the ignorant, wiser; and all better and happier together.

We made the experiment; and the fruit is before us. Look at it—think of it. Look at it in its aggregate grandeur, of extent of country and numbers of population—of ship, and steamboat, and trail.

* * *

From the first appearance of man upon the earth down to very recent times, the words "stranger" and "enemy" were quite or almost synonymous. Even yet, this has not totally disappeared. The man of the highest moral cultivation, in spite of all which abstract principle can do, likes him whom he does know much better than him whom he does not know. To correct the evils, great and small, which spring from want of sympathy and from positive enmity among strangers, as nations or as individuals, is one of the highest functions of civilization.

* * *

This is a world of compensation; and one who would be no slave must consent to have no slave.

Abraham Lincoln

Gentlemen,

While I receive with much satisfaction your address replete with expressions of affection and esteem; I rejoice in the opportunity of assuring you that I shall always retain a grateful remembrance of the cordial welcome I experienced in my visit to New Port....

The reflection on the days of difficulty and danger which are past is rendered the more sweet from a consciousness that they are succeeded by days of uncommon prosperity and security. If we have wisdom to make the best use of the advantages with which we are now favored, we cannot fail, under the just administration of a good government to become a great and a happy people.

The Citizens of the United States of America have a right to applaud themselves for having given to mankind examples of an enlarged and liberal policy, a policy worthy of imitation.

All possess alike liberty of conscience and immunities of citizenship. It is now no more that toleration is spoken of, as it was by the indulgence of one class of people, that another enjoyed the exercise of their inherent natural rights. For happily the government of the United States, which gives to bigotry no sanction, to persecution no assistance, requires only that they who live under its protection should demean themselves as good citizens, in giving it on all occasions their effectual support....

May the children of the Stock of Abraham, who dwell in this land, continue to merit and enjoy the good will of the other inhabitants, while every one shall sit in safety under his own vine and fig-tree, and there shall be none to make him afraid....

George Washington. A letter to the Hebrew Congregation in New Port, Rhode Island, 1790.

MEMORIAL DAY/VETERANS' DAY

The Young Dead Soldiers

The young dead soldiers do not speak.
Nevertheless they are heard in the still houses.
(Who has not heard them?)
They have a silence that speaks for them at night
And when the clock counts.
They say,
We were young. We have died. Remember us.
They say,
We have done what we could
But until it is finished it is not done.
They say,
We have given our lives
But until it is finished no one can know what our lives gave.
They say,
Our deaths are not ours,
They are yours,
They will mean what you make them.
They say,
Whether our lives and our deaths were for peace and a new hope
Or for nothing
We cannot say.
It is you who must say this.
They say,
We leave you our deaths.
Give them their meaning.
Give them an end to the war and a true peace,
Give them a victory that ends the war and a peace afterwards,
Give them their meaning.
We were young, they say.
We have died.
Remember us.

Archibald MacLeish

FOURTH OF JULY

May America remain loyal to the principles of the Declaration of Independence and apply them to ever widening areas of life.

May our country be free from oppression, persecution, and unjust discrimination; may we overcome religious, racial, and class conflicts; and may we be restored as a haven of refuge for the victims of injustice and deprivation.

May we learn the art of living together, and come to understand how to appreciate differences, to reconcile clashing interests, and to help one another achieve a harmonious and abundant life.

May we acquire the wisdom to choose honest and capable leaders who will govern us by democratic and ethical principles.

And may the enterprise of our American people be blessed that we may utilize the resources of our land for the good of all the world.

1945 Reconstructionist Sabbath Prayer Book (adapted)

The New Colossus

Not like the brazen giant of Greek fame,
With conquering limbs astride from land to land;
Here at our sea-washed, sunset gates shall stand
A mighty woman with a torch, whose flame
Is the imprisoned lightning, and her name
Mother of Exiles. From her beacon-hand
Glows world-wide welcome; her mild eyes command
The air-bridged harbor that twin cities frame.
"Keep, ancient lands, your storied pomp!" cries she
With silent lips. "Give me your tired, your poor,
Your huddled masses yearning to breathe free,
The wretched refuse of your teeming shore.
Send these, the homeless, tempest-tossed to me,
I lift my lamp beside the golden door!"

Emma Lazarus

We hold these truths to be self-evident: that all men are created equal; that they are endowed by their Creator with certain unalienable rights; that among these are life, liberty and the pursuit of happiness. That to secure these rights, governments are instituted among men, deriving their just powers from the consent of the governed. That whenever any form of government becomes destructive of these ends, it is the right of the people to alter or to abolish it, and to institute new government, laying its foundation on such principles and organizing its powers in such form, as to them shall seem most likely to effect their safety and happiness....

We, therefore, the representatives of the United States of America, in general congress assembled, appealing to the Supreme Judge of the world for the rectitude of our intentions, do, in the name, and by authority of the good people of these colonies, solemnly publish and declare that these United Colonies are, and of right ought to be free and independent States....And for the support of this Declaration, with a firm reliance on the protection of Divine Providence, we mutually pledge to each other our lives, our fortunes and our sacred honor.

The Declaration of Independence

LABOR DAY

In Palestine we must do with our own hands all the things that make up the sum total of life. We must ourselves do all the work, from the least strenuous, cleanest, and most sophisticated, to the dirtiest and most difficult. In our own way, we must feel what a worker feels and think what a worker thinks—then, and only then, shall we have a culture of our own, for then we shall have a life of our own.

It all seems very clear. From now on our principal ideal must be Labor. Through no fault of our own we have been deprived of this element and we must seek a remedy. Labor is our cure. The ideal of Labor must become the pivot of all our aspirations. It is the foundation upon which our national structure is to be erected. Only by making Labor, for its own sake, our national ideal shall we be able to cure ourselves of the plague that has affected us for many generations and mend the rent between ourselves and Nature. Labor is a great human ideal. It is the ideal of the future, and a great ideal can be a healing sun.

Aaron David Gordon

Fish Crier

I know a Jew[ish] fish crier down on Maxwell Street with a
  voice like a north wind blowing over corn stubble in January.
He dangles herring before prospective customers evincing a joy
  identical with that of Pavlowa dancing.
His face is that of a man terribly glad to be selling fish, terribly
  glad that God made fish, and customers to whom he may
  call his wares from a pushcart.

Carl Sandburg

The Operator

He's as absorbed in what he sews as though
this work is all he was created for.
Beyond the pane he sees no pigeons soar,
nor on the sunlit roofs the melting snow.

At the machines around him, row on row,
bent at their work like him sit many more.
As if under a heavy film they are.
His ear is shattered by a cry of woe.

To slaves of distant times he's brother sworn:
of Egypt, Babylon, Jerusalem
and Rome—an endless chain uniting him
with all the slaves that ever have been born.

And deep within his low and narrow brow
a fire darts about and shoots up strong;
as if the battle's being born inside his brain right now,
out of the uproar leaps a liberation song!

דער אָפּערייטער

ער איז אַזוי אַרייַנגעטון אין דעם גענייַ,
ווי ס'וואָלט מער קיין זאַך נישט געווען אין לעבן.
ער זעט נישט פאַר די פענסטער טויבן שוועבן,
און אַף די דעכער אין דער זון—דאָס שמעלצן זיך פון שנייַ.

אַרום אים, איבער די מאַשינען, רייַ נאָך רייַ—
אַסך נאָך אַנדערע ווי ער אַליין געבויגן.
ס'איז אַלץ ווי מיט אַ הייַטל שווער פאַרצויגן,
אין אויער רוישט אים פון געפּייַניקטע ס'געשרייַ. ←

מיט לאַנגע דורות קנעכט איז ער באַשוועךט.
ער זעט די קנעכט פון פּיתום אין מִצרַיִם,
אין בָּבל, רוים–די גולים פון ירושָלַיִם,–
אַ קייט, אַן ענדלאָזע, מיט קנעכט אַרום דער ערד.

און אין זיין שמאָלן, נידעריקן שטערן–
אַ פּייער בלאָנדזשעט אום און ברענט און בריט;
און ווי ער וואָלט אָט ערשט אַליין דעם קאַמף פֿאַרקלערן–
גייט אוף פון דעם געוויש דער קלאַנג פון פרייהייטליד.

Naftali Gross (translated by Aaron Kramer)

THANKSGIVING

She Was Like No Doll I'd Ever Seen...

When I sat down at the table for breakfast, the doll was at my place. Mama had made hair out of dark brown yarn and she'd embroidered eyes, a nose, and a mouth on the face. She had covered the yarn hair with a yellow kerchief embroidered with red flowers.

"She's gorgeous, Mama," I managed to murmur. "But she doesn't look like the Pilgrim woman in the picture."

"No?" Mama said.

"She looks like you in that photograph you have that was taken when you were a girl."

"Of course," Mama said. "I did that on purpose. What's a Pilgrim, *shaynkeit*? A Pilgrim is someone who came here from the other side to find freedom. That's me, Molly. I'm a Pilgrim!"

Barbara Cohen

...At P.S. 125..., as soon as October was folded back on the calendar, we began paying intense, if somewhat baffled, homage to the glories of Thanksgiving.

Most of us were the children of immigrants from Vilna or Minsk or Odessa, who rarely budged from Brooklyn, and we had to sing loud our praises for the gathering of the harvest and the prodigal bounty of the land as the trolley cars clanged by under the windows. Day after day...we devoted ourselves to that old American holiday first conceived, we were told, in a bleak place called New England, by the Pilgrims, also known as ancestors. These ancestors spoke English without an accent, did not have to pass through Ellis Island when they reached the golden land, and had come to these shores to escape from religious persecution....

We labored intently...making the first Thanksgiving—the huge Pilgrim family, at an enormously long table, in the clearing they had courageously hacked out of the ominous New England forest. With crayons and paints we smeared a lavish feast....

There was a song we sang only in November—"We gather together and ask the Lord's blessing. He chastens and hastens His will to make known." We sang it with loud and cheerful assurance as Miss Johnson thumped away on a piano....Like Christmas carols...this Thanksgiving hymn had the lure of the forbidden. I would come home on November afternoons, my face hectically pink from the autumn air and the grandeur of Thansgiving, and sing "We Gather Together" until my mother, who would be working on a dress for me or one of her customers and never seemed to be listening, would suddenly hear "the Lord's blessing" and exclaim, "What kind of a song is this for a Jewish girl to sing! Stop this minute, it's not nice somebody should hear you." ↩

For weeks before the holiday I brought the same lament home from school every afternoon...."But Mama, *why* can't we have turkey for Thanksgiving like everybody else?"

"Who's everybody?" my mother would say, without taking her eyes from the sewing machine. "The Feins eat turkey Thanksgiving? Doris Levine's mother goes on the subway to buy a turkey God knows where Thanksgiving?"

"Oh, honest to God, Mama. You're always making believe you don't understand one single word I'm saying. I meant like *Americans* have on Thanksgiving, not that dopey Doris...."

I knew it was useless to argue. I knew it before I began to try. But something urged me, every November, to try just this once more. How easy it seemed, how easy and beautiful and right, as I pictured it, mooning in my room....the round table in the living room swelled with the two leaves we dragged out from behind the sofa only at Passover time....At four in the afternoon, all the guests would assemble....This day would differ from other days because on Thanksgiving my brother and I would be glad to see our cousins, who for a change would not say, "What do you have to take dopey violin lessons for?" And after we had all kissed each other sweetly, we would sit down, with cheerful smiles, around the jolly table set exactly the way they showed in the *Ladies' Home Journal.* After we sang "We Gather Together," my mother would march in from the kitchen at just the right moment, holding the enormous, steaming brown bird aloft on a silver platter, which she placed reverently in front of my father, poised and ready with a carving knife handed down, of course, by ancestors. Then Papa would begin to carve with magnificent effortless skill, an art taught him by his father who had learned it from *his* father....

Pearl Kazin

DEATH, MOURNING AND MEMORY

Dirge Without Music

I am not resigned to the shutting away of loving hearts in the hard ground.
So it is, and so it will be, for so it has been, time out of mind:
Into the darkness they go, the wise and the lovely. Crowned
With lilies and with laurel they go; but I am not resigned.

Lovers and thinkers, into the earth with you.
Be one with the dull, the indiscriminate dust.
A fragment of what you felt, of what you knew,
A formula, a phrase remains, but the best is lost.

The answers quick and keen, the honest look, the laughter, the love,
They are gone. They are gone to feed the roses. Elegant and curled
Is the blossom. Fragrant is the blossom. I know. But I do not approve.
More precious was the light in your eyes than all the roses in the world.

Down, down, down into the darkness of the grave
Gently they go, the beautiful, the tender, the kind;
Quietly they go, the intelligent, the witty, the brave.
I know. But I do not approve. And I am not resigned.

Edna St. Vincent Millay

The Intention

Healing is both an exercise
and an understanding
and yet not of the will
nor of the intention
It is a wisdom
and a deeper knowledge
of the daily swing
of life and death
in all creation
There is defeat
to overcome
and acceptance of living
to be established
and always
there must be hope
Not hope of healing
but the hope which informs
the coming moment
and gives it reason
The hope which is
each man's breath
the certainty of love
and of loving
Death may live
in the living
and healing rise
in the dying
for whom the natural end
is part of the gathering
and of the harvest
to be expected ↩

To know healing
is to know that
all life is one
and there is no beginning
and no end
and the intention is loving

Margaret Torrie

In Many Houses

In many houses
all at once
I see my mother and father
and they are young
as they walk in.

Why should my
tears come,
to see them laughing?

That they cannot
see me
is of no matter:

I was once
their dream:
now
they are mine.

Author Unknown

## לְכָל אִישׁ יֵשׁ שֵׁם	## *Each Of Us Has a Name*
לְכָל אִישׁ יֵשׁ שֵׁם	Each of us has a name
שֶׁנָּתַן לוֹ אֱלֹהִים	given by God
וְנָתְנוּ לוֹ אָבִיו וְאִמּוֹ	and given by our parents
לְכָל אִישׁ יֵשׁ שֵׁם	Each of us has a name
שֶׁנָּתְנוּ לוֹ קוֹמָתוֹ וְאֹפֶן חִיּוּכוֹ	given by our stature and our smile
וְנָתַן לוֹ הָאָרִיג	and given by what we wear
לְכָל אִישׁ יֵשׁ שֵׁם	Each of us has a name
שֶׁנָּתְנוּ לוֹ הֶהָרִים	given by the mountains
וְנָתְנוּ לוֹ כְּתָלָיו	and given by our walls
לְכָל אִישׁ יֵשׁ שֵׁם	Each of us has a name
שֶׁנָּתְנוּ לוֹ הַמַּזָּלוֹת	given by the stars
וְנָתְנוּ לוֹ שְׁכֵנָיו	and given by our neighbors
לְכָל אִישׁ יֵשׁ שֵׁם	Each of us has a name
שֶׁנָּתְנוּ לוֹ חֲטָאָיו	given by our sins
וְנָתְנָה לוֹ כְּמִיהָתוֹ	and given by our longing
לְכָל אִישׁ יֵשׁ שֵׁם	Each of us has a name
שֶׁנָּתְנוּ לוֹ שׂוֹנְאָיו	given by our enemies
וְנָתְנָה לוֹ אַהֲבָתוֹ	and given by our love
לְכָל אִישׁ יֵשׁ שֵׁם	Each of us has a name
שֶׁנָּתְנוּ לוֹ חַגָּיו	given by our celebrations
וְנָתְנָה לוֹ מְלַאכְתּוֹ	and given by our work
לְכָל אִישׁ יֵשׁ שֵׁם	Each of us has a name
שֶׁנָּתְנוּ לוֹ תְּקוּפוֹת הַשָּׁנָה	given by the seasons
וְנָתַן לוֹ עִוְרוֹנוֹ	and given by our blindness
לְכָל אִישׁ יֵשׁ שֵׁם	Each of us has a name
שֶׁנָּתַן לוֹ הַיָּם	given by the sea
וְנָתַן לוֹ	and given by
מוֹתוֹ׃	our death.

Zelda (translated by Marcia Falk)

Life After Death

These things I know:
How the living go on living
and how the dead go on living with them
so that in a forest
even a dead tree casts a shadow
and the leaves fall one by one
and the branches break in the wind
and the bark peels off slowly
and the trunk cracks
and the rain seeps in through the cracks
and the trunk falls to the ground
and the moss covers it
and in the spring the rabbits find it
and build their nest
inside the dead tree
so that nothing is wasted in nature
or in love.

Laura Gilpin

To open eyes when others close them
to hear when others do not wish to listen
to look when others turn away
to seek to understand when others give up
to rouse oneself when others accept
to continue the struggle even when one is not the strongest
to cry out when others keep silent—
to be a Jew
it is that,
it is first of all that
and further
to live when others are dead
and to remember when others have forgotten.

Emmanuel Eydoux (translated from the French by Jonathan Magonet)

Connections are made slowly, sometimes they grow underground. You cannot tell always by looking what is happening. More than half a tree is spread out in the soil under your feet. Penetrate quietly as the earthworm that blows no trumpet. Fight persistently as the creeper that brings down the tree. Spread like the squash plant that overruns the garden. Gnaw in the dark and use the sun to make sugar.

Weave real connections, create real nodes, build real houses. Live a life you can endure: make love that is loving. Keep tangling and interweaving and taking more in, a thicket and bramble wilderness to the outside but to us interconnected with rabbit runs and burrows and lairs.

Live as if you liked yourself, and it may happen: reach out, keep reaching out, keep bringing in. This is how we are going to live for a long time: not always, for every gardener knows that after the digging, after the planting, after the long season of tending and growth, the harvest comes.

Marge Piercy

Birth is a Beginning

Birth is a beginning
And death a destination.
And life is a journey:
From childhood to maturity
And youth to age;
From innocence to awareness
And ignorance to knowing;
From foolishness to discretion
  And then perhaps to wisdom;
From weakness to strength
Or strength to weakness—
  And, often back again;
From health to sickness
  And back, we pray, to health again;
From offense to forgiveness,
From loneliness to love,
From joy to gratitude,
From pain to compassion,
And grief to understanding—
  From fear to faith;

From defeat to defeat to defeat—
Until, looking backward or ahead,
We see that victory lies
Not at some high place along the way,
But in having made the journey, stage by stage,
  A sacred pilgrimage.
Birth is a beginning
And death a destination
But life is a journey,
A sacred pilgrimage—
  To life everlasting.

Alvin I. Fine

LOSS OF A PARENT

All the Generations Before Me

All the generations before me
donated me, bit by bit, so that I'd be
erected all at once
here in Jerusalem, like a house of prayer
or charitable institution.
It binds. My name's
my donors' name.
It binds.

I'm approaching the age
of my father's death. My last
will's patched with many patches.
I have to change my life and death
daily to fulfill all the prophecies
prophesied for me. So they're not lies.
It binds.

I've passed forty.
There are jobs I cannot get
because of this. Were I in Auschwitz
they would not have sent me out to work,
but gassed me straightaway.
It binds. ↩

כָּל הַדּוֹרוֹת שֶׁלְּפָנַי

כָּל הַדּוֹרוֹת שֶׁלְּפָנַי תָּרְמוּ אוֹתִי
קִמְעָה קִמְעָה כְּדֵי שֶׁאוּקַם כָּאן בִּירוּשָׁלַיִם
בְּבַת אַחַת, כְּמוֹ בֵּית־תְּפִלָּה אוֹ מוֹסַד צְדָקָה.

זֶה מְחַיֵּב. שְׁמִי הוּא שֵׁם תּוֹרְמַי.
זֶה מְחַיֵּב.

אֲנִי מִתְקָרֵב לְגִיל מוֹת אָבִי.
צַוָּאָתִי מְטֻלֵּאת בְּהַרְבֵּה טְלָאִים,
אֲנִי צָרִיךְ לְשַׁנּוֹת אֶת חַיַּי וְאֶת מוֹתִי
יוֹם יוֹם כְּדֵי לְקַיֵּם אֶת כָּל הַנְּבוּאוֹת
שֶׁנִּבְּאוּ אוֹתִי. שֶׁלֹּא יִהְיוּ שֶׁקֶר.
זֶה מְחַיֵּב.

עָבַרְתִּי אֶת שְׁנַת הָאַרְבָּעִים. יֵשׁ
מִשְׂרוֹת שֶׁבָּהֶן לֹא יְקַבְּלוּ אוֹתִי
בְּשֶׁל כָּךְ. אִלּוּ הָיִיתִי בְּאוֹשְׁוִיץ,
לֹא הָיוּ שׁוֹלְחִים אוֹתִי לַעֲבֹד,
הָיוּ שׂוֹרְפִים אוֹתִי מִיָּד.
זֶה מְחַיֵּב.

Yehuda Amichai (translated by Harold Schimmel)

To My Father

You gathered incredible strength
in order to die
to seem calm and fully conscious
without complaint, without trembling
without a cry
so that I would not be afraid

Your wary hand
slowly grew cold in mine
and guided me carefully
beyond into the house of death
so I might come to know it

Thus in the past you used to take my hand
and guide me through the world
and show me life
so I would not fear

I will follow after you
confident as a child
toward the silent country
where you went first
so I would not feel a stranger there

And I will not be afraid.

Blaga Dmitrova

About my father

—he became a teetotaler out of his socialist convictions; during
the war he began to drink again
—he was casual; he kept his tie in his pocket till the last minute
before oral exams
—he left me on the street to be picked up by the nuns from the
orphanage; he watched me from a distant doorway
—once he refused to hit me; he told my mother his hand was
too large
—he wrote to his aunt that he hoped the baby would be a boy
—when he was a student, jews were not permitted to sit in the
front rows of lecture halls; he made it a point to stand through
the lectures; ultimately, jews were allowed to sit
—he was a discus thrower
—according to some, he got along with everyone: jews, goyim,
children
—he was caught a couple of times by the germans; they thought
he was a polish smuggler
—once he was put on a train for treblinka; he jumped, was shot
at and wounded, but got back to warsaw alive
—he believed in resistance

Irena Klepfisz

The son of a rabbi mourned the loss of his beloved father.
Day after day he went to the cemetery and prostrated himself
on his father's grave.
One day as the son gave in to waves of sorrow,
his father appeared to him in a vision and said:
"My son, do you think that you honor my memory with your
grief?
"Offer me no tribute of tears, nor monuments of sorrow.
"Do not weep for me. Instead, live for me.

"Show your love by walking the Way,
in devotion to commandment, faith, and people. This is the only memorial that
truly honors the departed."
The son rose from his father's grave
on hearing these words,
and went to make his father's memory a perpetual light to guide him
and a blessing to the world.

Rabbinic Tale

The Death of a Parent

Move to the front
of the line
a voice says, and suddenly
there is nobody
left standing between you
and the world, to take
the first blows
on their shoulders.
This is the place in books
where part one ends, and
part two begins,
and there is no part three.
The slate is wiped
not clean but like a canvas
painted over in white
so that a whole new landscape
must be started,
bits of the old
still showing underneath—
those colors sadness lends
to a certain hour of evening.

Now the line of light
at the horizon
is the hinge between earth
and heaven, only visible
a few moments
as the sun drops
its rusted padlock
into place.

Linda Pastan

I asked unanswerable questions a child asks
When a parent dies-for nothing. Only slowly
Did I make myself believe–or hope–they
Might all be swept up in their fragments
Together
And made whole again
By some compassionate hand
But my hand was too small
To do the gathering.
I have only known this feeling since
When I looked out across the sea of death,
This pull inside against a littleness—myself
Waiting for an upward gesture.

from *Gilgamesh* (translated by Herbert Mason)

First Rites

It was my mother initiated me,
Her dying, my first death,
Her kaddish had with me no precedent.
She loved me more than any child could bear,
And yet it fit somehow
That she who taught me

How to scale the world in octaves
Would plummet to a whisper's end
Rasping
"Survive," An omen
That I will. I will.

Diane Cole,

Metamorphosis

1. Night

The angel of death flies
low over my father's bed.
Only my mother sees. She and my father
are alone in the room.

She bends over him to touch
his hand, his forehead. She is
so used to mothering
that now she strokes his body
as she would the other children's,
first gently, then
inured to suffering.

Nothing is any different.
Even the spot on the lung
was always there.

2. Metamorphosis

My father has forgotten me
in the excitement of dying.
Like a child who will not eat,
he takes no notice of anything.

I sit at the edge of his bed
while the living circle us
like so many tree stumps.

Once, for the smallest
fraction of an instant, I thought
he was alive in the present again;
then he looked at me
as a blind man stares
straight into the sun, since
whatever it could do to him
is done already.

Then his flushed face
turned away from the contact.

3. For My Father

I'm going to live without you
as I learned once
to live without my mother.
You think I don't remember that?
I've spent my whole life trying to remember.

Now, after so much solitude,
death doesn't frighten me,
not yours, not mine either.
And those words, *the last time*,
have no power over me. I know
intense love always leads to mourning.

For once, your body doesn't frighten me.
From time to time, I run my hand over your face
lightly, like a dustcloth.
What can shock me now? I feel
no coldness that can't be explained.
Against your cheek, my hand is warm
and full of tenderness.

Louise Gluck

Kaddish

Mother of my birth, for how long were we together
in your love and my adoration of your self?
For the shadow of a moment, as I breathed your pain
and you breathed my suffering. As we knew
of shadows in lit rooms that would swallow the light.

Your face beneath the oxygen tent was alive
but your eyes closed, your breathing hoarse.
Your sleep was with death. I was alone
with you as when I was young
but now only alone, not with you,
to become alone forever, as I was learning
watching you become alone.

Earth now is your mother, as you were mine, my earth,
my sustenance and my strength,
and now without you I turn to your mother
and seek from her that I may meet you again
in rock and stone. Whisper to the stone,
I love you, Whisper to the rock, I found you.
Whisper to the earth, Mother, I have found her,
and I am safe and always have been.

David Ignatow

Family Tree

My father was a wandering Aramaean,
  he said
But when I brought him maps,
  begged him show me Aramaea,
He hesitated,
  then told me

That Aramaea was a wondrous place,
  with camels,
Wells and towns, cities
  strong and weak,
Tricksters and beauties, and
  cow-eyed girls.

He put his newspaper aside, rose
  from his chair, intense,
As though remembering the scene, as though
  reliving some childhood view
And told me on and on of Aramaea.

Of course I know it was made up, that
  Aramaea and my dad
Were centuries apart, that
  worlds divided them and us.
I wish instead I'd asked him how it was, wrestling.

Theodore L. Steinberg

Heirloom

My father bequeathed me no wide estate;
No keys and ledgers were my heritage;
Only some holy books with yahrzeit dates
Writ mournfully upon a blank page—

Books of the Baal Shem Tov, and of his wonders;
Pamphlets upon the devil and his crew;
Prayers against road demons, witches, thunders;
And sundry other tomes for a good Jew.

Beautiful: though no pictures on them, save
The scorpion crawling on a printed track;
The Virgin floating on a scriptual wave,
Square letters twinkling in the Zodiac.

The snuff left on this page, now brown and old,
The tallow stains of midnight liturgy—
These are my coat of arms, and these unfold
My noble lineage, my proud ancestry!

And my tears, too, have stained this heirloomed ground,
When reading in these treatises some weird
Miracle, I turned a leaf and found
A white hair fallen from my father's beard.

A.M.Klein

LOSS OF A GRANDPARENT

Gramma

My grandmother was like your grandmother:
she hung in there, played pinochle
and watched the Dodger games
until they took her to the hospital
and when I visited her (home from school)
I embarrassed the family
by vomiting in the corridor,
all those tubes, in the nose, in the arm,
of Gramma, who was tougher than I.
And when she came home to die,
after four days of not eating
asked for a half grapefruit and died
in Mother's arms. No one had seen her
get up, but in the closet were folded
neatly her burial clothes.
Old Gramma, she loved
heavy chairs, big trees, her old house.
A little lady, she demanded
little, gave much and
enjoyed what was available.
There's a lot to be said for hanging in there.

Peter Meinke

Funeral

When her coffin had been carried from the room,
the house remained exactly as she had arranged it—
her thoughts present in the position of each chair,
in the snapshots of the dead upon the mantel;
and by the kitchen door a smudge where her hand
had often rested. Her grandson, by himself
in the house, drags a chair over to that spot,
climbs up and just touches his tongue to the mark,
and in its salt and faint taste of cinnamon
a hundred bright occasions return to him.

With his eyes shut and his tongue pressed to the wood,
he can feel the house unfurl its wings, rise up
and glide over the fields of wheat and small farms
like a horned owl from the branch of a dead tree.
His heart quickens with excitement. No telling
where he is going, and will she be waiting?

Stephen Dobyns

LOSS OF A GAY OR LESBIAN LOVER

Our thoughts turn to those who have died; people of every race and nation whose lives have been a blessing, enriching our own.

O God, remember today our gay sisters and brothers who were martyred in years past: those who were murdered by fanatics in the middle ages, those who perished in the Holocaust, and those struck down in our own city, in our own time. Remember also those driven to despair by a world that hated them because of their love for one another, who took their own lives. And in mercy remember those who have wasted their lives by suppressing their true natures and refraining from sharing their love with one another. O God, accept the sacrifice of these martyrs, and help us bring an end to hate and oppression of every kind.

Author Unknown

Sister that I never held near
Comrade that I never embraced
Your memory is almost lost:

The one we don't talk about.
The loving one who never married.
The one for whom no Kaddish is said.

Your loneliness calls out to me:
I know of your struggles; we are not strangers,
And if my path is easier, I will not forget who walked it first.
We call you to mind, but did you not sometimes think of us,
Your children, lovers across the years,
Those who would follow and would think of you
And bless your memory, and call you to mind.

With David and Jonathan, we will not forget you,
With Ruth and Naomi, we will not forget you,
In the name of God you are our sisters and our brothers,
And we ask that you be remembered for peace. Author Unknown

LOSS OF A LOVED ONE

My Hereafter

Do not come when I am dead
To sit beside a low green mound,
Or bring the first gay daffodils
Because I love you so,
For I shall not be there.
You cannot find me there.

I will look up at you from the eyes
Of little children;
I will bend to meet you in the swaying boughs
Of bud-thrilled trees,
And caress you with the passionate sweep
Of storm-filled winds;
I will give you strength in your upward tread
Of everlasting hills;
I will cool your tired body in the flow
Of the limpid river;
I will warm your work-glorified hands through the glow
Of the winter fire; ↩

I will soothe you into forgetfulness to the drop, drop
Of the rain on the roof;
I will speak to you out of the rhymes
Of the Masters;
I will dance with you in the lilt
Of the violin,
And make your heart leap with the bursting cadence
Of the organ;
I will flood your soul with the flaming radiance
Of the sunrise,
And bring you peace in the tender rose and gold
Of the after-sunset.

All these have made me happy:
They are a part of me;
I shall become a part of them.

Juanita de Long

Hold on to what is good
even if it is
a handful of earth.
Hold on to what you believe
even if it is
a tree which stands by itself.
Hold on to what you must do
even if it is
a long way from here.
Hold on to life even when
it is easier letting go.
Hold on to my hand even when
I have gone away from you.

Nancy Wood

LIFE AND DEATH

Gravy

No other word will do. For that's what it was. Gravy.
Gravy these past ten years.
Alive, sober, working, loving and
being loved by a good woman. Eleven years
ago he was told he had six months to live
at the rate he was going. And he was going
nowhere but down. So he changed his ways
somehow. He quit drinking! And the rest?
After that it was *all* gravy, every minute
of it, up to and including when he was told about,
well, some things that were breaking down and
building up inside his head. "Don't weep for me,"
he said to his friends. "I'm a lucky man.
I've had ten years longer than I or anyone
expected. Pure gravy. And don't forget it."

Raymond Carver

Strange is our situation here upon earth.
Each of us comes for a short visit,
not knowing why,
yet sometimes seeming to divine a purpose.
From the standpoint of daily life, however,
there is one thing we do know:
That we are here for the sake of others...
Above all, for those upon whose smile and well-being our own happiness depends,
and also for the countless unknown souls
with whose fate we are connected by a bond of sympathy.
Many times a day I realize how much my own outer and inner life is built upon the labors of my
fellows both living and dead, and how earnestly I must exert myself in order to give in return as
much as I have received and am still receiving.

Albert Einstein (Adapted)

Kaddish (for Marilyn)

As long
as I speak
your name
you are
not dead

as long
as I think
your pain
I cannot
grieve

the granite marker
tells
your name
your age

the bleak horizon
scars
the barren hedge

as long
as I
you
are not dead

Hannah Kahn

In Praise Of The Living

Yitgadal ve'yitkadash shemey raba
This profound praise of the living
Praise for the generous gift of life.

Praise for the presence of loved ones,
the bonds of friendship, the link of memory.

Praise for the toil and searching,
the dedication and visions, the ennobling aspirations.

Praise for the precious moorings of faith,
for courageous souls, for prophets, psalmists, and sages.

Praise for those who walked before us,
the sufferers in the valley of shadows,
the steadfast in the furnace of hate.

Praise for the God of our fathers,
the Source of all growth and goodness,
the Promise of which we build tomorrow.

Yitgadal ve'yitkadash shemey raba

This, the profound praise we offer.
Praise for the generous gift of life.

Harvey J. Fields

We turn our thoughts to yesterday...to a world that lives only in our memory.
As we recall the days gone by, we know the past is irretrievable.
Yet—through the gift of memory, we recapture treasured moments and images.
We are thankful for the happiness we knew with those no longer here, with whom we lived and laughed and loved.
We praise the Eternal wellspring of life who links yesterday to tomorrow. We affirm that despite all the tragedy bound up with living, it is still good to be alive.
We understand that there can be no love without loss, no joy without sorrow. May we have the courage to accept the all of life—the love and the loss—the joy and the sorrow, as we remember them.

Evelyn Mehlman

Living Memory

All we can read is life. Death is invisible.
A yahrzeit candle belongs
to life. The sugar skulls
eaten on graves for the Day of the Dead
belong to life. To the living. The Kaddish is to the living,
the Day of the Dead, for the living. Only the living
invent these plumes, tombs, mounds, funeral ships,
living hands turn the mirrors to the walls,
tear the boughs of yew to lay on the casket,
rip the clothes of mourning. Only the living
decide death's color: is it white or black?
The granite bulkhead
incised with names, the quilt of names, were made
by the living, for the living.

I have watched
films from a Pathe camera, a picnic
in sepia, I have seen my mother
tossing an acorn into the air;
my grandfather, alone in the heart of his family;
my father, young, dark, theatrical;
myself, a six-month child.
Watching the dead we see them living
their moments, they were at play, nobody thought
they would be watched so.

Adrienne Rich (Excerpted)

Upon Israel and upon the rabbis
and upon the disciples and upon all the disciples of the disciples
and upon all who study the Torah in this place and in every place, to them and to you, peace;

Upon Israel and upon all who meet with unfriendly glances, sticks and stones and names—
on posters, in newspapers, or in books to last,
chalked on asphalt or in acid on glass,
shouted from a thousand thousand windows by radio;
who are pushed out of class-rooms and rushing trains,
whom the hundred hands of a mob strike,
and whom jailers strike with bunches of keys, with revolver butts; to them and to you
in this place and in every place
safety;

Upon Israel and upon all who live
as the sparrows of the streets
under the cornices of the houses of others,
and as rabbits in the fields of strangers
on the grace of the seasons
and what the gleaners leave in the corners;
you children of the wind—
birds that feed on the tree of knowledge
in this place and in every place
to them and to you
a living;

Upon Israel
and upon their children and upon all the children of their children in this place and in every place,
to them and to you
life!

Charles Reznikoff

Learning from Trees

If we could,
like the trees,
practice dying,
do it every year
just as something we do—
like going on vacation
or celebrating birthdays,
it would become
as easy a part of us
as our hair or clothing.

Someone would show us how
to lie down and fade away
as if in deepest meditation,
and we would learn
about the fine dark emptiness,
both knowing it and not knowing it,
and coming back would be irrelevant.

Whatever it is the trees know
when they stand undone,
surprisingly intricate,
we need to know also
so we can allow
that last thing
to happen to us
as if it were only
any ordinary thing,

leaves and lives
falling away,
the spirit, complex,
waiting in the fine darkness
to learn which way
it will go.

Grace Butcher

The Five Stages Of Grief

The night I lost you
someone pointed me towards
the Five Stages of Grief.
Go that way, they said,
it's easy, like learning to climb
stairs after the amputation.
And so I climbed.
Denial was first.
I sat down at breakfast
carefully setting the table
for two. I passed you the toast—
you sat there. I passed
you the paper—you hid
behind it.
Anger seemed more familiar.
I burned the toast, snatched
the paper and read the headlines myself.
But they mentioned your departure,
and so I moved on to
Bargaining. What could I exchange
for you? The silence
after storms? My typing fingers?
Before I could decide, *Depression*
came puffing up, a poor relation
its suitcase tied together
with string. In the suitcase
were bandages for the eyes
and bottles of sleep. I slid
all the way down the stairs
feeling nothing. ↵

And all the time Hope
flashed on and off
in defective neon.
Hope was a signpost pointing
straight in the air.
Hope was my uncle's middle name,
he died of it.
After a year I am still climbing,
though my feet slip
on your stone face.
The treeline
has long since disappeared;
green is a color
I have forgotten.
But now I see what I am climbing
towards: Acceptance
written in capital letters,
a special headline:
Acceptance,
its name is in lights.
I struggle on,
waving and shouting.
Below, my whole life spreads its surf,
all the landscape I've ever known
or dreamed of. Below
a fish jumps: the pulse
in your neck.
Acceptance. I finally
reach it.
But something is wrong.
Grief is a circular staircase.
I have lost you.

Linda Pastan

Above Everything

I wished for death often
but now that I am at its door
I have changed my mind about the world.
It should go on; it is beautiful,
even as a dream, filled with water and seed,
plants and animals, others like myself,
ships and buildings and messages
filling the air—a beauty,
if ever I have seen one.
In the next world, should I remember
this one, I will praise it
above everything.

David Ignatow

Death is not strange.
Strange is life,
That flesh can think,
And body believe,

That dust can sing;
That a clod of earth
For one's lifetime
Can house God.

That dead things live
When touched by God's breath,
Is the miracle,
Not death.

Adapted from a poem by Joseph Leftwich

Zot Tefilati / This Is My Prayer

This is my prayer to you, my gentle God—
let me not stray from my life's course,
let not my spirit fall into decay,
and may it never cease to thirst for you,
and for the energizing dew
that you have sprinkled on it
ever since my life was new.

And let my heart be open to
the downtrodden, and to the orphaned life,
and to all who stumble,
and to one entangled amid hidden sorrows,
and to one who struggles in the dark.

And bless my eyes, and let me merit
to behold the human beauty in this world.

Deepen my senses, widen their grasp
so they absorb a green and flowering
and budding world, and take from it
the secret blossoming within a silence.

Grant me with strength to yield
the best of fruits. Let my life grow
a wealth of word and deed, steeped
in the fountain of my being,
without my measuring all things
for only what they have to offer me.

And when my day shall come,
let me slip into the land of night,
without asking anything from others
or from you, God.

זֹאת תְּפִלָּתִי לְךָ, אֵל אֱלֹהַי:
שָׁמְרֵנִי לְבַל אֵשְׁטְ מִנְּתִיב חַיַּי,
לְבַל יַמַּק רוּחִי וּלְבַל יִדַּל
מִצִּמְאוֹנוֹ לְךָ וּמִן הַטַּל
עָלָיו הִזְלַפְתָּ בְּעוֹדֶנִּי רַךְ.

יְהִי לִבִּי פָּתוּחַ אֶל כָּל־דַּךְ,
אֶל כָּל־יְתוֹם חַיִּים, אֶל כָּל־כּוֹשֵׁל
נִפְתָּל בַּסֵּתֶר וּמְגַשֵּׁשׁ בַּצֵּל.

בָּרֵךְ עֵינַי, זַכֵּנִי לִרְאוֹת
יְפִי אָדָם עוֹלֶה בְּתֵבֵל זֹאת.

וְאֶת־חוּשַׁי בִּי הָעֲמֵק, הַרְחֵב
לִסְפֹּג עוֹלָם יָרֹק, נִצָּן וָאֵב,
לִקְלֹט מֵהֶם סוֹד הַלִּבְלוּב בְּדָמִי.

חָנֵּנִי אוֹן לָתֵת מֵיטַב כָּל־פְּרִי,
תַּמְצִית חַיַּי, בְּנִיב שִׁקּוּי לְשַׁדִּי
מִבְּלִי צַפּוֹת לִגְמוּל צָפוּי בַּעֲדִי.

וּכְבוֹא יוֹמִי — לַחֲמֹק לִרְשׁוּת הַלֵּיל
בְּלִי תְבֹעַ מָה מֵאִישׁ וּמִמְּךָ, אֵל.

Hillel Bavli (translated by Joel Rosenberg)

After a while, you learn the subtle difference
Between holding a hand and chaining a soul.
And you learn that love doesn't mean leaning,
And company doesn't always mean security,
And you begin to learn that kisses aren't contracts,
And presents aren't promises.

And you begin to accept your defeats
With your head up and your eyes open,
With the grace of a woman,
Not the grief of a child.

And you learn to build all your roads on today,
Because tomorrow's ground is too uncertain for plans,
And futures have a way of falling down in mid-flight.

After a while you learn
That even sunshine burns if you get too much.
So you plant your own garden and decorate your own soul,
Instead of waiting for someone to bring you flowers.

And you learn that you really can endure...
That you really are strong,
And that you really have worth.

And you learn and learn...

With every goodbye, you learn

Veronica A. Shoffstall

One day a rabbi gazed through the window of his study which looked out upon the marketplace. People were hurrying to and fro, each attending to his or her own particular business. Suddenly the rabbi saw a familiar face.

"Hikel!" he called. "Come in, I want to speak with you."

"Shalom, Rabbi, how are you?"

"Thank God, I am fine. Tell me, Hikel, what were you doing in the marketplace?"

"Oh, I'm very busy today. I have a lot of business to take care of." ↩

"Hikel," asked the rabbi, "Have you looked up at the sky today?"
"At the sky, Rabbi? No, of course not. I'm too busy to look at the sky."
"Hikel, look out the window and tell me what you see."
"I see people and horses and carriages, all rushing around doing business."
"Hikel," the rabbi said, "in fifty years there will be other people in other carriages, drawn by other horses, and we will not be here. And, Hikel, in a hundred years, neither the marketplace nor this town will even exist. Look at the sky, Hikel, look at the sky!"

Hasidic Tale

Four Things

These things are beautiful beyond belief:
The pleasant weakness that comes after pain,
The radiant greenness that comes after rain,
The deepened faith that follows after grief,
And the awakening to love again.

Author unknown

Real faith does not mean professing what we hold true in a ready-made formula....It means holding ourselves open to the unconditional mystery which we encounter in every sphere of our life and which cannot be comprised in any formula. It means that, from the very roots of our being, we should always be prepared to live with this mystery as one being lives with another. Real faith means the ability to endure life in the face of this mystery.

Martin Buber

There are stars whose light reaches the earth only after they themselves have disintegrated and are no more. And there are people whose scintillating memory lights the world after they have passed from it. These lights which shine in the darkest night are those which illumine for us the path...

Hannah Szenes (Translator Unknown)

After My Death

After I am dead
Say this at my funeral:

There was a man who exists no more.

That man died before his time
And his life's song was broken off halfway.
Oh, he had one more poem
And that poem has been lost
For ever.

He had a lyre,
And a vital, quivering soul.
The poet in him spoke,
Gave out all his heart's secrets,
His hand struck all its chords.
But there was one secret he kept hidden
Though his fingers danced everywhere,
One string stayed mute
And is still soundless.

But alas! all its days
That string trembled,
Trembled softly, softly quivered
For the poem that would free her,
Yearned and thirsted, grieved and wept,
As though pining for someone expected
Who does not come,
And the more he delays, she whimpers
With a soft, fine sound,
But he does not come,
And the agony is very great,
There was a man and he exists no more.
His life's song was broken off halfway.
He had one more poem
And that poem is lost,
For ever.

אַחֲרֵי מוֹתִי

אַחֲרֵי מוֹתִי סִפְדוּ כָּכָה לִי:
”הָיָה אִישׁ — וּרְאוּ: אֵינֶנּוּ עוֹד;
קֹדֶם זְמַנּוֹ מֵת הָאִישׁ הַזֶּה,
וְשִׁירַת חַיָּיו בְּאֶמְצַע נִפְסָקָה;
וְצַר! עוֹד מִזְמוֹר אֶחָד הָיָה־לּוֹ —
וְהִנֵּה אָבַד הַמִּזְמוֹר לָעַד,
אָבַד לָעַד!←

וְצַר מְאֹד! הֵן כִּנּוֹר הָיָה־לוֹ —
נֶפֶשׁ חַיָּה וּמְמַלְּלָה,
וְהַמְשׁוֹרֵר מִדֵּי דַבְּרוֹ בוֹ
אֶת־כָּל־רָזֵי לִבּוֹ הִגִּיד לוֹ,
וְכָל־הַנִּימִין יָדוֹ דוֹבְבָה,
אַךְ רָז אֶחָד בְּקִרְבּוֹ הִכְחִיד,
סְחוֹר סְחוֹר לוֹ אֶצְבְּעוֹתָיו פִּזְּזוּ,
נִימָה אַחַת אִלְּמָה נִשְׁאֲרָה,
אִלְּמָה נִשְׁאֲרָה עַד־הַיּוֹם!

וְצַר מְאֹד, מְאֹד!
כָּל־יָמֶיהָ זָעָה נִימָה זוֹ,
דּוּמָם זָעָה, דּוּמָם רָעֲדָה,
אֶל־מִזְמוֹרָהּ, דּוֹדָהּ גּוֹאֲלָהּ,
כָּמְהָה, צָמְאָה, עָגְמָה, נִכְסָפָה,
כַּאֲשֶׁר יֶעְגַּם לֵב לַמְזֻמָּן לוֹ;

וְאִם־הִתְמַהְמַהּ — בְּכָל־יוֹם חִכְּתָה־לוֹ
וּבִנְהִימָה טְמִירָה שִׁוְּעָה־לוֹ —
וְהוּא הִתְמַהְמַהּ אַף לֹא־בָא,
אַף לֹא־בָא!

וְגָדוֹל מְאֹד, מְאֹד הַכְּאֵב!
הָיָה אִישׁ — וּרְאוּ: אֵינֶנּוּ עוֹד,
וְשִׁירַת חַיָּיו בְּאֶמְצַע נִפְסְקָה;
עוֹד שִׁיר מִזְמוֹר אֶחָד הָיָה־לוֹ,
וְהִנֵּה אָבַד הַמִּזְמוֹר לָעַד,
אָבַד לָעַד!"

Ḥayim Naḥman Bialik (translated by A.C Jacobs)

I Don't Have Time

I don't have time
to have time for everything
I don't have seasons enough to have
a season for every purpose. Ecclesiastes
was wrong about that.

I need to love and to hate at the same moment,
to laugh and cry with the same eyes,
with the same hands to cast away stones and to gather them,
to make love in war and war in love.

And to hate and forgive and remember and forget,
to set in order and confuse, to eat and to digest
what history
takes years and years to do.

I don't have time.
When I lose I seek, when I find
I forget, when I forget I love, when I love
I begin to forget.

And my soul is experienced, my soul
is very professional.
Only my body remains forever
an amateur. It tries and it misses,
gets muddled, doesn't learn a thing,
drunk and blind in its pleasures
and in its pains.

I will die as figs die in autumn,
shriveled and full of ourselves and sweet,
the leaves growing dry on the ground,
the bare branches already pointing to the place
where there's time for everything. ↩

אָדָם בְּחַיָּיו

אָדָם בְּחַיָּיו אֵין לוֹ זְמַן שֶׁיִּהְיֶה לוֹ
זְמַן לַכֹּל.
וְאֵין לוֹ עֵת שֶׁתִּהְיֶה לוֹ עֵת
לְכָל חֵפֶץ. קֹהֶלֶת לֹא צָדַק כְּשֶׁאָמַר כָּךְ.

אָדָם צָרִיךְ לִשְׂנֹא וְלֶאֱהֹב בְּבַת־אַחַת,
בְּאוֹתָן עֵינַיִם לִבְכּוֹת וּבְאוֹתָן עֵינַיִם לִצְחֹק
בְּאוֹתָן יָדַיִם לִזְרֹק אֲבָנִים
וּבְאוֹתָן יָדַיִם לֶאֱסֹף אוֹתָן,
לַעֲשׂוֹת אַהֲבָה בַּמִּלְחָמָה וּמִלְחָמָה בָּאַהֲבָה.

וְלִשְׂנֹא וְלִסְלֹחַ וְלִזְכֹּר וְלִשְׁכֹּחַ
וּלְסַדֵּר וּלְבַלְבֵּל וְלֶאֱכֹל וּלְעַכֵּל
אֶת מַה שֶּׁהִסְטוֹרְיָה אֲרֻכָּה
עוֹשָׂה בְּשָׁנִים רַבּוֹת מְאֹד.

אָדָם בְּחַיָּיו אֵין לוֹ זְמַן.
כְּשֶׁהוּא מְאַבֵּד הוּא מְחַפֵּשׂ
כְּשֶׁהוּא מוֹצֵא הוּא שׁוֹכֵחַ,
כְּשֶׁהוּא שׁוֹכֵחַ הוּא אוֹהֵב
וּכְשֶׁהוּא אוֹהֵב הוּא מַתְחִיל לִשְׁכֹּחַ.

וְנַפְשׁוֹ לְמוּדָה,
וְנַפְשׁוֹ מִקְצוֹעִית מְאֹד
רַק גּוּפוֹ נִשְׁאָר חוֹבֵב
תָּמִיד. מְנַסֶּה וְטוֹעֶה
לֹא לוֹמֵד וּמִתְבַּלְבֵּל
שִׁכּוֹר וְעִוֵּר בְּתַעֲנוּגָיו וּבְמַכְאוֹבָיו. ←

מוֹת תְּאֵנִים יָמוּת בְּסְתָו
מְצֻמָּק וּמְלֵא עַצְמוֹ וּמָתוֹק,
הֶעָלִים מִתְיַבְּשִׁים עַל הָאֲדָמָה,
וְהָעֲנָפִים הָעֲרֻמִּים כְּבָר מַצְבִּיעִים
אֶל הַמָּקוֹם שֶׁבּוֹ זְמַן לַכֹּל.

Yehuda Amichai (Translator Unknown)

Tattered Kaddish

Taurean reaper of the wild apple field
messenger from earthmire gleaning
transcripts of fog
in the nineteenth year and the eleventh month
speak your tattered Kaddish for all suicides:

Praise to life though it crumbled in like a tunnel
on ones we knew and loved

Praise to life though its windows blew shut
on the breathing-room of ones we knew and loved

Praise to life though ones we knew and loved
loved it badly, too well, and not enough

Praise to life though it tightened like a knot
on the hearts of ones we thought we knew loved us

Praise to life giving room and reason
to ones we knew and loved who felt unpraisable

Praise to them, how they loved it, when they could.

Adrienne Rich

Another Tree

If a tree dies, plant another one.
Linnaeus

We sat in the yard where his house had burned.

Only I had seen the shadowed negative,
the X-ray of his brain. He squinted,

one eye too sensitive to the sun.

His right hand lay useless on his lap.
Optimism all that was left to him,

all of his grace.

For him, I'd rescued and rebuilt the place,
made a new house, planted another tree,

the little mimosa now two stories high.

In a few weeks, he'd be gone,
such was the rapaciousness of the cells,

so defenseless the nervous system.

This was the yard, this the driveway,
where one summer of Saturdays he'd gathered

a minyan to say Kaddish for his mother.

He admired every living thing; he loved
the mimosa, the pan-sized hibiscus

the woodpecker whose staccato knocks
are the punctuation of this memory.

I held his good left hand, still the dreamer,

"Look, what a miracle this hand is—"
he said, "seventy years I hardly used it,

and now, the things it's learning to do!"
We looked together at what was left,

at what was growing.

Gail Mazur

SOURCES

Except as indicated below, all English translation through page 430 is the work of Joel Rosenberg (contemporary poet, essayist, professor of Hebrew Literature and Judaic Studies at Tufts University). All calligraphy and other art work is by Betsy Platkin Teutsch. Citations for previously published commentary, and full attributions for unpublished material by Mordecai M. Kaplan (American rabbi, 1881-1983; founder of Reconstructionist Judaism), are included below. To avoid confusion, sometimes a title or initial phrase is given. Refer to the key on page viii for full names of commentators. Biographies of authors of original works appear below. Full credits for outside sources and commentary are located in ACKNOWLEDGMENTS, pages xi-xiii.

Page 5
Marcia Falk (contemporary poet) formulated the *beraḥah* version "*Nevareh et eyn haḥayim...*" See *Kol Haneshamah: Erev Shabbat* (First edition 1989), pages 150-179.

Page 18
Adapted from a sermon given by Mordecai M. Kaplan at the Jewish Center, October 1919.

Page 20
Adapted from Mordecai M. Kaplan, *Notes*.

Page 28
A prayer used by Mordecai M. Kaplan to open classes.

Page 37
Mordecai M. Kaplan, *Notes*.

Pages 62-63
Mary Oliver (contemporary American poet), "Morning Poem" in *Dream Work*.

Page 64
Adapted from Mordecai M. Kaplan, "What Psychology Can Learn

from Religion," *The Reconstructionist*, Volume XXXII, Number 6, April 1966.

Page 76
Interpretive Version adapted from the 1945 Reconstructionist *Sabbath Prayer Book*, page 114.

Page 77
Interpretive Version adapted from the 1945 Reconstructionist *Sabbath Prayer Book*, page 118.

Page 83
Mordecai M. Kaplan, *Diary*.

Page 85
Mordecai M. Kaplan, *Notes*.

Page 104
Adapted from Mordecai M. Kaplan, *Notes*.

Page 106
Adapted from Mordecai M. Kaplan, *The Future of the American Jew*, page 381.

Page 109
Adapted from Mordecai M. Kaplan, *Notes*.

Page 111
Adapted from Mordecai M. Kaplan, *Notes*.

Page 128
Guided meditation composed by Judith Kummer while she was a student at the Reconstructionist Rabbinical College.

Page 132
Shiviti Meditations composed by Devora Bartnoff (Reconstructionist rabbi).

Page 134
Adapted from Mordecai M. Kaplan, *The Meaning of God in Modern Jewish Religion*, page 165.

Page 150
Excerpted from Robin C. Goldberg (anthropologist and storyteller), "Seeing and Seeing Through: Myth, Metaphor, and Meaning," *The Reconstructionist*, Volume L, Number 7; June 1985.

Page 162
"A Prayer for Peace" attributed to Naḥman of Bratzlav (Hasidic rabbi, 1772-1810) by his disciple Nathan Sternhartz of Nemirov in *Likutey Tefilot*, part two, 53; translated by Joel Rosenberg; first used in this location by Jules Harlow in *Sim Shalom.*

Page 170
Mordecai M. Kaplan, "Sermon at S.A.J.," 1922.

"As the hand..." adapted from *Ten Rungs: Hasidic Sayings*, collected and edited by Martin Buber (European-Israeli religious philosopher, 1878-1965), page 39.

Page 173
"When senseless hatred..." adapted from *ibid.*, page 79.

Adapted from Mordecai M. Kaplan, *S.A.J. Review*, 1928.

Page 220
Adapted from Mordecai M. Kaplan, *Notes.*

Page 225
See source for page 106.

Page 227
See source for page 109.

Page 229
See source for page 111.

Page 238
Mordecai M. Kaplan, *The Meaning of God in Modern Jewish Religion*, page 360.

Page 239
Abraham Joshua Heschel, (European-American rabbi and theologian, 1907-1972), *God in Search of Man*, pages 49 and 48.

Page 245
Adapted from Mordecai M. Kaplan, *Notes*, 1940's.

Page 246
See source for page 134.

Page 252
See sources for page 170.

Page 255
See sources for page 173.

Page 260
Adapted from Mordecai M. Kaplan, *The Meaning of God in Modern Jewish Religion*, page 248.

Page 261
Ibid., page 249.

Page 262
Adapted from *Ten Rungs: Hasidic Sayings*, collected and edited by Martin Buber (European-Israeli religious philosopher, 1878-1965), page 29.

Page 264
Interpretive Version adapted by Joy D. Levitt from the 1945 Reconstructionist *Sabbath Prayer Book*, pages 28-29.

Page 265
Interpretive Version adapted from "Unending Love" by Rami M. Shapiro (Reconstructionist rabbi), published in *Tangents*.

Page 267
Adapted from Mordecai M. Kaplan, *Notes*, 1920s.

Page 268
Mordecai M. Kaplan, *Notes*.

Page 272
Mordecai M. Kaplan, *The Meaning of God in Modern Jewish Religion*, page 172.

Adapted from Mordecai M. Kaplan, 1970s.

Page 282
Rami M. Shapiro (Reconstructionist rabbi), "Who is Like You," in *Tangents.*

Page 286
Adapted from Mordecai M. Kaplan, *Notes*, 1940s.

Page 292
"Standing here..." by Sandy Eisenberg Sasso (Reconstructionist rabbi).

"Dear God..." by Sheila Peltz Weinberg (Reconstructionist rabbi).

Mordecai M. Kaplan, *Diary*, 1904.

Page 293
This *Shiviti* design is by Betsy Platkin Teutsch, a contemporary American artist, who did all the other artwork in this siddur. The *Shiviti* is a traditional Jewish art form used for meditation. It is based upon the biblical verse: "I have set (שִׁוִּיתִי / *Shiviti*) Yah always before me" (Psalm 16:8).

Page 297
See source for page 220.

Page 300
Mordecai M. Kaplan, *The Meaning of God in Modern Jewish Religion*, page 79.

Page 301
Abraham Joshua Heschel (European-American rabbi and theologian, 1907-1972), *The Sabbath: Its Meaning for Modern Man*, page 9.

Page 302
See sources for page 109.

Page 305
See sources for page 111.

Page 312
Pinḥas of Koretz was an eighteenth-century Hasidic rabbi.

Page 315
Mordecai M. Kaplan, *The Meaning of God in Modern Jewish Religion*, page 360.

Abraham Joshua Heschel (European-American rabbi and theologian, 1907-1972), *God in Search of Man*, pages 49 and 48.

Page 328
See sources for page 170.

Page 331
See sources for page 173.

Page 332
Alternative Version by Rami M. Shapiro (Reconstructionist rabbi), published as "It Is Up To Us" in *Tangents.*

Page 333
Alternative Version by Judy Chicago (contemporary American artist and poet), entitled "Merger." Capitalization is identical to that in the original.

Page 334
"Love is not changed..." from *Eurydice* by Edith Sitwell (British poet, 1887-1964).

Page 342
Mordecai M. Kaplan, *Journal* 1933.

Page 351
"*Miriam Hanevi'ah*" by Leila Gal Berner (Reconstructionist rabbi).

Page 356
"*Hamavdil*" by Isaac ibn Ghayat (eleventh-century Sephardic rabbi).

Page 414
Order of Counting the Omer from the 1963 Reconstructionist *Daily Prayer Book*, pages 108ff.

Page 431
Lea Goldberg (Israeli poet, 1911-1970), from "*Shirey Sof Hadereḥ* / Poems," translated by Pnina Peli.

Page 432
Solomon ibn Gabirol (eleventh-century Sephardic poet and philosopher), "*Sheḥi La'el* / Submit to God," translated by Reena Spicehandler.

Page 433
Ruth Firestone Brin (contemporary American poet), "In Praise/GENESIS 1, 2" in *Harvest: Collected Poems and Prayers.*

Moses ibn Ezra (medieval Sephardic poet and philosopher), *Ye'iruni Se'ipay Laḥazoteḥ*/My Thoughts Awaken Me to See You," translation adapted from that of Raymond P. Scheindlin in *The Gazelle: Medieval Hebrew Poems on God, Israel and the Soul.*

Page 435
"We cannot merely pray to God..." by Jack Riemer (contemporary American rabbi).

Page 436
Nancy Lee Gossels, "Somewhere Out of Time," in *Vetaher Libenu*, Congregation Beth El of the Sudbury River Valley, 1980, page 101.

Page 438
Ruth H. Sohn (contemporary American rabbi), "I Shall Sing to the Lord a New Song."

Page 440
"God, help me..." in *Forms of Prayer for Jewish Worship*, Volume III, page 3.

S. Y. Agnon (Israeli novelist, 1888-1970; recipient of the Nobel Prize for Literature), selections from *Yamim Noraim/Days of Awe*, translated by Judah Goldin, page 125.

Page 442
"The zodiac symbol..." *ibid.*, page 16.

"Do not say..." *ibid.*, page 119.

Page 443
"A tale is told..." *ibid.*, page 38.

"Everyone must prepare..." *ibid.*, page 18.

Page 444
"Everyone is given...," *ibid.*, page 115.

"The essence of repentance...," by Adin Steinsaltz (contemporary Israeli rabbi, Talmudist and scholar).

Page 445
S. Y. Agnon (Israeli novelist, 1888-1970; recipient of the Nobel Prize for Literature), selection from *Yamim Noraim/Days of Awe*, translated by Judah Goldin, page 22.

Page 446
"There was once a poor...," *ibid.*, page 22.

Page 449
Dana D. Shuster (member of the Jewish Reconstructionist Congregation in Evanston, Illinois), "Legacy."

Mani Leyb Brahinski (Yiddish-American poet, 1883-1953), excerpt from "They," translated from the Yiddish by David G. Roskies and Hillel Schwartz.

Page 451
A. L. Strauss (European-Israeli poet 1892-1953), "Lament for the European Exile," translated by A. C. Jacobs in *Voices Within the Ark*.

Page 453
Avraham Shlonsky (Israeli poet, 1900-1973), *Neder*/Pledge" from *Yalkut Shirim*. This translation is found on the wall of *Yad Vashem* in Jerusalem.

Page 454
Nelly Sachs (German-Jewish poet, 1891-1970), "Chorus of the Rescued" in *O The Chimneys*, translated by Michael Roloff.

Page 455
Hirsh Glik (poet and resistance fighter in the Vilna Ghetto, 1920-1944), "*Zog Nit Keynmol*/Never say." This poem, inspired by the Warsaw Ghetto uprising, was written in April 1943. As a song it became the hymn of the United Partisan Organization. The music is attributed to Dmitri Pokrass.

Page 457
Nahum Waldman (contemporary American rabbi and scholar), "To Touch Hands in Peace" in *Likrat Shabbat*, augmented edition, 1992.

Page 458
"Let us stand...," from an address given on *Yom Hazikaron*/Remembrance Day by David Ben Gurion, (first prime minister of Israel, 1886-1973).

Page 463
"*Yerushalayim Shel Zahav*/Jerusalem of Gold." Lyrics and music by Naomi Shemer (contemporary Israeli composer).

Page 466
Yehudah Halevi (twelfth-century Sephardic poet), "*Tziyon halo tishali...*/Zion ask now...," translated by Joel Rosenberg.

Page 471
"*Hatikvah*" by Naphtali Herz Imber (Hebrew poet, 1856-1909), translated by Judith Kaplan Eisenstein.

Page 475
Avigdor Hame'iri (Hebrew poet, novelist, and translator, 1890-1970), "*Me'al Pisgat Har Hatzofim*/From Mount Scopus's Crest."

Page 477
Primo Levi (Italian chemist and author, 1919-1987), "Song of Those Who Died In Vain," January 14, 1985.

Page 482
Archibald MacLeish (American poet, 1892-1982), "The Young Dead Soldiers."

Page 483
Adapted from the 1945 Reconstructionist *Sabbath Prayer Book*, page 546.

Emma Lazarus (American poet, 1849-1887), "The New Colossus."

Page 485
Aaron David Gordon (Zionist thinker, 1856-1922), excerpted from the essay "People and Labor" (1911) in *The Zionist Idea* edited by Arthur Hertzberg, page 374.

Carl Sandburg (American poet, 1878-1967), "Fish Crier."

Page 486
Naftali Gross (Yiddish-American poet and folklorist, 1896-1956), "The Operator," translated by Aaron Kramer in *A Century of Yiddish Poetry*.

Page 487
Barbara Cohen (contemporary American author), excerpt from *Molly's Pilgrim*.

Page 488
Pearl Kazin (American author), excerpt from "We Gather Together," *The New Yorker*, November 26, 1955, page 51.

Page 490
Edna St. Vincent Millay (modern American poet), "Dirge Without Music," in *Collected Poems*.

Page 491
Margaret Torrie (contemporary American poet), "The Intention," in *All in the End is Harvest*.

Page 493

Zelda Mishkowsky (Israeli poet, 1914-1984), "*Leḥol Ish Yesh Shem*/Each of Us Has a Name," translated by Marcia Falk.

Page 494

Laura Gilpin (contemporary American anthropologist), "Life After Death" in *The Hocus-Pocus of the Universe.*

Emmanuel Eydoux, pen name of Roger Eisinger (modern French Jewish author). This translation by Jonathan Magonet originally appeared in *Forms of Prayer for Jewish Worship*, page 402.

Page 495

Excerpted from "The Seven of Pentacles," in *To Be of Use* by Marge Piercy (contemporary American poet and novelist).

Pages 496

"Birth is a Beginning" by Alvin I. Fine (contemporary American rabbi). This poem originally appeared in *Gates of Repentance*, pages 283-284.

Page 497

Yehuda Amichai (contemporary Israeli poet), "*Kol Hadorot Shelefanay*/All the Generations Before Me," from *Aḥshav Bera'ash*, translated by Harold Schimmel.

Page 499

"To My Father." Believed to be the work of Blaga Dmitrova.

Page 500

Irena Klepfisz (contemporary Yiddish-American poet), "About My Father" from *A Few Words in the Mother Tongue – Poems Selected and New*, 1971-1990, page 48.

Page 501

Linda Pastan (contemporary American poet), "The Death of a Parent," in *A Fraction of Darkness.*

Page 502
"I asked unanswerable questions..." from the ancient Babylonian epic *Gilgamesh*, translated by Herbert Mason.

Page 502
Diane Cole (contemporary American poet), "First Rites," in "Ten by Seven: Contemporary Poems on Jewish Themes," *The National Jewish Monthly*, January 1977, page 16.

Page 503
Louise Gluck, "Metamorphosis," in *The Triumph of Achilles.*

Page 505
David Ignatow (contemporary American poet), "Kaddish," in *New and Collected Poems 1970-1985.*

Page 506
Theodore L. Steinberg (contemporary American poet), "Family Tree," in *Chazon: Vision*, edited by Reuven M. Ben Avraham, Molad Publications, Memphis, Tennessee, 1984, page 60.

Page 507
A. M. Klein (contemporary Canadian poet), "Heirloom," in *Collected Poems.*

Page 508
Peter Meinke (contemporary poet), "Gramma," in *The Night Train and the Golden Bird.*

Stephen Dobyns (contemporary American poet), "Funeral," in *Cemetery Nights.*

Page 510
"Do not come when I am dead..." by Juanita de Long (contemporary poet), in *The World's Greatest Religious Poetry.*

Page 511
Nancy Wood (contemporary American poet), "Hold on to What is Good," in *Many Winters.*

Page 512
Raymond Carver (American poet, 1938-1988), "Gravy," in *A New Path To The Waterfall.*

Page 513
Hannah Kahn (contemporary American poet), "Kaddish," in *CCAR Journal*, Autumn 1972, page 28.

Page 514
Harvey J. Fields (contemporary American rabbi), "In Praise of the Living."

Page 515
Evelyn Mehlman (Jewish musicologist and composer, 1915-1989; first woman graduate of the Cantor's Institute at The Jewish Theological Seminary). "We Turn our Thoughts..." first appeared in the Yizkor memory book of the West End Synagogue.

Page 516
Adrienne Rich (contemporary American poet), excerpted from "Living Memory," in *Time's Power: Poems 1985-1988.*

Page 517
Charles Reznikoff (American poet, 1894-1976).

Page 518
Grace Butcher (contemporary American poet), "Learning from Trees," from *Child, House, World* (Hiram Poetry Review) 1991, originally in *Poetry*, April 1991, page 32.

Page 519
Linda Pastan (contemporary American poet), "The Five Stages of Grief," in *The Five Stages of Grief.*

Page 521
David Ignatow (contemporary American poet), "Above Everything," in *New and Collected Poems, 1970-1985.*

"Death is not strange..." adapted and excerpted from *Years at the*

Ending by Joseph Leftwich (British poet, anthologist and translator, 1892-1983).

Page 522
"This is my prayer..." by Hillel Bavli (Hebrew poet, 1893-1961), translated by Joel Rosenberg. Originally appeared in *Mahzor for Rosh Hashanah and Yom Kippur,* edited by Jules Harlow, page 412.

Page 526
Ḥayim Naḥman Bialik (Hebrew poet, 1873-1934), "*Aḥarey Moti*/After My Death," translated by A. C. Jacobs in *Voices Within the Ark.*

Page 529
Yehuda Amichai (contemporary Israeli poet), "*Adam Beḥayav*/I Don't Have Time."

Page 531
Adrienne Rich (contemporary American poet), "Tattered Kaddish," in *An Atlas of the Difficult World: Poems 1988-1991.*

Page 532
Gail Mazur (contemporary American poet), "Another Tree," *Poetry,* April 1991, page 33.

INDEX

Acknowledgments xi
Adon Olam, 342
Afternoon Service, 212
Aḥat Sha'alti, 197, 337
Al Naharot Bavel, 472
Amidah
    Abbreviated Amidah, 106
    Amidah Meditations, 128-133
    Ma'ariv, 294
    Minḥah, 218
    Shaḥarit, 98
Ashrey, 40, 212
Avinu Malkeynu, 136
Bedtime Shema, 346
Beraḥot, alternative formulations, 5, 151
Birḥot Hashaḥar/Morning Blessings, 2, 14
Birkat Hagomel/Blessing for Deliverance, 154
Blessings
    Alternative formulations 5, 151
    Bedtime, 346
    Birḥot Hashaḥar/Morning Blessings, 2, 14
    Deliverance and Good Fortune, 154
    Gomel, 154
    Ḥanukah, 386
    Keriat Shema Al Hamitah/The Bedtime Shema, 346
    Lulav and Etrog, 358
    Megillah, 388
    Mi Sheberaḥ, 156
    Morning, 14
    Netilat Lulav, 358
    Torah, 151-153
    Torah Study, 24
Candlelighting (Ḥanukah), 386
Commentators, viii
Conclusion of Shivah, 428
Counting the Omer, 414
Eliyahu Hanavi, 351
Elohay Neshamah, 23

Elul Meditations, 440
Esa Eynay, 45
Etz Ḥayim Hi, 167
Evening Service, 260
Gomel/Blessing for Deliverance, 154
Hadlakat Nerot Shel Ḥanukah/Hanukah Candlelighting, 386
Ḥag Purim, 392
Hallel, 360
Hamavdil, 356
Ḥanukah, 386
Hatikvah, 471
Havdalah, 350
Hoshanot, 394
    Third Day of Sukkot, 398
    Fourth Day of Sukkot, 400
    Fifth Day of Sukkot, 402
    Sixth Day of Sukkot, 404
    Hoshanah Rabah, 406
Hoshi'ah Et Ameḥa, 397
Introduction, xiv
Kaddish
    Derabanan, 26
    Ḥatzi, 64
    Mourners', 204, 256, 334
    Titkabal, 144
Keriat Shema Al Hamitah/The Bedtime Shema, 346
Ki Mitziyon, 147
Lighting Candles for Ḥanukah, 384
Lulav and Etrog, 358
Ma'ariv, 206
Mah Tovu, 2
Ma'oz Tzur, 386
Me'al Pisgat Har Hatzofim, 475
Meditations
    Elul, 440
    Guided Amidah Meditations, 128
    Shiviti, 131, 132
Memorial
    Mourners' Kaddish, 204
    Readings, 490-532
Minḥah, 212

Min Hametzar, 379
Miriam Hanevi'ah, 351
Mi Sheberaḥ Prayers, 156
Mourners' Kaddish, 204, 256, 334
Netilat Lulav, 358
Notes on Usage, xvii
Omer, Counting the, 414
Pesukey Dezimrah/Verses of Praise, 32
Pilgrimage Festivals
    Hallel, 360
    Hoshanot, 394
    Netilat Lulav, 358
Pitḥu Li, 381
Prayer for Peace, 162
Prayer for Sustenance, 234
Prayer for Those Who Are Ill, 228
Prayer for Travel, 174
Preface, ix
Psalms
    Psalm 23, 340
    Psalm 24, 176
    Psalm 27, 196
    Psalm 30, 30
    Psalm 48, 180
    Psalm 49, 200
    Psalm 81, 190
    Psalm 82, 184
    Psalm 93, 194
    Psalm 94, 186
    Psalm 100, 38
    Psalms 113-118 (Hallel), 360
    Psalm 121, 44
    Psalm 126, 476
    Psalm 128, 46
    Psalm 130, 48
    Psalm 145 (Ashrey), 40, 212
    Psalm 146, 50
    Psalm 147, 52
    Psalm 148, 56

Psalm 150, 60
Elul, 196
Friday, 194
Monday, 180
Mourning, 200
Sunday, 176
Thursday, 190
Tuesday, 184
Wednesday, 186
Purim, 388
Readings
Death, Mourning and Memory, 490
Elul and Teshuvah, 440
Exodus, 438
Fourth of July, 483
Labor Day, 485
Life and Death, 512
Loss of a Gay or Lesbian Lover, 509
Loss of a Grandparent, 508
Loss of a Loved One, 510
Loss of a Parent, 497
Martin Luther King Day, 479
Meditations for Elul, 440
Memorial Day, 482
Nature, 433
New Year's Day, 478
Peace, 162
Prayer, 431
Presidents' Day, 480
Social Action, 435
Thanksgiving, 487
Tisha Be'av, 472
Torah Study, 436
Tu Bishevat, 448
Veterans' Day, 482
Yom Hasho'ah, 449
Yom Ha'atzma'ut, 457
Sefirat Ha'omer, 414
Shavu'a To'v, 357
Shivah, Conclusion of, 428

Shoshanat Ya'akov, 390
Sisu Et Yerushalayim, 461
Songs
    Adon Olam, 342
    Aḥat Sha'alti, 197, 337
    Al Naharot Bavel, 472
    Eliyahu Hanavi, 351
    Elohay Neshamah, 23
    Esa Eynay, 45
    Etz Ḥayim Hi, 167
    Ḥag Purim, 392
    Hamavdil, 356
    Hatikvah, 471
    Hoshi'ah Et Ameḥa, 397
    Mah Tovu, 2
    Ma'oz Tzur, 386
    Me'al Pisgat Har Hatzofim, 475
    Miriam Hanevi'ah, 351
    Psalm 150, 60
    Shoshanat Ya'akov, 390
    Sisu Et Yerushalayim, 461
    Veha'er Eyneynu, 81
    Yerushalayim Shel Zahav, 463
    Yevareḥeḥa, 47
    Yigdal, 206
Sources, 533
Taḥanun, 424
Tefilat Hadereḥ/Travelers' Prayer, 174
Torah Blessings, 151-153
Torah Service, 146
Travelers' Prayer, 174
Waving the Lulav, 358
Yerushalayim Shel Zahav, 463
Yevareḥeḥa, 47
Yigdal, 206

PUBLISHER'S NOTE

This book is published by the Reconstructionist Press which is sponsored by the Jewish Reconstructionist Federation. The JRF also publishes *Reconstructionism Today.* Founded in 1955, the JRF is the congregational arm of the Reconstructionist movement.. The JRF does outreach, provides a variety of services to its congregations and ḥavurot, and does regional and movement-wide programming.

To order copies of this book, or to obtain book lists or other information, please contact:

JEWISH RECONSTRUCTIONIST FEDERATION
Beit Devora
7804 Montgomery Avenue, Suite #9
Elkins Park PA 19027-2649

Phone: 1-215-782-8500 Fax: 1-215-782-8805 Toll-free: 1-877-JRF-PUBS
E-mail: Press@jrf.org Website: www.jrf.org